A Communicative
Grammar of English

A Communicative Grammar of English

Second edition

Geoffrey Leech and
Jan Svartvik

LONGMAN
LONDON AND NEW YORK

Addison Wesley Longman Limited,
Edinburgh Gate,
Harlow, Essex CM20 2JE, England
and Associated Companies throughout the world.

Published in the United States of America
by Addison Wesley Longman Inc., New York

First published 1975
Second edition 1994
Sixth impression 1998
ISBN O 582-23827 7 CSD
ISBN O 582-08573 X PPR

British Library Cataloguing-in-Publication Data

A catalogue record for this book is
available from the British Library

Library of Congress Cataloging-in-Publication Data

Leech, Geoffrey N.
    A communicative grammar of English / Geoffrey Leech, Jan Svartvik.
— 2nd ed.
        p.   cm.
    'Based on A Comprehensive Grammar of the English Language by Randolph Quirk,
Sidney Greenbaum, Geoffrey Leech, Jan Svartvik.'
    Includes bibliographical references and index.
        ISBN 0–582–238727–7 (cased). — ISBN 0–582–08573–X (pbk.)
        I. English language—Textbooks for foreign speakers.   2. English
language—Grammar. I. Svartvik, Jan. II. Grammar of contemporary
English. III. Title.
PEII28.L45   1994
428.2'4—dc20   93–45811
                                                          CIP

Set in 15 in 9½/12 pt Photina
Printed in Singapore through Addison Wesley Longman China Limited

Contents

Based on
A Comprehensive Grammar of the English Language
by Randolph Quirk,
Sidney Greenbaum,
Geoffrey Leech,
Jan Svartvik

Preface

This is a thoroughly revised edition of *A Communicative Grammar of English*. When the first edition appeared in 1975, 'communicative competence' was probably a new concept to many of our readers. Now in the 1990s, the communicative approach has established itself as an efficient and popular method for learning foreign languages and, within that framework, *A Communicative Grammar of English* has established itself as an innovative grammar.

This new edition of the grammar makes use of real examples and gives increased emphasis on spoken English. We also believe it is easier to use than the first edition. The presentation is more 'pedagogical' in giving simpler explanations, in providing more examples, and in making clear the distinctions between major and minor points. The basic design of the book remains the same, but the numbering of sections has been changed. Of the four parts of the first edition, the first two parts have been revised and combined, so that the new book is divided into three parts:

- Part One: A guide to the use of this book

- Part Two: Grammar in use

- Part Three: A–Z in English grammar.

We are confident that those who are used to the first edition will have little difficulty in adapting to this new version of the book.

This book is partly based on Randolph Quirk, Sidney Greenbaum, Geoffrey Leech and Jan Svartvik, *A Comprehensive Grammar of the English Language* (Longman, 1985). However, it cannot be regarded as a condensed version of that larger work since its arrangement is totally different, and it contains additional material (especially in Part Two). On the other hand, the structural or formal aspect of grammar is less comprehensively treated here than in the larger work and also Sidney Greenbaum and Randolph Quirk, *A Student's Grammar of the English Language* (Longman, 1990). We have therefore added to each entry in Part Three a reference to the most relevant sections of *A Comprehensive Grammar of the English Language*, so that, if required, a more detailed treatment of the topic can be consulted in that book. We have attempted to simplify grammatical terminology and classifications as far as possible, so that the terms and categories treated in Part Three do not in every case correspond to the same terms in the *Comprehensive Grammar*.

We are very grateful to Andrew Wilson, of Lancaster University, for his research work on computer corpora, to Freda Gidlow and Xu Xunfeng, also of Lancaster, and Ami Gayle of Lund University for their help in preparing the manuscript of the new edition.

GL and JS
Lancaster and Lund, February 1994

Symbols

( )   Items in round brackets are optional, i.e. the sentence is acceptable also if the bracketed words are left out:

> *She said she would come but she didn't (do so).*

can be read either as

> *. . . but she didn't do so*
> or as *. . . but she didn't.*

Round brackets are also used for cross-references:

> '(*see* 408)' means 'see section 408 in this grammar'
> '(*see* CGEL 14.2)' means 'see *A Comphrehensive Grammar of the English Language*, section 14.2'

[ ]   Numerals in square brackets appear after examples when required for cross-reference:

> As in sentence [5] . . .

Square brackets are also used to separate items, such as two adverbials:

> We go [*to bed*] [*early*].

/   A slash indicates a choice of items, such as between *some-* or *any-* pronouns:

> Did *somebody/anybody* phone?

{ }   Braces indicate a range of choices, such as between different relative constructions:

> The film $\begin{Bmatrix} \textit{which we liked best} \\ \textit{that we liked best} \\ \textit{we liked best} \end{Bmatrix}$ was . . .

~   A tilde indicates 'roughly equivalent', e.g. active and passive:

> *They published this paper in 1992.*
> ~ *This paper was published in 1992.*

A tilde is also used between related forms, e.g. verb forms or comparative forms:

> *give ~ gave ~ given*
> *big ~ bigger ~ biggest*

⟨ ⟩ Angle brackets are used around variety labels (*see* 44–55):

> ⟨formal⟩, ⟨informal⟩   ⟨spoken⟩, ⟨written⟩
> ⟨BrE⟩, ⟨AmE⟩   ⟨polite⟩, ⟨familiar⟩

*   An asterisk signifies that what follows is not 'good English', i.e. it is unacceptable usage:

> We can say *Ann's car*, but not **the car of Ann.*

‖   A double bar separates ⟨BrE⟩ from ⟨AmE⟩ usage:

> /ˈkʌlə/‖/ˈkʌlər/ (pronunciation)

S   subject (*see* 705)
V   verb phrase (*see* 735)
O   object (*see* 608)
C   complement (*see* 508)
A   adverbial (*see* 449)
SVO   subject + verb phrase + object
SVC   subject + verb phrase + complement
SVA   subject + verb phrase + adverbial

/ /   Slashes enclose phonemic transcriptions (*see* 43):

> *lean*/liːn/, *leant* /lent/

ˈ   A stress mark is placed before the stressed syllable of a word:

> ˈ*over*   (stress on the first syllable)
> *temp*ˈ*tation*   (stress on the second syllable)
> *transfor*ˈ*mation*   (stress on the third syllable)

__   Underlined syllables carry the nuclear tone (*see* 38):

> How could you d<u>o</u> that?

`   A falling tone: <u>yes</u>
ʹ   A rising tone: <u>yes</u>
ˇ   A fall-rise tone: <u>yes</u>

| A single vertical bar indicates tone unit boundary (*see* 37):

> |I <u>a</u>lmost phoned them <u>up</u> and said | Come a bit l<u>a</u>ter|

Part One

A guide to the use of this book

Introduction

1

It is sometimes argued that grammar is not important in a communicative approach to language. However, like Canale and Swain quoted here, we take the view that communicative competence rests on a set of composite skills, one of which is grammatical:

> Communicative competence is composed minimally of grammatical competence, sociolinguistic competence, and communication strategies, or what we will refer to as strategic competence. There is no strong theoretical or empirical motivation for the view that grammatical competence is any more or less crucial to successful communication than is sociolinguistic competence or strategic competence. The primary goal of a communicative approach must be to facilitate the integration of these types of knowledge for the learner, an outcome that is not likely to result from overemphasis on one form of competence over the others throughout a second language programme. (Michael Canale and Merrill Swain, 'Theoretical Bases of Communicative Approaches to Second Language Teaching and Testing', *Applied Linguistics* 1: 27, 1980)

There are several reasons for emphasizing the communication aspects of learning English grammar as we do in this book. Here, let us consider four reasons.

- **A new angle**

2

The type of student we have had in mind when writing this book is fairly advanced, for example a first-year student at a university or college of education. Often, such students already have grounding in the grammar of the language after several years of school English. Yet their proficiency in actually using the language may be disappointing. This, we believe, may be partly due to 'grammar fatigue'.

The student may therefore benefit from looking at grammar from another angle, where grammatical structures are systematically related to meanings, uses and situations, as we attempt to do in Part Two: Grammar in use. In this way we expect students to improve and extend their range of competence and their use of communication strategies in the language. In Part Three, called 'A-Z in English grammar', the book also supplies essential information about grammatical forms and structures, and can therefore be used as a general reference book or source book on English grammar. There we give references to relevant parts of *A Comprehensive Grammar of the English Language*, a standard grammatical description of English, where the advanced student can find extra information on topics which cannot be fully covered in this book.

• A better organization

3

The conventional way of presenting English grammar in terms of structure also has a certain drawback in itself. For example, in such a grammar, notions of time may be dealt with in as many as four different places: under the tense of the verb, under time adverbs, under prepositional phrases denoting time, and under temporal conjunctions and clauses. The student who is primarily interested in making use of the language rather than in learning about its structure (and this is true for the majority of foreign students) is not likely to find such an arrangement particularly helpful. In *A Communicative Grammar of English*, the central part deals with grammar in use, which makes it possible to bring similar notions, such as those involving time, together in one place.

• Spoken English

4

An important element in the communicative approach is the student's ability to use and understand the spoken language. This emphasis on speech is sometimes misunderstood, so that the communicative method is taken to imply focus on the spoken language. We do not share this view: 'communication' means communication in both speech and writing. Yet, since traditional grammar tends to concentrate on written language, we think it is important for a communicative grammar to describe and exemplify both types of language use. (On grammar in spoken and written English, *see* Sections 17–32.)

• Corpus data

5

The examples given in grammars have often been made up by grammarians rather than taken from real language in actual use. A made-up example may well serve to illustrate a particular grammatical point, but it can appear stilted or 'wooden', distancing the learning of grammar from real live usage. This is no doubt one reason why grammar is often considered to be a less important part of language in the communicative approach. We take the view that the grammar of a language is indeed of central concern to students, since it describes what makes language tick – how it can carry the meanings we want to communicate. In this revised edition of our grammar we have illustrated grammatical statements with the help of hundreds of authentic examples from English language corpora (for example, the Longman-Lancaster Corpus, the Brown University Corpus of American English, the Lancaster-Oslo/Bergen Corpus of British English, the London-Lund Corpus of Spoken English, the

Spoken English Corpus, and the British National Corpus). These corpora, stored on computers, provide access to many millions of words of spoken and written material in modern English. However, the corpus examples sometimes have to be simplified by the omission of distracting material. There can also be an advantage – for example, where precise contrasts have to be clearly indicated – in making use of made-up examples. We believe that in this book we have achieved the right balance between the use of authentic examples and the use of the clearest illustrative material.

The way this book is organized

6
The book is divided into three parts as follows:

- Part One: A guide to the use of this book (sections 1–56)
- Part Two: Grammar in use (sections 57–434)
- Part Three: A–Z in English grammar (sections 435–747)

Note that the book is organized in consecutively numbered sections (1–747), for ease of reference. At the end of the book, there is a detailed index which gives section numbers, rather than pages, as the most convenient means of looking up what you want.

We now give a brief overview of these three parts and what they contain.

Part One: A guide to the use of this book (sections 1–56)
7
In this first part, we try to explain the design of the book, and the apparatus of information you need in order to understand it, and to find what you need.

One of the major things you will need is a guide to the different labels we use for different kinds or varieties of English (44–56). Where English gives us a choice of grammatical forms or structures for a given purpose, the different structures available are often not equivalent, since they belong to different 'styles' or 'varieties'. An important part of communicative grammar is knowing the appropriate choice according to the situation you are in. For example, if you are communicating in **speech** your choices of grammar will often be different from the choices you make in **writing**. And when you are writing, if you are communicating in an **informal** situation, your choices will often be different from those that you choose in a **formal** situation. Throughout the book, therefore, we make use of 'variety labels' such as ⟨informal⟩, ⟨formal⟩, ⟨written⟩ and ⟨spoken⟩, whenever we want to make a point about the appropriateness of a grammatical form for this or that situation. Remember that the **angle brackets** ⟨...⟩, whenever they occur in this book, signal this kind of appropriate choice.

At the same time, it is as well to remember that English grammar is substantially the same, whatever the situation you are communicating in (*see* 16, 44).

One particular purpose of Part One is to explain and illustrate the symbols used in representing features of the spoken language. Most of us are used to the conventions for representing the written language on paper – the use of spelling, punctuation, and so on. But how do we capture on paper the nature of spoken language? For this, not only do we need symbols representing vowels and consonants in speech (*see* 43), but more important, we need symbols for representing features of stress and intonation, which are closely integrated with the grammar of spoken language (32–42). H. E. Palmer in his well-known pioneering *A Grammar of Spoken English* (First Edition 1924) went to the lengths of presenting the grammar of speech through phonetic transcription of all features of the language. This brave effort was a valuable correction to the assumption – all too common in those times – that grammar was synonymous with the study of the written language. But it increased the difficulty of using the book enormously, and paradoxically impeded the thing it was intended to promote – a widespread appreciation of the features of spoken language. Our position, in contrast to this, is that we need to reduce to a minimum the use of special symbols which students need to understand the facts of grammar. This means using phonetic symbols and symbols of stress and intonation rather sparingly, and in any case, only where they are important to understanding the use of grammar in the spoken language. For many purposes, we can most helpfully use the conventions of written language in the representation of speech.

Part Two: Grammar in use (57–434)
8

Part Two is the central part and largest part of the grammar. It is also the part which justifies our title 'Communicative Grammar', by presenting grammar through the eyes of the communicator. The question it tries to answer, in as much detail as space permits, is: Given that I want to communicate certain meanings in certain situations or contexts, which grammatical forms and structures can I use?

Communication is not a simple process. It is helpful, for our purpose, to think of four circles, one inside another, representing different kinds of meaning function and the different ways of organising such functions. The four circles in the figure below correspond to Sections A–D in Part Two.

	Type of meaning or meaning organization	Type of formal unit
	Section A: 'Concepts'	Word, phrase, or clause (pp. 39 – 124)
	Section B: 'Information, reality and belief'	Sentence (pp. 125 – 52)
	Section C: 'Mood, emotion and attitude'	Utterance (pp. 152 – 77)
	Section D: 'Meanings in connected discourse'	Discourse or text (pp. 177 – 211)

The right-hand column, stating 'types of formal unit', should not be interpreted too strictly. It is useful to see the relation between the different layers of meaning and a hierarchy of grammatical units, but there is much overlap of the types of unit, and other factors are important. For example, intonation has an important role in the expression of meaning in Sections B, C and D.

Section A: Concepts (57–239)
9
The first circle is that of notional or conceptual meaning. Here we find the basic meaning categories of grammar: for example, 'number', 'definite meaning', 'amount', 'time', 'manner', 'degree'. Such terms point to aspects of our experience of the world. The structural units we deal with here are smaller than the sentence, i.e. **words**, **phrases**, and **clauses**.

Section B: Information, reality and belief (240–97)
10
The second circle represents logical aspects of communication. Here we make use of the categories of Section A, but we judge them and respond to them in the light of concepts such as truth and falsehood, which we depend on in giving and receiving information. Such categories as 'statements, questions and responses' belong here. So do 'affirmation and denial', 'possibility' and 'certainty'. The formal unit we are chiefly concerned with is the **sentence**.

Section C: Mood, emotion and attitude (298–350)
11
The third circle involves the social dimension of communication, relating grammar to the attitudes and behaviour of speaker and hearer. At the speaker's end, language expresses attitudes and emotions, and is a means of carrying out social goals. At the receiving end, language can control or influence the actions and attitudes of the hearer. This 'controlling' aspect of communication is performed through such speech acts as commanding, requesting, advising, promising. Although the logical aspect of meaning (Section B) is made use of, it is extended, or perhaps even 'distorted' to perform different kinds of social function. Thus, on a logical level, a question is a means of eliciting information – of determining what is true and what is false. But questions can be adapted 'pragmatically' for the purpose of making an offer:

> *Would you like some more?*

or making a suggestion:

> *Why don't you come with me?*

or expressing a strong feeling:

> *Wasn't it a marvellous play?*

The unit of language we are mainly dealing with here is the **utterance**, which may or may not correspond to a sentence in length.

Section D: Meanings in connected discourse (351–434)
12
The fourth circle deals with the organization of communication. The question here is How shall we arrange our thoughts? i.e., in what order shall we put them, and how shall we bind them together, in order to communicate in the most appropriate or effective way? Grammar is flexible enough to offer a considerable choice in these matters. This is the aspect of the use of grammar which takes account of 'context' in the sense of 'the preceding or following aspects of the discourse'. Looking at sentences in isolation is not sufficient: the unit here, therefore, is the **text** or **discourse**.

The four circles of the diagram represent a rational progression from the most limited and detailed aspect of meaning to the most inclusive. This design underlies Part Two, but we have not stuck to it too rigidly. To have done so would often have meant inconvenient repetitions of material in different sections. In dealing with emotive meaning (Section C), for example, we have moved directly from the **expression** of emotion to the **description** of emotion, even though it might be argued that the description of emotion belongs more naturally to conceptual meaning (Section A). The overriding consideration, in arranging the material, is that of dealing with related communicative choices together.

Part Three: A–Z in English grammar (435–747)
13
If Part Two is the main 'communicative' part of the book, Part Three is complementary to it. We need to know not only the communicative choices which grammar offers (Part Two), but the structural grammatical choices through which communication is channelled (Part Three). The two sets of choices are to a large extent independent of one another, and so are dealt with separately. The entries in Part Three are arranged alaphabetically, for ease of access, and will be particularly useful in enabling students to find detailed explanations of grammatical terms (e.g. 'relative clause', 'phrasal verb') whose meaning may be unclear to them.

Cross-references and index
14
The reference apparatus is a very important part of every grammar book. In this grammar, with its innovative arrangement, it is essential to have numerous cross-references, and a comprehensive index. We have aimed to provide both. The index distinguishes between different kinds of references:

- References to individual words and phrases (e.g. *proper, because of*)
- References to grammatical terms (e.g. PROPER NOUN)

- References to functions or meanings (e.g. proportion, female person)
- References to language varieties (e.g. ⟨speech⟩, ⟨American English⟩)

In this way, multiple access is given to the information contained within the grammar.

Varieties of English

15

To use a language properly, we of course have to know the grammatical forms and structures and their meanings. (These are the subjects of Parts Two and Three.) But we also have to know what forms of language are appropriate for given situations, and for this purpose you will find in both those parts 'variety labels' such as ⟨spoken⟩, ⟨written⟩, ⟨AmE⟩ (for American English), ⟨BrE⟩ (for British English), ⟨formal⟩, ⟨informal⟩, ⟨polite⟩, ⟨familiar⟩. These labels are reminders that the English language is, in a sense, not a single language, but many languages, each belonging to a particular geographical area or to a particular kind of situation. The English used in formal written communications is in some ways different from the English used in informal conversation; the English used in the United States is somewhat different from the English used in Great Britain, in Australia, and so on. Obviously, in a general book of this kind we must ignore many less important differences. The purpose of this section of Part One is to explain briefly what is meant by the variety labels that you will meet, and to illustrate the varieties they refer to. If you wish to follow up a particular variety in detail, you may do so by means of the entries for variety labels in the index.

The 'common core'
16

Luckily for the learner, many of the features of English are found in all, or nearly all varieties. We say that general features of this kind belong to the 'common core' of the language. Take, for instance, the three words *children*, *offspring* and *kids*. *Children* is a '**common core**' term; *offspring* is liable to occur in a rather formal situation (and is used of animals as well as human beings): *kids* is likely to occur in an informal or familiar situation. It is safest, when in doubt, to use the 'common core' term: thus *children* is the word you would want to use most often. But part of knowing English is knowing in what circumstances it would be possible to use *offspring* or *kids* instead of *children*. Let us take another example, this time from grammar:

Feeling tired, she went to bed early. ⟨rather formal⟩	[1]
As she felt tired, she went to bed early.	[2]
She felt tired, *so* she went to bed early. ⟨rather informal⟩	[3]

Sentence [2] is a 'common core' construction. It could (for example) be used either in speech or in writing. Sentence [1] is rather formal, and typical of written language; [3] is rather informal, and is likely to occur in relaxed conversation. In this book, you can assume that features of English given no variety label belong to the 'common core'.

Grammar in spoken and written English

Different transmission systems
17

English, like other languages, makes use of two channels: speech and writing. They have different transmission systems. Speech is transmitted by sound-waves, originated in speaking and received in hearing. Writing is transmitted by letters and other visible marks, produced in writing and received in reading. Good, all-round communicative competence involves all four skills:

- speaking and writing (production)
- hearing and reading (reception)

Spoken and written English do not have different grammars, but the shared English grammar is used differently on the two channels. For the benefit of those who want to acquire good, all-round communicative competence we will therefore indicate in this book many such differences in the use of English grammar.

What is relevant to this book is how the different systems affect the grammar of spoken and written English. We treat the two channels as of equal importance. But sometimes, when we give intonation marks (*see* 33) or present examples of dialogue, it will be clear that we are thinking of spoken English.

Transitory speech and permanent writing
18

Normal speech is processed in real time and is transitory, leaving no trace other than what we may remember. Our memory being what it is, this is often limited to just the gist of a conversation or some particularly interesting points in a lecture. Writing, on the other hand, takes longer to produce and can be read not just once but many times. Writing leaves a permanent record. Moreover, writing that is made public in some way, such as in printed books and journals, leaves a record which can be read by millions of contemporary readers, and also by later generations.

Such differences between the two channels affect our language use in several ways. One is that spoken communication requires fast, almost instantaneous production and understanding. On the other hand, when we write, we usually have time to revise, check and rewrite what we have written. Likewise, when we receive a piece of writing we can read it, reread it, ponder over it, and discuss it.

19

In spontaneous speech we have no time to prepare what to say in advance, but we must shape our message as we go along. Here is an example of such speech:

> Well I had some people to lunch on Sunday and – they turned up half
> an hour early – (laughs) – I mean you know what [g] getting up
> Sunday's like anyway and – I'd – I was behind in any case – and I'd
> said to them one o'clock – and I almost phoned them up and said come
> a bit later – and then I thought oh they've probably left by now – so I
> didn't – and – twelve thirty – now that can't be them – and it was –
> and they'd they'd left plenty of time for all their connections and they
> got all their connections at once – and it was annoying cos they came
> with this – child – you know who was running all over the place and
> they kept coming in and chatting to me and I couldn't get on with
> things and I I get really erm – you know when when I'm trying to
> cook – and people come and chat I I get terribly put off – can't get on
> with things at all erm – and yet you feel terribly anti-social if you you
> do just stay in the kitchen anyway

On the audio-tape, this recording sounds natural and is quite easy to follow. However, when transcribed as here in written form, it looks fragmented, rambling, unstructured and is rather difficult to read. In this short extract from a conversation, we can note several features typical of informal talk:

- **silent pauses** (indicated by a dash –):

    they've probably left by now – so I didn't – and – twelve thirty – now that can't be them – and it was – and

- **voice-filled pauses** (indicated by *erm*) indicating hesitation:

    and I I get really erm – you know when when I'm trying to cook

- **repetitions**: *I I, when when, they'd they'd, you you*
- **false starts**: the speaker may fail to complete a sentence, or lose track of the sentence and mix up one grammatical construction with another:

    I mean you know what [g] getting up Sunday's like anyway and – I'd – I was behind in any case
    and I I get really erm – you know when when I'm trying to cook – and people come and chat I I get terribly put off

- **'fillers'**, i.e. certain words and phrases such as *well, you know*. The opening *well* in the extract is a typical spoken discourse item in this use of 'topic opener' (*see* 410). When we speak we often fill in gaps with 'fillers' (like *you know, you see, I mean, kind of, sort of*) to allow us to think of what next to say, or just to indicate that we intend to go on talking.
- **short forms** such as contractions of the negative *not* (*didn't*) and verb forms (*I'm, I'd, they've*), and *cos* for *because*.

In the next sections we will discuss why such features are so common in speaking.

Interactive and non-interactive uses of English
20
Spoken language is the most widely used form of language. Within spoken language there are many variations, but we will distinguish two main uses of spoken English. The first, and by far the most common use, is **conversation** with two or more participants taking their turns when talking to each other, either face-to-face or on the telephone. For the foreign student of English, this is a particularly important type to learn because it is the most common everyday use of speech. Moreover, it cannot be prepared in advance: conversation is impromptu, or spontaneous.

The second use of spoken English occurs with one person speaking at a time to an audience of people who do not talk back but just listen. We call this **public speaking** in contrast with conversation, which is **private speaking**. Conversation is typically **interactive**, and public speaking is less interactive, or even **not interactive** at all. Public speaking is intermediate between conversation and writing, in that a speech can be (and often is) prepared in advance in writing, and read aloud to an audience. In public speaking we include such spoken varieties as lectures, radio talks and T V news broadcasts. The figure below shows some of the different uses of English, and indicates that the relation between spoken and written English is more like a scale than a simple division. On the whole, the varieties of language towards the top of the diagram are more interactive than the varieties towards the bottom.

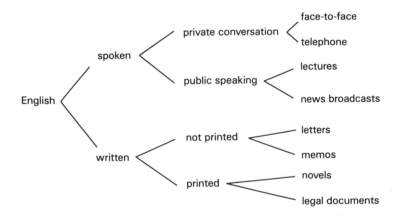

Cooperation in conversation
2 1
In a conversation, the speaker can check if the listener has understood by asking 'Do you see what I mean?', and the listener can ask the speaker for clarification: 'What did you mean by that?', etc. In writing we have no such direct contact between writer and reader and, in writing made public (as in newspapers, periodicals and books), we may not even have any idea who will

ever read what we write. This gives speaking an advantage in providing us with an opportunity for immediate feedback, to find out whether our message has been properly received, or is acceptable. This feedback can be verbal (*yes, uhuh, I see*, etc.) or non-verbal (a nod, raised eyebrows, etc.).

But, usually, a conversation is not just a matter of giving and receiving information. It is also, perhaps primarily, a form of social interaction, and **participant cooperation** is indeed a basic feature of conversation. There exists a give-and-take process which is manifested in several ways.

22

One is **turn-taking**, which means sharing out the role of speaker in the conversation, as one speaker takes a turn, then another. In this extract from a conversation with two speakers (A and B), notice the interplay of questions (*Are you playing the recorder too?*), answers (*I play the recorder too and I find this quite amusing*), and positive follow-up comments (*Yes, Precisely, That's right*):

[A] What are you writing? Are you copying out parts for a quartet or something, or what?
[B] I was transposing a trio written for two oboes and a cor anglais into recorders.
[A] Oh. Are you playing the recorder too?
[B] I play the recorder too and I find this quite amusing.
[A] Who do you play the recorder with?
[B] Erm – Do you know someone called Julie?
[A] Yes. She – her husband is an architect.
[B] Precisely.
[A] Yes, that's right.

23

Cooperation is also achieved by using **fillers**, which are a number of words and expressions typical of English spoken discourse – hence also called **discourse items**. Some of them (*yes, well, you see, precisely, that's right*, etc.) we have already met in the extracts above. Below we list some more such discourse items which are frequent in English conversation. We put them under three headings, indicating a scale from 'purely interactive' functions (which are above all characteristics of conversation) to 'also interactive' functions (which are more grammatical and frequently used also in public speaking and writing; *see* 249):

- Purely interactive: *ah, aha, mhm, oh, yes, yeah, yup, uhuh*
- Mainly interactive: *no, please, I see, I mean, you know, you see, OK, that's OK, all right, thank you, that's right, that's all right, well, sure, right*
- Also interactive: *anyway, in fact, maybe, perhaps, probably, absolutely, of course, certainly, obviously, indeed, really, honestly*

Most of these expressions are commonly used in conversations among native speakers, and it is therefore important for the foreign learner to be familiar with them and be able to use them quickly, and appropriately, in different situations.

Interactive expressions may add little information, but they tell us something of the speakers' attitude to their audience and to what they are saying.

Some grammatical features of spoken English
24
• *Tag questions.* A highly typical feature of speech is tag questions (*see further* 684). There are two main types:

> Positive + negative: We've *met* before, *haven't we?*
> Negative + positive: We *haven't met* before, *have we?*

Tag questions fit in nicely with the need for cooperation between speakers and the feature of turn-shift from one speaker to another. First the speaker asserts something (e.g. *It was a couple of years ago*), then invites the listener's response (*wasn't it?*), as in this example from the beginning of a conversation:

[A]   We've met before, haven't we?
[B]   Yes, we certainly have. It was a couple of years ago, wasn't it?
[A]   Oh yes, now I remember: at the Paris exhibition. How are you these days?

25
• *Ellipsis.* In some cases part of a sentence can be omitted, for example:

> Hope she's coming. ∼ I hope she's coming.
> Want a drink?   ∼ Do you want a drink?
> Better be careful.   ∼ You/We'd better be careful.
> Sounds fine to me. ∼ That sounds fine to me.

This type of omission, which is called 'initial ellipsis', is another characteristic of informal talk. It creates the sort of relaxed atmosphere that we try to achieve in a cooperative social situation.

26
• *Coordination.* A preference for coordination, rather than subordination of clauses (*see* 709), is a characteristic of speech. (We should of course add that coordination is widely used also in writing, just as certain types of subordination occur frequently in speech.) Compare these pairs of sentences: the first has coordination and is ⟨colloquial⟩, the second has subordination and is ⟨more formal⟩:

> Push the door hard and it'll open. ⟨colloquial⟩
> ∼ If the door is pushed hard, it will open. ⟨rather formal⟩
> He's now back in prison – and we'll have to try again. ⟨colloquial⟩
> ∼ Now that he is back in prison, we will have to try again. ⟨rather formal⟩

Another type of coordination that is common in impromptu speech can be seen in these examples:

I like to go sailing, and my wife does too. ⟨informal, spoken⟩
~ Both my wife and I like to go sailing. ⟨rather formal, written⟩
She doesn't work very hard, and that son of hers doesn't either. ⟨informal, spoken⟩
~ Neither she nor her son works very hard. ⟨rather formal, written⟩

27

● *Finite clauses.* In written English we often use non-finite and verbless clauses (*see* 494) as adverbials and modifiers, as in this example:

Feeling tired, the director went to bed early. ⟨rather formal, written⟩

Such constructions would be highly unlikely in speech, where finite clauses and coordination are preferred, as in

~ I felt so tired I went to bed early.
~ I felt tired and went to bed early.

Here are some other pairs of examples:

Lunch finished, the guests retired to the lounge. ⟨rather formal, written⟩
~ The guests all went into the lounge after lunch.
Ben, knowing that his wife was expecting, started to take a course on baby care. ⟨rather formal, written⟩
~ Ben got to know his wife was expecting, so he started to take a course on baby care. ⟨informal, spoken⟩
When fit, a Labrador is an excellent retriever. ⟨rather formal, written⟩
~ A Labrador is an excellent retriever if it's fit. ⟨informal, spoken⟩
Discovered almost by accident, this substance has revolutionized medicine. ⟨rather formal, written⟩
~ This stuff – it was discovered almost by accident – it's made an awfully big impact on medicine. ⟨informal, spoken⟩

28

● *Sign posts.* The grammar of spoken sentences is, in general, simpler and less strictly constructed than the grammar of written sentences. In writing we often indicate the structure of paragraphs by such 'sign posts' (or 'linking signals', *see* 351) as

firstly, secondly, finally, hence, to conclude, to summarize, e.g., viz.

Such expressions would not be used in informal talk where they would sound rather stilted and give the impression of a prepared talk. In a spontaneous talk we are more likely to introduce new points by such expressions as

and so, in other words, all the same, the first thing is . . .

For example:

> well – you know – the *first er* – *thing* that strikes me as odd about this whole business is – for example that . . .

29

- *Contracted forms.* When the auxiliary verbs *do, have, be* and some modal auxiliaries occur together with *not*, they can have either uncontracted or contracted forms (*see* 582):

do not ~ *don't*	*does not* ~ *doesn't*	*did not* ~ *didn't*
have not ~ *haven't*	*has not* ~ *hasn't*	*had not* ~ *hadn't*
are not ~ *aren't*	*is not* ~ *isn't*	
were not ~ *weren't*	*was not* ~ *wasn't*	

Uncontracted (or full) forms are typical of ⟨written⟩, especially ⟨formal⟩ English. The contracted forms are typical of ⟨spoken⟩ discourse, but they also occur in ⟨informal writing⟩. In some cases there is more than one contracted form available:

> I *have not* seen the film yet. ⟨typical of writing⟩
> I *haven't* seen the film yet. ⟨typical of speaking⟩ OR
> I'*ve not* seen the film yet. ⟨typical of speaking⟩

Later on in this book we will comment on other constructions that are used differently in ⟨spoken, informal⟩ and ⟨written, formal⟩ varieties, such as the subjunctive (*see* 706) and the passive (*see* 613).

Spelling v. pronunciation

30

In ⟨writing⟩ we have to observe a number of spelling changes (*see* 700), when we add a suffix to a word, for example

- replacing one letter by two, e.g. when adding *-s* or *-ly*:

they *carry*	B U T: she *carries*
a *lady*	B U T: several *ladies*
That's *easy*.	B U T: We did it *easily*.

- replacing two letters by one (e.g. when adding *-ing*):

they *lie*	B U T: they are *lying*

- adding letters (e.g. when adding *-s* or *-er*):

one *box*	B U T: two *boxes*
they *pass*	B U T: she *passes*
a *big* spender	B U T: *bigger* spenders, the *biggest* spenders

- dropping letters (e.g. when adding *-ing* or *-ed*):

love	B U T: *loving, loved*

In this respect, spoken English is simpler than written English. In fact, the reason why written English has such spelling rules is often to indicate the correct pronunciation of the inflected forms with suffixes. Note, for example, the following contrasts (for phonetic symbols, *see* 43):

hope/hoʊp/ ~*hoping*/'hoʊpɪŋ/ ~ *hoped*/hoʊpt/
hop/hɒp/   ~*hopping*/'hɒpɪŋ/ ~ *hopped*/hɒpt/

There are some differences between British and American English which do not affect speaking but only spelling: *centre∥center, levelled∥leveled,* etc. (*see* 703). There are some differences in pronunciation, too, but these are independent of the spelling differences. For example, /'kʌlə∥'kʌlər/ for *colour∥color.*

In nouns with regular plural, the written distinction between the genitive plural (*boys'*), the genitive singular (*boy's*), and also the common gender plural (*boys*) does not exist in the pronunciation /bɒɪz/ (*see* 664). To avoid ambiguity, the use of the genitive with nouns ending with the regular plural suffix -*s* tends to be avoided in speech, unless the number appears from the context (*the two boys' teacher,* etc.). However, there is no problem with irregular plurals: *the children's teacher.*

Written representation of speech

31
In some writing representing spoken English (for example comic strips) we can meet the form *got to* or even *gotta,* pronounced /'gɒtə/, as in

> You gotta be careful with what you say. ⟨non-standard in writing⟩

This is a representation of *have got to*:

> You've got to be careful with what you say. ⟨standard in speech and writing⟩

Similarly, *gonna,* pronounced /'gɒnə/, is sometimes the written form for ⟨standard written⟩ (*be*) *going to,* as in

> What (are) you *gonna do* now? ⟨non-standard in writing⟩
> What are you *going to do* now? ⟨standard in writing⟩

These non-standard written representations of the spoken form reflect a typical phonetic reduction of vowels and omission of consonants in everyday speech. However, the written language rarely captures these simplifications. For example, in

> They could have gone early

could have is commonly pronounced /'kʊdə/, but even in representations of the most casual speech, the non-standard written form *coulda* rarely occurs.

Punctuation v. chunking

32
We become familiar with the structure of written language through normal education: the way spoken language is structured is more difficult to observe

and to study. In writing we work with sentences. But it is often hard to divide a spoken conversation (such as the extract from a conversation in 19) into separate sentences. Part of the reason is that the speakers rely more on the hearers' understanding of context, and on their ability to interrupt if they fail to understand. Also, in 'getting across' their message, speakers are able to rely on features of intonation which tell us a great deal that cannot be rendered in written punctuation. Compare:

- **Punctuation in writing.** The written sentence is easily recognizable, since it begins with a capital letter and ends with certain punctuation marks (. ? !). Within the sentence we can indicate clause and phrase boundaries by commas (,), dashes (–), colons (:), and semi-colons (;).

- **Chunking in speaking.** Punctuation marks cannot be pronounced or heard but, in speaking, we use other devices to indicate what belongs together in an utterance. A piece of spoken information is packaged in **tone units** (also called **intonation units**, **chunks**, or **information units**). They are usually shorter than a sentence, averaging about 4–5 words, and have a separate intonation contour. The most heavily accented word in a tone unit contains a nucleus.

  There is no exact match between punctuation in writing and tone units in speaking. Speech is more variable in its structuring than writing. Chunking speech into tone units depends on such things as the speed of speaking, the emphasis given to a particular part of a message, and the length of grammatical units. (*See further* 397.) Note that:

- **Sentence adverbials** (such as *evidently*, *naturally*, and *obviously*) are often separated from what follows by a tone unit boundary in speech (indicated by a vertical bar '|') or a comma in writing. Compare:

  |*Obviously* | they expected us to be on time| ⟨spoken⟩
  Obviously, they expected us to be on time. ⟨written⟩

- **Non-restrictive apposition** (*see* 471) is usually set off by a separate tone unit in speaking, and by commas in writing:

  |Dr Johnson | *a neighbour of ours* | is moving to Canada| ⟨spoken⟩
  Dr Johnson, *a neighbour of ours*, is moving to Canada. ⟨written⟩

- **Comment clauses** are often marked off from other clauses, by having a separate tone unit in speech and commas in writing (*see further* 499):

  |*What's more* | we'd lost all we had| ⟨spoken⟩
  Moreover, we had lost all we had. ⟨written⟩

As a general comment, we may note that features marked as ⟨informal⟩ in this book are more likely to occur in ⟨speech⟩. On the other hand, ⟨formal⟩ features are more likely to occur in ⟨writing⟩ (*see further* 45).

Intonation

33

You will need some knowledge of English intonation patterns if you are to understand English grammar. This is because features of intonation are important for signalling grammatical distinctions, such as that between statements and questions. For example, a sentence like *They are leaving* can be a statement when said with falling intonation, but a question with rising intonation.

Here we concentrate on explaining those features of stress and intonation which play a significant role in grammar, and which therefore need to be discussed and symbolized in this book. The features we want to explain in the following sections are these:

- **Stress**, symbolized by a stress mark (' –*see* 34):

  '*over, an*'*alysis, transfor*'*mation*
  (stress on first, second and third syllable, respectively)

- **Tone units** with their boundaries marked by a vertical bar (|; *see* 37):

  |The task seemed difficult|

- **Nucleus**, i.e. the focal point of a tone unit, is symbolized by underlining the syllable carrying the nucleus (*see further* 36):

  |The task seemed di̐fficult|

- **Tones** are falling, rising or combinations of rising and falling. In our grammar the most important are these three (*see further* 38):

  A **falling tone** is marked: o̒bviously

  A **rising tone** is marked: o̓bviously

  A **fall-rise tone** is marked: o̬bviously

Stress

34

The rhythm of English is based on stress. In connected speech, we feel the rhythm of the language in the sequence of **stressed** syllables. Between one stressed syllable and another there may occur one or more **unstressed** syllables. The stressed syllables in these examples are preceded by the stress mark ', and the unstressed syllables are unmarked:

  I 'rang you on the 'way to the 'airport.
  It went 'off 'smoothly that 'long 'meeting of the ex'ecutive com'mittee.

This means that the syllables in SMALL CAPITALS below are stressed:

> I RANG you on the WAY to the AIRport.
> It went OFF SMOOTHly that LONG MEETing of the exECutive comMITtee.

The normal rules for placing stress are as follows. The syllables which are **stressed** are:

- a one-syllable word which belongs to one of the major word-classes (*see* 744), i.e. nouns (*WAY*), verbs (*RANG*), adjectives (*LONG*), adverbs (*OFF*).
- the accented syllables of words of more than one syllable of major word-classes, e.g. 'SMOOTHly, 'AIRport, com'MITtee.

The syllables which are **unstressed** are:

- a word belonging to one of the minor word-classes (*see* 745), e.g. prepositions (*to*), pronouns (*it*), articles (*the*).
- the unaccented syllables of words of more than one syllable, e.g. 'SMOOTHly, 'AIRport, com'MITtee.

35

There is no simple rule for which syllable is accented in a word which consists of more than one syllable. As we see above, accent varies from word to word, so that the accent falls on the first syllable of 'airport, but on the second syllable of com'mittee, and on the third syllable of transform'ation. The placing of stress is also variable according to sentence context, emphasis, speed of utterance, etc., and so the rules above are not without exceptions.

One point to notice is that a prepositional adverb (*see* 660) belongs to a major word-class, and is therefore stressed, whereas a one-syllable preposition is usually unstressed. Contrast:

> This 'bed has 'not been 'slept in. (*in* = preposition)
> The 'injured 'man was 'carried 'in. (*in* = prepositional adverb)

The same contrast is sometimes seen between the particle of a prepositional verb (*see* 632) and the particle of a phrasal verb (*see* 630):

> He's re'lying on our 'help. (*rely on* = prepositional verb)
> He's 'putting 'on a 'new 'play. (*put on* = phrasal verb)

But the particle may also be unstressed:

> 'Make up your 'mind!

In the examples in this book, stress will be marked only where it is necessary for the point illustrated.

The nucleus

36

Not all stressed syllables are of equal importance. Some stressed syllables have greater prominence than others, and form the **nucleus**, or focal point, of an intonation pattern. We may describe a nucleus as a strongly stressed syllable which marks a major change of pitch direction, i.e. where the pitch goes up or down. Here is an example to indicate pitch direction:

> She's going to the States.

The change of pitch on the nucleus is indicated by an arrow:

In this example, the nucleus marks a fall in pitch towards the end of the sentence. (The step-up in pitch before the nucleus *States* is something which will not concern us here.) As a nucleus is always stressed, there is no need to put a stress mark before it. Often in our examples, we simply indicate the nucleus by underlining without indicating the other stressed syllables:

> She's going to the <u>States</u>.

Tone units

37

The basic unit of intonation in English is the **tone unit**. (Other names you may meet are **intonation unit, chunk,** and **information unit.**) A tone unit is a stretch of speech which contains one nucleus. It may also contain other stressed syllables, normally preceding the nucleus. The boundaries of a tone unit are marked by a vertical bar |:

> |She's going to the <u>States</u>.|

In this example, the tone unit has the length of a whole sentence. But a sentence often contains more than one tone unit. The number of tone units depends on the length of the sentence, and the degree of emphasis given to various parts of it. This sentence

> This department needs a new chairperson

would normally have one tone unit:

> |This department needs a new <u>chairperson</u>|

But it might be pronounced with two tone units:

> |<u>This</u> department | needs a new <u>chairperson</u>|

The additional nucleus on *this* here expresses an emphasis on 'this *department* in contrast to other departments. The following sentence might be pronounced with either one or two or three tone units, as indicated:

|This is the kind of pressure that it's very difficult to re<u>sist</u>.|
|This is the kind of <u>pressure</u> | that it's very difficult to re<u>sist</u>.|
|This is the <u>kind</u> | of <u>pressure</u> | that it's very difficult to re<u>sist</u>.|

In general, we include tone unit boundaries in our examples only where they serve an illustrative purpose. Usually, we omit them.

Tones

38

By **tone** we mean the type of pitch change which takes place on the nucleus. The three most important tones in English, and the only ones we need distinguish here, are

the falling tone:	tòwn	Chàucer	|What's the name of this tòwn?|
the rising tone:	tówn	Cháucer	|Are you going to tówn today?|
the fall-rise tone:	tŏwn	bĭg tówn	|I can't allow you to do thăt.|

These sentences can also be represented in the following way:

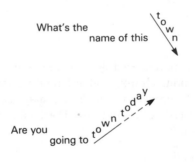

Here are two examples of the different tones in sequences of tone units:

|It's not like a lecture on Cháucer | or Éliot | or something of thăt kínd.|
|Our chair is very stròngly of the opínion | that we àll ought to go on téaching | to the end of tèrm.|

The tone of a nucleus determines the pitch of the rest of the tone unit following it.

- After a **falling tone**, the rest of the tone unit is at a low pitch:

  (Ann is getting a new job,) | but she hasn't to̖ld me about it. |

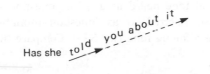

- After a **rising tone**, the rest of the tone unit moves in an upward pitch direction.

  (Ann is getting a new job.) | Has she to̗ld you about it? |

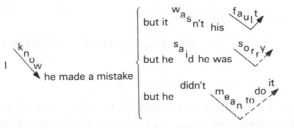

- The **fall-rise tone** consists of a fall in pitch followed by a rise. If the nucleus is the last syllable of the tone unit, the fall and rise both take place on one syllable – the nuclear syllable. Otherwise, the rise occurs in the remainder of the tone unit. Compare the following examples:

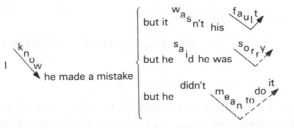

We symbolise these three tones as follows:

> |but it wasn't his fa̬ult.|
> |but he said he was so̬rry.|
> |but he didn't me̖an to do̗ it.|

Where the rise of the fall-rise extends to a stressed syllable after the nucleus, as· in the last example, we signal the fall-rise tone by placing a fall on the nucleus and a rise on the later stressed syllable. This will make it easier for you to follow the intonation contour when you read the examples.

The meanings of tones

39

The meanings of the tones are difficult to specify in general terms. Roughly speaking, the **falling tone** expresses 'certainty', 'completeness', 'independence'. Thus a straightforward statement normally ends with a falling tone, since it asserts a fact of which the speaker is certain. It has an air of finality:

| In this lecture I want to enlarge on the relation between grammar and lèxis. |

40

A **rising tone**, on the other hand, expresses 'uncertainty' or 'incompleteness' or 'dependence'.

- A *yes-no* question (*see* 682) usually has a rising tone, because the speaker is uncertain of the truth of what he or she is asking about:

  |Can I hélp you?|

Because the typical tone heard in a *yes-no* question is a rising tone, this intonation is often referred to as 'question-intonation'. However, most *wh*-questions have a falling tone (*see* 683). Compare the tones in these two questions:

  |Why are you lèaving?|

  |Don't you líke working here?|

- A question put in the form of a grammatical statement depends in speech on a question-intonation with a rising tone (*see* 244, 696):

  |You got home sáfely then?|

- Making a new start in the train of thought (*see* 353) often has a rising intonation:

  |Wéll | what do you suggest we do nòw?|

- Parenthetical and subsidiary information in a statement is also often spoken with a rising tone. The reason is that this information is incomplete and dependent for its full understanding on the main assertion:

  |If you líke | we can have dinner at mỳ place tonight.|

- Encouraging or ⟨polite⟩ denials, commands, invitations, greetings, farewells, etc. are generally spoken with a rising tone:

  [A] |Are you búsy?|
  [B] |Nó. | ('Please interrupt me if you wish') 'Do sit dòwn.|

Here a falling tone (Nò), which indicates finality, would sound ⟨impolite⟩.

41

A **fall-rise tone** combines the falling tone's meaning of 'assertion, certainty' with the rising tone's meaning 'dependence, incompleteness'. At the end of a sentence, it often conveys a feeling of reservation. It asserts something, and at the same time suggests that there is something else to be said. There is often an implied contrast:

  |That's not mỳ sígnature.| ('it must be somebody else's')

[A] |Do you like pόp-music?|
   [B] |Sǒmetimes,| ('but not in general')
[A] |Are you búsy?|
   [B] |Not rěally.| ('Well, I am, but not so busy that I can't talk to you')

At the beginning or in the middle of a sentence, the fall-rise tone is a more forceful alternative to the rising tone, expressing the assertion of one point, together with the implication that another point is to follow:

|Mòst of the tíme | we stayed on the bèach.|

|Most yǒung people | take plenty of èxercise.|

|He's not a relǎxed lecturer | but he's a drìving lecturer.|

A meaning which can be expressed by intonation may have to be expressed by a different grammatical construction in writing. Compare:

|You don't see a fox every dǎy.| ⟨speech⟩
It is not every day that one sees a fox. ⟨writing⟩

In both cases the implication is: 'it happens quite rarely'.

Conversation in transcription

42

After this brief survey of some basic features of spoken English and how intonation is represented in written transcription, it is time for an application of the system to a longer stretch of text than we have been able to offer in the isolated examples above. So, here again is the vivid account of the Sunday lunch (given in 19), but now with the intonation indicated as follows:

- **Tone units:** To highlight the chunking feature of speech, there is one tone unit per line (with | marking the end of each tone unit).

- **Tones:** There are three tone types: falling tone (dò), rising tone (dό), fall-rise tone (dǒ).

- **Pauses** are indicated by a dash (–).

   |Well I had some people to lunch on Sùnday|
   and – they turned up half an hour èarly | – (laughs) –
   I mean you know what [g] getting up Sùnday's líke |
   ǎnyway |
   and – I'd – I was behind in any càse | –
   and I'd said to them one o'clόck | –
   and I ǎlmost phoned them up and said |
   come a bit làter | –
   and then I thought oh they've probably lèft by nόw | –

so I dìdn't | –
and – twelve thírty | –
nòw | –
that càn't be thém | –
and it wàs | –
and they'd they'd lèft |
plenty of tìme |
for all their connĕctions |
and they got all their connĕctions |
at ónce | –
and it was annŏying |
cos they came with this – chìld | –
you knów |
who was running all òver the place |
and they kept coming in and chàtting to mé |
and I couldn't get òn with thíngs |
and I I get really erm – you know when when I'm trying to còok | –
and people come and chàt |
I I get terribly put òff | –
can't get on with things at àll |
erm – and yet you feel terribly anti-sŏcial |
if you you dò just stay in the kítchen |
ànyway |

If you read this extract aloud, giving emphasis to the pitch movements in the syllables with tone marks and making pauses where they are indicated, you will find this version less rambling and more coherent than the first version. Yet the text is identical in the two versions.

This goes to show that intonation is an important part of spoken language. But, of course, we can never manage to give an adequate written representation of what real speech is like. What we can do to get a better idea of real speech – not only of what was said, but also how it was said – is at least to indicate, as here, the main features of spoken discourse – by far the most widely used form of English.

A note on phonetic symbols
43

Phonetic symbols are used only occasionally in this text, where they are needed to illustrate a grammatical point or rule. We have tried to use a system of transcription which is not biased towards a particular kind of speech, but this is not easy since British and American English (the two national varieties we are mainly dealing with) differ more in pronunciation than in any other respect. To make things simple, we consider only one accent from each national variety: **Received Pronunciation**, or RP, which is commonly used as a standardized accent for the learning of British English pronunciation, and **General American** pronunciation, or GA, which has a somewhat comparable status in the United States of America. However, considering the limited use we make of phonetic symbols, other standardised varieties of speech (e.g. for Australian English) are also reasonably well represented. Phonetic symbols, where they occur, will be

Key to phonetic symbols

Vowels		Consonants	
iː	as in b*ea*d	p	as in *p*ig
ɪ	as in b*i*d	b	as in *b*ig
e	as in b*e*d	t	as in *t*wo
æ	as in b*a*d	d	as in *d*o
ɑː	as in c*a*lm	k	as in *c*ome, *k*ing
ɒ	as in c*o*t ⟨RP⟩	g	as in *g*um
ɔː	as in c*au*ght ⟨RP⟩	tʃ	as in *ch*eap
ʊ	as in p*u*ll	ʤ	as in *j*eep, bri*dg*e
uː	as in p*oo*l	f	as in *f*ew
ʌ	as in c*u*t	v	as in *v*iew
ɜː	as in b*i*rd ⟨RP⟩ (*see* Note)	θ	as in *th*ing
ə	as in *a*bout	ð	as in *th*en
		s	as in i*c*e, *s*ay
Diphthongs		z	as in e*y*e*s*, *z*oo
eɪ	as in f*ai*l	ʃ	as in pre*ss*ure, *sh*ow
oʊ	as in f*oa*l	ʒ	as in plea*s*ure
aɪ	as in f*i*le	h	as in *h*ot
aʊ	as in f*ow*l	m	as in su*m*
ɔɪ	as in f*oi*l	n	as in su*n*
ɪə	as in p*eer* ⟨RP⟩ ⎫	ŋ	as in su*ng*
eə	as in p*air* ⟨RP⟩ ⎬ (*see* Note)	l	as in *l*ot
ʊə	as in p*ure* ⟨RP⟩ ⎭	r	as in *r*ot
		w	as in *w*et
		j	as in *y*et

Note

Corresponding to the ⟨RP⟩ diphthongs /ɪə/, /ɛə/, /ʊə/ are the ⟨GA⟩ r-coloured diphthongs which may be transcribed: /ɪr/, /ɛr/, and /ʊr/. Similarly, corresponding to the ⟨RP⟩ long vowel /ɜː/ is the r-coloured vowel which may be transcribed: /ɜr/: e.g. klɑːk∥klɜrk for *clerk.*

enclosed in slant lines, for example: /k/, /ʊ/, /θ/, /mʌst/. We use the double bar (‖) to separate RP and GA pronunciations where necessary: e.g. /et‖eɪt/ for *ate*.

Geographical and national varieties: ⟨AmE⟩, ⟨BrE⟩

44

English is spoken as a native language by over three hundred million people: in the United States of America, Great Britain, Canada, Australia, the Caribbean, Ireland, New Zealand and other places. This means there is a great abundance of English dialectal variation throughout the world. But when we come to the study of grammar in standard varieties of English, the differences are small. Since the varieties of English used in the United States and in Britain are the most important in terms of population and use throughout the world, the only national varieties we shall distinguish in this book are American English ⟨AmE⟩ and British English ⟨BrE⟩. The grammatical differences between these two varieties (in comparison with differences in pronunciation and vocabulary) are not very great, and are almost negligible in ⟨formal, written⟩ usage. However, some brief examples here will show the kinds of difference which exist between ⟨AmE⟩ and ⟨BrE⟩, and which will be pointed out in Parts Two and Three.

- *got/gotten*: ⟨AmE⟩ has two past participle forms of *get*: *gotten* and *got*, whereas ⟨BrE⟩ has only one: *got* (*see* 559). (The past tense is *got* in both varieties.) For example:

  ⟨AmE⟩: Have you *gotten/got* the theater tickets?
  ⟨BrE⟩: Have you *got* the theatre tickets?

- **Simple past and present perfect:** There is also a tendency to use the simple past tense in ⟨AmE⟩ where in ⟨BrE⟩ the present perfect is used. For example, with *yet* or *already* (*see* 125, Note *a*):

  ⟨AmE⟩: *Did* you *eat* breakfast already?
  ⟨BrE or AmE⟩: *Have* you *eaten* breakfast already?

- **Subjunctive:** The use of the subjunctive after verbs like *demand, require, insist, suggest*, etc. is more common in ⟨AmE⟩ than in ⟨BrE⟩, where *should* + infinitive is preferred:

  ⟨typical of AmE⟩: They suggested that he *be* dropped from the team.
  ⟨typical of BrE⟩: They suggested that he *should be* dropped from the team.

- *different from/than*: The normal word after *different* is *than* in ⟨AmE⟩, but *from* in ⟨BrE⟩.

  ⟨AmE⟩: They're taking a very different attitude *than* their employers.
  ⟨BrE⟩: They're taking a very different attitude *from* their employers.

- *from ... through, from ... to*: There are some other differences in prepositional usage, such as the use of *from X through Y* in ⟨AmE⟩ to clarify that a period includes both *X* and *Y*:

> ⟨AmE⟩: The tour lasted *from* July *through* September.
> ⟨BrE⟩: The tour lasted *from* July *to* September (inclusive).

> (In ⟨BrE⟩ the word *inclusive* is sometimes added to make clear that the period includes the last-mentioned period, here September.)

Within each English-speaking country there are many differences of regional dialect (e.g. between the English spoken in the Southern States of the USA and in other parts of the same country). These differences rarely affect grammatical usage in written English or in standardized spoken English, and so we ignore them in this book.

Levels of usage:
formal and informal English (⟨formal⟩, ⟨informal⟩)

45

We turn now to the way English varies not according to geographical differences, but according to differences in the relation between speaker (or writer) and hearer (or reader) (we can refer to these as **levels of usage** – *see* 15–16).

Formal language is the type of language we use publicly for some serious purpose, for example in official reports, business letters, regulations, and academic writing. Formal English is nearly always ⟨written⟩, but exceptionally it is used in ⟨speech⟩, for example in formal public speeches or lectures.

Informal language (also called 'colloquial') is the language of ordinary conversation, of personal letters, and of private interaction in general. It is the first variety of language that a native speaking child becomes familiar with. Because it is generally more accessible to readers or listeners than formal English, it is used more and more nowadays in public communication of a popular kind: for example, in advertisements, popular newspapers, and broadcasting. Informality is typically found in ⟨spoken⟩ language, although it also occurs quite widely in the ⟨written⟩ medium, e.g. in diaries, personal letters and popular fiction.

An example of the formality scale
46

The difference between ⟨formal⟩ and ⟨informal⟩ usage is best seen as a scale, rather than as a simple 'yes or no' distinction. Consider the following example:

> There are many friends to whom one would hesitate to entrust one's
> own children. ⟨formal⟩   [1]

This is towards the formal end of the scale for a number of reasons:

- Use of *there are*, which, unlike the less formal *there's* or *there is*, maintains the plural concord with *many friends* as subject (*see* 547–9).
- Use of *many friends* itself, rather than the more informal *a lot of friends* or *lots of friends* (*see* 72-3).
- Use of the initial preposition to introduce a relative clause (*to whom*), rather than a construction with a final preposition *who(m) . . . to*. (Compare, for example, the formal *the firm for which she works* with the informal *the firm she works for* – *see* 686–94.)
- Related to the preceding feature is the use of *whom*, which is itself a rather formal pronoun (*see* 686–94) compared with *who* – for example, in *Whom did they meet?* compared with *Who did they meet?*
- Use of the generic personal pronoun *one* (*see* 98), rather than the more informal use of generic *you*.

47

If we replaced all these features of [1] by informal equivalents, the sentence would run as follows [1a]:

> There's lots of friends who you would hesitate to entrust your own children to. ⟨informal⟩   [1a]

However, it is significant that this sentence seems very unidiomatic. The reason is that a translation from one variety to another, like translation from one language to another, cannot be treated as a mechanical exercise. In practice, informal English prefers its own typical features, which include, for example, contracted forms of verbs (*there's* rather than *there is*, etc.), omission of the relative pronoun *who/whom/that*, and informal vocabulary rather than more formal vocabulary such as *entrust*. As an example of informal English, the following is a more natural-sounding sentence than [1a]:

> There's lots of friends you'd never trust with your own children.   [1b]

However, we could still make lexical changes to increase or decrease the formality of this sentence. For example, replacing *children* by *kids* would make the sentence even more informal:

> There's lots of friends you'd never trust with your own kids.   [1c]

On the other hand, the following, with its use of *there are* and *would*, is a more formal variant:

> There are lots of friends you would never trust with your own children.   [1d]

It is therefore possible to place the above sentences (leaving aside [1a]) on a scale of formality in the following order:

> There are many friends to whom one would hesitate . . . ⟨most formal⟩   [1]

There are lots of friends you would never trust with your
　　own children. [1d]
There's lots of friends you'd never trust with your own children. [1b]
There's lots of friends you'd never trust with your own kids
　　⟨most informal⟩. [1c]

However, it is difficult to be precise about degrees of formality and informality, so
that we often have to be content with relative phrases such as '⟨rather formal⟩'
or '⟨rather informal⟩'.

48
One reason for this vagueness is that formality, as a scale, can be applied on
the one hand to aspects of the situation in which communication takes place,
and on the other hand to features of language which correlate with those
aspects. There is a two-way relation here: not only does situation influence
the choice of language, but choice of language influences situation – or,
more precisely, the nature of the situation as perceived by the speaker and
hearer. Thus, someone answering the phone with the ⟨very formal⟩ question
To whom am I speaking? would, by that very utterance, establish a more
formal relationship with the other speaker than if the question had been *Who
am I speaking to?*

Formality of vocabulary and grammar
49
In English there are many differences of vocabulary between formal and informal
language. Much of the vocabulary of formal English is of French, Latin, or Greek
origin. In contrast, informal language is characterised by vocabulary of Anglo-
Saxon origin. Compare

　　commence, continue, conclude ⟨formal⟩
　　begin, keep (on/up), end ⟨less formal⟩

Many phrasal and phrasal prepositional verbs (*see* 630–4) belong to informal
English. Compare:

⟨formal or common core word⟩	⟨informal expression⟩
discover	*find out*
encounter	*come across*
enter	*go in(to)*
investigate	*look into*
surrender	*give in*

These differences show how formal and informal English provide the speaker
with substantially different resources for communication, and again illustrate
the difficulty of translating a sentence in one variety into an equivalent sentence
in the other. The choice of appropriate grammar is intimately connected to the
choice of vocabulary.

Impersonal style: ⟨impersonal⟩

50

Formal written language often goes with an impersonal style; i.e. one in which the speaker avoids personal references to speaker and/or hearer, such as *I*, *you*, and *we*. Some of the common features of impersonal language are passives (*see* 613–18), sentences beginning with introductory *it* (*see* 542–6), and abstract nouns (*see* 68–9). All these features are illustrated in:

> *Announcement from the librarian*
> It has been noted with concern that the stock of books in the library has been declining alarmingly. Students are asked to remind themselves of the rules for borrowing and return of books, and to bear in mind the needs of other users. Penalties for overdue books will in the future be strictly enforced.

The author of the above could have written a more informal and less impersonal message as follows:

> *Bring those books back!*
> Books in the library have been disappearing. Please make sure you know the rules for borrowing, and don't forget that the library is for *everyone's* convenience. From now on, we're going to enforce the rules strictly. *You have been warned!*

Polite and familiar language: ⟨polite⟩, ⟨familiar⟩

51

Our language tends to be more ⟨polite⟩ when we are talking to a person we do not know well, or to a person more senior in age or social position. Context also plays a role: for example, if we are asking a big favour, such as the loan of a large sum of money, this will induce greater politeness than if we were asking a small favour, such as the loan of a pen.

English has no special familiar pronouns or polite pronouns, like some languages (e.g. French *tu/vous*, German *du/Sie*). But familiarity can be shown in other ways. Thus, when we know someone well or intimately, we tend to drop polite forms of language. Instead of using a polite vocative such as *Mrs*, *Mr*, or *Ms* we tend to use first name (*Peter*) or a short name (*Pete*) or even a nickname or pet name (*Misty*, *Lilo*, *Boo-boo*, etc.). Interestingly, present-day English makes little use of the surname alone, except in third person reference (e.g. *Clinton*, *Eliot*, *Shakespeare*) to someone one does not know personally, but by repute, such as a famous author or politician.

52

Polite language behaviour is most observable in such speech acts as requesting, advising, and offering (*see* 333–5, 347–8). Compare, for example, these requests:

> Shut the door, will you? ⟨familiar⟩
> Would you please shut the door? ⟨rather polite⟩

I wonder if you would mind shutting the door. ⟨more polite⟩

The word *please* has the sole function of indicating politeness when one is making a request. But it has little effect in itself: to give a really polite impression, *please* usually has to be combined with devices of indirectness such as using a question, the hypothetical *could* or *would*, etc. (*see* 248, 333–4).

At the other end of the scale, slang is language which is very familiar in style, and is usually restricted to members of a particular social group, for example, 'teenage slang', 'army slang', 'theatre slang'. Slang is not easy to understand unless you are a member of a particular group or class of people. Because of its restricted use, and its short life, we will not be concerned with slang in this book.

Tactful and tentative language

53

Politeness and indirectness are linked with **tact**. To be tactful is to avoid causing offence or distress to another. Sometimes tact means disguising or covering up the truth. A request, suggestion or piece of advice can be made more tactful by making it more **tentative**. Compare:

> You'd better put off the meeting until tomorrow. ⟨informal, familiar⟩
> Look – why don't you postpone the meeting until tomorrow? ⟨informal⟩
> May I suggest you postpone the meeting until tomorrow? ⟨tactful, tentative⟩
> Don't you think it might be a good idea to postpone the meeting until tomorrow? ⟨more tactful, more tentative⟩

In other cases tentativeness is simply an indication of speakers' reluctance to commit themselves on given questions. For example, *might just* is a more tentative way of expressing possibility than *may*:

> Someone *may* have made a mistake.
> Someone *might just* have made a mistake. ⟨more tentative⟩

Literary, elevated or rhetorical language: ⟨literary⟩, ⟨elevated⟩, ⟨rhetorical⟩

54

Some features of English of limited use have a 'literary' or 'elevated' tone: they belong mainly to the literary or religious language of the past, but can still be used today by someone who wants to move or impress us. An example of elevated language comes from the Inaugural Speech of President Kennedy (1961):

> Let the word go forth from this time and place, to friend and foe
>   alike, that the torch has passed to a new generation of
>   Americans . . .

This begins with the elevated *let*-construction (*see* 498), and also contains old-fashioned words (archaisms) such as *forth* and *foe*.

In addition to the variety labels ⟨literary⟩ and ⟨elevated⟩, we occasionally use the similar label ⟨rhetorical⟩. This signifies a stylised use of language, consciously chosen for an emphatic or emotive effect. A good example of this is the so-called 'rhetorical question' (*see* 304), which is meant to be interpreted as an emphatic statement:

> Is it any wonder that politicians are mistrusted? (= 'It is no
> wonder . . .')

Although we meet them in the literature of earlier periods, literary, elevated and rhetorical forms of language tend to be unusual in the English of today (and noticeable for that very reason). We will refer to them only very occasionally in this book.

Levels of usage: a map of variety labels

55

Apart from the national varieties ⟨AmE⟩ and ⟨BrE⟩, the different types of English we have discussed are related to one another, and might go under the general title of '**levels of usage**'. We might attempt to place them on a scale running from 'elevated' English at one extreme to 'slang' at the other extreme. But it is probably better to think in terms of three pairs of contrasting values, as shown:

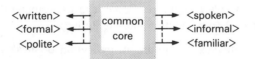

This diagram represents only the most important levels of usage, ignoring the more restricted variety labels, such as ⟨impersonal⟩ and ⟨elevated⟩. The features on the left tend to go together – likewise the features on the right – and this is conveyed by the vertical broken lines. But the lines are broken because the connection does not always hold: for example, it is possible to express oneself politely in spoken English, and it is possible to express oneself informally in written English.

The horizontal arrows represent scales of contrast. The common core of 'unmarked' usage occupies a middle area between the extremes of each of the three scales.

56

In Parts Two and Three we make free use of the labels for varieties of English, because we feel it is important to give as full guidance as possible on the 'appropriate use' of English grammatical forms and structures. Some speakers of English may disagree with some of our judgements on the uses of these labels. This is because our knowledge of 'levels of usage' still remains, today, very much a subjective matter, depending on the perceptions of people who use the language. For example, an older English speaker might regard as 'familiar' a form of language which might not seem so to a younger speaker. There are also differences of perception in different English-speaking countries. Thus, without considering these labels as descriptive of general standards of appropriateness, we would like you to use them for guidance in your own use of the language.

Part Two

Grammar in use

Section A: Concepts

Referring to objects, substances and materials

57
Through nouns and noun phrases, grammar organizes the way we refer to objects. We begin with **concrete nouns**, or nouns referring to physical objects and substances. (We use the word 'object' to refer generally to things, animals, people, etc.) Our first topic will be **count** and **mass** concrete nouns, and the various ways in which they are linked by *of*.

Singular and plural: one and many
58
Count nouns refer in the singular to one object, and in the plural to more than one object. As the name implies, count nouns can be counted: *one star, two stars*, etc. (*see* 597–601):

Singular	*Plural*		
a star	two stars	three stars	seven stars, etc.
one star			
a single star			

Groups of objects
59
We may refer to objects as belonging to a group or set, as follows:

a $\left\{ \begin{array}{l} \text{group} \\ \text{number} \end{array} \right\}$ of stars   a small group of stars   a large group of stars

Group nouns: *a group (of stars)*
60
Nouns like *group, set,* and *class,* which refer to a set of objects, are called **group nouns**. Like other count nouns, group nouns may be singular or plural; e.g.

one *group* of stars	three *groups* of stars
a *set* of tools	two *sets* of tools
a *class* of insects	several *classes* of insects

Often a special group noun is used with certain kinds of objects:

an *army* [of soldiers]	a *crew* [of sailors]
a *crowd* of people	a *gang* of thieves, bandits, etc.
a *herd* of cattle	a *pack* of cards
a *flock* of sheep	a *constellation* of stars
a *bunch* of flowers	a *series* of games

Many group nouns refer to a group of people having a special relationship with one another, or brought together for a particular reason: *tribe, family, committee, club, audience, government, administration, team, etc.* There is often a choice of whether to use a singular or plural verb (*see* 510):

- **singular**: when we treat the group as a single thing
- **plural**: when we treat the group as a collection of individuals

    The audience is/are enjoying the show.

Notice also the difference between *its mind* (singular) and *their minds* (plural) in this example:

$$\text{The government never} \begin{cases} \text{makes up its mind} \\ \text{make up their minds} \end{cases} \text{in a hurry.}$$

Part and whole: *part of the cake, a piece of cake*
61
Parts of objects can be referred to by

- **part nouns** like *part* (contrasted with *whole*), *half, a quarter, two thirds, etc*;
- **unit nouns** like *piece, slice*:

the (whole) cake	a slice of the cake	half (of) the cake	(a) quarter of the cake

part of the cake

Mass nouns: *milk, sand*, etc.
62
Mass nouns (sometimes called 'non-count' or 'uncountable' nouns) are so called because they cannot be counted like count nouns (*see* 597). They typically refer to substances, whether

> solid, e.g. *butter, wood, rock, iron, glass*
> liquid, e.g. *oil, water, milk,* or
> gas, e.g. *smoke, air, butane*

Mass nouns are always singular: it makes no sense to 'count' the quantity of a mass substance which cannot be divided into separate objects. You can say:

> There's no *milk* in the refrigerator.
> We had two *bottles of milk* to cook with.

BUT NOT: *There are no milks in the refrigerator.
> *We had two milks to cook with. (*see* 66)

Some mass nouns, we might argue, should 'really' be count, because the 'substance' consists of separate things: *furniture* consists of *pieces of furniture*, *grass* of separate *blades of grass, hair* of separate *strands of hair* (or *hairs*), *wheat* of separate *grains of wheat*. But **psychologically** we think of such things as indivisible when we use a mass noun.

Note
On mass nouns which can be 'converted' into count nouns (*two coffees, please*), *see* 66.

Division of objects and substances
Unit nouns: **a piece of bread, a block of ice,** *etc.*
63
As with single objects, masses can be subdivided by the use of nouns like *part*:

> Part of the butter has melted.

In addition, there are many countable **unit nouns**, as we call them, which can be used to subdivide notionally a mass into separate 'pieces'. *Piece* and *bit* ⟨informal⟩ are general purpose unit nouns, which can be combined with most mass nouns:

a *piece* of bread	a *piece* of paper	a *piece* of land
a *bit* of food	a *bit* of paint	a *bit* of air

There are also unit nouns which typically go with particular mass nouns:

a *blade* of grass	a *sheet* of paper
a *block* of ice	a *speck* of dust
a *pile* of rubbish	a *bar* of chocolate
two *lumps* of sugar	a *length* of new rope
several *cups* of coffee	a fresh *load* of hay

As with part nouns, unit nouns are linked to the other nouns by *of*. Sometimes, the word for a container (*cup, bottle,* etc) is used as a unit noun, as in *a cup of tea, a bottle of wine*.

Nouns of measure: a kilo of flour, *etc.*
64
Another way to divide a mass into separate 'pieces' is to measure it off into length, weight, etc:

DEPTH:	a *foot* of water	AREA:	an *acre* of land
LENGTH:	a *yard* of cloth		a *hectare* of rough ground
WEIGHT:	an *ounce* of tobacco	VOLUME:	a *pint* of beer
	a *kilo* of flour		a *litre*‖*liter* of milk

Species nouns: a type of, *etc.*
65
Here is another type of division: nouns like *type, kind, sort, species, class, variety* can divide a mass or a set of objects into 'types' or 'species':

> Teak is a *type* of wood.
> A Ford is a *make* of car.
> A tiger is a *species* of mammal. ⟨rather formal⟩

We usually place adjectives and other modifiers before the species noun rather than the noun which follows *of*:

> a Japanese make of car (NOT *a make of Japanese car)
> a delicious kind of bread.

Notice that the second noun, when count, usually has no indefinite article: *a strange kind of mammal* (NOT *a strange kind of a mammal*).

In ⟨informal⟩ English, there is a mixed construction in which the determiner (if any) and the verb are plural, although the species noun is singular:

> These kind of dogs are easy to train. ⟨informal⟩

Compare the normal construction: *This kind of dog is easy to train.*

Nouns which can be both count and mass
66
Quite a number of nouns can be both count and mass (*see* 597). *Wood*, for instance, is count when it refers to a collection of trees (= a forest), and mass when it refers to the material of which trees are composed:

> We went for a walk in the *woods*. [count]
> In America a lot of the houses are made of *wood*. [mass]

Many food nouns are count when they refer to the article in its 'whole' state, but are mass when they refer to the food in the mass, e.g. as eaten at table:

> There was *a* huge *cake* in the dining room.
> BUT: 'Let them eat *cake*', said the queen.

> She began peeling *potatoes*.
> BUT: She took a mouthful of *potato*.

> Do we have enough *food* for the weekend?
> BUT: Some of the tastiest *foods* are pretty indigestible.

> I'd like *a boiled egg* for my breakfast.
> BUT: I'd prefer *some scrambled egg* on toast, please.

In other cases English has a separate count noun and a separate mass noun referring to the same area of meaning:

Count	Mass
Do you have *a fresh loaf*?	Do you have *some fresh bread*?
Would you like *a meal*?	Would you like *some more food*?
She's looking for *a new job*.	She's looking for *some interesting work*.
There are too *many vehicles* on the road.	There is too *much traffic* on the road.

Sometimes words which are usually mass nouns are 'converted' into count unit nouns or count species nouns:

> Two more *coffees*, please. (= cups of coffee)
> Current London auctions deal with *teas* from 25 countries. (= kinds of tea)

Occasionally the opposite happens: count nouns are 'converted' into mass nouns after a noun of measure: *a few square metres‖meters of floor; an inch of cigarette*.

Concrete and abstract

67

Abstract nouns refer to qualities (*difficulty*), events (*arrival*), feelings (*love*), etc. Just like concrete nouns, abstract nouns combine with part nouns (*part of the time*), unit nouns (*a piece of information*), and species nouns (*a new kind of music*). Abstract nouns can be either count or mass, even though these notions cannot be understood in a physical sense.

In general, abstract nouns can more easily be both 'count' and 'mass' than concrete nouns. Nouns referring to events and occasions (*talk, knock, shot, meeting*, etc.) are usually count:

> There was *a loud knock* at the door.
> The committee has had *three meetings*.

But *talk* (with other nouns like *sound, thought*) can also be a mass noun:

> I had *a long talk* with her.
> In the country we now hear *talk* of famine.
>
> I couldn't hear a *sound*.
> These modern planes can fly faster than *sound*.
>
> What are your *thoughts* on this problem?
> He was deep in *thought*.

Other abstract nouns tend to be mass nouns only: *honesty, happiness, information, progress, applause, homework, research*, etc:

> Her speech was followed by loud *applause*.
> I have some *homework* to finish.
> He is engaged in scientific *research*.
> *Wealth* did not bring them *happiness*.

68

But again, many such nouns (e.g. *experience, difficulty, trouble*) can be either mass or count (with some difference of meaning):

> We had little *difficulty* convincing him.
> BUT: He is having financial *difficulties*.
> He is a policeman of many years' *experience*.
> BUT: Tell me about your *experiences* abroad.
> I have some *work* to do this evening. [*work* = labour, activity]
> BUT: They have played two *works* by an unknown French composer.
> [artistic or musical work]

Some nouns are mass nouns in English, but not in some other languages. Examples are *advice, information, news, shopping*:

> Can you give me *some good advice* on what to buy here?
> Do you have *any information* about the airport buses?
> What's *the latest news* about the election?
> The department stores stay open for *evening shopping*.

Partition and division with abstract nouns: *a useful bit of advice*
69
Part with abstract nouns is illustrated by:

> Part of his *education* was at the University of Cambridge.

Division is illustrated in these phrases:

Unit nouns:	We had *a (good) game of chess.*
	He suffered from *(terrible) fits of anger.*
	There was *a (sudden) burst of applause.*
	Let me give you *a (useful) bit of advice.*
	Here's *an (interesting) item of news.* (A L S O : *a news item*)
	This translation is one of *her best pieces of work.*
Measure nouns:	*three months of hard work*
	(also *three months' hard work*) (see 107)
Species nouns:	*an (exciting) type of dance*
	a (strange) kind of behaviour

Amount or quantity

Amount words (or quantifiers) (*see* 675–80): *all, some,* etc.

70

Amount words like *all, some* and *none* can be used with both count and mass nouns:

(A) **Used with singular count nouns like *cake, house*** they are equivalent to part nouns:

all of the cake   some of the cake   none of the cake
(= the whole of   (= part of the cake)
the cake)

(B) **Used with plural nouns like *stars*:**

all (of) the stars   some of the stars   none of the stars

(C) **Used with mass nouns like *land*:**

all of the land   some of the land   none of the land

Note these relations of meaning between *all, some* and *none*:

> *Some* of the stars were invisible.
>   = *Not all* (of) the stars were visible.
> *None* of the stars was visible.
>   = *All* (of) the stars were invisible.

Further examples:

> *Some of* the patients will have pain when they come to hospital.
>   (i.e. others will not)

None of their attempts so far has been wholly successful.
(i.e. All attempts have been unsuccessful.)

71
Amount words specify more precisely the meaning 'some':

A large quantity

> { They have lost *many* of their ***friends***. [count]
> { They have lost *much* of their ***support***. [mass]
> { *A lot of* our ***friends*** live in San Francisco. [count]
> { *A lot of* our ***support*** comes from city dwellers. [mass]
> { *A large number* of ***people*** have recently joined the party. [count]
> { They've been making *a great deal of **noise*** recently. [mass]

A small quantity

> { We managed to speak to *a few of* the ***guests***. [count]
> { Could you possibly spare *a little of* your ***time***? [mass]
> { She invited just a *small number of* her ***friends***. [count]
> { I'm afraid we've run into *a bit of **trouble***. [mass]

Not a large quantity

> { *Not many of **us*** would have been as brave as she was. [count]
> { I promise I'll take very *little of* your ***time***. [mass]

Notice that *few* and *little* without *a* have a negative bias. Compare:

> *A few* (= a small number, some of) of the students pass the examination.
> *Few* (= not many) of the students pass the examination.

Other words of quantity or amount:

> *One/two/three* (and other numerals, *see* 602) of our best players have been injured.
> *Half* (of) the money was stolen.
> *More* of your time should be spent in the office. (ALSO: *less* of your time)
> *Most* of our friends live locally.
> *Several* of the paintings (= 'slightly more than a few') are from private collections.

Note
With *a/the majority of* and *a minority of* (both ⟨rather formal⟩) it is normal to use plural and group nouns:

> *The majority of* farmers are the sons and grandsons of farmers (= Most of the farmers . . .)
> Only *a minority of* women feel able to report such attacks to the police. (= fewer than half . . .)

(On concord with the verb in these and similar cases, *see* 510.)

Many and *much*; *a lot of, lots of*

72

Many and *much* are often used in combinations with *as, too, so* (*as many/much as, too many/much, so many/much*) and in questions (*how many/much?*)

Compare the count and mass words in the questions and answers below:

Count	Mass
[A] *How many* of the rolls have you eaten?	[A] *How much* of the bread have you eaten?

	Count		Mass
	All of them		*All* of it
	Most of them		*Most* of it
	A lot of them		*A lot* of it
[B]	*Half* of them	[B]	*Half* of it
	Several of them		—
	A few of them		*A little* of it
	None of them		*None* of it

Indefinite use of amount words

73

For the amount of words above there is a definite 'total' (shown by the circles in the diagrams in 70) within which amounts are to be measured. Now we look at the general (indefinite) use of amount words, where no total is given. Here the amount word is used as a determiner e.g. *most people* (see 522), and *of* and *the* are generally omitted. (But *of* occurs with *a lot of, a great deal of, a number of, lots of people*, etc.)

Count	Mass
All crimes are avoidable.	*All violence is* avoidable.
(i.e. all of the crimes in the world)	
We didn't buy *many* things.	We didn't buy *much* food.

Count

All pupils should learn to ski.
We saw *several snakes* down by the river.
Most men don't know how to dance.
Few new writers have their first story accepted.
I want to ask Mr Danby *a few questions*.
I think people catch *fewer colds* these days.

Mass

There was *less excitement* in the gilt-edged market.
Plants in plastic pots usually need *less water* than those in clay pots.
The village can provide *no food* for the refugees.
It will take *a little time* to clear up the mess.
Put *a few pieces of butter* on top of the vegetables.

In ⟨informal⟩ style, *a lot of* (or *lots of*) is preferred to *many* or *much* in positive statements:

Many patients arrive on the surgical ward as planned admissions. ⟨formal⟩

You find *a lot of* nurses have given up smoking. ⟨informal⟩

There's *lots of spare* time if you need it.

But in questions and after negatives (*very*) *many* and *much* are not restricted to ⟨formal⟩ English:

> { Have you seen *much* of Julie recently?
> { I don't eat *much* in the mornings.
> { Do *many* people attend the meetings?
> { We don't get *many* visitors in the winter.

Words of general or inclusive meaning

74

All, *both*, *every*, *each*, and (sometimes) *any* are amount words of **general** or **inclusive** meaning. With count nouns, *all* is used for quantities of more than two, and *both* for quantities of two only:

> The western is a popular kind of movie with *both* sexes and *all* ages.

Every, each

75

Words like *every* and *each* can be called **distributive**, because they pick out the members of a set or group singly, rather than look at them all together. Apart from this difference, *every* has the same meaning as *all*:

> *All* good teachers study their subject(s) carefully.   [1]
> *Every* good teacher studies his or her subject carefully.   [2]

The 'distributive' meaning of *every* shows in the use of singular forms *teacher*, *studies*, *his or her* in [2]. (However, *see* 96 on the use of *he or she*, *his or her*, etc.)

76

Each is like *every* except that it can be used when the set has only two members. Thus *each* (unlike *all* and *every*) can sometimes replace *both*:

> She kissed her mother on { *each cheek.*
> { *both cheeks.*

Note also the difference between:

> She complimented *each/every* member of the winning team.   [3]
> She complimented *all* (the) members of the winning team.   [4]

Whereas [3] suggests that she spoke to each member of the team separately, [4] suggests that she made one speech, addressing all members of the team at once. Like *every* in meaning are *everyone, everybody, everything,* and *everywhere.*

Any, either

77
The most familiar use of the determiners *any* and *either* is in negative sentences and questions (*see* 697–9), but here we consider them as inclusive words. *Any* can sometimes replace *all* and *every* in positive sentences:

> *Any* new vehicle has to be registered immediately.   [5]

> (Compare: Every new vehicle *has* to . . .
>   All new vehicles *have* to . . .)

Here *any* has the same inclusive meaning as *all* and *every* in [1] and [2]. But *any* means something different in:

> You can paint the wall *any* colour you like.

Any colour means 'red *or* green *or* blue *or* . . .', while *every colour* means 'red *and* green *and* blue *and* . . . .' *Any* means 'it doesn't matter who/which/what . . . one chooses'.

78
When there are only two objects, *either* is used instead of *any*:

> You could ask *either* of my parents.
>   (= either my father or my mother)

Compare the use of *neither* for two objects, 379, 584: *Neither of my parents is keen on rock music.*

79
Any can also be used with mass nouns and plural count nouns:

> Àny land is valuable thése days.
> You're lucky to find àny shops open on Sŭnday.

As shown here, *any* often takes nuclear stress (*see* 36). Like *any* are *anyone, anybody, anything, anywhere, anyhow, anyway* and ⟨informal AmE⟩ *anyplace*:

> *Anyone* will tell you the way. (= Whoever you ask, he or she will . . .)
> He will eat *anything*. (= He will eat whatever you give him.)

Scale of amount

80
We can order the most common amount words roughly on a scale, moving from the inclusive words at the top, to the negative words at the bottom:

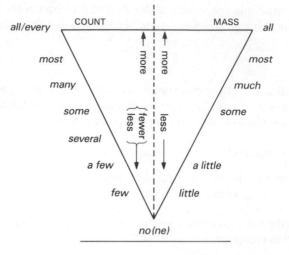

(*Any* we place separately, because its main use, in negative and interrogative contexts, does not fit into this scale.)

81

Positions on a scale of amount can be expressed not only through the words already discussed (which are determiners or pronouns) but by pronouns like *everybody, everything,* and by adverbs of frequency (*always*), degree (*entirely*), etc. We show some of the correspondences between different areas of meaning in the table opposite.

Of the columns of the diagram, A–D represent noun phrases, and E–G represent adverbials (to be dealt with later in 449–63). The rows are in ascending order of amount, from the inclusive word *all* to the non-committal word *any*. Here are some examples labelled according to their position in the table opposite:

A1   *All* stress increases the body's need for nutrients.
A2   *All* faculty members were given bonuses.
B2   Are there *many* other names which come to mind?
B3   *Some* of these patients will be nursed in a surgical ward.
C6   *Nobody* was reported injured. / *No one* was hurt.
C7   *Anyone* would be astonished to see the amount of public money wasted.
D6   *Nothing* has yet been decided.
D7   He would do *anything* to please her.
E3   You ought to come over to Cambridge *sometime*.
E4   Cook the vegetables slowly, stirring *occasionally*.

Definite and indefinite meaning: *the, a/an,* zero

82

When we use the definite article *the* we presume that both we and the hearer or reader know what is being talked about. Most of the words we have considered

A Mass	B Count	C Personal	D Non-Personal	E Frequency	F Duration	G Degree
(see 675–8)	*(see* 675–8)	*(see* 679)	*(see* 679)	*(see* 166)	*(see* 161–5)	*(see* 217–8)
1 all	all, every, each,	everyone, everybody	everything	always	always, for ever	absolutely, entirely etc.
2 much, a lot (of)	many, a lot (of)	(many people)	(many things)	often, frequently	(for) a long time	very, (very) much
3 some	some	someone, somebody	something	sometime	(for) sometime	rather, somewhat, quite
4 a little	a few	(a few people)	(a few things)	occasionally	(for) a while	a little, a bit
5 little	few	(few people)	(few things)	rarely, seldom	not . . . (for) long	scarcely, hardly
6 no(ne)	no(ne)	no one, nobody	nothing	never	—	not . . . at all
7 any	any	anyone, anybody	anything	ever	—	at all

in 70 81 are indefinite; but if we want to express indefinite meaning without any added meaning of amount, etc, we use the indefinite article *a/an* (with singular count nouns), or the zero indefinite article with mass nouns or plural count nouns (*see* 597): *Would you like a **drink**? Do you like **chocolate**?*

Uses of the definite article

To express definite meaning we use the definite article *the*. There are four main cases:

Unique use of the

83

When the object or group of objects is the only one that exists (or has existed): *the stars, the earth, the world, the sea, the North Pole, the equator, the Renaissance, the human race*:

> *The North Pole* and *the South Pole* are equally distant from *the equator*.

This **unique** use of *the* also arises where what is referred to is 'understood' to be unique in the context: *the sun, the moon, the kitchen, the town-hall, the Queen, the last President*, etc. We could, if we wanted, make the definite meaning clear by modification after the noun (*the moon belonging to this earth, the kitchen of this house, the Queen of this country*, etc.), but this would normally be unnecessary.

Back-pointing use of **the**
84
When identity has been established by an earlier mention (often with an indefinite article):

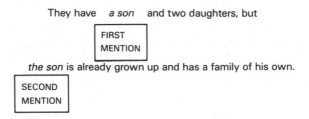

Forward-pointing use of **the**
85
When identity is established by a modifier, such as a relative clause or an *of-*phrase (*see* 641) that follows the noun:

> John returned the radio *he bought yesterday*.
> The wine *of France* is the best in the world.
> The wine *which France produces* is the best *in the world*.
> The discovery *of radium* marked the beginning of a new era of
>   medicine.

Conventional use of **the** (*for institutions, etc.*): **the radio, the paper**
86
When reference is made to an institution shared by the community: *the radio, the television, the telephone, the paper(s)* (i.e. *newspaper(s)*), *the train*, etc.

> What's in *the paper* today?
> She went to London on *the train*.

Most cases of this institutional use are connected with communications and transport. Sometimes (*see* 475) the article may be omitted with this use:

> What's on (*the*) *television* tonight?

Note
After a preposition, *the* is used before parts of the body in constructions like these:

She looked *him* in *the eye* and said 'No'.
Lev smiled and shook *me* by *the hand*.

Usually, in such cases, the direct object refers to the person who 'owns' the body-part (*see* 624).

Generic use of articles
87
The also has a **generic** use, referring to what is general or typical for a whole class of objects. This is found with count nouns:

> *The tiger* is one of the big cats; it is rivalled only by *the lion* in strength and ferocity. *The tiger* has no mane, but in old males *the hair* on *the cheeks* is rather long and spreading.   [1]

Here *the tiger* indicates tigers in general, not one individual. Thus [1] expresses essentially the same meaning as [2] and [3]:

> *Tigers* have no mane.   [2]
> *A tiger* has no mane.   [3]

[2] is the generic use of the indefinite plural form; [3] is the generic use of the indefinite singular. When we are dealing with a whole class of objects as here, the differences between definite and indefinite, singular and plural, tend to lose their importance. There is, however, a slight difference in the fact that *the tiger* (generic) refers to the species as a whole, while *a tiger* (generic) refers to any member of the species. We can say:

> The tiger is in danger of becoming extinct.
> Tigers are in danger of becoming extinct.

BUT NOT:
> *A tiger is in danger of becoming extinct

Specific versus generic meaning
88
In contrast to the **generic** use of *the*, all the other uses (*see* 83–6) may be called **specific**. For mass nouns, there is only one generic form, that with the zero article:

> *Water* is composed of *hydrogen* and *oxygen*.

The ways of expressing generic meaning with count and mass nouns are shown in the table:

	Count	Mass
generic meaning	*the tiger* *a tiger* *tigers*	*water*

As the table implies, *the* is always **specific** with mass nouns (*the water*) and also with plural nouns (*the tigers*) (with the exception of some nationality words, *see* 579). The following examples show generic meaning with three types of noun:

- *butter, Venetian glass, Scandinavian furniture*, . . . (concrete mass nouns)
- *music, English literature, contemporary art*, . . . (abstract mass mouns)
- *dogs, horses, classical languages*, . . . (plural nouns)

In specific use, these nouns take *the*.

Specific Use	Generic Use
• Pass *the butter*, please.	*Butter* is expensive nowadays.
• *The acting* was poor, but we enjoyed *the music*.	I simply love *music* and *dancing*.
• Before you visit Spain, you ought to learn *the language*.	The scientific study of *language* is called linguistics.
• Come and look at *the horses*!	*Horses* are my favourite animals.

89
Notice that English tends to treat mass nouns and plural nouns as generic when they have a modifier before them (*Chinese history*). But when they are followed by a modifier, especially by an *of*-phrase, *the* normally has to be present (*the history of China*). Compare:

Chinese history	*the* history of China
American society	*the* society of America
early mediaeval architecture	*the* architecture of the early middle ages
animal behaviour	*the* behaviour of animals

The tendency is strong with abstract mass nouns. It is less strong with concrete mass nouns and plural nouns. We can omit *the* in

eighteenth-century furniture	(*the*) furniture of the eighteenth century
tropical birds	(*the*) birds of the tropics

Compare:

She's one of the world's experts on { eighteenth-century furniture / (the) furniture of the eighteenth century.

Generic *the* with adjectives, nationality nouns, and group nouns
90
Adjectives are used with generic *the*:

- To denote a class of people (*the poor, the unemployed, the young, the handicapped*) (*see* 448):

  They should see to it that there's work for *the unemployed*, food for *the hungry*, and hospitals for *the sick*.

- To denote an abstract quality (*the absurd, the beautiful, the sublime*) (*see* 448):

  His behaviour on the platform borders on *the ridiculous*.

- With nationality adjectives ending in a sibilant *-ch, -ese, -sh* or *-ss* used to refer to a people as a whole: *the Dutch, the English, the French, the Japanese, the Vietnamese* (*see* 579):

  The French say they must sell more wine to Germany.

Generic *the* is also commonly used:

- With nationality or ethnic nouns (except those ending in *women* or *men*), e.g. *the Indians, the Poles, the Zulus*:

  The plan has received warm support from *the Germans*.

- With group nouns like *the middle class, the public, the administration, the government* (*see* 60), or collective plural nouns such as *the clergy, the police*:

  He was a socialist and believed in the right of *the working class* to control their own destiny.
  The public can help by reporting anything suspicious to *the police*.

Other words of definite meaning
91
Apart from common nouns (i.e. count and mass nouns) with *the*, the following words always or usually signal definite meanings:

Proper nouns (*see* 667): *Susan, Chicago, Tuesday, Africa*, etc.
Personal pronouns (*see* 619): *I, we, he, she, it, they, you*, etc.
Pointer words or **demonstratives** (*see* 521): *this, that, these, those*.

We shall deal with these in turn, bearing in mind the types of definiteness already discussed (*see* 83–6).

Proper nouns
92
Proper nouns are understood to have unique reference: *Africa* refers to one particular continent, and *Susan* (in a given conversation) refers to one particular person. Here no *the* comes before the proper noun (*see* 667), because definite meaning is 'built into' the noun itself. This also normally applies when a proper

noun is the first word in a two-word name, such as *Harvard University, Oxford Street.*

93
But when proper nouns change into common nouns, *the* can be used. This happens, for example, when we need to distinguish two or more things of the same name.

> *the Susan* next door (i.e. not the Susan who works in your office)   [4]
> *the Venice* of story books (i.e. not the Venice of reality)   [5]

In [5], we distinguish not so much two places of the same name, but two aspects of the same place. *The* is also sometimes used before modifiers + noun (*the young Catherine, the future President Kennedy*), but with place-names it is generally left out: *Ancient Greece, eighteenth century London, upstate New York.*
   In the same way proper nouns sometimes change to plural:

> I know several *Mr Wilsons* (= 'people called "Mr Wilson" ').
> He was a friend of *the Kennedys* (= 'the family named "Kennedy" ').

A proper noun may also sometimes follow the indefinite article:

> The prize was given by *a Dr Robertson.*

This means 'a certain Dr Robertson' (a person you won't have heard of).

Third person pronouns
94
Third person pronouns (*he, she, it, they*) are usually definite because they point back to a previous mention. In a sense, they 'replace' an earlier noun phrase:

I phoned *the police* and asked *them*   (*ie* the police) what to do.
FIRST MENTION   SECOND MENTION

Concrete nouns are replaced by *he, she, it,* or *they* as follows:

- *he* (*him, his,* etc.) refers to a male person (or animal)
- *she* (*her,* etc.) refers to a female person (or animal)
- *it* (*its,* etc.) refers to an inanimate thing (or an animal)
- *they* (*them,* etc.) is the plural pronoun, referring to either animate or inanimate.

95
He and *she* are used for animals when we think of them as having the personal qualities of human beings (e.g. family pets):

Nemo, the killer whale, who'd grown too big for *his* pool on Clacton
Pier, has arrived safely in *his* new home in Windsor safari park.

It is otherwise used for animals, and sometimes for babies and very young
children, especially when their sex is unknown.

The dog was barking in *its* kennel.
The baby kept on crying until *its* mother returned.

Mass nouns and singular abstract nouns are replaced by *it*:

I've washed *my hair*, and *it* won't keep tidy.
Life today is so busy that *its* true meaning often eludes us.

Note
She is sometimes used

- for inanimate objects (especially ships):

What a lovely boat you've got! How many does *she* sleep?

- for countries seen as political units:

Last year *France* increased *her* exports by 10 per cent.

Referring to male and female
96
When a human noun is replaced by a pronoun and the sex is not known or
specified, traditionally *he* is used rather than *she*:

A martyr is someone who gives up *his* life for *his* beliefs.

However, nowadays this bias towards the male term is widely avoided, and *he
or she* (or *him or her*, etc.) is often used instead:

A martyr is someone who gives up *his or her* life for *his or her* beliefs.

As this example shows, however, *he or she* (etc.) can have an awkward effect,
especially if repeated. Another method of avoiding sex bias, well established in
⟨spoken English⟩, is the singular use of *they*:

A martyr is someone who gives up *their* life for *their* beliefs.

This 'ungrammatical' mixing of singular and plural is making its way into
⟨informal⟩ writing, although those with a strict sense of grammar avoid it.

Since none of the above alternatives is entirely satisfactory, it is often possible
to avoid the problem of sex-neutral third-person reference by changing from the
singular to the plural:

Martyrs are people who give up *their* life/lives for *their* beliefs.

Here, of course, the use of *they* causes no problem in itself, although indirectly it
may cause other problems, such as whether to use *life* or *lives* in the above
example.

Note
Other solutions to the problem of how to avoid male bias include the use of the subjective pronoun form *s/he*, the use of *she* or *he*, and the use of *she* as a sex-neutral pronoun. The mixed form *s/he* is convenient in writing, but has the disadvantage of not having any oblique forms such as **s*him* or **s/his*. Another disadvantage is that its pronunciation is not distinguishable from that of *she*.

First and second person pronouns: *I, we, you*
97
The first and second person pronouns have reference to the situation as follows:

First person:

I (*me, my, mine*)	'the speaker'
we (*us, our, ourselves*)	'a group of people, including the speaker'

Second person:

you (*your,* *yourself, yourselves*)	*a* 'the hearer' (singular)
	b 'a group of people, including the hearer but excluding the speaker' (plural)

We sometimes **includes** the hearer (= 'you and I'), and sometimes **excludes** the hearer:

> Let*'s* go to the dance tonight, shall we? ('**inclusive** *we*')
> *We*'ve enjoyed meeting you. ('**exclusive** *we*')

Inclusive *we* (*us*) is often used by writers of books:

> *We* noticed earlier, on page 200, that . . .
> Let *us* now turn to another topic . . .

Generic use of pronouns: *one, you, they*
98
Three pronouns have a generic use, in reference to people in general.

- *One* (singular) is rather ⟨formal and impersonal⟩ meaning 'people in general including you and me'

  > *One* never knows what may happen. ⟨rather formal⟩
  > These days, *one* has to be careful with *one's* money. ⟨rather formal⟩

- *You* is its ⟨informal⟩ equivalent

  > *You* never know what may happen. ⟨informal⟩
  > All this exercise makes *you* hungry, doesn't it? ⟨informal⟩

- *They* can also be used generically in ⟨informal⟩ English, but with a different meaning from *one* and *you*. It means roughly 'people (excluding you and me)':

  > *They* say it's going to rain tomorrow. (= 'People say . . .')

Pointer words: *this, that,* etc.

99

We use the term **pointer words** for words like the demonstrative *this* and *that*, which refer by *pointing* to something in the context. They can have three different uses.

- Pointer words can be **situational**; i.e. they can point to something in the context outside language:

  > Would you like to sit in *this* chair (= 'the one by me') or in *that* one? (= 'the one away from me, over there').

This identifies something near the speaker (either physically, in terms of space or time, or psychologically). *That* identifies something not so near the speaker.

- Pointer words can be **back-pointing**; i.e. they can point to something mentioned earlier:

  > I then tried to force the door open, but *this/that* was a mistake.

- Pointer words can be **forward-pointing** (i.e. they can point to something to be mentioned later):

  > *This* is how you start a car: you make sure the gears are in neutral and that the hand brake is on, then turn the ignition key.

100

We may separate two classes of pointer words, those related to *this* (and having the 'near' meaning) and those related to *that* (and having the 'distant' meaning):

The *this*-type:	*this* (singular)	*here* (= at this place)
	these (plural)	*now* (= at this time)
The *that*-type:	*that* (singular)	*there* (= at that place)
	those (plural)	*then* (= at that time)
		(usually in the past)

This and *that* can replace each other with no difference of meaning in back pointing, but *this* is commoner in ⟨formal⟩ English. For forward-pointing, only *this*, and the *this*-type words *these, here,* and *thus* can be used (but *see* 101):

> *This* is what he wrote: ⎫
> *These* are the latest results: ⎬ **(forward-pointing)**
> Halliday and Hasan define cohesion *thus*: ⎭
> *This/That* was what Charles had said. ⎱ **(forward- or**
> *These/those women* knew what they wanted. ⎰ **backward-pointing)**

Notice the opening and close of a radio news bulletin:

Here is the news . . .	(forward-pointing)
. . . And *that's* the end of the news.	(back-pointing)

101

Those is forward-pointing when its meaning is defined by a following modifier: *those who are interested* (= 'people who are interested') (*see* 521).

This and *that* in ⟨familiar⟩ use can 'point back' in a vague way to some experience not necessarily shared by the speaker and hearer:

Have you seen *this* report about smoking? (= 'a report I know about').
It gives you *that* great feeling of clean air and open spaces (= 'the feeling we all know about').

This can also be used ⟨familiarly⟩ to introduce something new in a narrative: *I was walking along the street when this girl came up to me* . . . (= 'a girl I'm going to tell you about').

Relations between ideas expressed by nouns

Relations expressed by *of*

102

We have talked of *of* used in phrases of

- **partition**: *a part of the house* (*see* 61)
- **division**: *a kind of tree* (*see* 63)
- **amount**: *a lot of difficulty* (*see* 70–81)

Of is also used more generally to indicate various relations between the meanings of two nouns:

the roof of the house (the house has a roof; the roof is part of the house)
a friend of my father's (see 535) (my father has a friend)
the courage of the firefighters (the firefighters have courage; the firefighters are courageous)
the envy of the world (the world envies . . .)
the trial of the conspirators (someone tries the conspirators)
the causes of stress (stress is caused by . . .)
the virtue of thrift (thrift is a virtue)
a shortage of money (money is [in] short [supply])
a glass of water (the glass has water in it; the glass contains water)
people of the Middle Ages (people who lived in the Middle Ages)
the house of my dreams (the house which I see in my dreams)
the College of Surgeons (the College to which surgeons belong)

The 'have' relation

103

Both *of* and *with* can indicate a relation of 'having'.
From the sentence 'Noun1 has Noun2' we can get:

- **Noun2 of Noun1:**   *the roof of the house, the courage of the people.*
- **Noun1 of Noun2:**   *people of (great) courage*
- **Noun1 with Noun2:** *a house with a roof*

In the 'Noun1 + preposition + Noun2' construction, *of* is used where **Noun2** is abstract (*a performance of distinction, a country of enormous wealth*), and *with* is used where **Noun2** is concrete (*a woman with a large family, a man with a beard*).

The uses of the genitive

104

A genitive (ending *'s* or apostrophe only, *see* 530) can often be used with the same meaning as an *of*-phrase, especially where the genitive has human reference:

- **The have relation** (*'Dr Brown has a son'*)

Dr Brown's son (definite)	⎰ *a son of Dr Brown* or *a son of Dr Brown's* ⎱ (*see* 535) (indefinite)
the earth's gravity	*the gravity of the earth* (more usual)

- **The subject-verb relation** (*'His parents consented'*)

his parents' consent	*the consent of his parents*
the train's departure	*the departure of the train* (more usual)

- **The verb-object relation** (*'They released the prisoner'*)

the prisoner's release	*the release of the prisoner*
a city's destruction	*the destruction of a city* (more usual)

- **The subject-complement relation** (*'Everyone is happy'*)

everyone's happiness	*the happiness of everyone*
the country's beauty	*the beauty of the country*

105

In the following cases, the *of*-phrase is not normally used:

- **The origin relation** (*'The girl told a story'*, etc.)

  the girl's story (= a story that the girl told)
  John's telegram (= a telegram from John, a telegram that John sent)

- **Various classifying relations** (where the genitive behaves rather like a modifying noun or adjective)

  > *a women's college*   (= a college for women)
  > *a doctor's degree*   (= a doctoral degree)

Choice between an *of*-construction and the genitive
106

In general, the genitive is preferred for human nouns (*the girl's arrival*) and sometimes also for animal nouns (*horses' hooves*) and human group nouns (*the government's policy*). *Of* is usually preferred for mass nouns and abstract nouns (*the discovery of helium, the progress of science*). In general, also, the genitive is preferred for the subject-verb relation:

> Livingstone's discovery (= 'Livingstone discovered something')

and *of* for the verb-object relation:

> the discovery of Livingstone (usually = 'Somebody discovered
> Livingstone')

The subject function can also be indicated by a *by*-phrase. Hence the notion 'The army defeated the rebels' might be expressed in three ways:

> the army's defeat of the rebels
> the defeat of the rebels by the army
> the rebels' defeat by the army

(But *the rebels' defeat of the army* has to mean that the rebels defeated the army.)

The *of*-construction is also preferred (especially in ⟨formal⟩ English) to the genitive when the modifying noun phrase is long. We can easily say:

> the departure of the 4.30 train for Edinburgh

BUT NOT:

> ?* the 4.30 train for Edinburgh's departure (*see* 533)

107

Note two special cases of the genitive.

- Time nouns are frequently used in the genitive:

  > this year's crop of potatoes
  > two weeks' holiday
  > a moment's thought
  > today's menu (*or* the menu for today)

- Place nouns are also frequently used in the genitive, especially if followed by a superlative:

the town's oldest pub (*or* the oldest pub in the town)
Norway's greatest composer (*or* the greatest composer in Norway)
the world's best chocolate (*or* the best chocolate in the world)

Relations between people: *with, for, against*
108
With often means 'together with' or 'in company with':

> I'm so glad you're coming *with us*.   [1]
> Sheila was at the theatre *with her friends*.   [2]

Sentence [2] is not very different in meaning from

> Sheila *and her friends* were at the theatre.

Without is the negative of *with* in this sense:

> Sheila was ill, so we went to the theatre *without her*.

For conveys the idea of support (= 'in favour of'), and like *with*, contrasts with *against*:

> Are you *for* or *against* the President?

With, in a situation of conflict or competition, means 'on the same side as':

> Remember that every one of us is *with* you (= 'on your side').
> Are you *with* us or *against* us?

Note
Also notice: *the fight against pollution, the campaign against inflation*, etc. *With* conveys the idea of opposition between two people or groups in *fight with, argue with*, etc: *He's always arguing with his sister*.

Ingredient, material: *with, of, out of, from*
109
With verbs of 'making', use *with* for an ingredient, and *out of* or *of* for the material of the whole thing:

> A fruit cake is made *with* fruit, but a glass jug is made (*out*) *of* glass.

Made from means that one is derived from another:

> Beer is made *from hops*.
> Most paper is made *from wood-pulp*.

Of alone is used in postmodifying phrases: *a ring of solid gold* (i.e. . . . made out of solid gold), *a table of polished oak* (i.e. . . . consisting of polished oak). One noun in front of another can also refer to a material: *a gold ring, an oak table*.

Restrictive and non-restrictive meaning

110

Modifiers before or after a noun usually help to specify its meaning exactly:

(A)	(B)
the children	the children *who live next door*
a king	a king *of Denmark*
buttered toast	*hot* buttered toast
these books	these *history* books

In each case, phrase (B) tells us more precisely than phrase (A) what the noun refers to. **It narrows down** or **restricts** the meaning of the noun, by saying *what kind of* children, king, etc. the speaker is talking of. This type of modifier is called **restrictive**.

111

There is also a **non-restrictive** type of modifier which does not limit the noun in this way. Compare:

Children *who learn easily* | should start school as early as possible.|

(RESTRICTIVE)   [1]

Children,|*who learn easily*, | should start school as early as possible.|

(NON-RESTRICTIVE)   [2]

In [1], the relative clause is restrictive and tells us *what kind of* children ought to start school early. In [2], where the relative clause is non-restrictive, the speaker is talking about all children in general. This is typically signalled by a tone unit boundary (*see* 37) in ⟨speech⟩, or a comma in ⟨writing⟩, separating it from the preceding noun. The clause does not in any way limit the reference of *children*. The speaker tells us *a* that all children learn easily, and *b* that all children should start school early.

Non-restrictive adjectives

112

Adjectives, as well as relative clauses, can be non-restrictive. The clearest cases are adjectives before proper nouns: since a proper noun already has unique reference, it cannot be limited any further by the adjective (but *see* 93): *poor Bill, old Mrs Brown, the beautiful Highlands of Scotland*.

Non-restrictive adjectives are not so clearly marked by punctuation or intonation, and so ambiguities can occur:

The *patriotic* Americans have great respect for their country's
constitution.   [3]
The *hungry* workers attacked the houses of their *rich* employers.   [4]

We might ask: Does [3] mean that 'all Americans have great respect' (non-restrictive)? Or does it mean that 'only some Americans (those who are patriotic, as opposed to those who are not) have great respect'? Does [4] refer to *all* the workers and *all* the employers, or just to the hungry workers (as opposed to those with enough to eat), and to the rich employers (as opposed to the poor ones)? These sentences could have either meaning, but the non-restrictive meaning is more likely.

Note
The ordering of modifiers can make a difference to meaning:

her last great novel	[5]
her great last novel	[6]

In [5] *great* is restrictive, while in [6] *great* is non-restrictive. The meaning of [5] is therefore 'the last of her great novels', and the meaning of [6] is 'her last novel, which was great'.

Time, tense and aspect

113
We turn now to meanings expressed by the verb phrase. Tense and aspect (*see* 740–2) relate the happening described by the verb to time in the past, present, or future.

States and events

114
We must first give some attention to the different kinds of meaning a verb may have. Broadly, verbs may refer

- to an event, i.e. a happening thought of as a single occurrence, with a definite beginning and end e.g. *become, get, come, leave, hit*
- to a **state**, i.e. a state of affairs which continues over a period, and does not need to have a well-defined beginning and end, e.g. *be, remain, contain, know.*

She *became* unconscious.	[event]
She *remained* unconscious.	[state]

The difference between **event** and **state** verbs is similar to the difference between count and mass nouns. As we saw in 62 for count and mass, these categories are based not so much on the world itself, as on the way our minds look at the world. The same verb can change from one category to another, and the distinction is not always clear: *Did you remember his name?* could refer either to a state or to an event. To be more accurate, then, we should talk of 'state uses of verbs' and 'event uses of verbs'; but it is convenient to keep to the simpler terms 'state verb' and 'event verb'.

115
The distinction between 'state' and 'event' gives rise to the following three basic kinds of verb meaning (illustrated in the past tense):

————	(1)	STATE	Napoleon was a Corsican.
•	(2)	SINGLE EVENT	Columbus discovered America.
• • • • • • • •	(3)	SET OF REPEATED EVENTS (HABIT)	Paganini played the violin brilliantly.

The 'habit' meaning combines 'event' meaning with 'state' meaning: a habit is a state consisting of a series of events. We often specify 'state' meaning by adding an adverbial of duration (161–5):

Queen Victoria reigned *for sixty-four years.*

We specify 'habit' more precisely by adding an adverbial of frequency (166–9) or an adverbial of duration:

He played the violin *every day from the age of five.*

(All three types of meaning can be clarified by an adverbial of time-when, *see* 151–60.)

To these three a further type of verbal meaning can be added:

(4)   the **temporary** meaning expressed by the progressive aspect (*see* 132, 740–1):

She *was cooking* the dinner.

Present time: *I adore your drawings!*
116
The following are the main ways of referring to something which occurs at the present time:

(A)   PRESENT STATE (the Simple Present Tense)

I'*m* hungry.
Do you *like* coffee?

The state may stretch indefinitely into the past and future, and so this use of the simple present tense applies also to general truths such as *The sun rises in the east.*

117

(B)   PRESENT EVENT (the Simple Present Tense)

I *declare* the meeting closed.
She *serves* – and it's an ace!

This use is rather specialized, being limited to formal declarations, sports commentaries, demonstrations, *etc.* In most contexts, one rarely has the occasion to refer to an event begun and ended at the very moment of speech.

118

(C)   PRESENT HABIT (the Simple Present Tense)

> We *work* for a major company.
> I *travel* to London quite often.
> It *rains* a lot in this part of the world.

By 'habit' here, we mean a repetition of events.

119

(D)   TEMPORARY PRESENT (the Present Progressive)

> Look! *It's snowing*!   [1a]
> The children *are sleeping* soundly now.   [2a]
> They *are living* in a rented house (temporarily – for a short period)   [3a]

The meaning of the progressive aspect is 'limited duration'. Compare the meaning of the simple present in these examples:

> It *snows* a lot in northern Japan. (habit)   [1b]
> The children usually *sleep* very soundly. (habit)   [2b]
> They *live* in a rented house. (permanently)   [3b]

For single events, which in any case involve a limited time-span, the effect of the progressive is to emphasize the durational aspect of the event:

> The champion *serves*. It's another double fault!
> The champion *is serving* well. (the service is a continuing activity)

With states, the effect of the progressive is to put emphasis on the **limited** duration of the state of affairs:

> She *lives* with her mother. (permanently)
> She's *living* with her mother. (at the moment)

120

(E)   TEMPORARY HABIT (the Present Progressive)

> I'*m playing* golf regularly these days.
> She's not *working* at the moment.
> He's *walking* to work while his car is being repaired.

This use combines the 'temporary' meaning of the progressive with the repetitive meaning of the habitual present.

Other ways of referring to present time

121

Three rather less important ways of referring to the present are these:

- We can use the progressive aspect with *always* or a similar adverb, to emphasize that an action is continuous, or persistent:

  Those children *are* always (= continually) *getting* into trouble.

This use carries with it some feeling of disapproval.

- Temporary and habitual meaning can be combined to indicate a repetition of temporary happenings:

  He'*s chewing* gum whenever I see him.

- In special circumstances, the past tense can be used to refer to the present:

  Did you *want* to speak to me? (= 'Do you want . . .')
  I *wondered* whether you would help me. (= 'I wonder . . .')

Here the past tense is an indirect and ⟨more tactful⟩ alternative to the simple present tense (*see* 136).

Past time: *I've read your book – and I loved it!*
122
Along with the present-time meanings in 116–121 above there are similar past-time meanings: we have already illustrated some of these (*see* 115).

But there is a special problem of past-time reference in English: the question of how to choose between the use of the past tense and the use of the perfect aspect. The **past tense** is used when the past happening is related to a definite time, in the past, which we may call '**then**'. Hence the simple past tense means 'past-happening-related-to-past-time'.

  He *was* in prison for ten years. (= 'Now he's out')

In contrast, the **perfect aspect** is used for a past happening which is seen in relation to a later event or time. Thus the present perfect means 'past happening-related-to-present-time'. For example:

  He *has* been in prison for ten years. (= 'He's probably still there.')

The past tense: *The parcel arrived last week*
123
The past tense refers to a **definite** time in the past, which may be identified by

    a   a past-time adverbial in the same sentence,
    b   the preceding language context, or
    c   the context outside language.

(On these aspects of definite meaning, compare the use of *the* (*see* 83–5).) Examples of the three types are:

    a   Haydn *was* born in 1732.   The parcel *arrived* last week.

b Joan *has become* engaged; it *took* us completely by surprise. (Here the past tense *took* can be used, because the event has already been identified in the first clause: *has become . . .*)

c *Did* you get any letters? (Here we can use the past tense without language context, because it is understood that the mail arrives at a given time in the day.)

Note

[a] Because of its definite meaning, a proper noun can provide the conditions for the past tense: *Rome wasn't built in a day.* (a saying); *Caruso was a great singer.* (Here it is implied that Caruso is dead, or at least is no longer a practising singer.)

[b] The past tense can sometimes be used when no definite time 'then' is easily apparent: *Hello, how are you?* They **told** *me you were ill.* Perhaps this is like *c* above, in that the speaker is *thinking* of a definite time in the past.

124

The past tense also implies a gap between the time referred to and the present moment:

His sister *suffered* from asthma all her life. (i.e. She's now dead)

His sister *has suffered* from asthma all her life. (i.e. She's still alive)

Adverbials referring to a past point or period of time normally go with the past tense.

The building *was dedicated* as a church *in the seventh century.* (*see* 129)

The present perfect: *I have written the letter*

125

Four related uses of the present perfect may be noted:

(A) PAST EVENT WITH RESULTS IN THE PRESENT TIME

The taxi *has arrived.* (i.e. 'it's now here')

All police leave *has been cancelled.* (i.e. 'the police remain on duty')

Her doll *has been broken.* (i.e. 'it's still not mended')

(Compare: Her doll was broken, but now it's mended.)

This is the most common use of the present perfect.

(B) INDEFINITE EVENT(S) IN A PERIOD LEADING UP TO THE PRESENT TIME

Have you (ever) *been* to Florence?

All my family *have had* measles (in the last five years).

(C) HABIT IN A PERIOD LEADING UP TO THE PRESENT TIME

She *has attended* lectures regularly (this term).

He's *played* at Wimbledon since he was eighteen.

(D) STATE LEADING UP TO THE PRESENT TIME

That supermarket – how long *has it been* open?

She's always *had* a vivid imagination.

In these instances (except for (B)) the states, habits, or events may be understood to continue at the present time; for example, the first sentence in (D) assumes '. . . it is still open'.

Note

[a] In sense (B), the present perfect often refers to the **recent** indefinite past: *Have you eaten* (*yet*)? *I've studied your report* (*already*). In such cases, ⟨AmE⟩ prefers the past tense: *Did you eat yet?*

[b] There is an idiomatic use of the past tense with *always*, *ever* and *never* to refer to a state or habit leading up to the present:

> *I always said* (= have said) he would end up in jail.
> *Did* you *ever see* such a mess?

The perfect progressive: *I have been writing a letter*
126

The present perfect progressive (*have been writing*, etc.) has the same sort of meaning as the simple present perfect, except that the period leading up to the present typically has **limited duration**:

> *I've been studying* for the exams.
> He *has been attending* lectures regularly.
> She *has been explaining* to me what you are doing.

The perfect progressive, like the simple perfect, can suggest that the results of the activity remain in the present: *You've been fighting!* (i.e. I can see that you have been fighting, because you have a black eye, torn clothes, etc.). In such cases the activity has continued up to the **recent past**, not up to the present. Unlike the present perfect, however, the present perfect progressive with event verbs usually suggests an action continuing into the present:

> *I've read* your book (= 'I've finished it').
> *I've been reading* your book (normally = 'I'm still reading it').

The past perfect: *I had written the letter*
127

The past perfect (simple or progressive) means 'past in the past'; that is, a time further in the past as seen from a definite time in the past:

> The house *had been* empty for several months (when we bought it).
> The goalkeeper *had injured* his leg, and couldn't play.
> It *had been* raining, and the streets were still wet.
> Their *relationship had been* ideal until Claire's announcement 'I'm leav-ing – there's someone else'.

The past perfect is neutral as regards the differences expressed by the past tense and present perfect. This means that if we put the events described in [2] and [3] further into the past, they both end up in the past perfect [2a, 3a].

They tell me that
    the parcel *arrived* on April 15th.   [2]
    the parcel *has* already *arrived.*   [3]
They told me that
    the parcel *had arrived* on April 15th.   [2a]
    the parcel *had* already *arrived.*   [3a]

When describing one event following another in the past, we can show their relation by using the past perfect for the earlier event, or else we can use the past tense for both, relying on the conjunction (e.g. *after, when*) to show which event took place earlier:

> When the guests *had departed*, Sheila *lingered* a little while.
> ~ When the guests *departed*, Sheila *lingered* a little while.
> After the French police *had* successfully *used* dogs, the German
>   authorities too *thought* of using them.
> ~ After the French police successfully *used* dogs, the German
>   authorities too *thought* of using them.

In these pairs of examples, both sentences have roughly the same meaning. Each sentence indicates that the first happening preceded the second.

Perfect aspect with infinitives and participles: *to have eaten, having eaten*
128

Infinitives and participles (*see* 738) have no tense, and so cannot express the difference between past tense and perfect aspect. Instead, the perfect expresses general past meaning:

He seems *to have missed* the point of your joke.   [1]
More than 1,000 people are said *to have been arrested.*   [2]
She is proud of *having achieved* stardom while still a child.   [3]
Lawes was convicted of *having aided* the rebels by planting bombs.   [4]

Sentence [1] could be alternatively expressed. *It seems that he has missed the point* or *It seems that he missed the point*. Sentence [3] could be otherwise expressed: *She is proud that she has achieved stardom* or *She is proud that she achieved stardom*. In [4], an alternative way of describing the happening would be to use the past perfect (see 127): *Lawes's crime was that he had aided the rebels by planting bombs*. There is no difference in the form of the participle, although the implied time and aspect may change. The same is true, for example, for the perfect infinitive following a modal auxiliary:

He *may have left* yesterday. (i.e. Perhaps he *left* yesterday)
He *may have left* already. (i.e. Perhaps he *has* left already)

Adverbials in relation to the past and the present perfect
129

Some adverbials go with the past and others with the present perfect, for example:

- **The past** (point or period of time which finished in the past):

  I *rang* her parents *yesterday* (*evening*).
  My first wife *died some years ago*.
  The fire *started* just *after ten o'clock*.
  A funny thing *happened* to me *last Friday*.
  I think someone *mentioned* it to her *the other day*.
  In the evening he *attended* an executive meeting of the tennis club.
  The conference *opened on Monday, October 30th*.
  School *began in August*, the hottest part of the year.
  In 1989 a new law *was introduced*.

- **The present perfect** (period leading up to present, or recent past time)

  Since January, life *has been* very busy.
  I *haven't had* any luck *since I was a baby*.
  Plenty of rain *has fallen* here *lately*.
  Sixty-six courses *have been held so far*.
  Up to now her life *hasn't been* altogether rosy.

- **Either the past or the present perfect**

The following pairs have almost the same meaning. However, in the first pair, the choice of the perfect suggests the speaker is speaking during the morning. The choice of the past, on the other hand, suggests that the morning is already [...] hard-and-fast rule.

[...]*een* a lot of horses *this morning*.
[...] lot of horses *this morning*.

[...] to speak to you about this *today*.
[...]peak to you about this *today*.

[...] *spoken* to him *recently?*
[...]*eak* to him *recently?*

State or habit in the past: *used to* and *would*
130

Used to (*see* 485) expresses a state or habit in the past, as contrasted with the present:

My uncle *used to keep horses*. (i.e. 'He once kept horses'.)
I *used to know* her well (when I was a student).

Would (*see* 291) can also express a past habit, with the particular sense of 'characteristic, predictable behaviour':

He *would wait* for her outside the office (every day).

This use of *would* is typical of narrative style, and is found mainly in ⟨written⟩ English.

The simple present tense with past meaning
131
There are two special uses where the simple present tense is used with past meaning:

- **The 'historic present'** is sometimes used in past-time narrative, when we want to describe events vividly as if they are happening in our presence:

  > Then in *comes* the barman and *tries* to stop the fight.

- The present is used **with verbs of communication** (*hear*, *inform*, etc.), where more strictly the present perfect would be expected:

  > I *hear* you've finished the building project.
  > I *am informed* that your appointment has been terminated. ⟨formal⟩

The progressive aspect
132
The progressive aspect (*see* 119, 739–42) refers to activity **in progress**, and therefore suggests

> (A) that the activity is **temporary** (i.e. of limited duration)
> (B) that it **need not be complete**.

The second element of meaning (B) is most evident in the past tense or in the present perfect:

> He *wrote* a novel several years ago (i.e. he finished it).
> He *was writing* a novel several years ago (but I don't know whether he finished it or not).

> I *have mended* the car this morning (i.e. the job's finished).
> I *have been mending* the car this morning (but the job may not be finished).

With verbs referring to a change of state, the progressive indicates movement towards the change, rather than completion of the change itself:

> The girl *was drowning* (but at the last moment I rescued her).

When linked to a non-progressive event verb, or to a point or period of time, the progressive normally shows that the activity or situation described by the verb is still in progress, i.e. has started but has not yet finished:

> When I went downstairs they *were* (already) *eating* breakfast.

Other examples:

> I knew the person who *was working* here last year.
> High winds and heavy seas *have been causing* further damage (today).
> As I came in, Agnes looked up from the book *she was reading*.
> I'm happy to say my arthritis *is getting better*.

Verbs which take, or do not take, the progressive

133

The verbs which most typically take the progressive are verbs denoting **activities** (*walk, read, drink, write, work,* etc.):

> A small boy in a blue jacket *was walking* along the street.
> I'*m writing* a letter to my sister in England.

or **processes** (*change, grow, widen, improve,* etc.):

> Alec *was growing* more and more impatient.
> I believe the political situation *is improving.*

Verbs denoting **momentary** events (*knock, jump, nod, kick,* etc.), if used in the progressive, suggest repetition:

> He *nodded.* (one movement of the head)
> He *was nodding.* (repeated movements of the head)

134

State verbs often cannot be used with the progressive at all, because the notion of 'something in progress' cannot be easily applied to them. The verbs which normally do not take the progressive include the following.

135

Verbs of perceiving

Feel, hear, see, smell, taste. To express continuing perception, we often use these verbs with *can* or *could*:

> I *can see* someone through the window, but I *can't hear* what they're saying. (NOT *I am seeing . . . *I'm not hearing . . .)

Verbs which have as their subject the thing perceived, such as *sound* and *look,* can also be included here:

> You *look* ridiculous, in that hat.
> It *sounds* as if the concert's finished.

136

Verbs referring to a state of mind or feeling

Believe, adore, desire, detest, dislike, doubt, forget, hate, hope, imagine, know, like, love, mean, prefer, remember, suppose, understand, want, wish, etc.

> I *suppose* I'd better buy them a Christmas present. (NOT: *I am supposing . . .*)
> I *hope* I haven't kept you all waiting.
> I *doubt* whether the standards of the schools are improving.

The verbs *seem* and *appear* may also be included here:

> He *seems/appears* to be enjoying himself.

137
Verbs referring to a relationship or a state of being
Be, belong to, concern, consist of, contain, cost, depend on, deserve, equal, fit, have, involve, matter, owe, own, possess, remain, require, resemble, etc.

> She *belongs* to the Transport and General Workers' Union.
> Most mail these days *contains* nothing that could be truly called a
>   letter.

Notice that all these verbs are used without the progressive even when they refer to a temporary state:

> I'*m* hungry.
> I *forget* his name for the moment.

Note
The verb *have*, when it is a state verb, does not go with the progressive: *He has a good job* (NOT: **He is having a good job*). But *have* can go with the progressive when it denotes a process or activity: *They were having dinner.*

138
Verbs referring to an internal sensation
There is a fourth group of verbs, those referring to internal sensation (*hurt, feel, ache,* etc.). These can be used either with the progressive or the non-progressive with little difference of effect:

$$\text{My back} \begin{cases} \textit{hurts.} \\ \textit{is hurting.} \end{cases} \qquad \text{I} \begin{cases} \textit{felt} \\ \textit{was feeling} \end{cases} \text{ill.}$$

Exceptions where the progressive is used
139
The types of verb in 134–7 above may be labelled 'non-progressive' but there are special cases in which you hear them used with the progressive. In many such cases, one can say that the state verb has changed into an 'activity verb' (referring to an active form of behaviour). Thus, in place of *see* and *hear*, we have the equivalent activity verbs *look* (*at*) and *listen* (*to*):

> Why *are* you *looking* at me like that?
> She *was listening* to the news when I entered.

But for *smell, feel,* and *taste,* there is no special activity verb, so these verbs have the role of expressing activity meaning as well as state meaning:

> The doctor has *been feeling* her pulse [activity].
> He says it *feels* normal. [state]
> (Compare: The doctor *has been listening to* her pulse. He says it *sounds*
>   normal.)
> We've *been tasting* the soup. It *tastes* delicious.

In the same way, *think, imagine, remember*, etc. can sometimes be used as 'mental activity' verbs:

> I'*m thinking* about what you're saying.
> He'*s hoping* to finish his training before the end of the year.

The verb *be* can go with the progressive when the adjective or noun which follows it refers to a type of behaviour, or to the role a person is adopting:

> He's (just) *being awkward* (= 'causing difficulty').
> John is *being a martyr* (= 'acting like a martyr').

Note
Another exceptional case is the use of the progressive with *hope, want*, etc. to express greater ⟨tentativeness⟩ and ⟨tact⟩. *We are hoping you will support us. Were you wanting to see me?*

Future time
140
There are five chief ways of expressing future time in the English verb phrase. The most important future constructions are those which use *will* (or *shall*) and *be going to* (A and B below).

(A) Will/shall (see 483)
141
Will (often reduced to *'ll*), or sometimes *shall* ⟨rather formal⟩ (with a first person subject) can express the neutral future of prediction:

> Temperatures tomorrow *will be* much the same as today.
> We *shall hear* the results of the election within a week.

It is particularly common in the main clause of a conditional sentence (*see* 207–14):

> If the book has real merit, it *will sell*.
> Wherever you go, you *will find* the local people friendly.
> In that case, I guess I'*ll have* to change my plan.

But with personal subjects, *will/shall* can also suggest an element of intention:

> I'*ll see* you again on Tuesday.
> They'*ll make* a cup of coffee if you ask them.

(B) Be going to
142
Be going to + INFINITIVE tends to indicate the future as a fulfilment of the present. It may refer to a future resulting from a present intention:

> *Are* you *going to put* a coat on?
> She said that she'*s going to visit* Vic at two o'clock.
> She says she'*s going to be* a doctor when she grows up.

It may also refer to the future resulting from other causative factors in the present:

> I think I'*m going to faint* (i.e. I already feel ill).
> It'*s going to rain* (i.e. I can already see black clouds gathering).
> I'm afraid we'*re going to have to* stop the meeting now.

In sentences like these last three, *be going to* also carries the expectation that the event will happen **soon**.

(C) *Progressive aspect*

143

The present progressive is used for future events arising from a present plan, programme, or arrangement:

> We'*re inviting* several people to a party.
> She'*s going* back to Montreal *in a couple of days*.
> What *are* you *doing* for lunch?

Like *be going to*, this construction (especially when there is no time adverbial such as *in a couple of days*) often suggests the **near** future: *The Smiths are leaving* (= soon).

(D) *Simple present tense*

144

The simple present tense is used for the future in certain types of subordinate clause, especially adverbial time clauses (*when she comes in*) and conditional clauses (*if she comes in*) (160, 207):

> I'll get her to phone you *when/if/before* she *comes* in.

Notice, however, that the verb in the **main** clause has *will*. Some of the conjunctions which go with the present tense in this way are *after, as, before, once, until, when, as soon as, if, even if, unless, as long as*. *That*-clauses following *hope, assume, suppose*, etc. can also contain a verb in the present tense referring to the future:

> I hope the train *isn't* late.
> ~ I hope the train *won't be* late.

Apart from these cases, the simple present is used (but not very often) for future events which are seen as absolutely certain, because they are determined in advance by calendar or timetable, or because they are part of an unalterable plan:

> Tomorrow *is* Wednesday.
> The term *finishes* at the beginning of July.
> Actually the match *begins* at three on Thursday.
> Miss Walpole *retires* at the end of the year.

In these sentences, the speaker treats the event as a fact, and puts aside the doubt one normally feels about the future. Compare:

> When *do* we *get* there? (e.g. according to the train timetable)
> When *will* we *get* there? (e.g. if we travel by car)

(E) Will/shall + progressive aspect
145
Will (or *'ll* or *shall*) followed by the progressive can be used in a regular way to add the temporary meaning of the progressive to the future meaning of the *will* construction (*see* 141):

> Don't call her at seven o'clock – she'*ll be eating* dinner then.

But in addition, we can use the *will* + progressive construction in a special way to refer to a future event which will take place 'as a matter of course':

> *Will* he *be coming* by car?
> We *will be taking part* in an international conference on the space
>   project on January 30th.

This is particularly useful for avoiding the suggestion of intention in the simple *will*-construction. It can therefore be ⟨more tentative and polite⟩:

> When *will* you *visit* us again?   [4]
> When *will* you *be visiting* us again? ⟨more tentative⟩   [5]

Sentence [4] is most likely to be a question about the hearer's intentions, while sentence [5] simply asks the hearer to predict the time of the next visit.

Be to, be about to, be on the point of
146
Some less common ways of expressing future meaning are illustrated here:

> The German Chancellor *is to visit* France.
> I'*m about to write* the director a nasty letter.
> She *was* just *on the point of moving* when the message arrived.

Be + *to*-infinitive signifies an arrangement for the future (especially an official arrangement), while both *be about to* and *on the point of* emphasize the nearness of a future event.

The future in the past
147
We can put the future constructions already mentioned (except the simple present) into the past tense. We then arrive at a 'future in the past' meaning (i.e. future seen from a viewpoint in the past). But such a meaning, e.g. with

was going to and *was about to*, usually conveys the idea that the anticipated happening did not take place:

> They *were* just *going to punish* him, when he escaped.
> The priceless tapestry *was about to catch fire*, but was fortunately saved through the prompt action of the fire service.

Was/were to and *would* can refer to the fulfilled future in the past, but in this sense they are rare and rather ⟨literary⟩ in style:

> After defeating Pompey's supporters, Caesar *returned* to Italy and proclaimed himself the permanent 'dictator' of Rome. He *was to pay* dearly for his ambition in due course: a year later one of his best friends, Marcus Brutus, *would lead* a successful plot to assassinate him.

However, for a series of events like this, the ordinary past tense can also be used throughout: *returned, . . . paid, . . . led*, etc.

Note
The future in the past is often expressed by *would, was going to*, etc. in reported speech (*see* 264–8).

The past in the future
148
The past in the future is expressed by *will* + Perfect Infinitive:

> I am hoping that by the end of the month you *will have finished* your report.
> In three months' time, the plant *will have taken* root.

In subordinate clauses which allow the simple present for future time (*see* 144), the present perfect can express past in the future:

> Phone me later, when you *have finished* your dinner.

Summary
149
In conclusion, here is a table summarising some of the commonest meanings expressed through tense and aspect. The symbols used are explained first.

single event	•
state	————
habit or series of events	• • • • • • • •
temporary state or event	∿∿∿∿
temporary habit	ᴠᴏᴠᴏᴠᴏ

The time dimension is expressed by a left-to-right arrow chain:
(→ → → → → →).
A definite point of time ('NOW' or 'THEN') is expressed by a dotted vertical line (⋮). The broken arrow (-----→) indicates anticipation of something happening at a later time.

150

Table: Tense and aspect

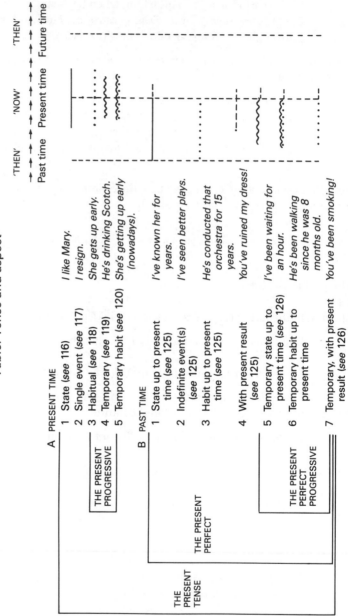

A PRESENT TIME

1 State (*see* 116) — *I like Mary.*
2 Single event (*see* 117) — *I resign.*
3 Habitual (*see* 118) — *She gets up early.*
4 Temporary (*see* 119) — *He's drinking Scotch.*
5 Temporary habit (*see* 120) — *She's getting up early (nowadays).*

B PAST TIME

1 State up to present time (*see* 125) — *I've known her for years.*
2 Indefinite event(s) (*see* 125) — *I've seen better plays.*
3 Habit up to present time (*see* 125) — *He's conducted that orchestra for 15 years.*
4 With present result (*see* 125) — *You've ruined my dress!*
5 Temporary state up to present time (*see* 126) — *I've been waiting for an hour.*
6 Temporary habit up to present time — *He's been walking since he was 8 months old.*
7 Temporary, with present result (*see* 126) — *You've been smoking!*

THE PRESENT PROGRESSIVE

THE PRESENT PERFECT

THE PRESENT PERFECT PROGRESSIVE

THE PRESENT TENSE

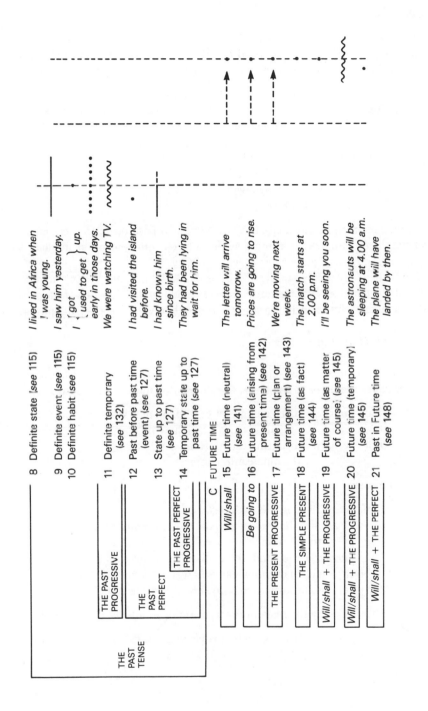

THE PAST TENSE

THE PAST PROGRESSIVE

THE PAST PERFECT

THE PAST PERFECT PROGRESSIVE

8	Definite state (see 115)	I lived in Africa when I was young.
9	Definite event (see 115)	I saw him yesterday.
10	Definite habit (see 115)	I got / used to get } up early in those days.
11	Definite temporary (see 132)	We were watching TV.
12	Past before past time (event) (see 127)	I had visited the island before.
13	State up to past time (see 127)	I had known him since birth.
14	Temporary state up to past time (see 127)	They had been lying in wait for him.

C FUTURE TIME

Will/shall

Be going to

THE PRESENT PROGRESSIVE

THE SIMPLE PRESENT

Will/shall + THE PROGRESSIVE

Will/shall + THE PROGRESSIVE

Will/shall + THE PERFECT

15	Future time (neutral) (see 141)	The letter will arrive tomorrow.
16	Future time (arising from present time) (see 142)	Prices are going to rise.
17	Future time (plan or arrangement) (see 143)	We're moving next week.
18	Future time (as fact) (see 144)	The match starts at 2.00 p.m.
19	Future time (as matter of course) (see 145)	I'll be seeing you soon.
20	Future time (temporary) (see 145)	The astronauts will be sleeping at 4.00 a.m.
21	Past in Future time (see 148)	The plane will have landed by then.

Time-when

151

Notions of time-when are expressed either by tense, aspect, and auxiliaries in the verb phrase, or by adverbials. The adverbial can be of a number of types:

I fixed it *yesterday*.	(ADVERB)
She phoned *on Thursday*.	(PREPOSITIONAL PHRASE)
Jennifer's coming to lunch *next week*.	(NOUN PHRASE)
Twelve months ago he found himself without a job.	(NOUN PHRASE + *ago*, *back*, etc.)
We met several years ago *while I was working in China*.	(ADVERBIAL CLAUSE)

Such time expressions normally have an adverbial position in the sentence (*see* 451), but occasionally they can act as the subject, complement, or modifier of a noun phrase: *The day after tomorrow will be Friday*.

Time-when adverbials answer the question 'When?' Thus all the adverbials listed above could answer the questions *When did you fix it? When did she phone?*, etc. It is most useful to begin the study of time-when with prepositional phrases.

At, on, in and *during*

152

At is used for points of time, and *on* and *in* for periods of time. In general, *on* is used for days, and *in* (or *during*) for periods longer or shorter than a day:

Clock time:	at 10 o'clock, at 6.30 p.m., at noon
Days:	on Sunday, (on) the following day
Other periods:	in/during the morning/April/spring/1973/ the nineteenth century

Some examples:

Her father arrived home *at six o'clock*.
A meeting will be held *at 12.45 p.m.* in the Committee Room.
We're going to the cottage *on Sunday*.
In the summer, roses climb the walls of the courtyard and *in autumn* the country smell of burning leaves hangs in the air.
Many varieties of shrubs blossom *during April and May*.

For periods identified by their beginning and ending points, *between* is used:

Between 1918 and 1939 many people in the West lost their faith in democracy.

In and *during*

153

In and *during* are more or less equivalent:

> He had been an airman *in/during the Second World War*.
> You can come back tomorrow *in/during visiting hours*.
> The Mayor always falls asleep *during the after-dinner speeches*.

Only *during* can be used to mean 'in the course of' before nouns like *stay, visit, meal, conversation*, etc. referring to an event lasting some time:

> We went to the zoo *during our stay in Washington*.
> *During the peace talks*, there was a complete news blackout.

Note

The preposition *in* (or *within* ⟨more formal⟩) can have the meaning 'before the end of':

> He travelled round the world *in eighty days*.
> Phone me again *within a week*.

Exceptions: *at, on,* and *by*

154

- *At* can be used for periods identified vaguely, as in *at that time, at breakfast time, at night*; also for short holiday periods (*at Christmas, at Easter*). In ⟨BrE⟩, *at the weekend* is used, but in ⟨AmE⟩ *on the weekend*.

  > Cars belonging to visitors at a local beauty spot were broken into *at* ‖ *on* the weekend.

- *On* is used before *morning, afternoon, evening,* and *night* when these periods are identified by the day of which they are a part: *on Monday night, on the following evening,* but *in the evening/night*. (On the omission of the definite article in such time expressions, *see* 475.)

  > A Yamaha motorbike was stolen from the Kwik Save car park *on Saturday morning*.

- *By day* and *by night* are idioms which can replace *during the day/night* with some activities such as travelling:

  > We travelled *by night* and rested *by day*.

Omitting the preposition

155

We almost always leave out the preposition before phrases beginning *last, next, this, that*; also before *today, yesterday, tomorrow*:

> He enjoyed coming out with us *last Saturday*.
> *Next time you're in town*, phone me at this number.
> We can't afford to go abroad *this year*.

That day I had nothing important to do.
See you *tomorrow*!

The phrases *at this/that time*, *on this/that occasion* are however exceptions.

On that occasion the government was saved by the intervention of the
Liberal Democrats. ⟨rather formal⟩

In ⟨informal⟩ English, we also usually leave out the preposition in phrases
pointing to a time related indirectly to the present moment, or to a time before
or after a definite time in the past or future:

I met her (*on*) *the day after her birthday*.
She got married (*in*) *the year after her graduation*.
The week before last, I was at a conference in Warsaw.
The festival will be held (*in*) *the following spring*.

The preposition is also sometimes omitted directly before days of the week:

I'll see you (*on*) *Wednesday*, then.
Well, Iris is there (*on*) *Wednesdays and Fridays*.

This omission is especially common in ⟨informal AmE⟩.

Time relationships: *before, after, by,* etc.
156

- *Before* and *after* (as prepositions, adverbs, and conjunctions) indicate relations between two times or events, as in:

The service was so much better *before the war*. (*before* = preposition)
We'd never met her *before*. (*before* = adverb = 'before that time')
Before she had gone very far, she heard a noise. (*before* = conjunction)
The secretary had left immediately *after the meeting*. (*after* =
    preposition)
After they had gone, there was an awkward little silence. (*after* =
    conjunction)

Before and *after* have opposite meanings, so the following are equivalent:

She arrived *after* the play started.
~ The play started *before* she arrived.

- *By* identifies a time when the result of an event is in existence ('not later
than'):

By Friday I was exhausted. (i.e. I became exhausted before Friday, and I
    was still exhausted on Friday)
Please send me the tickets *by next week*. (i.e. I want to have the tickets
    not later than next week)

- *Already, still, yet,* and *any more* are related in meaning to *by*-phrases.

Already and *yet* require the perfect aspect (or the Simple Past in ⟨AmE⟩) when referring to a single event: *They have already left*; *Have you eaten yet?* With state verbs and with the progressive aspect, they can occur with the present tense: *I know that already*; *He's not yet working.*
Note the negative relation of *already* and *yet* to *still* and *any more*:

> He *still* works here. (= He hasn't stopped working here *yet*.)
> He's *already* stopped working. (= He isn't working *any more*.)

• We use *by now* often when we are not certain that the event has happened:

> The wound should have healed *by now*. (. . . but I'm not sure)

Otherwise we prefer to use *already*:

> We've *already* done everything we can.

Comparing prepositions of time
157
Here, for comparison, are some examples of time phrases with a particular noun, *night*:

> What are you doing, throwing stones into our yard *in the middle of the*
>   *night?*
> It often rains quite heavily *in the night*. (*see* 153)
> *During the night* the rain stopped. (*see* 153)
> *At night* I relax. (*see* 154)
> *By night*, Dartmouth was a dazzling city. (*see* 154)
> I shall have to work *nights*.
> I'll be there *by Friday night*. (*see* 156)
> *For several nights* he slept badly. (*see* 161)
> They walked *all night*. (*see* 162)
> We're staying on the island *over night*. (*see* 163)

Measuring time: *ago, from now*, etc.
158
Ago following a noun phrase of time measure means '. . . before now': *We met a year ago*. For a similar measurement into the future, we use *from now*, or *in* + measure phrase, or *in* + genitive measure phrase + *time*;

$$\text{I'll see you} \begin{cases} \text{in three months.} \\ \text{(in) three months from now.} \\ \text{in three months' time.} \end{cases}$$

In measuring forwards from a point of time in the past, only the first alternative is available:

> They finished the job *in three months*. (i.e. from when they started it)

Before and *after*, and the adverbs *beforehand* and *afterwards*, *earlier* and *later*, can also follow a measure phrase:

> I had met them *three months before(hand)*.
> *Ten years after his death*, he suddenly became famous.

Time-when adverbs
159
There are two main groups of time-when adverbs (*see* 456):

> [A] *again*, *just* (= 'at this very moment'), *now*, *nowadays*, *then* (= 'at that time'), *today*, etc.
>
> [B] *afterwards*, *before(hand)*, *first*, *formerly*, *just* (= 'a very short time ago/before'), *late(r)*, *lately*, *next*, *previously*, *recently*, *since*, *soon*, *subsequently* ⟨formal⟩, *then* (= 'after that') *ultimately* ⟨formal⟩, etc.

Group A identifies a point or period of time directly; Group B identifies a time indirectly, by reference to another point of time understood in the context.
   Examples:

> [A]   Prices in the UK are *now* the second lowest in Europe.
>   She's not in town much *nowadays*.
>   Is the show *just* starting?
>
> [B]   We'll see the movie first, and discuss it *afterwards*.
>   Lucy has/had *just* made the tea.
>   Mr Brooking was *previously* general sales manager at the
>   company.
>   Anna was *recently* offered a job as top fashion designer for
>   Harrods.
>   At the next election he lost his seat, and has not turned to
>   politics *since* (= 'since that time').

Time-when conjunctions
160
The main time-when conjunctions are *when*, *as*, *before*, *after* (*see* 156), *while* (*see* 164), *as soon as*, *once*, *now* (*that*):

> It was almost totally dark *when they arrived*.
> We'll let you know *as soon as we've made up our minds*.
> *Once you have taken the examination*, you'll be able to relax.

Duration: *for, over, from . . . to*, etc.

161
Phrases of duration answer the question 'How long?' Compare:

> [A] *When* did you stay there?   [B] *In the summer*. (TIME-WHEN)
> [A] *How long* did you stay there?   [B] *For the summer*. (DURATION)

The phrase *in the summer* here indicates that the stay was **included** in the summer period. The phrase *for the summer* indicates that the stay lasted **as long as** the summer period.

For with this meaning can also precede phrases of time measurement, e.g. *for a month, for several days, for two years.*

Omitting *for*: *I'll be at home all day*
162

The preposition *for* is often left out:

> I went to Oxford in the autumn of 1989, and was there (*for*) *four years.*
> The snowy weather lasted (*for*) *the whole winter.*

For must be omitted before *all*:

> Except for about half an hour, I'll be at home *all day* today.

For is generally not omitted when it comes first in the sentence: *For several years they lived in poverty*; or when it follows a negative: *I haven't seen him for eight years.*

Note
With the verbs *spend* and *take, for* is never used: *We spent two weeks at the seaside; It'll take years to rebuild the palace.*

Other uses of prepositions meaning duration
163

- *Over* can be used instead of *for* for short periods such as holidays.

  > We stayed with my parents *over the holiday/weekend.*
  > She had such an unhappy time *over Christmas.*
  > What have you been doing with yourself *over the New Year?*

- *From . . . to* identify a period by its beginning and end: *from nine to five; from June to December.*

  > Hayes worked for the CIA *from 1949 to 1970.*

- *From . . . through*, in ⟨AmE⟩, are used to make clear that the whole period includes the second period named. Thus *from June through December* means '. . . up to and including December'.

- *Up to* often specifies that the longer period does *not* include the period named:

  > He worked *up to Christmas* (i.e. but not over Christmas).

- *Until* (or *till*) (see 164) can replace *to* in the construction *from . . . to . . .*: *from Monday until Friday.* But, with *from* absent, *to* cannot be used. *We stayed until five* (NOT: *We stayed *to five*).

While, since *and* until
164

- *While* as a conjunction can mean either (*a*) 'duration' or (*b*) 'time-when', depending on the kind of verb meaning (*see* 114–5).
  - *a* I stayed *while the meeting lasted* (i.e. for the duration of the meeting).   (*stay* is a **state verb**)
  - *b* I arrived *while the meeting was in progress* (i.e. in the course of the meeting).   (*arrive* is an **event verb**)
- *Since* as a conjunction or preposition also has these two functions:
  - *a* He's lived here (*ever*) *since he was born* (i.e. for his whole life, from his birth up to now).   (*live* is a **state verb**)
  - *b* They've changed their car twice *since 1990* (i.e. between 1990 and now).   (*change* is an **event verb**)

It is important to notice that *since* normally requires the perfect aspect in the verb of the main clause:

> I've *been* here in the laboratory since four o'clock. (NOT: *I am in the laboratory . . .)

- *Until* (or *till*) as preposition and conjunction has a meaning comparable to example *a* of *since* (the STATE VERB sense). But it names the end-point (rather than the beginning point) of a period:

> You're to stay in bed *until next Monday* (i.e. from now to next Monday).

In the negative, *until* can occur with event verbs, and is similar in meaning to *before*:

> He didn't start to read *until he was ten.*
> ∼ He didn't start to read *before he was ten.*

Adverbs and idioms of duration: *always, recently,* etc.
165
The following adverbs and idiomatic phrases indicate duration:

> *always, for ever* (both meaning 'for all time') (but *see also* 166)
> *since* ('since then'), also *recently, lately* (both meaning 'since a short time ago')
> *temporarily, for the moment, for a while* (all meaning 'for a short time')
> *for ages* ⟨informal⟩ ('for a long time').

Examples:

> There's something I've *always* wanted to ask you.
> They thought their city would last *for ever.*
> I've been suffering from sleepless nights just *lately.*
> *For the moment* there was no woman in his life.
> I waited *for ages* but your phone was apparently engaged.

Since, lately, and *recently* indicate either time-when or duration according to the type of verb meaning:

> They got married only *recently* (= 'a short time ago').
> He's *recently* been working nights (= 'since a short time ago').
> ⟨informal⟩

Frequency

166

Expressions of FREQUENCY answer the question 'How many times?' or 'How often?' The upper and lower limits of frequency are expressed by *always* ('on every occasion') and *never* ('on no occasion'). Between these extremes, a rough indication of frequency (INDEFINITE FREQUENCY) can be given by:

most ↑	*nearly always, almost always*
frequent	*usually, normally, generally, regularly* (= 'on most occasions')
	often, frequently (= 'on many occasions')
	sometimes (= 'on some occasions')
	occasionally, now and then ⟨informal⟩ (= 'on a few occasions')
least	*rarely, seldom* (= 'on few occasions')
frequent	*hardly ever, scarcely ever* (= 'almost never')

(Compare 80–1.)

Being more precise about frequency
167

A more exact measurement of frequency (**definite frequency**) can be expressed in one of the following three ways:

- *once a day, three times an hour, several times a week* (sometimes *per* ⟨formal, official⟩ is used instead of *a(n)* here: *once per day*):

> They ate only *once a day.*
> I go to the office *five times a week.*

- *every day* (= 'once a day'), *every morning, every two years*:

> We went for long walks *every day.*
> The board meets *every week* in Chicago.

- *daily* (= 'once a day'), *hourly, weekly, monthly, yearly. Daily, weekly,* etc. can act as adjectives as well as adverbs:

> I read *The Times daily.*   A *daily* newspaper.
> She is paid *monthly* in arrears.   A *monthly* magazine.

Notice the equivalence of:

$$\text{He visits me} \left\{ \begin{array}{l} \textit{once a week} \\ \textit{every week} \\ \textit{weekly} \end{array} \right\} = \text{He pays me a } \textit{weekly} \text{ visit.}$$

We can also say *once every day*, *twice weekly*, etc. *Every other day/week* etc. means '*every two days/weeks*'.

- A further type of frequency expression involves the use of quantifiers like *some, any, most, many* (*see* 80, 675):

  Some days I feel like giving up the job altogether.
  Come and see me *any time* you like.
  We play tennis *most weekends*.
  He's been to Russia *many times* as a reporter.

On . . . occasions
168
Frequency phrases generally have no preposition: we say *every week*, NOT **in every week*. One exception is when we use the word *occasion(s)* ⟨rather formal⟩:

  On several occasions the President has refused to bow to the will of
    Congress.
  It has been my privilege to work with Roy Mason *on numerous
    occasions*.

Abstract frequency
169
Frequency phrases sometimes lose much of their time meaning, and get a more abstract meaning, referring to **instances** rather than **times**. *Always* and *sometimes* (for example) can be interpreted 'in every case', 'in some cases', rather than 'on every occasion', 'on some occasions':

  Medical books *always* seem to cost the earth.
  The young animals are *sometimes* abandoned by their parents.
  Children *often* ('in many cases') dislike tomatoes. (roughly = 'Many
    children dislike tomatoes')
  Students *rarely* ('in few cases') used to fail this course. (roughly = 'Few
    students used to fail this course')

Place, direction and distance

170
Expressions of place and direction are chiefly adverbials and postmodifiers. They answer the question *Where?*, so that all of the following could be answers to the question *Where did you leave the bicycle?*:

$$I\ left\ it \begin{cases} (over)\ there. & (\text{ADVERB} - see\ 454,\ 469) \\ in\ the\ park. & (\text{PREPOSITIONAL PHRASE} - see\ 654\text{-}6) \\ two\ miles\ away. & (\text{NOUN PHRASE} + away,\ back,\ \text{etc}. \\ & \quad - see\ 595\text{-}6) \\ where\ I\ found\ it. & (\text{ADVERBIAL CLAUSE} - see\ 495) \end{cases}$$

On occasions, place expressions can also act as subject or complement of a sentence:

Over here is where I put the books. ⟨informal⟩

You will see that the range of grammatical structures and functions for expressing place is similar to that for expressing time (*see* 151). You will also notice that some forms (e.g. the prepositions *at*, *from*, and *between*) have related meanings in the two fields.

Prepositions of place

171

Apart from general adverbs like *here*, *there*, and *everywhere*, by far the most important words for indicating place are prepositions. The choice of preposition is often governed by the way we see an object, i.e. whether we see it:

(A) as a point in space   ×   (*see* 163)

(B) as a line

(C) as a surface   } (*see* 164 – 5)

(D) as an area

(E) as a volume   } (*see* 166 – 7)

The difference between 'surface' and 'area' will be explained below (*see* 174-5, 183).

We may distinguish

- '*at*-type' prepositions, which indicate a point (A)
- '*on*-type' prepositions, which indicate a line or a surface (B or C),
- '*in*-type' prepositions, which indicate an area or a volume (D or E).

Some prepositions (such as *across*) belong to more than one of these types.

At-type prepositions

172

(A) **The place is seen as a** POINT (i.e. a place which is identified quite generally, without being thought of in terms of length, width, or height).

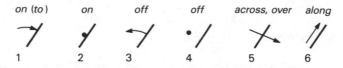

	to	at	(away) from	away from
	→x	·x	x→	x ·
	1	2	3	4

1 We went { to Stratford. / to the hotel. / to the door.

2 We stayed { at home. / at an inn. / at the entrance.

3 We came (away) { from the theatre. / from the house. / from the bus-stop.

4 We stayed { away from home. / away from England. / away from the village.

On-type prepositions

173

(B) **The place is seen as a** LINE, i.e. is a place thought of in terms of length, but not breadth or height (depth):

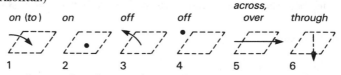

on (to)	on	off	off	across, over	along
1	2	3	4	5	6

1. The wagon rolled back *on to the road.* (ALSO written *onto.*)
2. The company headquarters was at a town *on the Mississippi River.*
3. We turned *off Greenville Avenue* onto Cherry Hill Road.
4. They were a hundred miles *off the coast of Sri Lanka.*
5. Another man tried to swim *across the river.*
6. The power was off in houses *along Smith Street.*

On-type prepositions: *surface*

174

(C) **The place is seen as a** SURFACE, i.e. is thought of in terms of length and width, but not height (or depth). (The surface need not be flat or horizontal.)

on (to)	on	off	off	across, over	through
1	2	3	4	5	6

The surface is often the *top* of some object (*on* = *on top of*): *He was lying on the bed; The book fell off the table.*

1. fall *on* (to) the floor
2. the label *on* the bottle
3. take the picture *off* the wall

4. a place *off* the map
5. a walk *across* the fields
6. looking *through* the window

Note

[a] *On* etc. is also used for public transport:
There were few passengers *on the bus/train/plane.*

We can also say *He travelled by bus/train/plane*, etc. (*see* 197, 475)

[b] Notice also *an apple on a tree, the ring on her finger* (where *on* = 'attached to' or 'adhering to').

In-type prepositions: *area*

175

(D) **The place is seen as an** AREA (usually an area of ground or territory enclosed by boundaries).

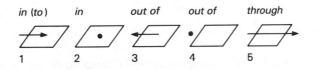

1. Crowds pour *into the city* from the neighbouring villages.
2. They had found suitable lodgings for her *in the town*.
3. The manuscript was smuggled *out of the country*.
4. He stayed *out of the district*.
5. We went for a walk *through the park*.

In-type prepositions: *volume*

176

(E) **The place is seen as a** VOLUME, i.e. is thought of in terms of length, width, height (or depth):

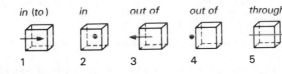

1. He ran *into the house*.
2. The food *in the cupboard*.
3. He climbed *out of the water*.

4. He was *out of the room*.
5. The wind blew *through the trees*.

Inside, outside, within

177

Inside and *outside* are sometimes used instead of *in(to)* and *out of*:

> Were you *inside the house* when the fire started?
> She was sitting just *outside the surgery*.

Within is a slightly more ⟨formal⟩ word than *in*, and often indicates a location bounded by limits, or by a given distance (*within 3 miles*, etc.):

> Many prisoners died *within the walls of the castle*. (= inside)
> He lives *within a stone's throw of the office*. (= not beyond)

Put in, put on, etc.
178
Some common transitive verbs such as *put, place, lay, stand* are followed by *on* and *in* rather than *on to* and *into*:

> Jane *put* each object back *in* its allotted place.
> She *placed* her hand *on* Kate's hair.

Also, *arrive* goes with *at, on,* or *in: The train arrives at/in Brussels at 7.15 (see* 171, 180).

Overlap between types of preposition
179
We can often use different prepositions with the same noun. But in such cases, the meaning will be slightly different.

> My car is *at the cottage.* (POINT, i.e. the cottage as a general location)
> They are putting a new roof *on the cottage.* (SURFACE)
> There are only two beds *in the cottage.* (VOLUME)

Overlap between *at*-type and *in*-type prepositions
180
For towns and villages, either *at* or *in* is used, depending on point of view. *At Stratford* means we are seeing Stratford simply as a place on the map; *in Stratford* means we have a 'close up' view of the place as a town covering an area, and containing streets, houses, etc. A very large town or city is generally treated as an area: *in New York. At New York* would be used only in a context of worldwide travel:

> We stopped to refuel *at New York* on our way to Tokyo.

Parts of cities also require *in: in Chelsea* (part of London); *in Brooklyn* (part of New York).

For continents, countries, states, and other large areas we use *in: in Asia, in China, in Virginia.* However, the directional words *to* and *from* are preferred to *into,* etc. even for large territories, except where those territories border one another:

> He sailed *from* Europe *to* Canada.
> We crossed the Rhine *into* Germany.

At/in the post office, etc.
181
For buildings or groups of buildings, you can use either *at* or *in,* but it is better to use *at* when thinking of the building as an institution rather than simply as a place. (Many such nouns with *at* take no definite article: *at school,* etc. – *see* 495.)

> You can buy stamps *at the post office.*
> BUT: I left my purse *at/in the post office.*
> The princess, aged 24, is now studying history *at Cambridge* (= the university).
> BUT: She is staying with a friend *at/in Cambridge* (= the city).

Shout to, shout at, etc.
182
At is used instead of *to* when the following noun indicates a target:

> He threw the ball *at me* (i.e. 'He tried to hit me').
> Eddie threw the ball *to Phil* (i.e. 'for him to catch').

Note also a similar contrast between:

> 'Hey, you', the man shouted *at her* (suggests that he was angry with her).
> Peter shouted *to me* (suggests that Peter was trying to communicate with me at a distance).

Other contrasts of the same general kind are seen in:

> He pointed his pistol *at Jess.*
> She passed/handed a note *to me.*

Similar cases are: *aim (a gun) at, hand (a ball) to.*

Overlap between *on*-type and *in*-type prepositions: *Sit on/in the grass*, etc.
183
There is a difference between 'surface' and 'volume' in:

> We sat *on the grass.* (SURFACE: i.e. the grass is short)
> We sat *in the grass.* (VOLUME: i.e. the grass is long)

Another difference (between 'surface' and 'area') is seen in:

> Robinson Crusoe was marooned *on a desert island* (SURFACE: i.e. the island is small).
> It's the most influential newspaper *in Cuba* (AREA: i.e. Cuba is a large island, and a political unit with boundaries).

Position: *over, under, in front of, behind*, etc.
184
Position is a relation between two objects, and can best be explained by a picture. Imagine a car standing on a bridge:

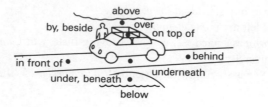

- **Over** and **under** tend to indicate a direct vertical relationship, or nearness:

  The injured girl had a bad cut *over the left eye*.
  The doctor was leaning *over her*.

  On the other hand, *above* and *below* may mean simply that one object is on a higher or lower level than the other. *Underneath* often means that one object is actually touching the other. In this respect it is the opposite of *on top of*:

  The children evaded capture by hiding *underneath a pile of rugs*.

- **By** and **beside** mean 'at the side of', but can also be used more generally to indicate the nearness of one object to another:

  Uncle Harry chose a big chair *by* (= 'near') *the fireplace*.

Prepositional adverbs of place: *overhead*, etc.
185
The following prepositional adverbs (*see* 660) or fixed phrases correspond to the prepositions of position we have just dealt with:

overhead	(over)	*above*	(above)
underneath	(under)	*below*	(below)
in front	(in front of)	*behind*	(behind)
on top	(on top of)	*beneath*	(beneath)

Examples:

Florentines are delicious, with bumpy nuts and cherries *on top*, and silky chocolate *underneath*.
The sky *overhead* was a mass of stars.
Huge waves are crashing on the rocks *below*.
Mr Smart drove to church with a guard of mounted police *in front* and *behind*.

Some other positions: *between*, *among*, *opposite*, etc.
186

- **Between**, **among** and **amid** are related: *Between* normally relates an object to two other objects, and *among* to more than two:

The house stands *between two trees.*

The house stands *among trees.*

But *between* can relate to more than two objects, if we have a definite set in mind:

> Manila lies on the shore of Manila Bay, *between the sea, the mountains, and a large lake called Laguna de Bay.*

- *Amid* ⟨formal⟩ means 'in the midst of', and like *among*, can apply to an indefinite number of objects: *The house stands amid trees.* Unlike *among*, it can also be followed by a mass noun:

> *Amid the wreckage of the plane* they found a child's doll.

- *Opposite* means 'facing':

> His house is *opposite mine* (i.e. 'facing mine, on the other side of the street').

- *(A)round* refers to surrounding position or motion:

> The police were standing on guard *around the building.*

About and *around* in ⟨informal⟩ English often have a vaguer meaning of 'in the area of' or 'in various positions in':

> The guests were standing *about/around the room.*
> There's quite a lot of woodland *about/around here.*

In ⟨AmE⟩, *about* is rarer in this sense than *around*.

Motion from one place to another
187
In 173–6, those meanings illustrated by diagrams 1, 3, 5, and 6 involve **motion**. The prepositions in the other diagrams (2 and 4) indicate **state**. Different aspects of motion can be pictured as follows:

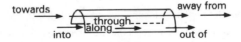

The train sped *towards/into/etc the tunnel.*

But the prepositions used to indicate position in 184–6 can also signify **motion** to the position concerned:

> 1 The bush was a good hiding-place, so I dashed *behind it.*
> 2 When it started to rain, we all ran *underneath the trees.*

Passage: *We drove past the town hall*
188

The same prepositions can also be used, like *through* and *across*, to indicate motion towards, then away from a place (i.e. **passage**):

1 The photographers ran *behind the goal-posts.*
2 I crawled *underneath the fence.*

Other prepositions can be used similarly:

1 We drove *by/past the town hall.*
2 We passed *over/across the bridge.*
3 We turned *(a)round the corner.*

Around and *round* can also refer more generally to circular motion: (*round* is more common in ⟨BrE⟩, and *around* in ⟨AmE⟩):

The earth moves *(a)round the sun.*

Direction: *up, down, along, across,* etc.
189

Up, down, along, and *across/over* represent motion with reference to a direction or axis.

HORIZONTAL AXIS   VERTICAL AXIS

I went silently *along the passage.*
He ran *across the lawn* to the gate.
She flung open the french windows and ran *over the sodden grass.*
They were rolling *down the hill* without brakes.
The royal couple went *up the steps* together.
She walked very quickly *up/down the street.*

The last sentence here does not necessarily mean that the street was on a hill: ⟨informally⟩, we use *up* and *down* with practically the same meaning as *along.* (*Downtown* ⟨AmE⟩ means simply the central or business part of a town.)

Note
We can express **repeated motion** by joining two prepositions with *and*:

He walked *up and down the room* (in one direction and then in another).
The oars splashed *in and out of the water.*
They danced *round and round the room.*

In such cases we can omit the noun phrase after the prepositions: *They danced round and round.*

Combining space and motion
190

• **Viewpoint:** The preposition *beyond* makes reference not only to two objects, but to a third factor, the 'viewpoint', or place at which the speaker is standing (in reality or in imagination):

> I could see the town *beyond the lake* (i.e. 'on the other side of the lake [from me]').

We can also express a 'viewpoint' meaning by using *across, over, through, past,* etc. in a sense similar to their 'passage' or 'direction' sense (*see* 188–9):

<table>
<tr><td>the people who live *over the road*</td><td>the cafe *round the corner*</td></tr>
<tr><td>an office *along the corridor*</td><td>the garage *past the supermarket*</td></tr>
<tr><td>friends *across the sea*</td><td>the hotel *down the road*</td></tr>
<tr><td>the house *through the trees*</td><td>a man *up a ladder*</td></tr>
</table>

We can, if we like, specify the viewpoint by using a *from*-phrase:

> He lives up/down/along/across the road *from me.*

● **Resulting place meaning**
Prepositions which have the meaning of 'motion' can also have a 'state' meaning, indicating the state of having reached a particular destination:

> The horses are *over the fence* (i.e. 'have jumped the fence').
> The divers are *out of the water* already.

● **Pervasive meaning**
Over and *through* can have 'pervasive' meaning, especially when preceded by *all*:

> He painted (*all*) *over the walls* (i.e. 'he covered the walls with paint').
> The noise could be heard *all over/through* the building.

Through is restricted to areas and volumes (*see* 175–6).
Throughout can be used instead of *all through:*

> His views were widely echoed *throughout Germany.*

Abstract place meaning

191
Place prepositions are often used in more abstract senses, which relate to their basic sense by metaphor. Some examples are:

In, out of (condition or inclusion): *in danger, out of danger; out of practice; in a race, in plays, in a group*

> People never behave *in real life* as they do *in plays.*

Above, below, beneath (levels on a scale)

> His grades are *above the average.*
> He rejects such activity as *beneath* (= not worthy of) him.

Over, under (power, surveillance, scale): *under suspicion, under orders, over* (= 'more than') *ten miles.*

The King had absolute power *over his subjects.*

Up, down (movement on a scale): *up the scale, down the social ladder.*
From, to (giving and receiving):

Did you get a letter *from Leslie* about this?
He gave a lot of money *to his family.*

Between, among (involving two or more people):

My sister and I share the place *between us.*
They agree *among themselves.*

Past, beyond (going too far):

Modern times have changed the world *beyond recognition.*
I'm *past* (= too old for) *falling in love.*

Place adverbs and their relation to prepositions
192
Most place prepositions (except the *at*-type prepositions) correspond in form to prepositional adverbs (*see* 660), and in general their meanings correspond as well. Here are some examples:

We stopped the bus and got *off* (i.e. '*off* the bus').
Have you put the cat *out* (i.e. 'out of the house')?
The child ran *across* in front of the car (i.e. 'across the road').
When they reached the bridge, they crossed *over*, looking *down* at the water *beneath.*

But some prepositional adverbs have special uses:

They travelled *on* (i.e. 'they continued their journey').
The thieves snatched her handbag and ran *off* (= 'away').
A man came *up* (i.e. 'approached') and introduced himself.
You don't see many parrots *about* nowadays (i.e. 'about the place').
⟨informal BrE – AmE prefers *around*⟩

In this last example, *about* is so vague as to be almost meaningless.

Note
In addition to *up* and *down*, the following adverbs of direction can be noted: *upward(s),*
downward(s); forward(s), backward(s); inward(s), outward(s); homeward(s).

Distance
193
Distance can be expressed by noun phrases of measure such as *a foot, a few metres∥meters, ten miles, a long way,* etc. These phrases can modify a verb of motion:

He ran *several kilometres.*   [1]

They can also precede and modify an adverbial of place:

> They live *a long way away*.   [2]
> The valley lay *two thousand feet below them*.

Here the meaning is one of static location. Notice the question forms corresponding to [1] and [2]:

> *How far* did he run?

B U T: *How far away* do they live?

Manner, means and instrument

Answering the question '*how*'
194
If you want to specify **how** an action is performed or **how** an event takes place, you can use an adverbial of **manner**, **means**, or **instrument**:

> [A]   *How* did you write the letter?
>
> [B]   I wrote it $\begin{cases} \text{(very) } \textit{hurriedly.} & (\text{MANNER}) \\ \textit{by hand.} & (\text{MEANS}) \\ \textit{with a red ball-point pen.} & (\text{INSTRUMENT}) \end{cases}$

You can ask a more specific question about the instrument with which an action is performed as follows:

> *What* did you write it *with*? ⟨rather informal⟩
> *What tools did the artist use* to create this remarkable effect?

Manner
195
The three chief ways of expressing manner are:

[A]   **adverb** (usually ending in *-ly*),
[B]   **in a . . . manner** (or **way**),
[C]   **with + abstract noun phrase**.

Most adjectives have matching *-ly* adverbs, and many adjectives have matching abstract nouns. Thus there may be three ways of expressing the same idea:

> He spoke $\begin{cases} \text{[A]} & \textit{confidently.} & \text{(most common)} \\ \text{[B]} & \textit{in a confident manner.} & \langle\text{more formal}\rangle \\ \text{[C]} & \textit{with confidence.} & \langle\text{formal}\rangle \end{cases}$

Examples of manner adverbs and manner phrases are:

> She stirred her coffee *thoughtfully* before answering.
> The task was done *in a workmanlike manner/way*.
> His father stopped and looked *in a startled manner* at his mother.
> Joanna stubbed out her cigarette *with unnecessary fierceness*.

I answered *without hesitation*. (i.e. 'unhesitatingly')
'Next year', she replied *gently, with a smile*.

Like this, like that (or *this way, that way*) are phrases with the meaning 'in this/that manner':

I'm sorry you had to hurt yourself *like this*.
Please, Ralph, don't talk *like that*.

Notice that *in* can be omitted before *way* in certain 〈informal〉 constructions:

Monica and her sister do their hair (*in*) *the same way*.
She prepared the dish (*in*) *the way he liked*, with slices of oil-bean and fish.
You can cook turkey (*in*) *a number of different ways*.

Combining manner with comparison
196

A manner phrase sometimes expresses a comparison:

She sings *like a professional* (i.e. 'in the manner of a professional, as well as a professional')
Sarah Morgan came into the room *like a ghost*.

Manner clauses introduced by *as* can be used in a similar way. Compare:

Pat cooks turkey ⎰ *as my mother did.*
                  ⎨ *in the way that my mother did.* 〈formal〉
                  ⎱ *the way my mother did.* 〈informal〉
They hunted him *as a tiger stalks its prey*. 〈formal〉

Comparisons with unreal situations can be expressed by a clause beginning *as if* or *as though*:

She treats me ⎰ *as if*   ⎱ *I were one of the family*.
               ⎨ *as though* ⎰

(On the verb form *were* here, *see* 277.)

Means and instrument: *by* and *with*
197

- **Means** is expressed by a phrase introduced by *by*:

  You're going to France *by car* are you? (*see* Note [b] below)
  She slipped into the house *by the back gate*.
  We managed to sell the house *by advertising it in the paper*.

- **Instrument** is expressed by a phrase introduced by *with*:

  She reached down and touched the lace *with her fingers*.
  The young man had been attacked *with an iron bar*.

The verb *use* and its object also convey the idea of instrument:

> She always opens her letters *with a knife.*
> ~ She always *uses a knife* to open her letters.

The non-use of an instrument can be expressed by *without*:

> You can draw the lines *without (using) a ruler.*

Notes

[a]   We sometimes prefer to replace a *by*-phrase of means by a different type of prepositional phrase, e.g. one of place:

[A] How did he get in?	[B] He came in *through the window.*
	(more usual than *by the window*)
[A] How did you hear the news?	[B] I heard it *on the radio.*

[b]   The article is omitted in *by*-phrases denoting communication: *by car, by train, by letter, by fax, by post‖mail, by radio (see 475).*

Cause, reason and purpose

Direct cause: actors and causative verbs
198
There are many different answers to the question 'What causes such-and-such an event?' The means and instrument, just discussed, may be said to be kinds of direct cause. More important, though, is the *person* who causes an event to take place, i.e. the **actor**. The actor is usually specified by the subject of a clause ([B] below), or by the agent in the passive ([C]) (*see* 613–5):

> [A]   How did the fire start?
> [B]   *Some children* started it (i.e. 'caused it to start').
> [C]   It was started by *some children.*

Start in the second sentence here may be called a **causative verb**, and *some children* names the actor.

Many adjectives and intransitive verbs in English have a corresponding causative verb. The causative verb may match them in form (*open, grow, blow up, narrow* (adj) and *narrow* (verb)), or may be different in form (*fall, fell; die, kill; come, bring*):

The dam *blew up.*	The terrorists *blew up* the dam.
The road became *wider.*	They *widened* the road.
The tree has *fallen.*	Someone has *felled* the tree.
The supplies *came in* yesterday.	They *brought* the supplies *in* yesterday.

199
Sometimes, when the actor is not mentioned, the instrument or means takes the position of subject, i.e. the role of the 'causer' of the action:

> They killed him *with his own gun.*   *His own gun* killed him.
> They brought the supplies *by*   *The train* brought the supplies.
>   *train.*

In the passive, the actor can be expressed by a *by*-phrase (*see* 613–5):

> The dam was blown up *by terrorists.*

The same is true of instrument:

> He was killed *by* his own gun.

Cause and result: *because*, etc. (*see also* 365)
200

In answer to the question 'why?', you may indicate cause or reason by an adverbial *because*-clause, or by a prepositional phrase beginning *because of, on account of* ⟨formal⟩, *from, out of*:

Because:

> The accident occurred *because the machine had been poorly maintained.* [1]

Because of:

> She can't go to work *because of the baby.*   [2]

On account of ⟨formal⟩:

> Many fatal accidents occurred *on account of icy road conditions.*   [3]

From, out of (mainly to express motive, i.e. psychological cause):

> He did accept the award, not *from/out of pride*, but *from/out of a sense of duty.*   [4]

Other prepositions of cause are *for* (mainly with nouns of feeling) and **through**:

> He jumped *for joy.*
> The car crashed *through the driver's carelessness.*   [5]

Indirect cause as subject
201

We can often make the 'cause' the subject of the sentence, using a general causative verb like *cause* or *make*. Compare [5] in 200 above with:

> The driver's carelessness *caused the crash.*   [active]
> ~ *The crash was caused by* the driver's carelessness.   [passive]

Other verbal constructions expressing cause are these:

> Such slipshod security is bound to *lead to* trouble.
> Many of these prosecutions *result in* acquittals.

We are trying *to bring about* equal rights for all people.
He argues that higher wages inevitably *give rise to* higher prices.

We can also express cause with a noun like *effect*:

The *effect* of higher wages is to raise prices.

Result
202
Result is the opposite of cause (compare [3] in 200):

The icy conditions *caused* many accidents.   [cause]
~ Many accidents *resulted from* the icy conditions.   [result]

Notice also that *result in* and *result from* are opposites:

The celebrations *resulted in* a serious riot.
~ A serious riot *resulted from* the celebrations.

Result can be expressed by a clause beginning with *so that*, or just *so* (which is
⟨informal⟩):

I ignored his objections, *so* (*that*) he flew into a rage.

This is another way of saying:

He flew into a rage *because* I took no notice of him.

So is more ⟨informal⟩ than *so that*.

Purpose
203
The intended result (*see* 323) or PURPOSE of an action is described by an
adverbial of purpose, usually a *to*-infinitive clause:

He left early *to catch the last train.*
Penelope leaned forward *to examine the letter more closely.*
To improve the railway service, they are electrifying all the main lines.

An adverbial of purpose may also be a finite verb clause beginning *so that*:

They advertised the concert *so that everyone should know about it.* (The
so that-clause often contains *would* or *should*, see 280.)

In order that is a ⟨more formal⟩ alternative for *so that*: *in order that everyone
should know about it.* In ⟨informal BrE⟩, *in case* can introduce the idea of
negative purpose (compare 208):

He left early *in case he should miss the last train* (i.e. '... so that he
should not miss it').

Reason and consequence: *because (of)*, *as, since*, etc.
204
Because, because of, and *on account of* can express **reason** as well as cause. Cause and reason are overlapping notions (both answering the question *Why?*), but the difference between them is that cause concerns the events themselves, while reason concerns the way a person interprets the events, and acts upon this interpretation:

> We have lunch early on Saturday *because the girls are always in a hurry to go out.*
> We decided to go home early, *because of the storm.*
> The contest was abandoned *on account of bad weather conditions.*
>   ⟨formal⟩

Reason can also be expressed by *as*-clauses and *since*-clauses:

> *As Jane was the eldest,* she had to look after her brothers and sisters.
> The report is out of date – which is hardly surprising, *since it was published in 1979.*

The main clause indicates the **consequence** of the reason clause. Another way to express the same idea would be:

> The city is situated near the sea and *consequently* enjoys a healthy climate. ⟨rather formal⟩

Now that *and* seeing that, *etc.*
205
Now that and *seeing that* are conjunctions which have a meaning very close to *as* and *since,* except that *now that* has also an element of time meaning:

> We hope to see much more of you *now that you're living in Vicksburg.*
> *Seeing that he could not persuade the other members of the committee,* he gave in to their demands.

Another ⟨more formal⟩ way to express the same idea is a participle clause (*see* 493):

> *The weather having improved,* the game was enjoyed by players and spectators alike. ⟨formal⟩
> *Being a man of fixed views,* he refused to listen to our arguments. ⟨rather formal⟩

Yet another construction expressing reason is a *for*-phrase, following certain adjectives and verbs of emotion and attitude:

> She laughed at herself *for being so silly and self-pitying.*
> They were praised *for their outspoken defence of free speech.* ('because of their . . .')

Linking adverbials: **therefore, hence,** *etc.*
206
Also important are linking adverbials of cause or reason (*see* 365) meaning 'because of that' or 'for that reason': *Therefore, thus, accordingly, hence,* and *consequently* are ⟨formal⟩, whereas *so* is ⟨informal⟩:

> Very shortly afterwards, however, he began to suffer from attacks of angina pectoris. *Accordingly,* he was excused all serious exertion. ⟨formal, written⟩
> After all, Glasgow was where she really belonged. *So* this year she had decided to spend her annual holiday in the city. ⟨informal⟩

A linking adverbial corresponding to *seeing that* (205) is *in that case*:

> [A]   The weather has improved.
> [B]   *In that case,* we can go out and enjoy our game.

Condition and contrast

Open and hypothetical conditions: *if,* etc.
207
Conditional clauses are related to reason clauses, but they discuss the consequence of something which may or may not be a real event. Notice the difference between:

> I'll lend Peter the money *because he needs it.*   [1]
> I'll lend Peter the money *if he needs it.*   [2]

The speaker of sentence [1] knows that Peter needs the money, while the speaker of [2] does not know whether he does. A sentence like [2] expresses what we call an **open** condition, because the truth or falsehood of what the sentence describes is 'open', i.e. unknown. The conditional clause often precedes the main clause:

> *If you feel seasick,* take one of these pills.

There is another type of conditional sentence, which expresses an unreal or **hypothetical** condition; i.e. for this type of sentence the speaker assumes the falsehood or unlikelihood of what is described:

> I would lend Peter the money *if he needed it.*

The speaker's assumption here is 'but he doesn't need the money'. As this example shows, the hypothetical meaning is signalled by the use of the hypothetical past tense (*see* 275).

In case (of), on condition that, provided that
208
Condition can also be expressed by the conjunctions *in case, on condition that, provided that,* and the preposition *in case of* ⟨formal⟩:

- *In case* names a future condition which may or may not arise:

> Take these pills, *in case you feel ill on the boat.*
> I had to watch where I put my feet *in case I fell.*

- *On condition that* specifies a condition to which a person must agree:

> I'll lend you the money *on condition that you return it within six months.*

- *Provided that* and *so long as* are like *on condition that* in expressing a strong condition 'if and only if . . .'.

> *Provided that* ⎫
> *So long as* ⎬ *they had plenty to eat and drink,*
>   ⎭
>   the crew seemed to be happy.

- *In case of* is a preposition expressing condition:

> *In case of emergency*, the simplest thing is to flick off the switch.

Negative condition: *unless*
209
Unless expresses a negative condition. Thus we could change the emphasis of *I'll lend Peter the money if he needs it* (*see* 207) by saying:

> I won't lend Peter the money *unless he needs it.*

Note the equivalence of:

> *Unless* Paul *improves* his work, he'll fail the exam.
> ~ If Paul *doesn't improve* his work, he'll fail the exam.
> You can take a book out of the library and keep it for a whole year *unless it's recalled.*

Negative hypothetical conditions can be expressed by *but for* + noun phrase:

> *But for Jenny*, we would have lost the match (i.e. 'If it hadn't been for Jenny'; 'If Jenny hadn't played well', etc.).

Unless cannot be used in this type of context.

Otherwise is a sentence adverb expressing negative condition (*see* 367):

> I'm sorry I had a previous engagement: *otherwise*, I'd have been here much earlier.

Use of *any, ever,* etc.
210
Because they indicate uncertainty, conditional clauses often contain *any*-words like *any, ever, yet,* etc. (rather than *some*-words like *some, always, already* – *see* 697–9):

If you *ever* have *any* problems, let me know.
Unless *anyone* has *any* questions, the meeting is adjourned.

But to express special positive bias (*see* 243), conditional clauses can contain *some*-words:

Help yourself if you want *something* to eat.

Clauses of contrast: *although*, etc. (*see also* 361)
211
A further type of adverbial meaning overlapping with conditional meaning is that of **contrast**, also called **concession**. If two circumstances are in contrast, it means that the one (*b*) is **surprising** or **unexpected** in view of the other (*a*):

{	*a*	The weather is bad.	{	*a*	He hadn't eaten for days.
	b	We are enjoying ourselves.		*b*	He looked strong and healthy.

We can link the contrasting ideas *a* and *b* by using the coordinating conjunction *but*.

The weather is bad, *but* we're enjoying ourselves.
He hadn't eaten for days, *but* he looked strong and healthy.

We can also put *a* and *b* together by making one of them into a subclause beginning *although* or *though* ⟨informal⟩:

We are enjoying ourselves, *although/though the weather is bad*.
(*Even*) *though he hadn't eaten for days*, he looked strong and healthy.

(*Even though* is slightly more emphatic than *although*.)
   The conjunctions *while* and *whereas* can express contrast between two equivalent ideas:

While we welcome his support, we disagree with a lot of his views.
Elizabeth was lively and talkative, *whereas her sister was quiet and reserved*.

Note
There are special constructions for expressing the meaning of 'even though':

Much as I would like to help, I have other work I must do. ('Even though I would like to help very much . . .')
Absurd as it may seem, she grew tired of being a success. ('Even though it may seem absurd . . .')

In sentences like these, the conjunction *as* occurs in the middle of the subclause, after an emphatic adjective (*absurd*) or an adverbial (*much*). Sometimes *though* is used instead of *as*: *Absurd though it may seem* . . . These constructions can sound rather ⟨elevated⟩ and ⟨rhetorical⟩:

Unarmed as/though he was, he bravely went forward to meet his enemies.

Phrases and adverbs of contrast: *in spite of*, etc.

212

In spite of, *despite* ⟨formal⟩, *notwithstanding* ⟨very formal⟩, *for all* are prepositions of contrast:

> We are enjoying ourselves *in spite of the weather*.
>
> *Despite her fabulous wealth*, Sara's only property is a humble house in the oldest part of Seville.
>
> *Notwithstanding state aid*, the local governments are continuing to seek extra revenue. ⟨formal⟩
>
> *For all his skill*, he has accomplished very little. (= 'Despite his great skill . . .')

There are also a number of sentence adverbials (*see* 361, 462) expressing the meaning 'in spite of this/that': *yet*, *however*, *nevertheless* ⟨formal⟩, *all the same* ⟨informal⟩, *still*, *even so*:

> The weather was absolutely dreadful; *however*, the children enjoyed themselves.
>
> Britain was mopping up yesterday after one month's rain fell overnight; *yet* we're still in the middle of a drought.
>
> He has, presumably, the main weight of local opinion behind him, not to mention the considerable resources of the French government. *Nevertheless*, the omens are not good. ⟨rather formal, written⟩

Yet can be used in the main clause to reinforce the contrast made by the subclause:

> *Although* he hadn't eaten for days, *yet* he looked strong and healthy.

Note

The adverb *even* is used to imply a contrast with what we might usually expect:

> My father won't give me the money – he won't *even* lend it to me.

The contrast here is with the usual expectation that fathers are willing to lend money to their children.

Condition + contrast

213

The ideas of condition (*if*) and implied contrast (*even*) come together in the conjunction *even if*:

> I always enjoy sailing, *even if the weather is rough*.
>
> ('You wouldn't expect me to enjoy sailing in rough weather, but I do.')
>
> We will take appropriate action, *even if we have to go it alone*.

The meaning of *even if* is sometimes conveyed by *if . . . (at least)*:

> *If nothing else*, at least two good things came out of the project. ('Even if nothing else came out of the project . . .')

The same contrastive meaning is expressed in hypothetical conditions by *even if*:

> She wouldn't give me the money, *even if I begged* her for it.

Alternative conditions: *whether . . . or, whatever*, etc.
214

Condition is combined with the meaning of *either . . . or* in the parallel conjunctions *whether . . . or*, which specify two contrasting conditions:

> *Whether we win or lose*, the match will be enjoyable. ('If we win or even if we lose . . .')
> They were guaranteed 40 hours' pay per week *whether they worked or not*. ('If they worked or even if they didn't.')

The meaning of 'contrary to expectation' is also present here, as the examples show.

A similar meaning is present in the *wh*-words *whatever, whoever, wherever*, etc.:

> I'll buy those shoes, *whatever the cost*.   [3]
> I intend to support the nominee of the party at St Louis, *whoever that may be*.   [4]
> *Wherever he goes*, he makes friends.   [5]

The meaning is that the statement in the main clause is true on **any of the conditions** covered by the subclause. Again, contrasting meaning is present, in that [3] implies, for example, 'I'll buy them, *even if* they cost a fortune'. The same meaning can be expressed by an adverbial clause beginning *no matter wh-*:

> I'll buy them, *no matter what they cost*.   [3a]

Two general adverbials with this type of meaning are *anyway* and *in any case* (= 'whatever the circumstances'):

> I don't know how much they cost, but I'll buy those shoes *anyway/in any case*.   [3b]

Degree
215

Expressions of **degree** usually modify the meaning of a particular word in the clause. Degree is largely expressed by adverbs, which either act as **modifiers** of adjectives, adverbs, etc. (*see* 464–9), or else act as **adverbials** in clause structure.

- **modifying degree adverbs** (*see* 465)

> [A] *How* hungry are you?   [B] (Actually I'm) *very* hungry.
> [A] *How* soon are they leaving?   [B] (They're leaving) *quite* soon.

- **degree adverbs as adverbials** (*see* 459). Here the degree adverbs usually modify the meaning of the verb (here *agree*):

    [A]   *How far* do they agree?   [B]   (They agree) *completely*.

Applied to nouns, degree is expressed by quantifiers like *much* (*see* 220, 232):

    [A]   *How much* of a dancer is he?   [B]   (He's) *not much* of one.
                                                  ⟨rather informal⟩

Degree expressions can answer the questions *How?* (for adjectives and adverbs); *How much?* (for verbs); and *How much of?* (for nouns). More ⟨formal⟩ questions of degree are *To what degree?* and *To what extent?* Applied to verbs, degree adverbials sometimes answer the question *How far?* and sometimes *How much?*:

    [A]   *How far* do you disagree with me?   [B]   (I disagree with you)
                                                      absolutely.
    [A]   *How much* did she enjoy the ballet?   [B]   (She enjoyed it)
                                                      immensely.

Gradable words and degree
216

Not all verbs, adjectives, etc. can be modified by a degree expression. Degree applies only to **gradable words**, i.e. words whose meaning can be thought of in terms of a **scale**. Most pairs of words of opposite meaning, like *old* and *young*, are gradable:

    [A]   *How old* is your dog?   [B]   He's *very old/quite young*.

If you want to make the degree more exact, you can use a measure phrase (*five years*, *six foot*, etc.) as a degree expression: *She's five years old. He's six foot tall.*
    There are two main kinds of gradable words:

- S C A L E words indicate a relative position on a scale (e.g. *large*, *small*)
- L I M I T words indicate the end-point of a scale (e.g. *black*, *white*):

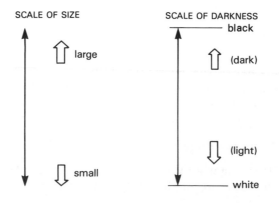

(For the idea of darkness, we also have the scale words *dark* and *light*.)

Degree with scale words

217

The same degree expression can sometimes act either as a modifier or as an adverbial:

> She was *absolutely* crazy about him. [MODIFIER] ⟨informal⟩
> I must say I agree with you *absolutely*. [ADVERBIAL]

In other cases a different adverb has to be used in the different functions: for example, *very* and *too* are limited to the modifying function. The most important differences concern scale words and are given in this table, which also shows the differences between types of adverbs modifying scale words:

Degree expressions with adjectives and verbs as scale words

WITH ADJECTIVE SCALE WORDS	WITH VERB SCALE WORDS
(A) Indicating extreme position on the scale	
very (*see* 220): He's very friendly. It's a very tall building.	(*very*) *much* (*see* 220) *a lot* ⟨informal⟩, *a great deal*: I like her very much.
(B) Intensifying the meaning slightly	
quite, rather, fairly; *pretty* ⟨informal⟩: She's still quite young. It's rather expensive. It's a fairly modern motel. She was pretty annoyed.	*considerably, rather;* *quite, a lot* ⟨informal⟩: I quite enjoy the job. Prices have increased considerably. We talked a lot about old times. I rather like her.
(C) Toning down or decreasing the effect of the scale word	
a bit ⟨informal⟩, *a little, slightly*: She's a bit upset. The journey was slightly uncomfortable. It's a little surprising.	*a bit* ⟨informal⟩, *a little, slightly*: I've read a bit about it. Prices have fallen slightly. I know him a little.

Degree with limit words

218

With limit words (*see* 216) the same adverbs can function as modifiers and as adverbials. The two main classes of such adverbs are:

- Adverbs indicating that the limit word's meaning is used to its fullest extent: *absolutely, altogether, completely, entirely, quite, totally, utterly*:

> I'm *absolutely* positive it's the truth.
> I *completely* disagree with you.
> I don't *entirely* agree with what Mr Turner says.
> We were *utterly* powerless to defend ourselves.

- Adverbs indicating a position near the limit of the scale: *almost, nearly, practically* ⟨informal⟩, *virtually*:

> Mr Player was *almost* in tears.
> I've *nearly* finished my work.
> At the beginning of this term, she *virtually* had a nervous breakdown.
> Johnny Mercer *practically* grew up with the sound of jazz and the blues in his ears.

Note
Notice that *quite* has two uses: *quite* (= 'considerably') goes with scale words, and *quite* (= 'absolutely') goes with limit words.

Degree with comparatives and superlatives
219
The same degree words which modify adjectives can also modify adverbs. But comparative adjectives and adverbs are modified by the degree words which function elsewhere as adverbials (*see* 217):

$$\text{I am feeling} \left\{ \begin{array}{l} \textit{much} \\ \textit{a great deal} \\ \textit{a lot} \langle \text{informal} \rangle \end{array} \right\} \text{more healthy than I was.}$$

Superlatives can be intensified by degree adverbs like *altogether* and *absolutely* which apply to limit words:

> It is *altogether/absolutely* the best show in town.

But *very* can also have an intensifying effect if placed directly before the superlative word (but not before *most*):

> We want to pick the *very* best candidate for the job.

Very and *much*
220
We have seen (*see* 217) that *very* acts as a modifier, whereas *much* acts as an adverbial. However, the adverb *much* on its own is of limited occurrence. It normally has to be preceded by another degree word such as *very* or *so*. Compare:

> The novel has some *very enjoyable* characters in it. (MODIFIER)
> I *very much* hope that you will accept. (MID-POSITION ADVERBIAL)
> I enjoyed the party *very much*. (END-POSITION ADVERBIAL)

Many verbs cannot go with *much* alone: we can say (for example) *I much prefer . . .*, but not **I much like . . . . I very much like . . .*, on the other hand, is acceptable:

> [A]   I *very much like* her latest recording.
> [B]   I *(very) much preferred* her earlier ones.

Positive and negative attitude
221
Some degree adverbs, although they have the same meaning with respect to 'scale' and 'limit', tend to be distinguished in terms of positive and negative **attitude**:

POSITIVE ATTITUDE	NEGATIVE ATTITUDE
It's *quite* warm today.	It's *rather* cold today.
She's *entirely* satisfied.	That is *completely* wrong.
The project looks *fairly* promising.	He felt *utterly* exhausted.

Fairly (= 'considerably'), *quite* (= 'considerably') and *entirely* sometimes suggest a positive or 'good' meaning, whereas *rather*, *completely*, and *utterly* sometimes suggest a negative or 'bad' meaning. Thus *fairly warm* implies that warmth is a good thing; if someone said *It's rather warm today*, on the other hand, he or she would probably be thinking that the weather was a little **too** warm. The expressions *a bit* and *a little* also tend to go with negative meanings: *These boxes are a bit/little heavy.*

Other aspects of degree adverbs
222

- Some words can be used both as scale words and as limit words, e.g. the adjectives *new*, *full*, and *empty*:

> The furniture looked $\left\{ \begin{array}{l} \textit{very} \text{ new.} \\ \textit{absolutely} \text{ new.} \end{array} \right.$
>
> The glass is $\left\{ \begin{array}{l} \textit{very} \text{ full.} \\ \textit{absolutely} \text{ full.} \end{array} \right.$

- We can have a **scale word and a different limit word dealing with the same area of meaning**:

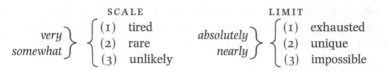

	SCALE		LIMIT
very	(1) tired	*absolutely*	(1) exhausted
somewhat	(2) rare	*nearly*	(2) unique
	(3) unlikely		(3) impossible

- A scale word often corresponds to one or more limit words, **which intensify its meaning,** and add emotive emphasis: for example, *terrible* intensifies the meaning of *bad*:

	ORDINARY			INTENSIFIED	
very	(1)	good	*absolutely*	(1)	perfect/marvellous
	(2)	bad		(2)	terrible/awful
	(3)	large		(3)	massive/colossal
	(4)	annoyed		(4)	infuriated

Note

[a] You can also intensify meaning by repeating the word *very*, or by adding *very . . . indeed*:

> He was a *very, very* special man.   That is *very* strange *indeed*.

[b] Scale words and limit words are sometimes difficult to separate, because there is a tendency to 'convert' limit words to scale words in everyday language. Hence we sometimes hear expressions like *too perfect* and *rather unique*. Some speakers, however, regard such expressions as illogical and 'bad English'.

223

- In addition there are **negative** degree adverbs (*barely*, *hardly*, and *scarcely* – see 584), and the **any-word** (*see* 697–8) degree adverbial *at all*:

> I *scarcely* noticed him (= 'I almost didn't notice him').
> I didn't notice him *at all* (= 'I totally failed to notice him').
> Was it *at all* enjoyable?   The text wasn't *at all* difficult.

- Apart from the degree adverbs listed so far, **there are many degree adverbs which are more restricted in their use**. These tend to intensify a particular set of gradable words, e.g. *badly* goes with the verbs *need* and *want*; *thoroughly* goes with the verbs *enjoy*, *disapprove*, *dislike*, etc.; *hard* goes with the verbs *work*, *try*, etc.:

> They were both *thoroughly enjoying* their first tour of Greece.
> I welcome this scheme, which is *badly needed*. (= 'needed very much').

Role, standard and point of view
224

A gradable word can also have its meaning qualified in terms of **role** or **standard**. By *at* or *as* you can specify the **role** which the gradable word implies; by *for* you can specify the **standard** by which the speaker is judging its use:

> Anna is **clever**.
> Anna is *very* **clever**.   (DEGREE)
>
> Anna is **clever** *at swimming*.   ⎱
> *As a swimmer*, she's **outstanding**. ⎰   (ROLE)

Anna is a **good** swimmer *for a youngster.* ⎫
For a learner, she swims **well.** ⎭ (STANDARD)

(Here the gradable words are in **bold type.**)

Further, you can specify the **point of view** from which a word or phrase is understood:

Morally, it was not an easy problem (i.e. 'From a moral point of view . . .').
In a way, I was very resentful about leaving. (i.e. 'In one respect/from one point of view . . .').
He is a good swimmer *in a technical sense* (i.e. 'from a technical point of view').
These trials were termed 'political cases' *in that the trial itself was a political act.* ⟨formal⟩

You can also name the person(s) whose point of view it is:

To his parents, his behaviour was astonishing.

Comparison
225

To compare two things with respect to their position on a scale of degree or amount, use comparative words *taller, happier,* etc. or comparative phrases *more careful, less careful,* etc. (*see* 500). A following phrase or clause introduced by *than* can indicate the 'standard' against which the comparison is made.

Jack is *taller than* Jill (is).   [1]
Jill is *shorter than* Jack (is).   [2]
Jill is *less tall than* Jack (is).   [3]
Jack is *less short than* Jill (is).   [4]

Sentences [1]–[4] have the same meaning, but are listed in order of their likelihood. A sentence like [4] is very unusual, and would only be said if we were comparing Jack and Jill in terms of their shortness.

Equal comparisons
226

For an equal comparison, e.g. when Jack and Jill are the same height, we use *as . . . as* instead of *more . . . than:*

Jack is *as* tall *as* Jill (is).
~ Jill is *as* tall *as* Jack (is).

To negate equal comparison, we say *not as . . . as,* or *not so . . . as:*

Jill is *not as* tall *as* Jack (is).   [5]
~ Jack is *not so* short *as* Jill (is).   [6]

Again, sentences [5] and [6] have the same basic meaning as [1]–[4].

Comparative and superlative
227
When comparing only two things, we use the comparative forms:

> Jill is *the shorter* of the two children.
> Jack is *the taller* of the two children.

When comparing more than two objects we use superlative forms *tallest, most useful, least tall*, etc.:

> Susan is *the tallest* of the three.
> Jill is the *shortest* of the three.
> That's the *most reasonable* theory.
> Things were being done in the *least efficient* way.

To name the objects, you use *of*, as above, followed by a noun phrase:

> Miller scored *the best goal of the game.*
> Luxembourg is the *smallest* of the *countries* of the European Union.

The *of*-phrase is sometimes placed for emphasis at the beginning of the clause:

> *Of all the capital cities in the world,* Bangkok is the one I would *most* like
> to visit.

To name the sphere or range of comparison use *in* with a singular noun phrase:

> He was the ablest man *in* the civil service.
> It was the worst moment *in my life.* (A L S O: *of my life.*)

Other constructions which can specify the range of comparison with superlatives
are possessive pronouns, genitives, adjectives and relative clauses:

> *my* best friend
> *the world's* highest mountain
> the greatest *living* composer
> the most boring speech *I ever heard*

Comparison with a definite norm
228
Sometimes a comparison is made between an object and a definite standard or
'norm' understood in context (often through back-pointing). In such cases, use
than that or *as that*:

> [A]   Jack must be six foot tall.   [B] $\Big\{$ No, he's taller (*than that*)   [7]
>   Is he really as tall *as that?*   [8]

In [7] you can omit the comparative part *than that* altogether. For [8], you can also say: *Is he* THÁT *tall?* ⟨informal⟩.

The *than*-phrase is usually omitted when we are comparing not two different things, but the same thing at an earlier and at a later time:

> All over the world the crime rate is growing *worse* (i.e. 'worse than it was'), but in many cases the criminal is becoming *more difficult* to catch (i.e. 'more difficult than before').

229

To express continuing change, repeat the comparative word with *and*:

> Germany's position as our principal ally grows *stronger and stronger*.
> Many painters feel *more and more* out of tune with modern society.
> *Fewer and fewer* families are working on the land these days.

Enough and *too*
230

Enough and *too* are words indicating 'as much as' and 'more than' some (usually desirable) norm. The norm to which these words refer can be indicated by a *to*-infinitive clause (*see* 493):

> This new boat is *big enough to cross the Atlantic*.
> This just sounds *too good to be true*.
> Some of the new laws are *too complex for the ordinary citizen to grasp their full import*. ⟨formal⟩

The viewpoint or standard for judging what is 'enough' or 'too much' can be expressed by a *for*-phrase:

> Is the room *warm enough for you?*
> The portrait was *too big for the room*.

Where the meaning is obvious, reference to norm and viewpoint can be omitted:

> Are you *warm enough?*
> We have been looking at all kinds of new properties, but they're all *too expensive*.

So . . . (that) and *such . . . (that)*
231

Degree or amount constructions with *so . . . (that)* and *such . . . (that)* (*see* 716) express a meaning similar to *enough* and *too*:

> It moved *so* quickly *that we didn't see anything* (meaning roughly 'too quickly for us to see anything').
> The little girl was *so* restless *that she couldn't bear to sit still*.
> He's *such* a miser *that he doesn't even stick stamps on his letters*.

The *so* . . . (*that*) and *such* . . . (*that*) constructions also add a meaning of result (*see* 202), expressed by a *that*-clause:

> Mrs Lewis was beaten up – kicked *so* hard *that three ribs were broken.*
> The interview was *such* a nightmare *that I prefer to forget all about it.*

So and *such* in these sentences add emotive emphasis, and this emphasis can also be expressed without the *that*-clause:

> The delay was 'such a nuisance!
> I'm 'so hungry! (*see* 300).

Comparison with nouns: *more of a success*, etc.
232
The various types of comparison just illustrated can be applied to gradable countable nouns (like *success, fool, coward*) by the use of *more of a, as much of a, less of a,* etc.:

> I'm *more of a socialist* now than before.
> It was *as much of a* success as I hoped (it would be).
> You're *less of a* fool than I thought (you were).
> He's *too much of a* coward to tell the full story.

Proportion
233
To compare equivalent tendencies, you can use an adverbial clause of **proportion** introduced by *as*:

> Things got worse and worse *as time went on.*
> *As children get older* women are more likely to work outside the home.

There is a more ⟨formal⟩ construction in which *so* is added to a following main clause:

> *As* the equations became more involved and detailed, *so* their connection to the basic phenomenon grew more tenuous. ⟨formal⟩

Yet another construction expressing proportion consists of two clauses beginning with *the* + a comparative word:

> Kids! *The* older they get, *the* more trouble they become.
> Sandra couldn't deny that, *the more* she thought about the question *the more* curious it became.

Notice that *the* here is a conjunction, and not the definite article. The comparative element of the clause has to come first after *the*, and so often requires a change from normal word order. Compare:

> { *He takes little notice* at the best of times. [SVO]
> { BUT: *The more* you argue with him, *the less notice* he takes.
> {   [ASVA], [OSV]

The subject and verb of the second clause, or of both clauses, can be omitted if their meaning is obvious:

> The more tickets you can sell, the better (i.e. . . . the better it will be).
> The more the merrier. (proverb)
> We'll have to begin our journey early tomorrow; in fact, the earlier, the better.

Addition, exception and restriction

Addition

234

To express **addition** we can use the prepositions *in addition to*, *as well as*, and *besides*:

> They stole three valuable paintings, *in addition to* the money.   [1]
>
> *As well as* ⎱ eating a four-course meal, they drank three bottles of
> *Besides*   ⎰ wine.   [2]

In a coordinate construction, the idea of addition can be simply conveyed by *and*, or (with more emphasis) by *not only . . . but (also)* (*see* 520). Thus [1] is equivalent to:

> ∼ The money (was stolen) and three valuable paintings were
>   stolen.   [1a]
> ∼ Not only the money, but (also) three valuable paintings were
>   stolen.   [1b]

The adverbials *also*, *too* ⟨informal⟩, *as well* ⟨informal⟩, and *in addition* ⟨rather formal⟩ all have the meaning 'in addition to that' (where *that* points back to something mentioned earlier):

> They ate a four-course meal: they *also* drank three bottles of wine.
>   (i.e. 'in addition to eating a four-course meal')
> ∼ they drank three bottles of wine, *too/as well*.
> ∼ *in addition*, they drank three bottles of wine.

The preferred positions of these adverbials are different: *also* prefers mid-position (*see* 451), *too* and *as well* end-position, and *in addition* front-position (but *see* 238).

So am I, etc.

235

So can be placed first in the sentence and followed by inversion (415) of subject and operator. It then combines the meaning of *also* or *too* with the function of a substitute form (*see* 418):

> I live close to the office. *So does my secretary* (= 'and my secretary does too').

If the fascists had gained time to prepare for war, *so had their enemies.*

While, *so, too,* etc. have a positive meaning, *neither* and *nor* have the correspond-ing negative meaning. For negative clauses, there is also the corresponding *any-*word (*see* 697) and adverb *either* ⟨informal⟩, which occurs at the end of a clause. Note that *so, neither,* and *nor* cause inversion (*see* 417–8):

$$
\begin{array}{ll}
[\text{A}] \quad \text{I'm hungry.} & \left. \begin{array}{ll} [\text{B}] & \text{I am, } \textit{too} \\ [\text{B}] & \textit{So} \text{ am I.} \end{array} \right\} \text{POSITIVE}
\end{array}
$$

$$
\begin{array}{ll}
[\text{A}] \quad \text{I'm not hungry.} & \left. \begin{array}{ll} [\text{B}] & \textit{Neither} \text{ am I.} \\ [\text{B}] & \textit{Nor} \text{ am I.} \\ [\text{B}] & \text{I'm not, } \textit{either.} \end{array} \right\} \text{NEGATIVE}
\end{array}
$$

Exception: *except (for)*, *apart from*, etc.
236
Exception is the opposite of addition: it indicates 'subtraction' from a total. This meaning can be expressed by a number of prepositions: *except, except for, apart from, bar, but* (*but* occurs only as part of a modifier):

> None of us had any money *except (for) James.*
> *Apart from herself and the MacGregors,* the house appeared to be empty.
> In everything *but title,* he is deputy Premier.
> They stole everything *bar the typewriter.* (less common)

We can also use an adverbial clause beginning with the conjunction *except* (*that*):

> The expedition was working well, *except that* no one could figure out who was the leader.

Otherwise and *else* are adverbs of exception:

> You have a good tan, but *otherwise* (= 'apart from that') you don't look like a man fresh back from sunny Italy.
> I noticed that the attic door had been forced open but everything *else* (= 'apart from that') seemed to be intact.

In this sense, *otherwise* occurs only as a sentence adverb, whereas *else* occurs as a modifier following a pronoun.

The adverb *even* expresses the negation of exception ('not excepting') normally with an effect of surprise and emphasis (*see* 213):

> They stole everything – *even* the clothes in the cupboard ('not excepting the clothes in the cupboard').

Even is also closely related to the notion of addition:

> He knows several languages; he even claims to speak Chinese ('that in addition to all the others').

Restriction: *only*, etc.
237
The word *only* is **restrictive**: it combines negative meaning with the idea of exception:

> He was wearing *only* his shorts (= 'he was wearing *nothing but* his shorts').
> *Only* James had any money (= 'no one except James . . .')

With expressions of amount (*see* 70–80) and degree (*see* 215–22) etc., *only* means 'no more than . . .':

> *Only a few* banks have published their balance sheets (= 'no more than a few . . .').
> I know her *only slightly* (= '. . . no more than slightly').

Other words with a meaning similar to *only* are *just, merely, simply*:

> This offer is more to me than *just* a job.
> Curt's visit to the stable had been *merely* a precaution, in case anyone should be watching.
> I don't mind who wins the contest: for me it's *simply* a matter of curiosity.

The restrictive meaning of *only* can be applied, in a slightly different way, to time:

> I saw her *only last week* (= 'no earlier than', 'as recently as').

Notice the contrast between *only* and *even*:

> *Only my coat* was wet ('that and nothing else').
> *Even my underclothes* were soaked ('those as well as everything else').

Ambiguity with *also, only*, etc.
238
Adverbs of addition, exception and restriction (like *also, even, only*) often 'focus' their meaning on a particular part of the sentence, such as a noun phrase or a verb or the whole of the sentence following the subject. A sentence can be ambiguous, depending on the element that is 'focused': *I only lent her the books.* But contrastive intonation (*see* 400) can help to clarify the meaning:

> (I didn't g̀ive her anything –) I only lènt her the books.   [1]
> (I didn't lend her the týpewriter –) I only lent her the bòoks.   [2]

An example with *also* is:

> (He's not only a g̀ood áctor –) He's also a succèssful actor.
> (He's not only a successful prodǔcer –) He's also a successful àctor.
> (He's not only a wrǐter –) He's also a successful àctor.

(The parts underlined are those which are 'focused'.) In writing, it is best to put the focusing adverb as near to the focused element as possible. Put *only* and *even* before it, and *also* and *too* after it. Thus you could pick out the meaning [2] by writing *I lent her only the books*, instead of *I only lent her the books*.

Only and *even* in front-position focus on the next element of the sentence – usually the subject:

> Only *one of us* had a sleeping bag.
> Even *the BBC* makes mistakes sometimes.

Compare:

> *His wife* ˋalso has a degree.
> *I* ˋtoo thought he looked ill.

Subject matter: *about* and *on*
239

About and *on* can both indicate the subject of a communication or discussion:

> She *told* me *about* her adventures.
> She gave *a lecture on/about* European history.
> Have you *any books on/about* stamp-collecting?

Some verbs and nouns go with *about* or *on*, others go with *about* only:

speak about/on	teach (someone) about
lecture about/on	learn about
argue about/on	read about
write about/on	quarrel about
a book about/on	a story about
a discussion about/on	ignorance about

On, unlike *about*, tends to be limited to deliberate, formal acts of speaking and writing, and also suggests a more definite focusing on the subject matter or topic. *About* can also be used of mental states: *think about, know about, be sorry about*, etc.

Note
Of is sometimes used instead of *about*: *I wouldn't dream of asking him; All you think of is money.* But notice the difference between *He thought about the problem* (= 'He considered the problem') and *He thought of the problem* (= 'He brought the problem to his mind').

Section B: Information, reality and belief

Statements, questions and responses

240
Why do we need to use language? Probably the most important reason (but not the only one) is that we wish to give some piece of information to someone who (we think) doesn't know about it already. **Statements** (*see* 696) are typically sentences which give information. **Questions** (*see* 681–4, 696) are typically sentences by which someone asks the hearer to give information. In this section, we discuss the ways in which information is given and received and we also consider people's attitudes to information, and the reality it deals with. This means considering such notions as truth, belief, probability, and indirect speech.

Questions and answers

241
In conversation, both statements and questions often evoke a **response**. For questions, the most natural response is an answer to the question, giving the speaker the information needed:

Yes-no **questions** (*see* **682**)

> [A] Is the dinner nearly ready?
> $\left\{\begin{array}{l}\text{[B]\ \ Yes, it's already cooked.\ \ (POSITIVE ANSWER)}\quad\text{[1]}\\\text{[B]\ \ No, it's not cooked yet.\ \ (NEGATIVE ANSWER)}\quad\text{[2]}\end{array}\right.$

You can generally shorten the answer by omitting some or all of the information already contained in the statement. Thus a shorter version of [1] is: *Yes, it is* or simply *Yes*. Shorter versions of [2] are:

> No, it isn't.
> No, not yet.
> Not yet.
> No.

Wh-**questions** (*see* **683**)

> [A] Where are you going?   [B] (I'm going) to the office.

Here again, part of the answer (the part in brackets) can be omitted.

Questions about alternatives
242
Yes-no questions are **limited**: only one of two answers (positive or negative) is possible. *Wh*-questions are **unlimited**, because any number of answers can be given, so long as they give information required by the *wh*-word (*who, what, when, where, how*, etc.; *see* 536-41). Another type of limited question is one which expects as an answer one of two or more alternatives mentioned in the question:

[A]   Shall we go by tráin or by
     bùs?   [B]   By bùs.

[A]   Would you like cóffee, téa,
     or còcoa?   [B]   Cóffee, pléase.

Notice that the intonation rises on each alternative except the last, on which it falls.

There is a type of alternative question which is like a *yes-no* question in expecting a positive or negative answer:

yes-no   Are you cóming?

alternative { Are you cóming or nòt?
              Áre you coming or àren't you (coming)?

Such alternative questions have a rather impatient tone.

Another type of alternative question is more like a *wh*-question in form:

What would you like to drìnk? Cóffee, téa, or còcoa?

Questions with positive or negative bias

Questions with **some, always, already,** *etc.*
243
Yes-no questions are mostly neutral as between positive and negative replies, e.g. when they have *any*-words like *any, ever, yet*, etc. (*see* 697-9). You can, however, use forms like *some, sometimes, already*, etc., to indicate that you expect a positive answer to your question:

Did *someone* cáll last night? ('Is it true that someone called last night?
     I have reason to believe that they did.')
     (Compare: Did *anyone* call last night? (neutral))

Has she gone to bed *alréady*? ('Am I right in thinking that she's gone to bed already?')

     (Compare: Has she gone to bed *yet*? (neutral))

Do you *sometimes* regret giving up your jób?

     (Compare: Do you *ever* regret giving up your job?)

For ⟨politeness⟩, use *some*-forms in making an offer:

Would you like *something* to éat? ('I expect you would!')

Do you need *some* money for the phóne?

The response here is assumed to be positive, and so the speaker politely encourages acceptance rather than refusal.

Questions in statement form
244
You can strengthen the positive bias of a question by putting it in the form of a statement (using, however, the rising tone of a question):

You got home sáfely then?

I take it the guests have had something to éat?

These questions are rather casual in tone, as if you are assuming in advance that the answer is 'Yes'. With a negative, such questions assume the answer 'No': *The shops weren't ópen?* (You might say this on seeing someone come home with an empty shopping basket.)

Tag questions: requests for confirmation
245
Tag questions (*see* 684) added to the end of a statement ask for confirmation of the truth of the statement. The answer expected is

- 'Yes' if the statement is positive.
- 'No' if the statement is negative.

(If the statement is positive, the tag question is negative, and vice versa.)

He likes his jòb, dóesn't he? ('I assume he likes his job. Am I right?')

Nobody was wàtching me, wére they? ('I assume nobody was watching me. Am I right?')

If the tag question has a falling tone, the positive or negative bias is stronger, and the tag question merely asks the hearer to confirm what the speaker is already sure of. The sentence is more like a statement than a question.

It's beautiful wèather, ìsn't it?

You have mèt my wìfe, hàven't you? (said by a man introducing his wife to another person)

(*See* 246 Note on how negative questions are answered in English.)

Note
There is a less common type of tag question for which both statement and question are positive: *You've mànaged to telephone, háve you?* Here the statement expresses a conclusion which the speaker has arrived at from the situation. We may call them 'just checking' questions. The tone is sometimes ironic: *So you call that hard wòrk, dó you?*

Negative questions
246

One might suppose that *yes-no* questions with a negative form assume a negative answer. In fact, such questions have a mixture of positive and negative bias:

> Haven't you had bréakfast yet? ('Is it really true that you haven't had breakfast? You ought to have had it by now!')   [3]
>
> Can't you dríve straight? ('I thought you could, but apparently you can't!')   [4]
>
> Won't ànyone help us to clear úp?   [5]

As the examples suggest, this construction usually expresses some degree of surprise (or even annoyance). The speaker, it implies, would normally assume the positive meaning, but now expects the negative. Thus a situation in which you would say [3] might be: you visit Mary at 10.30 a.m. and find that she is still preparing breakfast. Your earlier (and normal) assumption is that she has had breakfast; your later assumption (when you see her preparing breakfast) is that she hasn't.

Note

Some languages answer questions in a different way to English. To the question *Isn't she here yet?*, the English answer *No* means 'She is *not* here, while *Yes* means 'She is here': the answer is given to the underlying meaning rather than to the negative grammatical form of the question.

Questions with more than one *wh*-word
247

It is possible (though unusual) to have more than one *wh*-word in the same *wh*-question. In this case, only one of the *wh*-elements is moved to the front of the sentence (unless the two *wh*-elements are coordinated):

[A] *Who's* bringing *whát?*
[B] I'm bringing the drinks, and Gary's bringing the sandwiches.

[A] *How* and *when* did you arrìve?
[B] I arrived by train, on Friday.

[A] *Who* did you send those bòoks to, and *whỳ?* ⟨informal⟩
[B] I sent them to Tanya, because she asked me for them.

Polite questions
248

You can make a question more ⟨polite⟩ (e.g. when addressing a stranger) by adding *please*, or by using an introductory formula like *Could you tell me*:

What's your n`a´me, ple´ase?
Would you mind telling me your n´ame?
Please can I have your address and te´lephone number?
May/could I ´ask you if you are driving to the st`a´tion?

(On *can*, *may*, and *could* here, *see* 325.) These four questions are listed in order of politeness.

Responses to statements: backchannels

249

Unlike a question, a statement does not demand a response. But in conversation, we often make a response to a statement in order to express interest, surprise, pleasure, regret, *etc.*, or simply to show the speaker that we are still attending:

> [A] I've just had a phone call from the travel agent . . . [B] Ye´s? [A] . . . you know those plane tickets to Sydney that you ordered for next Tuesday. [B] Mm´? [A] well, he says they are now ready to be collected . . . [B] Oh, that's n`ice. [A] . . . but unfortunately, he says there's been a mistake . . . [B] Oh d`ear. [A] Yes, apparently the plane doesn't arrive in Australia until 9.00 a.m. on Wednesday. [B] I s`ee.

Mm /m/, *Mhm* /mhm/, *Uh-huh*/əhə/ and *Yeah*/jeə/ are casual alternatives to *Yes*. These 'backchannels' are particularly important in telephone conversations.
    Other signals of this kind are *Oh?* and *Really?*, to express surprise and interest:

> [A] I hear Paul's getting married.   [B] Re´ally?

Other backchannels are:

> *Ah, sure, quite, right, good heavens, oh God, that's right.*

Short questions

250

Questions can be used as responses to statements, when the hearer wants more information. Like other responses, these questions are often shortened by omitting repeated matter. They can often be shortened to the question word alone:

> [A]   The old lady's buying a house.
>
> [B]   Wh`en?/Wh`ere?/Wh`y?/Wh`ich house?/Wh`at old lady?

There are also two-word questions with an end-placed preposition:

> [A]   I'm going to write an adventure story.
>
> [B]   What f`or?/Who f`or?/What ab`out?

Similar questions are: *Who with?*, *Where to?*, etc. (These questions with end-placed prepositions are ⟨informal⟩ in style: in ⟨formal⟩ English we would say *With whom?*, etc., (*see* 537). All these shortened questions are rather ⟨familiar⟩

and abrupt. For greater ⟨politeness⟩, use a fuller question: *When is she going to buy it?*, etc.

Such questions can also be used when what the speaker says isn't clear in some respect, e.g. where the meaning of a definite word like *this* or *the* is not specified:

[A]   Were you there when they erected *the new* s͞igns?

[B]   *Wh͟ich* new signs?

Note

For a negative statement, use *Why not?* rather than *Why?*

[A]   Joan is very ups͞et.   [B]   Why?

[A]   She hasn't been inv͟ited.   [B]   Why n͟ot?

Echo questions: requests for repetition
251

Another type of response question is an **echo question**. Here we ask the speaker to repeat some information (usually because we failed to hear it, but sometimes also because we can't believe our ears):

[A]   I didn't enjoy that meal.

[B]   Did you say you didn't enj͞oy it?

Here the request is explicit, but we can leave out *Did you say*, and simply 'echo' part or all of what has been said, using a (sharply rising) question intonation: *You didn't enj͞oy it?* In these examples, brackets show how some repeated elements may be omitted:

[A]   The Browns are emigrating.   [B]   (They're) ͞emigrating?

[A]   Switch the light off, please.   [B]   (Switch) the l͞ight (off)?

You can also use a **wh-echo question**, indicating by the *wh*-word which part of the sentence that you didn't hear:

[A]   It cost five dollars.   [B]   H͞ow much did (you say) it cost? [6]

[A]   He's a dermatologist.   [B]   Wh͞at is he?   [7]

Note that the nucleus occurs on the *wh*-word in these questions.

Note

The *wh*-word can also be placed later in the sentence, in its statement position. Thus instead of [6] and [7], you could say: *It cost h͞ow much? He's (a) wh͞at?* But such questions, again, are ⟨familiar⟩ and often ⟨impolite⟩, unless preceded by an apology or mark of politeness:

Sorry, wh͞at was his job?

I'm sorry, I didn't quite hear: wh͞at does he do?

General requests for repetition

252

General requests for repetition are very commonly used:

[A]   I'll make some coffee.

[B]   ((I beg your) párdon?
[B]   Excúse me? ⟨AmE⟩
[B]   Sórry? ⟨BrE⟩
[B]   Whát? ⟨familiar, often impolite⟩

A more explicit general request for repetition (e.g. where you have heard most, but not all, of what was said) can take one of the following forms:

I'm sorry, I didn't quite hear/follow what you s`ai`d.

Sorry, I didn't quite g`e`t that. ⟨informal⟩

Sorry, would you mind repéating that?

I'm very sorry, would you mind saying that agáin?

Omission of information

253

The last section has already illustrated the general rule that we omit information which is already obvious from the preceding context. The rule is further illustrated by the following statement and six possible replies:

[A]   This country must economise if it's going to increase its prosperity.

[B]

I ag`re`e.
Absol`u`tely.
Certainly n`o`t.
N`o`nsense!
True enˇough, but the problem is h`o`w to economise.
And the only way to do it is by greater tax`a`tion.

All these responses in some way lack the structure of a 'complete sentence' (*see* 695–6), but are acceptable because the structure omitted contains information already understood.

'Incomplete' sentences and formulae

254

Elsewhere, it is the situation outside language which makes certain information unnecessary. Examples are the brief 'incomplete' or formulaic utterances you may hear in various situations:

Commands. C`a`refúl! `O`ut with ít! F`a`ster! Not so f`a`st!

Questions. More cóffee? How about jóining us? Any gráduate students here?

Slogans: Republicans òut; Republicans for èver.

Exclamations: Goal! Good! Excellent! You lucky boy! What a pity! Shame! Oh God, what an experience! Poor you! Oh for a drink! Now for some fun!

Alarm calls: H̲ė̲l̲p̲! F̲ì̲r̲e̲!

Sometimes, in casual ⟨familiar⟩ speech, you will notice that words are omitted from the beginning of a sentence. These are usually words which carry little information, such as a pronoun subject and/or an auxiliary verb. They are bracketed in the following examples:

Beg your p̲ár̲don. (I . . .)	Want a dr̲ìn̲k? (Do you . . .)
Serves you r̲ìg̲ht. (It . . .)	Sorry I m̲ìs̲sed you. (I am . . .)
No w̲ò̲nder he's late. (It is . . .)	See you l̲à̲ter. (I will . . .)

255

In public notices, headings *etc.*, a noun phrase, nominal clause, or adjective phrase often stands on its own:

Exit	Where to eat in London
College Officers – Private	Fresh Today
Members' Handbook	Setting the new agenda

Prohibition notices are often put in the form of a noun phrase: No Smoking, No Entry, No Parking, *etc.*

Also in some broadcasting situations, such as sports commentaries, a great deal of grammatical structure is omitted. This extract could be from a television football commentary:

> Jagtman to Jaeger: a brilliant pass, that. And the score still: Holland 1, Germany 0. The ball in-field to – oh, but beautifully cut off, and . . .

Reported statements and questions

Reported statements
256

To report what somebody has stated, you can use either quotation marks (**direct speech**) or a *that*-clause (**indirect speech**) (*see* 589):

> She said: 'I need more money'. (**direct speech**)
> She said that she needed more money. (**indirect speech**)

She said (in this example) can be called the **reporting clause**, and the rest of the sentence can be called the **reported clause**. In direct speech, the reporting clause can also be placed after the reported clause or in the middle of it.

$$
\text{'I need more } \underset{\backslash}{\text{money'}}, \left\{ \begin{array}{ll} \text{Marie exclaimed.} & [1] \\ \text{exclaimed Marie.} & [2] \\ \text{she exclaimed.} & [3] \end{array} \right.
$$

The subject can be placed after the verb of saying, as in [2], unless the subject is a pronoun. In modern English, *exclaimed she is not an option.

Indirect speech

257

In narrative, the reporting verb is usually in the past tense. In this case, certain changes are normally made in converting from direct speech to indirect speech:

1. Change present tense verbs into the past tense (to match the reporting verb).
2. Change 1st and 2nd person pronouns into the 3rd person.
3. (Sometimes) change pointer words (*see* 99–100): e.g. change *this* into *that*, *now* into *then*, *here* into *there*, *tomorrow* into *the next day*, and *ago* into *before*.

Examples:

Direct speech (i.e. what the speaker actually said)	**Indirect speech** (i.e. reporting it from the narrator's viewpoint)
'I *moved* here two years ago.'	~ He explained that *he had moved* there two years before. [1]
'Our team *has won*.'	~ They claimed that their team *had won*. [2]
'I *will* see you tomorrow.'	~ She promised that she *would see* him the next day. [3]
'They *can sleep* in this room.'	~ She suggested that they *could sleep* in that/this room. [4]

Notice that the change to the past tense applies not only to ordinary present tense verbs, but to the present perfect (*has won/had won*) (*see* 127), and to modal auxiliaries (*will/would, can/could*, etc.) (*see* 483). The shifting of a verb to an earlier time reference generally applies also to past tense verbs, which are shifted to the past perfect (the pluperfect) in indirect speech. Thus

> 'I *saw* them yesterday'
> ~ He told me that he *had seen* them the day before.

But sometimes the shift does not take place (*see* 258 (3)).

Special cases

258

There are four special cases to bear in mind in the shifting of tense in indirect speech.

(1) **Past perfect verbs** in direct speech are not changed in indirect speech: these verbs cannot be shifted 'further into the past'.

'I *had left* before they arrived.'   ~ She said (that) she *had left* before they (had) arrived.

(2) **Modal auxiliaries** like *must*, *should*, and *ought to* do not normally change since they have no past tense. But *must* can also be reported as *had to*:

'You *must go*.'   ~ She said that they $\begin{cases} must\ go. \\ had\ to\ go. \end{cases}$

'You *should be* more careful.'   ~ He said that they *should be* more careful.

(3) **When the idea expressed in the reported statement can also be applied to the time of reporting**, there is no need to change the tense or other forms:

'The world *is* flat.'   ~ Ancient philosophers argued that the world *is/was* flat.

This is because the question of whether the world is flat or round can apply as much to the present time as to the ancient world.

(4) **Some verbs of saying** used in direct speech narrative cannot be easily used in indirect speech. For example:

'The game is up,' growled Trent.

is fully acceptable, but not:

Trent growled that the game was up.

These verbs include verbs which emphasize vocal effect (like *gasp*, *grunt*, *laugh*, *shout*):

'Give the poor girl a chance to get a word in!', Jean *laughed*.
'I'm done', he *gasped*.
'See for yourself', *shouted* Derieux.

Other verbs like *answer*, *declare*, *reply*, *say* can be readily used for both direct and indirect speech, while verbs like *assert*, *confirm*, *state* occur mainly with indirect speech:

Stacey *replied* that it would bankrupt Forbes.
The club *confirmed* that Irons was one of its leading members.

Indirect questions
259
The rules for indirect speech apply to indirect questions as well as to indirect statements. The only difference is that for indirect questions, a *wh*-clause (*see* 590–1) is used instead of a *that*-clause:

Direct speech	Indirect speech
'*Do you líve* here?'	~ She asked him if (*or* whether) he
	lìved there. [5]
'*Did* our team wín?'	~ They asked if (*or* whether) their
	team *had* wòn. [6]
'Why *won't* you come wìth us?	~ He asked her why she *wouldn't*
	come wìth *them*. [7]
'Which chair *shall I sìt* in?'	~ He wondered which chair he
	should sìt in. [8]

Indirect *yes-no* questions ([5], [6]) are introduced by *if* or *whether* (*see* 591). Indirect *wh*-questions are introduced by the *wh*-word which begins the question in direct speech.

260

Questions about alternatives (*see* 242) behave in the same way. The *yes-no* type of alternative question is generally introduced by *whether* in indirect speech:

'Is it yóur turn or Sùsan's?'
~ She asked him whether it was his turn or Sùsan's.

There is also a type of indirect question in which the reported clause is a *to*-infinitive clause beginning with a *wh*-word:

I asked him what to dò (= 'I asked him what I ought to do').
He wondered whether to lèave (= 'He wondered whether he ought to leave'). (Compare commands: *see* 336).

Denial and affirmation

Negative sentences
261

When speakers want to deny the truth of something, they use a **negative sentence** containing one of the negative items *not* (or *n't*), *no, nothing, nowhere,* etc. (*see* 581–4). The part of a sentence or clause which follows the negative word is called the **scope of negation**, and it is this part of the sentence that is negated. The scope of negation is here signalled by **bold type**:

He definitely hasn't tàken the job. ('It's definite that he hasn't').   [1]
He hasn't definitely taken the jòb. ('It's not definite that he has').   [2]

In these examples, the meaning is different because in [1] *definitely* is outside the scope of negation, while in [2] *definitely* is within the scope of negation. A final adverbial may or may not be in the scope of negation:

They weren't at hóme | for the whole dày. ('For the whole day, they weren't at home.')

They weren't **at home for the whole dᵥay.** ('It's not true that they were at home for the whole day.')

(On the intonation here, *see* 33–41, 397–8.) Notice the difference in meaning between the first and second sentence in the following pairs:

{ Crime necessarily **doesn't pay.**   (= 'Crime never pays.')
{ Crime **doesn't necessarily pay.**   (= 'It doesn't always pay.')
{ I really **don't mind waiting.**   (= 'I don't mind at all.')
{ I **don't really mind waiting.**   (= 'I DO mind, but not too
                                           much.')

262
Inside the scope of negation, *any*-words like *any, yet, ever* (*see* 697–9) are used:

I **didn't attend à̱ny of the lectures.** ('I attended none of the lectures'). [3]
We **haven't had dì̱nner yet.**   [4]

But we can also use *some*-words like *some, already, sometimes* after the negative word, and these words lie outside the scope of negation. Therefore the meaning of [3] is different from that of [5]:

I **didn't attend s̱o̱me of the léctures.** ('There were some lectures that I didn't attend.')   [5]

263
Occasionally a negative word does not apply at all. Instead, it applies its meaning to a phrase or part of a phrase elsewhere in the sentence:

No food at all is better than unwholesome food. (i.e. 'Eating nothing at all is better than eating . . .').
We *not infrequently* go abroad. (i.e. 'We quite often go abroad.')
They stayed at a *not very* attractive hotel. (i.e. '. . . at a rather unattractive hotel')

Affirmation
264
To place emphasis on the positive meaning of a sentence, we put the intonation nucleus on the operator (or first auxiliary of the verb phrase, *see* 609–12). This is done especially for contrast, when someone has suggested or assumed the negative:

[A] So you two haven't met   [B] *Well,* we hᵥave met – but it
     before?   was àges ago.
[A] What a pity Mary isn't here! [B] (But) she ì̱s here.

If the response is not a straightforward denial, but contains new positive information, the new information is stressed by a fall-rise tone (*see* 43):

[A]   Surely they wouldn't have   [B]   Nò, but they còuld have
        stolen it?   taken it by mistǎke.

If there is no other operator, use *do* as dummy operator (*see* 611):

Oh, so you dìd stay after àll. I thought you were leaving èarly.

I'm afraid I don't know much about cooking. But I dǒ bake my own
    brěad.

Denial
265
To DENY what someone has suggested or supposed, you can again place the
nucleus on the operator, but this time on the negative (*can't, didn't*, etc.):

So you hàven't lost your keys! ('I thought you had.')

[A]   When did he pass his exàm?   [B]   Well, actually, he dìdn't pass
                                            it.

When the negative is not contracted, the nucleus falls on *not*:

Well, actually, he did nòt pass it.

Short affirmations
266
There is a shortened type of affirmation in which everything is omitted after the
operator. This is usual when you are simply affirming a question or statement,
and do not need to repeat what has already been said:

[A]   This book is interesting.   [B]   Yes, it ìs. (i.e. 'It ìs
                                            interesting')
[A]   I assume John will be late.   [B]   Yes, he wìll.
[A]   Can you speak German?   [B]   Yes, I càn.
[A]   Have I missed the bus?   [B]   Yes, I'm afraid you háve.

To agree with a negative statement, use a negative operator:

[A]   Your mother doesn't look   [B]   No, she dòesn't, I'm afráid.
        wèll.

Short denials
267
Shortened statements (in the negative) are also used to deny a statement:

[A]   You worry too much.   [B]   No, I dón't.   [6]
[A]   I'll probably fail my driving [B]   No, you wǒn't.   [7]
        test.

Notice that when we deny or contradict a statement, as in [6] and [7], we use a
rise or fall-rise tone. Similar shortened statements are used to answer a
question:

[A]   Can you speak German?   [B]   No, I'm afraid I càn't.
[A]   The line's engaged. Will you   [B]   No, I wòn't, thanks.
      hold?

More ⟨formal⟩ or emphatic sentences contain operator + *not*. In these cases the nucleus is on *not*:

[A]   Did she fail the test?   [B]   No, she did nòt.

To deny a negative statement, use the positive operator with a rising or fall-rise tone:

[A]   I understand most people   [B]   Yes, they díd.
      didn't agree with me.
[A]   I won't pass the exam.   [B]   I bet you wǐll.

268

A denial can seem blunt and ⟨impolite⟩ unless we tone it down in some way. We can make a denial more ⟨tactful⟩ by only ⟨tentatively⟩ expressing the contrary view:

[A]   He's married, isn't he?   [B]   Actually, I don't think he ìs.
                                     [B]   Ìs hé? I thought he was a
                                           bàchelor.
                                     [B]   Are you súre? I had the
                                           impression that he was still
                                           sìngle.

Denial combined with affirmation
269

The construction *not* (or *n't*) . . . *but* is used to deny one idea and to affirm another, contrasting, idea:

I do*n't* agree with his principles, *but* at least he's sincere.
The land does*n't* belong to me, *but* to the government.

We can also say:

The land belongs *not* to me, *but* to the government.
The land belongs to the government, *not* to me.

Notice a nucleus can be on the operator in both the positive and negative clause:

I dòn't like mathemǎtics, but dò enjoy biòlogy.

Agreement and disagreement

Agreement
270
It is all the more necessary to be ⟨polite⟩ when the other person's **judgement** or **opinion** is in question.

In agreeing with an unfavourable opinion, you may wish to qualify your agreement with an expression of regret, etc:

[A]   His speech was so boring.

- [B]   Yes, I'm afraid it w`a`s.
- [B]   Yes, I have to agree that it w`a`s.
- [B]   I must say I f`ou`nd it s`o`.

In other cases, you can be as enthusiastic as you like in expressing your agreement:

|A| It was an interesting exhibition, wasn't it?

[B]   (Yes,) It was superb/absolutely splendid, etc.

[A]   A referendum will satisfy everybody.

[B]   (Yes,)
- d`e`finitely.
- qu`i`te.
- absol`u`tely.

[A]   A referendum won't satisfy everybody.

|B|
- Definitely n`o`t.
- It certainly w`o`n't.
- You're absolutely r`i`ght, it w`o`n't.
- I agr`e`e (that it won't).

Tactful disagreement
271
When you deny or contradict what someone else has stated, the effect is often ⟨impolite⟩, unless the denial is softened in some way. You can soften it by an apology or by adjusting to the speaker's point of view:

[A]   English is a difficult language to learn.

- [B]   I'm afraid I disagr`e`e with you: some languages are even m`o´`re difficult, I th`i`nk.
- [B]   Tr`u`e, but the gr`a`mmar is quite e`a´`sy.
- [B]   Y`e`s, but it's not so difficult as R`u`ssian.
- [B]   Do you th`i`nk so? Act`u`ally, I find it quite `e`asy.

[A]   The book is tremendously well wr`i`tten.

[B]   Yès, (well written) as a whŏle – but there are some rather
boring pàtches, don't you thínk?

Partial or qualified agreement

272

In discussion and argument, there is often a need to agree with one aspect of a
speaker's view, and to disagree with another. Here are some of the methods you
might use to express this sort of qualified agreement (X and Y here stand for
statements, and x and y for noun phrases).

Certainly it's true that X, but on the other hand Y.

I realize that [X] *every form of taxation has its critics*, but surely [Y] *this
is the most unfair and unpopular tax that was ever invented.*

I'm in total agreement with you/Joan/etc. about [x] the need for
international action, but we also have to consider [y] *the right of
nations to take charge of their own internal affairs.*

Agreed, but if we accept x, then it must (also) be true that y.

Strengthened agreement

273

We can also agree, and add a further point to strengthen the argument:

[A]   The government will have to take steps to limit the number of
cars on the road.

[B]   Yes, in fact [X] *I believe public opinion is now in favour of banning
cars in the central areas of major cities.*

Other ways of strengthening agreement are:

Yes, and what is more, X.

I agree, and in fact one might go so far as to say X.

Absolutely. Actually, I would go further, and say X.

Fact, hypothesis and neutrality

274

We have considered the truth and falsehood of statements in terms of affirmation, denial, negation, etc. but there are many cases where truth or falsehood is
ASSUMED rather than directly stated.

Compare:

I'm glad that the minister has agreed (FACT)   [1]

I wish that the minister had agreed. (HYPOTHESIS)   [2]

In [1], the speaker assumes the truth of the statement *the minister has agreed*,
while in [2], the speaker assumes its falsehood. We will call something assumed
to be false **hypothetical**.

Hypothetical meaning
275

- A **fact** (or factual meaning) is usually expressed by a finite verb clause, as in [1], or by an -*ing* clause (*see* 493):

  > I'm surprised *that he made that mistake.*
  > ~ I'm surprised *at his making that mistake.*

- A **hypothesis** (or hypothetical meaning) is usually expressed by the past tense in dependent clauses, as in [2], and by *would* (or '*d*) + infinitive in main clauses. These two constructions can be seen in the conditional subclauses and in the main clause of hypothetical conditions (*see* 207):

  SUBCLAUSE

  If we *saw* anything strange, we *would let* you know.

  MAIN CLAUSE

Notice that the past tense (*had, would*) here has nothing to do with past time: reference is to PRESENT or FUTURE time.

Past time, when combined with hypothesis, is expressed by the perfective construction *have* + -*ed* participle:

> If we'*d seen* anything strange, we *would have let* you know.

Would in the verb of the main clause can be replaced by another past tense modal auxiliary:

> If Monty *hadn't been* there, you *could have told* ('would have been able to tell') the whole story.

Other constructions containing hypothetical clauses
276

Apart from conditional clauses, hypothetical meaning may occur in a few other special constructions. The main ones are illustrated here:

> *It's time* you were in bed. ('but you're not in bed')
> He behaves *as if* he owned the place. ('but he doesn't own . . .')
> It's not *as if* you were all that fond of Alice. ('You're not fond . . .')
> *Suppose* that the United Nations had the power to impose a peaceful solution. ('It does not have the power . . .')
> *If only* she had kept her eyes open. ('She didn't keep them open')
> *In your place*, I would have taken a taxi.

Very often *would* is used where there is no *if*-clause, but where a conditional 'if I is implied:

> I can't let anyone see the letters – it *wouldn't* be right, *would* it? ('. . . if I let them see them')

(On the special hypothetical use of modal auxiliaries for tentative meaning, *see* 286, 322, 325.)

Other ways of expressing hypothetical meaning
Were, were to, should
277
In addition to the past tense, there are three less common ways of expressing hypothetical meaning in subclauses:

- **The *were*-subjunctive** (*see* 708).

> I'd play football with you if I *were* younger.
> If I *were* Home Secretary, I would impose no restriction whatsoever in such matters.

In ⟨informal⟩ style the ordinary past tense *was* can replace *were*.

- ***Were to*** (or ***was to*** ⟨informal⟩) + **infinitive:**

> If it *were to rain* tomorrow, the match would be postponed. ⟨rather formal⟩

(This construction expresses hypothetical future.)

- ***Should*** + **infinitive**

> If a serious crisis *should arise*, the government would have to take immediate action. ⟨rather formal⟩

The last two constructions are slightly ⟨formal or literary⟩, and suggest ⟨tentative⟩ conditions. They are in general limited to conditional clauses (and constructions related to conditions, like *Suppose he were to see us!*).

Conditionals with inversion
278
Another type of hypothetical conditional clause has no *if*, but instead begins with an operator (609) placed before the subject (inversion – *see* 416). The three operators which occur in this construction are *had*, subjunctive *were*, and putative *should* (*see* 280 above):

> *Had they known*, they would have been more frightened. ('If they had known . . .') ⟨formal⟩
> *Were a serious crisis to arise*, the government would have to act swiftly. ('If a serious crisis were . . .') ⟨formal⟩
> *Should you change your mind*, no one would blame you. ('If you should . . .')

These clauses with *were* and *should* are rather ⟨literary⟩ in tone, and can always be replaced by an *if*-clause: *If they had known*, etc.

Note
In the negative of clauses beginning with *had*, *were* and *should*, there is no contracted form: instead of *Hadn't I known*, etc. we must say *Had I not known*, etc.

Neutrality

279

In addition to fact and hypothesis, there is a third type of situation, in which the speaker assumes neither truth nor falsehood. We will call this situation **neutrality**. For example:

> It's best *for Sarah to be patient.*   [1]
> I want *all of us to agree.*   [2]

In sentence [1], we do not know whether Sarah will be patient or not; in sentence [2], whether all of us will agree or not. In this sense, the assumptions are **neutral**. Infinitive clauses often express neutrality.

Open conditions are another case of a construction which is **neutral** with regard to truth and falsehood:

> It's best *if Sarah is patient.*   [3]

Sentences [1] and [3] have the same effect. Also neutral are *wh*-clauses, which in this respect sometimes contrast with *that*-clauses:

> Did you know *that* the minister has agreed? ('The minister has agreed.')
> Do you know *whether* the minister has agreed? ('Please tell me')

There is a similar contrast between:

> He told me *that* he had passed the exam.
> He told me *whether* he had passed the exam.

To the second sentence, a listener would be inclined to reply with a question: *Well, and did he pass it? Doubt* is another verb that can be followed by either a *that*-clause or a *wh*-clause. *Not* + *doubt*, on the other hand, expresses certainty, and so takes a *that*-clause:

> I doubt whether
> I don't doubt that } James will cooperate with us.

Putative *should*

280

We have already said that *should* expresses a tentative condition in *if*-clauses. This is true not only for hypothetical conditions, but for OPEN conditions (*see* 207):

> If you { *hear*
> *should hear* ⟨tentative⟩ } the news, Jane, please let me know.

(We do not know from this whether or not Jane will hear the news.)

In other dependent clauses, too, *should* is used neutrally, to represent something as a neutral 'idea' rather than as a 'fact'. We call this use of *should* **putative**. Contrast these two sentences:

FACT: The fact is that the referendum will be held next month.
We know that the referendum will be held next month.

IDEA: The idea is that the referendum *should* be held next month.
Someone is suggesting that the referendum *should* be held next month.

281

Putative *should* occurs quite widely in *that*-clauses (*see* 589), especially in ⟨BrE⟩:

It's a pity that you *should have* to leave.   [4]
I'm surprised that there *should be* any objection.   [5]
It's unthinkable that he *should resign*.   [6]
What worries me is that men *should be able* to threaten
    ordinary peaceful citizens with bombs and bullets.   [7]

In some of these sentences, there is no neutrality: for example, the speaker of [5] assumes that 'somebody objects'. Even so, there is a difference between [5] and the factual sentence *I'm surprised that there is an objection*, because in [5] it is the 'very idea' of the objection that surprises me, not the objection as a fact.

Note
[a]   Putative *should* is also found in some questions and exclamations:
        How should I know?
        Why should she have to resign?
        Who should come in but the mayor himself!
[b]   In some sentences, putative *should* is difficult to distinguish from *should* in the sense of 'ought to' (292, 328): *He has urged that private firearms should be banned.*

The subjunctive
282
The subjunctive (*see* 706–8) also has neutral meaning. It can be used:

● **In some *that*-clauses,** where the clause expresses an intention (this is especially common in ⟨AmE⟩):

    Congress has *voted/decided/decreed/insisted* that the present law *continue* to operate.

Here *should* + infinitive can also be used: . . . *should continue* to operate.

● **In some conditional and contrast clauses** (*see* 207–14):

    Whatever *be* the reasons for it, we cannot tolerate disloyalty.
    (= 'Whatever the reasons for it may be . . .') ⟨formal, elevated⟩

● **In certain idioms,** in main clauses:

    God *save* the Queen!

So be it then.
Heaven *forbid!*

These idioms tend to be rather ⟨elevated or archaic⟩.

Degrees of likelihood
283

Instead of thinking of truth and falsehood in black-and-white terms, we can think in terms of a **scale of likelihood**. The extremes of the scale are **impossibility** and **certainty** (or **logical necessity**). Other intermediate concepts to be considered are **possibility, probability, improbability**, etc. These notions are expressed in various ways:

- most importantly, by modal auxiliaries (*can, may, must*, etc., *see* 501):

    I *may* be wrong.   He *may* try to phone us.

- more ⟨formally⟩, by a sentence with introductory *it* and a *that*-clause:

    It is possible that you are right (*see* 542).

- by an adverbial such as *probably, perhaps, necessarily* (*see* 461–3):

    Perhaps there was some mistake.

We show these various constructions in 284-92. We give special attention, where necessary, to the use of auxiliaries in negative sentences, in questions, in reference to past time, and in hypothetical clauses.

Auxiliaries such as *can, may*, and *must* can refer to the future as well as to the present: *You may feel better tomorrow* (= 'It's possible that you will feel better').

Possibility
Can, may, could, might
284

- **Possibility of the fact** (*factual*)

    The railways *may be* improved.   [1]

    It is possible that the railways will be improved.   [2]

    Perhaps/possibly/maybe the railways will be improved.   [3]

- **Possibility of the idea** (*theoretical*)

    The railways *can* be improved.   [4]

    It is possible for the railways to be improved.   [5]

Theoretical possibility (*can*) is 'weaker' than factual possibility (*may*). Sentence

[4], for example, says merely that **in theory** the railways are 'improvable', i.e. that they are not perfect. Sentence [1], on the other hand, could suggest that there are definite plans for improvement.

Note
In general (habitual) statements of possibility, *can* has roughly the same meaning as *sometimes*: *A good leather bag can last* (= 'sometimes lasts') *a lifetime*; *She's very helpful, but she can be short-tempered*; *Lightning can be dangerous.*

285

- **Negation:** For impossibility, use *cannot* or *can't* (but not *may not*):

  He *can't* be working at this time! ('It is impossible that he is working...')

  He may not be working, on the other hand, means 'It is possible that he is not working'.

- **Questions:** Use *can* (not *may*): *Can he be working?* (= 'Is it possible that he is working?')

- **Past time:** For something which was possible in the past, use *could*:

  In those days, you *could* be sentenced to death for a small crime.

  For the (present) possibility of a past happening, use *may* + the perfect:

  Krasnikov *may* have made an important discovery. ('It is possible that he (has) made a ...')

- **Hypothetical:** For hypothetical possibility, use *could* or *might*:

  If someone were to come to the wrong conclusion, the whole plan *could/might* be ruined.

Tentative possibility (could, might)
286
Could and *might* in their hypothetical sense often express ⟨tentative⟩ possibility, i.e. they refer to something which is possible, but unlikely:

  He *could/might* have been telling lies. ('It is just possible that he was/has been telling lies'.)
  I wonder if there *could be* a simpler solution to the problem.

Ability (can, be able to, be capable of, *etc.*)
287
The notion of 'ability', also expressed by *can*, *be able to*, and *be capable of*, is closely related to 'theoretical possibility':

  She *can* speak English fluently.
  Will you *be able to* meet us in London tomorrow?

She *is capable of* keeping a secret when she wants to.
Every secretary should *know how to* type a letter.

- **Negation:** Use *cannot, can't* (or *be unable to,* or *be incapable of*):

   He *can't* speak German very well.
   I *cannot* explain what happened.
   Maria *was unable to* speak and *incapable of* moving.

- **Questions:** *Can you drive a car? Do you know how to unlock this door?*

- **Past time:** *Could* sometimes means 'knew how to': it refers to a permanent or habitual ability:

   He *could* already play the piano when he was five.

Was/were able to often combines the ideas of 'ability' and 'achievement':

   By acting quickly, we *were able to* save him from drowning. ('We could, and did save him'.)

- **Hypothetical:** I'm so hungry, I *could* eat two dinners!

Certainty or logical necessity (*must, have to,* etc.)
288
Must + infinitive and *have* + *to*-infinitive (or, *have got to*) can express certainty or logical necessity:

   There *must* have been some misunderstanding.
   You *have to* be joking! ALSO: You've *got to* be joking!
   The bombing's *got to* stop sometime.
   It *is* (almost) *certain that* the hostages will be released.
   Many people will *certainly/necessarily* lose their jobs.
   ~ Many people are *certain/sure/bound* to lose their jobs.
   Inevitably, some changes will take place.

The contrasting relation between possibility and certainty can be seen in:

   She's over ninety, so
      her father *must* be *dead.*
      ~ her father *can't* still be *alive.*
      ~ it is *impossible* that her father is still *alive.*
      ~ it is *certain* that her father is *dead.*

All four sentences have in effect the same meaning.

289

- **Questions:**

   Does there *have to* be a motive for the crime?
   ~ Is there *necessarily* a motive for the crime?

- **Negation:**

> Strikes *don't have to* be caused by bad pay (they can also be caused by
> bad conditions, etc.).
> Strikes are *not necessarily* caused by bad pay.
> You *don't need* to worry about it.

Note

The modal auxiliary *need* (484) is used < *esp* in BrE >, in place of *must* in questions and
negatives:

> You *needn't* wait for me. ('It is unnecessary . . .')

However, this use of *need* is not common, and *need to* + infinitive or *have to* + infinitive can be
used instead: *You don't need/have to wait for me.*

290

- **Past time:** We have to distinguish a past certainty (*had to*) from a certainty
  about the past (usually expressed by *must* + the perfect):

> Don't worry. Someone *had to* lose the game. ('It was necessary, by the
> rules of the game, for someone to lose'.)
> John *must* have missed his train. ('It appears certain that John missed
> his train'.)

- **Hypothetical:** Use *have to*:

> If I *had to* choose, I'd prefer this job to any other.
> You *would have to* be brilliant, to win a prize.

Prediction and predictability (*will, must*)
291

As already seen (*see* 288), *must* often expresses a feeling of certainty when we
draw a conclusion from evidence. On hearing the phone ring, a man might say
*That **must** be my wife* = '. . . I **know** that she is due to phone at about this time,
and I therefore **conclude** that she is phoning now'). In a similar way, you can
use *will* to express a '**prediction**' about the present (just as you can use *will* to
make a prediction about the future – *see* 141): *That **will** be my wife.* There is
little difference here between *must* and *will*:

> They *will* have arrived by now. (ALSO: They *will* have arrived by tomor-
> row.)
> They *must* have arrived by now.
> (BUT NOT: *They *must* have arrived by tomorrow.)

This sort of prediction with *will* often occurs with conditional sentences:

> If litmus paper is dipped in acid, it *will* turn red.

Will can also be used in a habitual sense, to express the idea of 'predictability' or
'characteristic behaviour':

Accidents *will* happen. (a saying)
A lion *will* only attack a human being when it is hungry.

We have noted (*see* 130) the equivalent use of *would* to express habitual or characteristic ('predictable') behaviour in the past:

She *would* often go all day without eating.

Probability (*should, ought to*, etc.)

292

The auxiliaries *should* and *ought to* (*see* 483) can express 'probability'; they are weaker equivalents of *must* (= 'certainty'). Compare:

Our guests *must* be home by now. ('I am certain')

Our guests $\left\{ \begin{array}{l} should \\ ought\ to \end{array} \right\}$ be home by now. ('They probably are but I'm not certain.')

Should is more frequent than *ought to*. Other ways of expressing probability are:

It is quite *probable/likely* that they didn't receive the letter.
He is *probably* the best chess player in the country.
They have *very likely* lost the way home. (Here *likely* is an adverb.)
The concert is *likely* to finish late. (Here *likely* is an adjective.)

- **Negation**: Improbability can be expressed by *shouldn't, oughtn't to*, or *it is improbable/unlikely that*:

There $\left\{ \begin{array}{l} shouldn't \\ oughtn't\ to \end{array} \right\}$ be any difficulties.
~ It *is unlikely that* there will be any difficulties.

- **Questions** (rare):

Should there be any difficulty in getting tickets?

Note
People have a natural tendency to overstate their convictions. Therefore *must* and *will* (*see* 291) are sometimes used in a weakened sense that one feels is nearer to 'probability' than to 'certainty':

You'*ll* be feeling hungry after all that work.
They *must* have spent years and years building this cathedral.
I'm sure that they can all be trusted.

Attitudes to truth

293
We now consider the ways in which people may be committed or uncommitted to the truth or reality of something. The people concerned may be the speaker

('I') or another person, or a group of people. To express such attitudes, we often use:

- a ***that*-clause**: I know *that his answer will be 'No'.*
- a ***wh*-clause** (expressing a neutral attitude – *see* 279):
  I know *what his answer will be.*
- Sometimes **adverbials**: e.g. *obviously*, *without doubt*:
  Without doubt, she is one of the best teachers in the school.
- **Other constructions**, such as the type of parenthetical clauses we call **comment clauses** (*see* 499), e.g. They can all be trusted, *I hope*.

Note

In ⟨impersonal⟩ style, people prefer to use the methods of expressing certainty, probability, etc. discussed in 288–92, rather than those which involve a 1st person pronoun. Thus *It is certain . . .* and *It is unlikely . . .* can be impersonal alternatives to *I am certain . . .* or *I doubt . . .*

Certainty
294

Polly *knew* (that) she was being watched.
You *know* what I'm like: I hate a big fuss.
I am *certain/sure* (that) the party will be a success.
~ The party will be a success, I'm *sure.*
They were (absolutely) *convinced* ⎰ (that) they would succeed.
⎱ of their success.
It is *obvious/clear/plain* (to us all) that he has suffered a great deal.
~ He has *clearly/obviously/plainly* suffered a great deal.
We *do not doubt* that he is honest.
~ We *have no doubt* of his honesty.
Doubtless it doesn't always rain at Barnard Castle: that's just the way it seems.

Doubt or uncertainty
295

Doubt is the opposite of certainty.

I am *not certain/sure/convinced* that he deserves promotion.
~ I am *not certain/sure* whether he deserves promotion.
They were *uncertain/unsure* (*of*) who was to blame.
I *doubt* if many people will come to the meeting.
~I *don't think* many people will come to the meeting (*see* 587).
There were some *doubts about* your pricing policy.
We have *doubts about* the risks everyone is taking.
They were *uncertain of/about* the best course to take.

Belief, opinion, and similar meanings
296

- **Belief, opinion**

> *I believe* (that) the lecture was well attended.
> ~ The lecture was well attended, *I believe*.
> She *thinks* (that) she can dictate to everybody.
> It was everybody's *opinion* that the conference was a success.
> It's my *belief* that cars will disappear from our roads one day.
> *In my opinion*, he was driving the car too fast.
> You may *consider* yourselves lucky. (On the use of an object complement
> here, *see* 508, 733.)
> She was *thought/believed/considered* to be the richest woman in Europe.

Tag questions (684), especially with a falling tone, can be used to express an opinion:

> He was driving too f`a`st, w`a`sn't he?

Note
There is a slight difference between 'opinion' and 'belief': an opinion is usually something that someone arrives at on the basis of observation and judgement:

> It's my belief that he drinks too much. ('I don't know how much he drinks, but . . .')
> It's my opinion that he drinks too much. ('I know how much he drinks, and in my
> judgement, it's too much'.)

- **Assumption**

> We *assume/suppose* that you have received the package.
> All the passengers, *I presume*, have been warned about the delay.
> ~ All the passengers have *presumably* been warned about the delay.

Will in the sense of 'present prediction' (*see* 291) can be used here:

> *I assume* you *will* all have heard the news.

- **Appearance**

> It *seems/appears* (to me) that no one noticed his escape.
> ~ No one *seems/appears* to have noticed his escape.
> ~ *Apparently*, no one noticed his escape.
> It *looks as if* he's ill. ⟨rather informal⟩ (Here *looks* may refer to visual
> appearance only.)

Note
Like can replace *as if* in the last example in ⟨informal AmE⟩. In ⟨BrE⟩ this use of *like* as a conjunction is less acceptable.

297
In *that*-clauses of the types shown in 296 above, transferred negation (*see* 587) is common. Thus instead of *I think he hasn't arrived*, we prefer to say *I don't think he has arrived*.

Notice that in shortened reply statements of these three categories, the clause which is the object of belief, etc. can usually be replaced by *so* (*see* 386):

[A]   Has the race been postponed?   [B]
- I think *so*.
- I suppose *so*.
- It seems *so*.
- Apparently *so*.
- I don't think *so*.

(Here *so* replaces '(that) the race has been postponed'.)

Section C: Mood, emotion and attitude

298

In Section B, we looked at the English language as a means of giving and receiving information. But language is more than this: it is communication *between people*. It often expresses the emotions and attitudes of the speaker, and the speaker often uses it to influence the attitudes and behaviour of the hearer. These are the aspects of English we consider in this section.

Emotive emphasis in speech

Interjections

299

In this part of Section C, we shall be dealing mainly with ⟨familiar⟩ forms of English.

Interjections are words whose only function is to express emotion. Common English interjections are:

> *Oh* /oʊ/ (surprise):
>> *Oh*, what a beautiful present.
> *Ah* /ɑː/ (satisfaction, recognition, etc.):
>> *Ah*, that's just what I wanted.
> *Aha* /əˈhɑː/ (jubilant satisfaction, recognition):
>> *Aha*, these books are exactly what I was looking for.
> *Wow* /waʊ/ (great surprise):
>> *Wow*, what a fantastic goal!
> *Yippee* /ˈjɪpiː/ (excitement, delight):
>> *Yippee*, this is fun!
> *Ouch* /aʊtʃ/:
>> *Ouch*, my foot!
> *Ow* /aʊ/ (pain):
>> *Ow*, that hurt!

Ugh /ʌx/(disgust):

> *Ugh*, what a mess.

Ooh /uː/(pleasure, pain):

> *Ooh*, this cream cake's delicious.

Other ways of giving emotion emphasis
300

- **Exclamations** (*see* 528)

> What a wonderful time we've had!
> How good of you to come! ⟨rather formal⟩

Exclamations are often shortened to a noun phrase or an adjectival phrase:
What a girl! ('What a girl she is!'); *How funny!* ('How funny it is!').

- **Emphatic *so* and *such*** (*see* 528)

> The whole place was 'such a mèss!
>
> I'm 'so afraid they'll get lòst.
>
> I didn't know he was 'such a nice màn.

These have an emotive emphasis similar to that of exclamations, but their
tone can be rather 'gushy'. The words *so* and *such* are stressed, and for extra
emphasis, may receive nuclear stress.

- **Repetition** (which also denotes degree = *extremely*)

> This house is 'far, 'far too expensive.
>
> I agree with *every* word you've said – 'every 'single 'word.
>
> I think that the lecturers are 'very 'very boring.
>
> You 'bad, 'bad boy! (spoken to a naughty child)

Note the use of stress (') to emphasize the repetition.

- **Stress on the operator** (*see* 609–12)

> That wìll be nice!
> What áre you dòing?
> We hàve enjoyed ourselves!

The operator often has nuclear stress. *Do* can be used as a dummy auxiliary
to express emphasis (*see* 611–12):

> You dò look pretty.
> You 'did give me a frǐght.

There is a similar use of *do* to give persuasive emphasis to a command:

> 'Do be quìet! ⟨impolite⟩
> Dò come éarly.

- **Nuclear stress on other words**
  > I wìsh you'd sée to it.
  > I'm tèrribly sǒrry!

Intensifying adverbs and modifiers
301
As we noted in 217–18, many degree adverbs and other degree expressions intensify the meaning of the word they modify:

> Well, that's *very* nice *indeed*.
> We are *utterly* powerless.
> It's this sort of thing that makes me look an *absolute* fool.

In ⟨familiar⟩ speech, some adjectives and adverbs (such as *terrific, tremendous, awfully, terribly*) have little meaning apart from their emotive force. Thus *terrific, great, grand, fantastic* are simply emphatic equivalents of *good* or *nice*: *The weather was terrific; It was a great show*; etc. Notice that *awfully* and *terribly* can be used in a 'good' sense, as well as in a 'bad' sense:

> She's *terribly* kind to us.

In addition to degree adverbs, certain adverbs like *really* and *definitely* have an emphatic effect:

> We *really* have enjoyed ourselves.
> He *definitely* impressed us.
> It was *truly* a memorable occasion.
> She *literally* collapsed with laughter. ⟨familiar⟩

Emphasis
302
You can intensify the emotive force of a *wh*-question by adding *ever, on earth,* etc. to the *wh*-word:

> How *ever* did they escape? ('I just can't imagine')
> Why *on earth* didn't you tell me? ('How silly of you!')
> What *in heaven's name* does he think he's doing? ('The idiot!')

These forms are typical of ⟨informal or familiar speech⟩. In ⟨writing⟩, *ever* is sometimes spelled as part of the *wh*-word: *whoever, wherever*, etc., but so spelled, these words have other uses apart from intensifying (*see* 214, 592). *Why ever* is always spelled as two words.

Emphatic negation
303

- **You can intensify a negative sentence** by adding *at all* either directly after the negative word, or in a later position in the sentence.

    The doctors found nothing *at all* the matter with him.
    She didn't speak to us *at all*.

Other negative intensifiers are *a bit* ⟨informal⟩ and *by any means* (both adverbials of degree); and *whatever* (modifier after a negative noun phrase):

    They weren't *a bit* apologetic.
    You have no excuse *whatever*.

Further examples of negative intensifiers are:

    I didn't sleep *a wink*. ⟨informal⟩
    He didn't give me *a thing* (= 'anything at all'). ⟨informal⟩

- **A negative noun phrase beginning** *not a* can be used for emphasis:

    We arrived *not a* moment too soon (= We didn't arrive one moment too soon).

- **Fronted negation**

Another rather ⟨rhetorical⟩ form of negative emphasis is often combined with the forms already mentioned. This is to place the negative element at the beginning of the clause:

    Not a penny of the money did he spend.
    Never have I seen such a crowd of people. ⟨rather formal⟩

As the examples show, the operator (*did, have*, etc.) is placed before the subject (unless the negative element is itself the subject: *Not a single word passed her lips*) (*see* 417).

Exclamatory and rhetorical questions
304
An **exclamatory question** is a *yes-no* question spoken with an emphatic falling tone, instead of the usual rising tone. The most common type has a negative form:

Hasn't she grown! ('She's grown very very much!')	[1]
Wasn't it a marvellous concert!	[2]
[A] The picture's faded. [B] Yes, isn't it a pity.	[3]

Here the speaker vigorously invites the hearer's agreement; the effect of [2] is similar to:

    It was marvellous concert, wasn't it? (*see* 245)

Another type of exclamatory question is positive in form, with stress on the operator and subject:

> 'Am 'I hu̱ngry! ('I'm very very hungry'.)
> 'Did 'he look anno̱yed! ('He certainly looked very annoyed'.)
> 'Has 'she gro̱wn! ('She's grown such a lot!')

305
A **rhetorical question** is more like a forceful statement than an exclamation.

• **Positive**

A *positive* rhetorical question is like a strong *negative* statement:

> Is this a reason for saving nó one? ('Surely that is not a reason . . .')

• **Negative**

A *negative* rhetorical question is like a strong *positive* statement:

> Didn't I te̱ll you he would forgét? ('You know I told you . . .')

There are also rhetorical *wh*-questions:

> What di̱fference does it make? ('It makes no difference.')
> How many employees would refuse a rise in pay?
> ('Very few or none.')

As the name suggests, rhetorical questions are often rather ⟨rhetorical⟩ in tone. They challenge the hearer to deny what appears obvious.

Describing emotions

306
We come now to the description or reporting of emotive behaviour. An emotive reaction to something can be expressed by the preposition *at*:

> I was *alarmed at* his behaviour.   [1]
> An audience will always *laugh at* a good joke.   [2]
> She was very *surprised at* your resignation from the club.   [3]

In ⟨BrE⟩, *with* is often used instead of *at* when what causes the reaction is a person or object rather than an event:

> I was *furious with* him for missing that penalty.
> Is she *pleased with* her present?

Other prepositions used are *about* and *of*: *worried about, annoyed about, resentful of,* etc. (*see* 239).

> As a former champion, he was *annoyed about* his own failures, and *resentful of* the successes of others.

The cause of the emotion is often expressed by a *to*-infinitive clause or a *that*-clause (with or without *should*, *see* 280), and in these cases the preposition is omitted (*see* 655):

> They were alarmed *to find the house empty*.
> She is sorry *to have missed the show*.
> He was delighted *to see them so happy*.
> We're anxious *that everything should go smoothly*.

307
The cause of emotion may also be expressed by the subject (or, in the passive, by the agent). Compare [3] above with:

> Your resignation from the club surprised her very much.
> ~ She was very surprised by your resignation from the club.

Other constructions for describing emotions do not specify the person affected, and are therefore more ⟨impersonal⟩:

> The accommodation was *satisfactory/delightful*, etc.   [4]
> The news from the front is *very disturbing*.   [5]
> *It's amazing* that so many passengers were unhurt. (*see* 438, 542)   [6]
> *It is a pity* that the government should ever have been led to
>   abandon its principles.   [7]
> *It's a pity* to leave the party before the fun starts.   [8]

In most of these cases, the person affected is likely to be 'me' (the speaker). The person affected can sometimes be made clear by a phrase introduced by *to* or *for*: *satisfactory for most people*, *disturbing to me*, etc. Thus [6] can be expanded:

> *To me*, it's amazing that so many passengers were unhurt.

Sentence adverbials expressing emotion
308
Some sentence adverbials (including comment clauses, *see* 499) can express an emotional reaction or judgement:

> *To my regret*, he did not accept our offer. (i.e. 'I regretted that he did not
>   accept the offer.')
> *Surprisingly*, no one has objected to the plan. (i.e. 'It is surprising
>   that . . .')
> She is *wisely* staying at home today. (i.e. 'She is wise to stay . . .')
> The children were rather noisy, *I'm afraid*.

Other sentence adverbs similar to *surprisingly* and *wisely* are *amazingly*, *strangely*, *regrettably*, *fortunately*, *luckily*, *happily*, *hopefully*, *preferably*, *foolishly*, *sensibly*. For example:

> *Amazingly*, the dog survived.

Fortunately we were outside the building when the fire started.
Hopefully all my problems are now behind me.

Liking and disliking
309
Verbs such as *like, love, hate,* and *prefer* can be followed either by a noun phrase object [9], by a *to*-infinitive clause [10] or by an *-ing* clause [11] (*see* 515):

$$
\text{She likes/loves/hates} \begin{cases} \textit{parties.} & [9] \\ \textit{to give parties.} \\ \text{(i.e. 'She likes etc. the idea of it', etc.)} & [10] \\ \textit{giving parties.} \\ \text{(i.e. 'She likes it when she does it', etc.)} & [11] \end{cases}
$$

Some English speakers see a slight difference between [10] and [11]: the infinitive clause expresses an 'idea', while the *-ing* clause expresses a 'fact' (*see* 274). Thus in some contexts (but not in [10]), the infinitive clause may have **neutral** meaning (*see* 279):

$$
\text{He likes me } to\ work \text{ late.} \begin{cases} \text{'. . . and that's why I do it.'} \\ \text{OR} \\ \text{'. . . but I never do it.'} \end{cases}
$$

He likes me *working* late.   ('. . . and that's why I do it.')

When the main verb is hypothetical, usually only the infinitive clause can be used:

[A]   Would you like *to have* dinner now?
[B]   No, I'd prefer *to eat* later.

Note
Enjoy, dislike, and *loathe* take only *-ing* clauses: *He enjoys/dislikes/loathes working.*

Preference
310
Prefer means 'like more' or 'like better'. The rejected alternative is introduced by a *to*-phrase, or by a clause introduced by *rather than,* which may be followed by an infinitive (with or without *to*) or by an *-ing* participle:

Most people prefer trains *to* buses.
They prefer renting a car *to* having one of their own.
~ They prefer to rent a car *rather than* to have one of their own.
~ *Rather than* buy a car of their own, they prefer to rent one.
She has always preferred making her

$$
\text{own clothes,} \begin{cases} \textit{rather than} \\ \textit{instead of} \end{cases} \text{buying them in the shops.}
$$

Would prefer + *to*-infinitive (hypothetical preference) can be replaced by *would rather* + bare infinitive, which may be followed by a *than*-construction (*see* 715):

> I'*d prefer to stay* in a house *rather than* in a hotel.
> ~ I'*d rather stay* in a house *than* in a hotel.

Some other emotions
311
Here are some of the ways of expressing other emotions. Many of them have already been discussed and exemplified. Notice that adverbs of degree (*see* 217–26) can be used to indicate the 'strength' of the emotion. Many of the sentences are ⟨informal and familiar⟩.

Hope
312

> I (very much) hope (that) he $\left\{ \begin{array}{l} \text{will arrive} \\ \text{arrives} \end{array} \right\}$ on time.

> I am hoping that they get that letter tomorrow. ⟨tentative⟩ (*see* 139)
> I was hoping we would get a bit more time. ⟨more tentative⟩ (*see* 121, 139)
> I hope to see you soon.
> Hopefully, next spring will bring an improvement in the economic situation.

Anticipation of pleasure
313

> I am looking forward to receiving your reply.
> I know we'll enjoy meeting you again.

Disappointment or regret
314

> I'm (rather/very) disappointed that the match has been cancelled.
> It is (somewhat) disappointing that over half the tickets are unsold.
> It's a (great) shame/pity that this is the last party.
> I'm (very) sorry to hear that you have to leave.
> I had hoped that she would change her mind. (unfulfilled hope) (*see* 275)
> I wish (that) someone had let me know. (unfulfilled wish) (*see* 321–2)
> If only I had known! (*see* 322)
> Unfortunately we're having trouble with the builder.

Approval
315

I (very much) approve of $\begin{cases} \text{the plan.} \\ \text{your asking for his opinion. } \langle \text{formal} \rangle \end{cases}$

It wasn't a bad movie, was it? ⟨familiar⟩ (mild) (684)
I (rather) like the new boss.

I $\begin{cases} \text{love} \\ \text{do like} \end{cases}$ your dress. (enthusiastic)

What a great/terrific/marvellous/. . . play! (enthusiastic) (528)

Disapproval
316

I don't like the way she dresses (very much).
I don't (much) care for iced tea, actually.

I didn't think $\begin{cases} \text{much of the orchestra.} \\ \text{the orchestra was much/very good.} \end{cases}$

I thought the novel was poor/dreadful/appalling, didn't you.
It would have been better, I think, if you hadn't mentioned it.
You shouldn't have bought such an expensive present. (*see* 328)
You could have been more careful.
I don't think you should have told the children.
I had hoped you would have done more than this.

Disapproval can often be expressed more ⟨tactfully⟩ by means of a question:

Did you have/need to work so late?
Why did you do a thing like that?
Was it really necessary to be so rude to the waiter?
Don't you think it would have been better if you had told me in advance?

Surprise
317

It's (rather) surprising/amazing/astonishing that so many people come to these meetings.
I am/was (very) surprised that so many turned up.
What a surprise!
How strange/odd/astonishing/amazing that you both went to the same school!
Wasn't it extraordinary that the child was totally unhurt? (*see* 304)
Surprisingly/strangely/incredibly, James slept soundly through the whole affair.

Concern, worry
318

> I am (a bit) concerned/worried that our money will be used unnecessarily.
> I am (rather) worried/concerned about what will happen to the union.
> It's (very) disturbing/worrying that no one noticed the break-in.
> I find his behaviour very disturbing/worrying.
> Her health gives (some) cause for anxiety. ⟨formal, impersonal⟩

Volition

319
We distinguish four types of volition: **willingness, wish, intention, insistence**. These are listed in order of increasing 'strength'.

Willingness
320
Willingness can be expressed by the auxiliary *will* (or *'ll* ⟨informal⟩):

> [A] *Will* you lend me those scissors for a moment?
> [B] OK, I *will* if you promise to return them.
> The porter *will* help if you ask him.

Here the future meaning of *will* is mixed with that of volition (*see* 129). For past or hypothetical willingness, use *would*:

- **Past time:** We tried to warn them about the dangers, but no one *would* listen.
- **Hypothetical:** My boss is so greedy, he *would* do anything for money.

Won't and *wouldn't* express the negative of willingness, i.e. **refusal**:

> She *won't* take any notice. (= 'She refuses/declines to take any notice.')
> They *wouldn't* listen to me. (= 'They refused . . .')

Wish
321
For neutral volition, **want** is a less ⟨formal⟩ verb than **wish**:

> I *want* (you) to read this newspaper report.
> Do you *want* me to sign this letter?
> The manager *wishes* (me) to thank you for your cooperation. ⟨rather formal⟩

For a hypothetical circumstance, use only *wish*:

> I wish (that) you would listen to me! ('. . . but you won't')

322

The exclamatory construction *If only* . . . can also be used for hypothetical meaning:

> *If only* I could remember his name!
> ~ I 'do *wish* I could remember his name!

When expressing your own wishes, or inviting the wishes of others, you can make the wish more ⟨tentative⟩ and ⟨tactful⟩ by using *would like, would prefer,* or *would rather* (*see* 309–10):

> *Would* you *like* me to open these letters?
> I *would like* to stay in an inexpensive hotel.

(*Should* can replace *would* in the 1st person.) Another way to consult someone's wishes is to use a question with *shall,* or more ⟨tentatively⟩, with *should:*

> *Shall* I make you a cup of coffee? ('Would you like me to . . .?')
> What *shall* we do this evening?
> *Shall* we cancel the order if it's not needed?
> *Should* we tell him that he's not wanted?

Note

1st and 3rd person commands with *let* (*see* 498) also express a kind of wish: *Let's listen to some music* (*, shall we?*); *Let everyone do what they can.*

Intention

323

The verbs *intend, mean, plan* and *aim* (+ infinitive clause) express intention:

> He *intends/plans/aims* to arrest them as they leave the building.   [1]
> That remark was *meant/intended* to hurt her.   [2]

Intention can also be expressed by *be going to* (*see* 142) or, in the 1st person, by *will/shall* (*see* 141) or the contraction '*ll*:

> *Are* you *going to* catch the last train?
> We *won't* stay longer than two hours.

These forms also have an element of prediction, and so are more definite about the fulfilment of the intention than [1] and [2]. (On clauses and phrases of purpose, or 'intended result', *see* 203.)

Insistence

324

> He *insists* on doing everything himself.
> We *are determined* to overcome the problem.

Insistence is occasionally expressed by *will/shall* with strong stress:

> He 'will try to mend it him`self`. ('He insists on trying . . .')
> I `won't` give in!

Permission and obligation

Permission: *can, may*, etc.

325

> *Can* we sit down in here? Yes, you can/may.
> *May* I speak to you for a minute? ⟨more formal, polite⟩
> *Are we allowed to* use the swimming pool?
> *Is it all right if* we smoke in here? ⟨informal⟩
> They have *allowed/permitted him to* take the examination late.
>   (*permit* is ⟨more formal⟩ than *allow*)
> They *let* him do what he wants.

- **Past:** *could*

> The prisoners *could* leave the camp only by permission of the governor.
>   ('. . . were allowed to . . .')

- **Hypothetical**

> If you were a student, you *could* travel at half-price.
>   ('. . . would be allowed to . . .')

You can also use hypothetical *could* (and rarely *might*) in ⟨tactful⟩ requests for permission:

> *Could* we ask you what your opinion is?
> I wonder if I *could* borrow your pen?

Another construction for asking and giving permission involves the verb *mind*:

[A]   *Would you mind* { if I opened a wíndow?
                          opening a wíndow for me?

[B]   No, { I *don't mind* at àll.
             not at àll. (= 'certainly you may').

Again, the hypothetical form is more ⟨tactful⟩.

Obligation or compulsion: *must, have to*, etc.

326

> You *must*   ⎱ be back by 2 o'clock – (I want you to do some
> You'll *have to* ⎰ cleaning).   [1]
> You *have to* sign your name here (otherwise the document isn't
>   valid).   [2]
> I've *got to* finish this essay by tomorrow. ⟨informal⟩   [3]
> The university *requires* all students to submit their work by a date.
>   ⟨formal, written⟩   [4]

Must and *have (got) to* + infinitive (*see* 288, 483) both express obligation, but some English speakers feel a difference between them. For such speakers, *must* involves the speaker's authority (*see* [1]), while *have (got) to* may involve some other authority than the speaker; e.g. official regulations (*see* [2]). With a first person subject, *must* expresses my authority over myself, e.g. my sense of duty:

> I *must* phone my parents tonight. ('They'll be worrying about me.')   [5]
> We *must* invite the Stewarts to dinner. ('It's months since we saw them'.)

- Past: *had to*

> They *had to* work six days a week in those days. ('were obliged to . . .')

- Hypothetical:

> If you went abroad, you *would have to* earn your own living.
> ('. . . would be obliged to . . .')

327

- Questions: *have got to, have to, need to,* etc.

> Why *have* you *got to* work so hard?
> Do you *have to* be so strict?
> Does anyone *need to* leave early?

- Negation:

> We don't *have to* hurry.
> You don't *need to* pay that fine.
> There's no *need to* buy the tickets yet.

Note

[a] *Must* sometimes occurs in questions expecting a negative answer:

> *Must* you leave already? ('Surely you don't have to!')

[b] Especially in ⟨BrE⟩, *need* as an operator is used instead of *must* in questions and negatives:

> *Need* you work so hard?; We *needn't* hurry.

Other ways of expressing obligation: *should, ought to,* etc.
328

- *Should* and *ought to* (*see* 292) express an obligation which may not be fulfilled. Compare [4] and [5] in 326 above with:

> All students *should* submit their work by a given date ('. . . but some of them don't!').
> I *ought* to phone my parents tonight ('but I probably won't have time').

- *Need to* + **infinitive** (where *need* is a main verb, not an auxiliary, *see* 484) indicates 'internal obligation' caused by the state of the person referred to:

> He *needs to* practise more if he is to improve his game of golf.

We can also use *need* with a direct object:

He *needs* more practice.

- *Had better* (or *'d better*) ⟨informal⟩ + **infinitive** (without *to*) has the meaning of 'strong recommendation or advisability':

$$\text{You}'d \text{ better be quick} \begin{cases} \text{or you'll miss the train.} \\ \text{if you want to catch the train.} \end{cases}$$

He*'d better not* make another mistake.
I suppose I*'d better* lock the door.

- *Shall* in the sense of 'obligation' is normally limited to official regulations and other ⟨formal⟩ documents:

> The Society's nominating committee *shall* nominate one person for the office of President. ⟨formal⟩

Prohibition (and negative advice)

329

Prohibition is the negation of permission ('He/she is not allowed to do something'). *Can* and *may* (= 'permission') and *must* (= 'obligation') can all have the meaning of 'prohibition' with a negative:

> [A] *Can* the children play here?   [B] No, I'm afraid they *can't* ('they're not allowed to') – it's against the rules.
> You *may not* go swimming ('You're not allowed to . . .'), unless you have a certificate.
> You *mustn't* keep us all waiting. ('You're obliged not to . . .?)

A weakened prohibition (more like negative advice) can be expressed by *shouldn't*, *oughtn't to* ⟨esp BrE⟩, and *had better not*:

> She *shouldn't* be so impatient.
> You *oughtn't to* waste all that money on smoking.
> We*'d better not* wake the children up.

Influencing people

Commands

330

- With the aim of getting someone to do something, a **direct command** can be used: *Shut the door; Follow me; Just look at this mess;* etc. (*see* 497). A negative command has the effect of forbidding an action: *Don't be a fool; Don't worry about me.*

- In addition, with a 2nd person subject, the **verb forms expressing obligation and prohibition** (*see* 326, 329) can have almost the same effect as a command: *You must be careful; You mustn't smoke here.*

- The construction *be to* + **infinitive** can convey a command given either by the speaker, or (more usually) by some official authority:

He *is to* return to Germany tomorrow. ('He has been given orders to
   return to Germany.')

You *are to* stay here until I return. ('These are my instructions to you.')

Note

[a] Some verbless sentences have the effect of brusque commands: *Out with it! This way! Here!*
(= 'Bring/put it here'). Another type is especially used in addressing children and pets: *Off you
go! Down you get! Up you come!* ⟨familiar⟩

[b] *Will* in its future sense can sometimes be used (e.g. in military contexts) with the force of a
severe command:

Officers *will* report for duty at 0600 ('six hundred') hours.

You *will* do exactly as I say.

Commands with grammatical subjects, etc.

331

You can specify the people who have to obey the command by putting a 2nd or
3rd person subject in front of the imperative verb (*see* 497), or else by using a
vocative:

'You take thís tray, and 'you take thàt one. (pointing to the people
   concerned; note that *you* is stressed)

Jack and Susan stand over thère.

Somebody open this dòor, pléase.

Come hère, Míchael.

Elsewhere, a command with *you* has a tone of impatience:

You mind your own bùsiness!

Another form of impatient command begins with *will*:

Will you be quìet!

Although this has the grammatical form of a question, its falling intonation
gives it the force of a command. In many circumstances, commands are
⟨impolite⟩, and therefore we shall consider in 332–5 various ways of toning
down the effect of a command.

Note

However, it is ⟨not impolite⟩ to use a command when you are telling someone to do
something for his or her own good: *Have another chocolate; Make yourself at home; Just leave
everything to me; Do come in.* These are in effect offers or invitations rather than commands.

Weakened commands

332

One way to tone down or weaken the imperative force of a command is to use a
rising or fall-rise tone, instead of the usual falling tone:

Be cǎreful.

Don't forget your wállet.

Another way is to add *please*, or the tag question *won't you*:

> Plèase hurry úp.
>
> Look after the chíldren, wòn't you.
>
> Thìs way, pléase.

However, none of these alternatives is particularly ⟨polite⟩.

Note
Two other tags, *why don't you* and *will you* (after a negative command), can tone down a command:

> Have a drínk, why don't you.
>
> Don't be lǎte, wìll you.

But after a positive command, *will you* has rising intonation, and usually expresses impatience (*see* 331).

> Sit dòwn, wíll you.

Requests

333
It is often more ⟨tactful⟩ to use a request rather than a command: i.e. to ask your hearer whether he or she is willing or able to do something. The auxiliaries *will*/*would* (= willingness) and *can*/*could* (= ability) can be used:

> [A] *Will* you make sure the water's hòt?   [B] Yès, okáy. ⟨familiar⟩
>
> [A] *Would* you please tell me your phòne number?   [B] Yès, cèrtainly, it's . . .
>
> [A] *Can* anyone tell us what the tíme is?
>
> [A] *Could you* lend me a pén.   [B] Okày. ⟨familiar⟩ Hère it ís.

(These examples also show some typical replies.) *Would* and *could* are more ⟨tactful⟩ than *will* and *can*. You can also use a negative question, which expects a positive answer (*see* 246), and is to that extent less ⟨tentative⟩ and more persuasive;

> Won't you come in and sit dówn?
>
> Couldn't you possibly come anóther day?

Other ⟨polite⟩ forms of request

334
There are many more indirect ways of making a ⟨polite⟩ request; e.g. you can make a statement about your own wishes. The following are listed roughly in order of least to most ⟨polite⟩:

> I wouldn't mind a drínk, if you háve one.
>
> Would you mind starting agáin?
>
> I wonder if you could put me on your màiling list, please.
>
> Would you be good/kind enough to let me knów?

> I would be (extremely) grateful if you would telephone me this afternoon.
> I wonder if you would kindly write a reference for me.

These sentences are typical of ⟨spoken⟩ English. In formal letters, useful formulae are: *I would be very grateful if you would . . .*; *I would appreciate it if you could . . .*; *Would you kindly . . .*

Advice and suggestions
335
As ways of influencing other people, **advice** and **suggestions** are milder than commands. Strictly, these leave the decision about what to do in the hands of the hearer. But in practice, as the examples show, they are often ⟨tactful⟩ ways of giving commands or instructions.

- **Advice**

  > You *should* stay in bed until you start to recover.
  > You *ought* to keep your money in a bank.
  > There's a new book you *ought* to see.
  > You'd *better* take your medicine.
  > I'd *advise* you to see a doctor.
  > *If I were you, I'd* sell this car.

- **Suggestions**

  > I *suggest* they take the night train.
  > You *can* read these two chapters before tomorrow (if you like).
  > You *could* be cleaning the office while I'm away.
  > You *might* have a look at this book.
  > *Why don't you* call on me tomorrow?

Could and *might* indicate ⟨tentative⟩ suggestions.

- **Suggestions involving the speaker**

  > I *suggest* we go to bed early, and make an early start tomorrow.
  > *Shall we* listen to some music?
  > *Let's not* waste time.
  > *Why don't we* have a party?
  > *How about* a game of cards?
  > *What about* having a drink?

Reported commands, requests, etc.
336
Commands, like statements and questions (*see* 264–8), can be reported either in direct speech or in indirect speech:

Direct speech: 'Put on your space-suits,' he said.

Indirect speech: He told/ordered/commanded/instructed them to put on their
space-suits.

In indirect speech, put the command in the form of a *to*-infinitive clause. The
hearer can be indicated by an indirect object (*see* 608, 730) – *them* in the above
examples. Note the passive construction:

They *were told* to put on their space-suits.

The same construction can be used for advice, requests, permission, obligation,
persuasion, invitations, etc.:

She *advised* me to read this book.	[1]
He *asked/begged* me to help him with his homework	[2]
She *allowed* him to borrow her car.	[3]
They *compelled* him to answer their questions.	[4]
Mary has *persuaded* me to resign.	[5]
We were *invited* to attend the performance.	[6]
They *recommended* us to stay at this hotel.	[7]

Notice also direct object constructions:

The doctor *advised* a rest.
He *begged* our forgiveness.
I (can) *recommend* the local cuisine.

337

Not all verbs for 'influencing people' take an infinitive. *Suggest* takes a *that*-
clause (often with putative *should* or with the subjunctive, *see* 280–2):

He *suggested* that they (should) play cards.

This construction may also follow other verbs, such as *recommend*:

The doctor *recommends* that you do/should not tire yourself.

Requests, acts of permission, etc. can also be put in the form of indirect
statements and questions. Thus instead of [2] and [3] you could say:

He *asked* me if I would help him with his homework.	[2a]
(DIRECT: 'Will you help me with my homework?')	
She *said* he could borrow her car.	[3a]
(DIRECT: 'You can borrow my car.')	

The rules for changing into the past tense, etc. (*see* 256–7) for indirect statements
and questions apply also to indirect commands, requests, etc. (except that there
is no tense-change in the infinitive clauses). After a past-tense reporting verb,
will, shall, can, may and *have to* change to their past tense forms *would, should,
could, might,* and *had to* (*see* [2a], [3a]) but *must, ought to, should,* and *had better*
do not change:

'You *must* be careful.'	I told them they *must* be careful.
'You *ought to* stay in bed.'	I said that he *ought to* stay in bed.

Reported prohibitions, refusals, etc.
338
The verbs *forbid* ⟨formal⟩, *prohibit* ⟨formal⟩, *dissuade*, *refuse*, *decline*, *deny* and *prevent* already contain a negative meaning, so the clauses which follow them are normally positive:

> They were *forbidden* to smoke.   ⎱ ('They were ordered not to
> They were *prohibited* from smoking. ⎰   smoke')
>
> She *dissuaded* him from leaving the country. ('She persuaded him not to . . .')
> The minister *refused/declined* to comment on the press report.
> He *denied* that any promises had been broken.
> They were *prevented* from taking part.

Warnings, promises and threats
339
Finally, we turn to three types of utterance involving future time:

- **Warnings**

> Mind (your head)!
> Look out!
> Be careful (of your clothes).
> I warn you it's going to be foggy.
> If you're not careful, that pan will catch fire.

Short warnings are often spoken with a fall-rise intonation: Mǐnd!

- **Promises**

> I'll let you know tomorrow.
> I promise (you) it won't hurt.
> You won't lose money, I promise (you).
> Assuming that the order reaches our office by tomorrow, our firm will undertake to supply the goods by the weekend. ⟨formal, written⟩

- **Threats**

> I'll report you if you do that.
> Don't you dare tell lies.
> You dare touch me!
> Do that, and I'll tell your mother (*see* 366).
> Stop eating those sweets, or I'll take them away (*see* 367).

Warnings, promises and threats in reported speech
340

- **Reported warnings**

> He *warned* us to be careful.

They *warned* us of/about the strike.
We were *warned* that the journey might be dangerous.

- **Reported promises**

  He *promised/undertook* to let me know.
  He *promised* that he wouldn't bet on horses.
  They *promised* him that he would not lose his job.
  Her boss ⟨familiar⟩ has *promised* her a rise.
  She has been *promised* a rise.

- **Threats**

  She *threatened* to report me to the police.
  The manager has *threatened* that they will lose their jobs.
  He has *threatened* them with dismissal.

Friendly communications

341
Let us now look at some of the simple acts of communication whereby people establish and maintain friendly relations with one another. Common intonations are given where they are important (*see* 33–42).

Beginning and ending conversation
342

- **Greetings**

  Good morning/afternoon/evening. ⟨polite⟩
  Hello. Hi. ⟨familiar⟩

  Hello (with a rising tone) is also used in answering the phone.

- **Farewells** (temporary)

  Goodbye.
  (Bye)-bye. ⟨very familiar⟩
  See you. ⟨very familiar⟩
  See you at six o'clock. ⟨familiar⟩
  Cheerio. ⟨familiar BrE⟩; Cheers. ⟨very familiar, BrE⟩
  See you later. ⟨very familiar⟩
  See you tomorrow. ⟨familiar⟩
  Good-night (final word before parting for the night or before going to
    bed).

- **Farewells** (more permanent): Goodbye.

Other remarks may be added for politeness:

It's been nice knowing you.

(I hope you) have a good journey.

- **Introductions**

    May I introduce (you to) Miss Brown? ⟨formal⟩

    This is John Smith.

    Meet my wife. ⟨familiar⟩

    I don't think you've met our neighbour, Mr Quirk.

- **Greetings on introduction**

    How do you do? ⟨formal⟩   How are you?

    Glad to meet you.   Hello. ⟨informal⟩

    Hi. ⟨familiar, especially AmE⟩

'Small talk'

343

After a greeting, a conversation may continue with a polite inquiry about health, etc:

How are you?

How are you getting on? ⟨familiar⟩

How's things? ⟨very familiar⟩

How are you doing? ⟨familiar, esp. AmE⟩

Common replies to such questions are:

(I'm) fine. How are you?

Very well, thank you. And you?

If someone is liable to poor health, you might begin: *How are you feeling today/ these days?* or *I hope you're well.*

Especially in Britain, opening remarks about the weather are common:

[A] (It's a) lovely day, isn't it? (*see* 245)

   [B] Yes, isn't it beautiful. (*see* 304)

[A] What miserable weather! (*see* 528)

   [B] Dreadful!

Beginning and ending letters

344

- **Example of a ⟨formal⟩ official letter**

    Dear Sir,/Dear Madam,

    With reference to your letter of ....

Yours faithfully.
A R Smith
(Manager)

- **Example of a ⟨less formal⟩ letter**

    Dear Dr Smith,/Miss Brown,/George,

    Thank you for your letter of ....
    ....

    (With best wishes)
      { Yours sincerely, ⟨BrE⟩
      { Sincerely (yours), ⟨AmE⟩
    James Robertson

- **Example of an ⟨informal⟩ letter between acquaintances**

    Dear George,

    ....

    (Best wishes)
    Yours (ever),
    Janet

More intimate letters may begin and end with endearments:
  My dear George, Dearest George, . . . Love from Janet, etc.

Thanks, apologies, regrets
345

- **Thanks**

    Thánk you.   Thanks very múch.
    (Many) thánks.   Ta. ⟨BrE slang⟩

- **Responses to thanks**

    Not at àll.   You're wélcome.
    Thàt's all ríght.

Note that in English such responses are not so common (esp. in ⟨BrE⟩) as in some other languages. Often the 'giver' makes no reply. In shops, etc. the customer will say *Thank you* for the article bought, and the shopkeeper will often likewise say *Thank you* in return, on receiving the money.

- **Apologies**

    (I'm) sǒrry.   (I beg your) párdon.   Excùse me.

Excuse me is an apology in ⟨AmE⟩, but in ⟨BrE⟩ is limited to mild apologies for routine impolite behaviour; e.g. for interrupting, for sneezing, for pushing in front of somebody. One would say *I beg your pardon* for mishaps such as treading on someone's toe. More lengthy apologies are:

I'm extrèmely sorry $\begin{cases} \text{(about that létter).} \\ \text{(for forgetting to send that létter).} \end{cases}$

Will you forgive/excuse me if I have to leave éarly?

I hope you will forgive/excuse me if I have to leave ĕarly.

- **Responses to apologies**

    Thàt's all ríght.   Please don't wórry.

- **Regrets**

    I'm sorry I couldn't come to the meeting. ⟨informal⟩

    I regret that I was unable to provide the assistance you required.
    ⟨formal, written⟩

Good wishes, congratulations, condolences
346
These are normally spoken with a falling tone.

- **Good wishes**

    Good luck!

    Best wishes for your holiday ‖ vacation.

    Have a nice day ⟨esp. AmE⟩.

    Have a good time at the theatre.

    I wish you every success in your new career. ⟨more formal⟩

- **Good wishes sent to a third person**

    Please give my best wishes to Sally.

    Please remember me to your father.

    Please give my kindest regards to your wife. ⟨formal⟩

    Give my love to the children. ⟨informal⟩

    Say hello to Joe. ⟨informal, esp. AmE⟩

- **Seasonal greetings**

    Merry Christmas.   Happy New Year.

    Happy birthday (to you).   Many happy returns (of your
                                        birthday).

- **Toasts**

    Good health. ⟨formal⟩   Your health. ⟨formal⟩

    Cheers! ⟨familiar⟩   Here's to your job. ⟨familiar⟩

    Here's to the future. ⟨familiar⟩

- **Congratulations**

    Well done! ⟨familiar⟩ (for a success or achievement).

    Congratulations on your engagement.

I was delighted to hear about your success/that you won the
competition.
I congratulate *The Times* on the high quality of its reporting.
May we congratulate you on your recent appointment. ⟨formal⟩

- **Condolences, sympathy**

    Please accept my deepest sympathy on the death of your father.
    ⟨formal⟩
    I was extremely sorry to hear about your father/that your father has
    been so ill. ⟨informal⟩

Offers

347

In making an offer, you can make use of questions about the wishes of the
hearer (*see* 319–24):

Would you like another helping of turkey?	[1]
Would you like me to mail these letters?	[2]
Shall I get you a chair?	[3]
Can I carry your bags upstairs?	[4]

In answering an offer in the form of a question, we say

either   Yes, please. (acceptance)
or   No, thank you. (refusal)

More ⟨polite⟩ acceptances:

Yes, please. That's very kind of you.
Yes, thank you, I'd love some more.

Note that *thank you* can be used in accepting, as well as refusing.
More ⟨polite⟩ refusals include an explanation of the refusal:

That's very kind of you, but I couldn't possibly manage any more.
[answer to 1 above]
No, thank you very much. I'm just leaving. [answer to 3]

In ⟨familiar⟩ English, commands are often used in making offers:

Have some more coffee.
Do sit down. (*see* 497)
Let me get a chair for you. (*see* 498)

After the offer has been accepted, the other person need not say anything when
he/she performs the service. Especially in ⟨BrE⟩, quite often people just smile, or

say *Here you are* (e.g. on bringing some food), or *There you are* (e.g. on opening a window, bringing a chair, etc.).

Invitations
348

Come in and sit dówn. ⟨familiar⟩

Would you like to come with mé?

How would you like to come and spend a wèek with us next yèar?

May I invite you to dìnner next Saturday? ⟨formal, polite⟩

Here is a typical sequence:

[A] Are you doing anything tomorrow évening?

[B] Nó.

[A] Then perhaps you'd be interested in joining us for a mèal at a restaurant in tówn.

[B] Thank you very mùch. ⎰ That ìs kind of you.
⎱ I'd lòve to.

In ⟨politely⟩ refusing the invitation, [B] might say:

Well, that's very kĭnd of you – but I'm afraid I have already arranged/ promised to . . . What a pìty, I would have so much enjŏyed it.

Vocatives

349
To get someone's attention, you can use a vocative such as *John, Mrs Johnson, Dr Smith*:

Jŏhn, I wànt you.

Plèase, Jenny, stòp.

Now just a mòment, Mr Wílliams.

Thànk you, Dr Gomez.

Vocatives can be used more generally to mark the speaker's relation to the hearer.

Sir and *madam* are vocatives which mark respect to a stranger:

Did you order a tàxi, mádam? ⟨formal⟩

Other titles of respect, and some professional titles, can be used as vocatives: *Ladies and gentlemen!* (⟨formal⟩ opening of a speech); *My Lord* (to a peer, a bishop, a British judge, etc.); *Your honor* (to an American judge); *Your Excellency* (to an ambassador); *Mr President; Prime Minister; Father* (to a priest); *Doctor* (to a medical doctor); etc.

In contrast, the following are some of the many examples of the ⟨familiar⟩ use of vocatives: *dad(dy)*; *mum(my)*; *(you) guys* ⟨familiar AmE⟩; *(my) dear*; *(my) darling*; *honey* ⟨AmE⟩.

350
English is restricted in forms of address to strangers. *Sir* and (especially) *madam* are too ⟨formal⟩ to be used in most situations. *Miss* as a vocative is by many considered ⟨impolite⟩. Many people even feel that occupational vocatives like *waiter* or *driver* are ⟨rather impolite⟩, although others, like *nurse* (= 'nursing sister') or *operator* (telephone operator) are acceptable:

> Would you help me, please, *operator*? I'm trying to get through to a
> number in Copenhagen.

Thus to get the attention of a stranger, you have to rely on *Excuse me!* or in ⟨AmE⟩ *Pardon me!*

Section D: Meanings in connected discourse

351
In Sections A, B and C we have considered aspects of meaning in isolation, but in this final section we will think about how meanings may be put together and presented in a spoken or written discourse. That is, we shall be discussing style and presentation of ideas. We start with the organization of connections within and between sentences.

Linking signals

352
Whether in speech or in writing, you help people to understand your message by signalling how one idea leads on from another. The words and phrases which have this connecting function are like 'signposts' on a journey. Most of them in English are sentence adverbials, and they generally come at the beginning of a sentence. Their most important functions are as follows.

Making a new start
353
Well and *now*, placed at the front of an utterance in ⟨speech⟩, signal a new start in the train of thought:

> [A] You remember that puppy we found?
> [B] Yes.
> [A] W̌ell, we adopted it, and now it has some puppies of its own.

Well here means roughly 'I am now going to tell you something new'.

Well is particularly common when the speaker is asked for an opinion:

> [A] What did you think of that play?
> [B] *Well*, I wasn't really happy about the translation into the television medium.

Now often signals a return to an earlier train of thought:

> Well, that finishes th\`at. *Now* what was the \`other thing I wanted to ask you?

Changing the subject

354

Incidentally or *by the way* ⟨informal⟩ can be used to change the subject:

> I think I've been a bit absent-minded over that letter. *Incidentally,/By the way*, this fax machine doesn't seem to be working properly.

Listing and adding

355

In ⟨writing⟩ and ⟨formal speech⟩:

- You can list a series of points by such adverbs as *firstly* (or *first*), *second(ly)*, *next*, *last(ly)* (or *finally*).

- Phrases such as *to begin with*, *in the second place*, and *to conclude* can also be used.

- Similar to these adverbials are *also, moreover, furthermore, what is more*, etc. which indicate that an additional point is being made (*see* 238):

> Several reasons were given for the change in the attitude of many students in the 1960s. *To begin with*, they feared the outbreak of nuclear war. *Secondly*, they were concerned over the continuing pollution of the environment. Not enough progress, *moreover*, had been made in reducing poverty or racial discrimination ... And *to conclude*, they felt frustrated in their attempts to influence political decisions. ⟨formal, written⟩

Reinforcement

356

Besides, in any case ⟨informal⟩, *in fact* and *anyway* ⟨informal⟩ are other sentence adverbials indicating an additional point in an argument. They are used to reinforce an argument in a situation where a preceding argument might not seem sufficient:

> Ray won't have any proof of my guilt. *Besides*, he doesn't suspect me of having any connection with the recent robberies.

Furthermore ⟨more formal⟩ and *what is more* can be used in a similar way.

Summary and generalization

357

To lead into a brief summary of points already made, you can write *in a word*, *in short*, or *to sum up*:

> The Foundation could be custodian of a central fund of charities. It could plan and finance a stock of books, tapes and films. *In a word*, it could do plenty.

Here is another example, from a book review:

> The techniques discussed are valuable. Sensible stress is laid on preparatory and follow-up work. Each chapter is supported by a well-selected bibliography. *In short*, this is a clearly written textbook that should prove extremely valuable to teachers.

Other linking phrases serve to indicate a generalization from points already made: *in all*, *altogether*, *more generally*, etc. These are used in a similar way to the summary signals. Thus *in all* could replace *in short* in the quotation above.

Explanation

358

A point already made can be explained in three ways:

- by **expanding** and **clarifying** its meanings: *that is, that is to say, i.e.*
- by giving a more **precise description**: *namely, viz.*
- by giving an **illustration**: *for example, for instance*:

> It is important that young children should see things, and not merely read about them. *That is*, the best education is through direct experience and discovery.
> Role-playing can be done for quite a different purpose: to evaluate procedures, regardless of individuals. *For example*, a sales presentation can be evaluated through role-playing.

These forms can also link two structures in apposition (*see* 470–2) in the middle of a sentence:

> A good example is a plant, proverbial for its bitter taste, *namely* wormwood.

Note

The Latin abbreviations *i.e.*, *viz.* and *e.g.* are mainly found in ⟨formal written⟩ texts. They are normally read aloud as 'that is', 'namely', and 'for example', respectively.

Reformulation

359

Sometimes, to make our ideas clearer, we explain or modify them by putting them in other words. Such **reformulation** can be introduced by an adverbial like *in other words, rather, better*:

Be natural. *In other words,* be yourself.
We decided, or *rather* it was decided, to pull the place down.

Linking clauses and sentences

360

We can think of a clause – the unit which may express a statement – as the basic unit of meaning in a discourse. Grammar provides three main ways of putting such units together:

[A] COORDINATION: You can coordinate them by the conjunctions *and, or, but, both . . . and,* etc. (*see* 515–20).
[B] SUBORDINATION: You can subordinate one clause to another (i.e. make it into a subclause, *see* 709–17), using such conjunctions as *when, if,* and *because.*
[C] ADVERBIAL LINK: You can connect the two ideas by using a linking sentence adverbial (*see* 479), such as *yet, moreover,* and *meanwhile.*

Contrast
361

The three methods (coordination, subordination, and adverbial link) are illustrated below for the relation of **contrast** (*see* 211):

[A] The conversation went on *but* Rebecca stopped listening.
[B] *Although* Quebec did not break its ties with the rest of Canada, it did not feel itself part of the Confederation.
The country around Cambridge is flat and not particularly spectacular, *though* it offers easy going to the foot traveller.
[C] In theory, most companies would like to double their profits in a year.
However, few could really handle it, and most companies wouldn't even try.

Note
For a stronger and more emphatic link, occasionally one finds a combination of a sentence adverbial with coordination or subordination:

[A] + [C] He was extremely tired, *but* he was *nevertheless* unable to sleep until after midnight.
[B] + [C] *Although* he was suffering from fatigue as a result of the long journey, *yet* because of the noise, he lay awake in his bed, thinking over the events of the day until the early hours of the morning. ⟨formal, rather rhetorical⟩

Choice between coordination, subordination and linking adverbial
362

[A] **Coordination** is often a 'looser' connection than the others, because it is more vague (*see* 371) and less emphatic. It is more characteristic of ⟨informal⟩ than of ⟨formal⟩ style.

[B] **Subordination** tends to give a clause a less important part in the information conveyed by a sentence. Thus an adverbial subordinate clause is often used when the information in that clause is already wholly or partly known or expected by the hearer (*see* 405–7):

> They gave her something warm to wear, and she went to change in the bathroom. *When she came back*, the dinner was already on the table.

[C] **Adverbial links** are often used to connect longer stretches of language, perhaps whole sentences which themselves contain coordinate or subordinate clauses (*see* example [C] in 361).

Other relations of meaning
363
Here are some other examples of meaning-links to show how English offers a choice between coordination, subordination, and adverbial links. In the case of coordination (and sometimes of subordination), we place an adverbial in brackets where it can be added to make the link more specific. (Cross-references are given to where these meaning-links are discussed in Section A.)

Time-when (*see* 151–60)
364

[A] Penelope stopped the car *and* (*then*) rolled down the windows.
[B] *After* chatting to Davidson for a few minutes longer, he went back to his office.
(C) She studied the letter for a long time. *Then* she turned back to Wilson and smiled.

Cause, reason, result (*see* 197–207)
365

[A] She ran out of money, and (*therefore*) had to look for a job.
[B] *Since* a customer had arrived in the shop, Samantha said no more.
The prisoners had a secret radio, so (*that*) they could receive messages from the outside world.
[C] When children reach the age of 11 or 12, they start growing fast. They *therefore* need more protein.

Positive condition (*see* 207–8)
366
The conjunction *and* can express a condition, but only in some contexts such as commanding, advising, etc.:

[A] Take this medicine, and (*then*) you'll feel better. ⟨informal⟩
[B] *If* you take this medicine, you'll feel better.
[C] You ought to take your medicine regularly, as the doctor ordered. You'd feel better, *then*. ⟨informal⟩

Negative condition (*see* 209)
367
Or can be used to express a negative condition in the same contexts as in 366[A].

[A] You'd better put your overcoat on, *or* (*else*) you'll catch a cold. ⟨informal⟩
[B] *Unless* you put on your overcoat, you'll catch a cold.
[C] I should wear an overcoat if I were you; *otherwise*, you'll catch a cold.

Condition + contrast (*see* 213–4)
368

[B] *However* much advice we give him, he (*still*) does exactly what he wants.
[C] It doesn't matter how much advice we give him: he *still* does exactly what he wants.
(Coordination alone cannot indicate this meaning.)

Addition (*see* 238–42)
369
[A] She's (*both*) a professional artist *and* a first-rate teacher (*see* 520).
   ~ She's *not only* a professional artist, *but* (*also*) a first-rate teacher.
[B] *As well as* (being) a professional artist, she's (*also*) a first-rate teacher.
[C] She's well known all over the country as a professional artist. *What's more*, she's a first-rate teacher.

Alternatives (compare 242)
370

[A] We can (*either*) meet this afternoon, *or* (*else*) we can discuss the matter at dinner (*see* 520).
[C] Would you like us to have a meeting about the matter this afternoon? *Otherwise* we could discuss it at dinner.
   I may be able to cross the mountains into Switzerland. *Alternatively*, I may get a boat at Marseilles.

(This meaning cannot be expressed by subordination.)

'General purpose' links

371
As you can see from 364–6, 369, *and* is a 'general purpose' linking word, which can adapt its meaning according to context. Any positive link between two ideas can be expressed by *and*. English has three other methods of vague or 'general purpose' connection of this kind. They are:

[A] **Relative clauses** (*see* 686–94)
[B] **Participle and verbless clauses** (*see* 493–4).
[C] Grammatically **unlinked** clauses.

Relative clauses
372
Notice the equivalence between a coordinate clause with *and*, and a **non-restrictive** relative clause (*see* 110–11, 693):

> We have arrived at the hotel, and find it very comfortable.
> ~ We have arrived at the hotel, *which we find very comfortable.*

The same equivalence is seen in **sentence relative** clauses (*see* 694). Here the relative pronoun points back to a whole clause or sentence:

> He's spending too much time on sport, and that's not good for his school work.
> ~ He's spending too much time on sport, *which is not good for his school work.*

Restrictive clauses also have a flexible connecting function. In the sentences [1–3], the implied links are reason, time-when, and condition:

- **Reason:**
  I don't like people *who drive fast cars.*   [1]
  ('Because they drive fast cars, I don't like them')
- **Time-when:**
  The man *I saw* was wearing a hat.   [2]
  ('When I saw him, he was wearing a hat')
- **Condition:**
  Anyone *who bets on horses* deserves to lose money.   [3]
  ('If anyone bets on horses, he or she deserves to lose money')

Participle and verbless clauses
373
These clauses (*see* 493–4), more characteristic of ⟨formal written⟩ English, also have a varied 'general purpose' linking function, as these examples show:

- **Reason:**
  Being a farmer, he has to get up early.
  ('As he is a farmer . . .')
- **Time-when:**
  Cleared, the site will be very valuable. ⟨rather formal⟩
  ('When it is cleared . . .')
- **Condition:**
  Cleared, the site would be very valuable. ⟨rather formal⟩
  ('If it were cleared . . .')
- **Means:**
  Using a sharp axe, they broke down the door. ⟨rather formal⟩
  ('By using a sharp axe . . .')

- **Reason:**

    She stared at the floor, *too nervous to reply.* ⟨rather formal⟩
    ('. . . because she was too nervous . . .')

Unlinked clauses

374

Two neighbouring clauses may be grammatically unlinked. For example, they may be separated in writing by a period (.) or a semi-colon (;) a colon (:) or a dash (–). But this does not mean there is no connection of meaning between them; it means, rather, that the connection is implicit, and has to be inferred by the hearer or reader.

In ⟨informal speech⟩, a speaker frequently relies on such implied connections, whereas in ⟨writing⟩, the writer would often make the connection clear by sentence adverbial or coordination. These examples may be compared with the [C] sentences of 364–70 (the 'missing link' is indicated in small type in [square brackets]):

> He loaded the pistol carefully; [then] he took aim . . . a shot rang out. (TIME)
> He had to look for a job – [because] he had run out of money. (REASON)
> Take this medicine: [if you do] it'll make you feel better. (CONDITION)

Cross-reference and omission

375

Clauses are often connected not only because of a meaning-link of the kinds we have considered, but because they SHARE some content, e.g. they may be talking about the same person:

> *My brother* was wearing a raincoat. So *my brother* didn't get wet.

We can, if we like, link these two sentences into one sentence, linking them with an adverb like *so*, without changing them: *My brother was wearing a raincoat, so my brother didn't get wet.* But generally, we avoid repeating the shared words and content, either

- by **cross-reference** (using a pronoun such as *he*); or

- by **omitting** the repeated element(s):

> *My brother* was wearing a raincoat, and so (*he*) didn't get wet.

Cross-reference and omission are very useful and important: (A) they shorten the message, and (B) they can make the connections of meaning more easy to grasp. We may say that they make the structure of the sentence 'tighter'. The general rule is: CROSS-REFER AND OMIT WHEREVER YOU CAN, EXCEPT WHERE THIS LEADS TO AMBIGUITY. We now consider some of the ways in which the English language allows these things. We consider cross-reference and omission together, and see how repetition can be avoided by these methods. Sometimes one method is available, sometimes the other, and sometimes both.

Cross-reference to noun phrases
3rd person pronouns
376
The personal pronouns *he, she, it, they,* etc. (*see* 619–22) cross-refer to noun phrases, and agree with them in number and/or gender (*see* 529, 597–601). In these examples, the noun phrase and the pronoun are in *italics*:

> *Henrietta* looked down at *her left hand. It* was covered with blood.
> *The new psychology professor* kept *her* distance. *She* did not call *students* by *their* first names.
> *Bill* gave an inward groan. *He* felt that the situation was getting beyond *him.*
> *Millions of flies* were on *their* way towards us.

Notice that the plural pronouns *they, them,* etc. substitute not only for plural noun phrases, but for coordinated singular noun phrases such as *Red* and *Handley*:

> I know *Red and Handley* well. *They* are both painters.
> In the morning, *Power and Ross* rose at dawn and began *their* day's work.

Note
[a] On the choice between *he, she* and *they* when sex is unspecified, *see* 96.
[b] Reflexive pronouns (*himself, themselves,* etc.) (*see* 626–8) and relative pronouns (*see* 686–94) behave in a similar way to personal pronouns in signalling cross-reference:

> *He* hurt *himself.*/*She* hurt *herself.*/*They* hurt *themselves.*
> *The man who* was injured . . ./*The house that* was destroyed . . .

1st and 2nd person pronouns
377
Occasionally, 1st and 2nd person pronouns substitute for coordinate noun phrases. If a 1st person pronoun is present in the noun phrase, agreement is with the 1st person:

> *You and I* ought to get together sometime and share *our* ideas.
> *My wife and I* are going to Argentina. *We* hope to stay with some friends.

If a 2nd person pronoun is present without a 1st person pronoun, agreement is with the 2nd person pronoun:

> *You and John* can stop work now. *You* can both eat your lunch in the kitchen.
> Do *you and your husband* have a car? I may have to beg a lift from *you.*

Special cases
378

- **Quantifiers** (*see* 675–80). Sometimes a plural pronoun cross-refers to quantifier pronouns like *everybody*, *somebody*, *no one*, and *anyone*.

    Everybody looked after *themselves*.

This compares with the more ⟨formal⟩ use of singular pronouns such as *he or she* (*see* 96):

    One of the most important things anyone can do in business is consider *his or her* future connections.

- **Group nouns**. For cross-reference a singular noun referring to a group of people can be treated as a singular inanimate noun (when we are thinking of the group as a unit):

    It is a family *which* traces *its* history from the Norman Conquest (*see* 510).

It can also be treated as a plural human noun (when we are thinking of the members of the group):

    They are a family *who* quarrel among *themselves*.

Quantifier pronouns as substitutes for noun phrases
379
Other pronouns such as *one*, *some*, *each*, *none* (*see* 676) can act as **substitutes** for a noun phrase (we could alternatively treat most of these cases as omissions of some part of the phrase):

- **Substitution for singular count noun phrases**
    [A] Would you like *a cup of tea*?
    [B] No, thanks – I've just had *one*. (*one* = 'a cup of tea')

- **Substitution for plural count noun phrases**

    Can you give me *a few stamps*? I need *some* for these postcards. ('some stamps')
    The museum has *twenty rooms*, *each* portraying a period in the country's history. ('each room')
    We lost *most of the games*, but not quite *all*. ('all of them')
    Proust and James are great novelists, but I like Tolstoy better than *either*. ('either of them')
    Two members of the panel later told the Court about receiving anonymous telephone calls. *Neither* was seated on the jury. ('Neither of the two members')
    These books are heavy. You carry one *half*, and I'll carry the *other*. ('You carry half of them, and I'll carry the other half of them')

John and I went looking for *mushrooms*. He found *a few*, I found *several more*, and we soon had *enough* for breakfast.

- **Substitution for mass noun phrases**
  Some of the equipment has been damaged, but *none* has been lost.
  I'd like *some paper*, if you have *any*.

380

- **Substitutes for nouns and parts of noun phrases**
  The pronoun *one* (680) can substitute for a noun, as well as for a whole noun phrase:

  Have you seen any *knives*? I need a sharp *one*. ('a sharp knife')
  She moved down the row of freight cars, checking for the serial
      number which corresponded to the *one* ('serial number') Teufel
      had written down for her.

The plural of *one* in this sense is *ones*:

  Plastic *pots* are usually more expensive than clay *ones*.

Notice that *one* cannot replace mass nouns; instead, they are omitted: *Which wine would you like? The red or the white?* ('The red wine or the white wine?')

381
Sometimes there is a choice (with count nouns) between *one* and omission:

  This house is bigger than my last (one).
  Navneet had a shop in Hong Kong and another (one) in Bombay.
  His bus broke down, and he had to wait for over two hours for the next
      (one).
  I know her two older children, but I don't know the youngest (one).

382
With following modifiers, the pronouns *that* and *those* can act as substitutes with definite meaning (= 'the one', 'the ones'). *That* as a substitute pronoun always has non-personal reference:

  The hole was about as big as *that* ('the hole') made by a rocket. ⟨rather
      formal⟩
  The paintings of Gaugin's Tahiti period are more famous than *those*
      (= 'the ones') he painted in France. ⟨rather formal⟩

That can also be used as a substitute with a mass noun:

  The plumage of the male pheasant is far more colourful than *that*
      (= 'the plumage') of the female. ⟨rather formal⟩

These uses of *that* and *those* are rather ⟨formal⟩, and are largely restricted to ⟨written⟩ English.

Substitutes for structures containing a verb
The auxiliary verb do
383
The dummy auxiliary verb *do* (479) can act as a substitute for the whole of a clause apart from the subject:

> He cooks as well as she̱ does. ('as she cooks')
>
> [A] Did you read that book in the end?   [B] Yes I di̱d.
>
> [A] Who wants to play tennis this afternoon? $\begin{cases} \text{I do.} \\ \text{I don't.} \end{cases}$

You can also omit the whole clause following the subject:

> He can *cook* as well as $\begin{cases} \text{she. } \langle\text{formal}\rangle \\ \text{her. } \langle\text{informal}\rangle \end{cases}$
>
> [A] Who wants to play tennis?   [B] $\begin{cases} \text{Me. } \langle\text{informal}\rangle \\ \text{Not me. } \langle\text{informal}\rangle \end{cases}$

Notice that in ⟨informal⟩ English, the pronoun subject is changed from *I* (etc.) to its objective form (*me*, etc.) when the rest of the sentence is omitted.

Do can also substitute for the part of a clause excluding subject and adverbial:

> [A] *Have* you *written to your father* yet?
>
> [B] Yes, I *did* last week. ('I wrote to my father . . .')

Occasionally *do* acts as a substitute for a verb phrase alone:

> She likes him better than she *does* me. (*does* = 'likes')

Omission following an operator
384
In cases like those in 383, you can use other auxiliaries in a parallel position to *do*. That is, you can omit the whole or part of the sentence following an auxiliary:

> I'*ll open a bank account* if you̱ wi̍ll. (= '. . . if you will do so')
>
> He *can cook* as well as she̱ can. (= 'can cook')
>
> [A] He *is working* late this week.   [B] Yes, he *was* la̍st week, to̍o.
> (= . . . 'was working late last week, too')
>
> You *can play* in the garden, but you *mustn't* in the garage.
> (= '. . . mustn't play in the garage')

Do and the other auxiliaries are unstressed, except in cases of affirmation and denial (*see* 264–5), or where they have some sort of contrastive meaning:

[A] Are you going to clean the car?

[B] I cŏuld, and ŏught to, but I don't think I wĭll.

The omission also occurs after two or three auxiliaries:

[A] Is the kettle boiling?   [B] It mày bé. ('. . . be boiling')

[A] Did you lock the door?   [B] No, I shŏuld háve, but I forgot.

Note

[a] *Be* as a main verb (*see* 482) cannot be omitted after an auxiliary:
   If they're not asleep, they shŏuld be. (= '. . . be asleep')

[b] In ⟨BrE⟩, *do* or *done* is sometimes added after another auxiliary:
   He can't promise to come tonight, but he mày *do*.
   [A] Would you please unlock the door?   [B] I hàve *done*.

The main verb do: do it, do that, do so
385

The main verb *do* (*see* 479) acts as a substitute for a main verb, normally a verb denoting some action or activity. *Do* requires an object, which may be *it, that,* or *so*:

If we want to preserve our power, this is the way to *do it*.

They have promised to increase pensions by 10 per cent. If they *do so*, it will make a big difference to old people.

Do that is generally more emphatic and ⟨informal⟩:

They say he sleeps in his shoes and socks. Why ever does he *do thàt?*

It's easy for you to talk – you travel around the world. We would like to *do that* too.

Substitutes for *that*-clauses

So *after a verb, and omission after a verb*
386

So is a substitute for *that*-clauses representing reported statements, beliefs, assumptions, emotions, etc.:

The government won't provide the money – I have heard the minister *say so*. ('. . . say that the government won't . . .')

It's silly, childish, running after them like that. I *told Ben so*. ('. . . told him that it's silly . . .')

[A] Has Ivan gone home?

[B] I thĭnk só./I suppòse só./I hòpe só./I'm afrăid só.

Not replaces *so* in negative clauses: I *hope not*, I'm *afraid not*, etc. But, with verbs taking transferred negation (*see* 587), it is more natural to say: I *don't think so*; I *don't suppose so*; etc.:

[A] Are there any questions you want to ask us, Ms Blake?
[B] No, *I don't think so.*

In sentences expressing certainty and doubt (*see* 294–5) we cannot use *so*, but have to say: *I'm sure they are*; *I'm sure of it*; *I doubt if they are*; *I doubt it*; etc.

In comparative clauses (505), the whole of a *than*-clause can be omitted:

He's older than I thought ('. . . than I thought he was').
The journey took longer than we had hoped.

Also, after the verbs *know*, *ask*, and *tell*, a whole *that*-clause is frequently omitted in conversation:

[A] She's having a baby.   [B] I *know.*

[A] { How did you *hear?*   [B] She *told* me (so) herself. Why
    { How did you *hear that?*   do you *ask?*

So cannot be used after *know* and *ask*.

Substitutes for *wh*-clauses
387
The whole of a *wh*-clause following the *wh*-word can be omitted:

Someone has hidden my notebook, but I don't know *who/where/why*.
(= 'I don't know who has hidden my notebook', etc.)

This cannot be done with *whether* and *if*.

Substitutes for *to*-infinitive clause
388
With infinitive clauses, you can omit the whole of the clause following *to*:

[A] Why don't you come and stay with us?
[B] I'd love to (do so).

You can *borrow* my pen, if you want to (do so).

If this pain gets much worse, I shan't be able to *move around* much.
    The doctor has told me not to (do so), anyway.
Somebody ought to *help you*. Shall I ask Peter to (do so)?

As we see, there is a choice between including *do so* ⟨more formal⟩ and omitting it. With some verbs, such as *want* and *ask*, the whole of the infinitive clause, including *to*, can be omitted, especially in ⟨informal⟩ English:

You can borrow my pen, if you want. ⟨informal⟩
Shall I ask Peter? ⟨informal⟩

It, that, this as clause substitutes
389
The definite pronouns *it*, *that*, and *this* are widely used as substitutes for clauses as well as for noun phrases (*see* 94, 99, 376):

> *If you make a sound*, you'll regret *it*. ('regret making a sound')

> [A] *She's having a baby.*
> [B] How do you know th*a*t? (i.e. '. . . know that she's having a baby')

> After many weeks of rain, *the dam burst. This* resulted in widespread flooding and much loss of livestock and property. ('The bursting of the dam resulted in . . .')

Other strategies of omission
390
Other structures which allow us to shorten a sentence by omission are coordinated structures, non-finite clauses, and verbless clauses. All these structures will be further discussed in Part Three (515–20, 493–4), so here we merely give a few examples of the varied types of omission that occur in them, showing how these provide briefer alternatives to substitution and repetition.

Omission through coordination
391
(The elements which are or can be omitted in coordination are in *italics*.)

> Freda ate the food but left the drink.
>   ('Freda ate the food, but *she* left the drink.')
> Particular attention was given to the nuclear tests conference and to the question of disarmament.
>   ('Particular attention was given to the nuclear tests conference and *particular attention was given* to the question of disarmament.')
> Peter cut himself a slice of bread and some cheese.
>   ('Peter cut himself a slice of bread; *he* (also) *cut himself* some cheese'.)
> She is not only a trained mathematician, but a good singer.
>   ('She is not only a trained mathematician, but *she is* a good singer.')
> Either Germany or Brazil will win the World Cup.
>   ('Germany will win the World Cup; or (else) Brazil *will do so*.')
> Tom washes and irons his own shirts.
>   ('Tom washes his own shirts; he irons *them* (too).')

In general, the same omissions cannot be made when one of the clauses is subordinate to the others. Compare:

> She was exhausted and went to sleep.

BUT NOT:

> *She was so exhausted that went to sleep.

In the subclause we have to repeat the subject:

> She was so exhausted (that) *she* went to sleep.

But there are a few cases where subclauses follow the coordinate clause pattern:

> The rain stopped, *though* not the wind.

Omission in non-finite clauses
392
Non-finite clauses (*see* 493) have no operator (*see* 609–12), and most of them have no conjunction or subject. Thus in comparison with finite subclauses they are more economical and avoid repetition; *-ing* clauses and *-ed* clauses, probably for this reason, are particularly favoured in ⟨formal or written⟩ styles of English. We now illustrate these points with equivalent finite clauses.

- *to*-INFINITIVE CLAUSE: I hope *to get in touch with you soon.*
  (= 'I hope *that I will get in touch with you soon*'.)

- *-ing* CLAUSE: *Coming home late one evening*, I heard something which made my blood freeze in horror. (= '*When I was coming home . . .*')

- *-ed* CLAUSE: The man *injured by the bullet* was taken to hospital.
  (= 'The man *who was* injured by the bullet . . .')

393
The same applies to non-finite clauses introduced by a subordinator:

- *-ing* CLAUSE: It's a trick I learned *while recovering from an illness.*
  (= '. . . *while I was recovering . . .*')

- *-ed* CLAUSE: *Though defeated*, she remained a popular leader of the party.
  ⟨rather formal⟩ (= 'Though *she had been* defeated . . .')

Omission in verbless clauses
394
Verbless clauses (*see* 494) have no verb and usually no subject.

> *Whether right or wrong*, he usually wins the argument.
>   (= 'Whether *he is* right or wrong . . .')
> *A man of few words*, Uncle George declined to express an opinion.
>   ⟨formal⟩
>   (= '*Being* a man of few words/*As he was* a man of few words . . .')

Verbless clauses, like participial clauses, often belong to a more ⟨formal⟩ style, and belong mainly to ⟨written⟩ English.

Note
Not all subordinators can introduce participial and verbless clauses. For example, *because, as,* and *since* (as conjunctions of reason) cannot. Compare:

| *Since she left school*, she's had several different jobs. | [1] |
| *Since you know the answer*, why didn't you speak up? | [2] |

In [1], the clause of time can be replaced by *Since leaving school*, but in [2], the clause of reason cannot be replaced by * *Since knowing the answer*.

Presenting and focusing information

395
We now deal with the ways in which meanings can be presented and arranged for effective communication. For a message to be properly understood,

- the message has to be cut up into individual pieces of information (*see* 396–8)
- the ideas have to be given the right emphasis (*see* 399–409)
- the ideas have to be put in the right order (*see* 410–32).

Pieces of information

396
In ⟨written⟩ English, a **piece of information** can be defined as a piece of language which is separated from what goes before and from what follows by punctuation marks (.,:;–?!), and which does not itself contain any punctuation marks. In ⟨spoken⟩ English, a piece of information can be defined as a **tone unit** (*see* 37), i.e. a unit of intonation containing a **nucleus** (*see* 36). Notice the difference, in ⟨written⟩ English, between:

| Mr Average has a wife and two children. | [1] |
| Mr Average has a wife; he also has two children. | [2] |

In a sense (*see* 369, 374) [1] and [2] 'mean the same', but [1] presents the message as ONE piece of information, while [2] presents it as TWO pieces of information, separated by a punctuation mark (;). In ⟨speech⟩, the same contrast is seen in:

| He has a wife and two chìldren \| | ONE TONE UNIT | [1a] |
| He has a wìfe\|he also has two chìldren\| | TWO TONE UNITS | [2a] |

Dividing the message into tone units

397
There is no exact match between punctuation in ⟨writing⟩ and tone units in ⟨speech⟩. Speech is more variable in its structuring of information than writing. Cutting up speech into tone units depends on:

- the speed at which you are speaking,
- what emphasis you want to give to parts of the message,
- the length of grammatical units.

A single sentence may have just one tone unit, like [1a]; but when the length of a sentence goes beyond a few words, it is difficult not to divide it into two or more separate pieces of information.

|The man to̱ld us|we could park he̱re.|

|The man to̱ld us|we could pa̱rk|at the ra̱ilway station.|

|The man to̱ld us|we could pa̱rk|in that stṟeet|over the̱re.|

398
For guidance, the following general rules are useful in knowing when to start a new tone unit:

- If a sentence begins with a **clause or adverbial phrase**, give the clause or adverbial element a separate tone unit:

    |*Last yéar*|the warfare gre̱w.|

- If a sentence contains a **non-restrictive modifier** (*see* 99–102), e.g. a non-restrictive relative clause (*see* 693), give the modifier a separate tone unit:

    |The emergency services were hampered by thick smo̱ke, | *which spread quickly*|*through the sta̱tion.*|

- Similarly, give any **medial phrase or clause** a separate tone unit:

    |The go̱vernment, | *in Mr Hǒwell's view,*|must ensúre | that we have enough e̱nergy.|

- A **vocative** or **linking adverb** usually has its own tone unit (or at least ends a tone unit):

    |Mǎry|are you cóming?|

    |The poli̱ce | *howéver* | thought she was gu̱ilty.|

- Give a separate tone unit to **a clause or long noun phrase acting as a subject**:

    | *What we néed* | is plenty of ti̱me.|

- If **two or more clauses are coordinated**, give them each a separate tone unit:

    |He opened the dóor | and walked straight i̱n.|

But the overriding rule is: give a separate tone unit to each separate piece of information.

End-focus and contrastive focus
399
The nucleus is the most important part of a tone unit: it marks the **focus of information**, or the part of the unit to which the speaker especially draws the hearer's attention. Normally, the nucleus is at the end of the tone unit; or, to be more precise, on the last major-class word (noun, main verb, adjective, or

adverb (*see* 744), in the tone unit. Which syllable of the word is stressed, if it has more than one syllable, is determined by ordinary conventions of word stress: to'*day*, '*working*, '*photograph*, *conver*'*sation*, etc. This neutral position of the nucleus, which we see in nearly all the examples in 413, we call **end-focus**.

Note
Two or more nouns together (*see* 651) often behave, for stress purposes, like a single word (i.e. like a noun compound), with the main stress on the first noun: '*export records*; '*building plan*; '*traffic problem*. (But this is not an invariable rule: contrast *town* '*hall*, *country*'*house*, *lawn*'*tennis*, etc.)

400

But in other cases you may shift the nucleus to an earlier part of the tone unit. You may do this when you want to draw attention to an earlier part of the tone unit, usually to contrast it with something already mentioned, or understood in the context. For this reason, we call earlier placing of the nucleus **contrastive focus**. Here are some examples:

[A] |It must have been last Monday.|

[B] |No.|It's next Monday.| [1]

Have you ever driven a sports car? |Yes,| I've often driven one.| [2]

In cases like the following examples, contrastive meaning is signalled by a fall-rise tone (*see* 41), with a fall on the nucleus and a rise on the last stressed syllable in the tone unit:

Those parcels – one of them has arrived.|(But the other one hasn't

arrived) [3]

|After you get married,|people stop giving you things.|

(In a discussion of wedding presents.)   [4]

In other sentences, there can be a double contrast, each contrast indicated by its own nucleus:

|Her father|is Austrian,|but her mother|is French.| [5]

401

Sometimes contrastive focus draws attention to a whole phrase (e.g. *her mother* in [5]); at other times, it is a single word that receives the focus (e.g. *often* in [2]). Even words like personal pronouns, conjunctions, prepositions, and auxiliaries, which are not normally stressed at all, can receive nuclear stress for special contrastive purposes:

(I've never been to Paris)|but I will go there|*some* day.| [6]

[A] (What did she say to Kath?)

[B] |She was speaking to me|(not to Kath).   [7]

I know he works in an office,|but who does he work *for?*| [8]

(I don't know if you mean to see Peter.)|But *if* you sée him, please

give him my good wishes.   [9]

In some cases, e.g. [7] and [8], contrastive focus comes later rather than earlier than normal end-focus. Thus the normal way to say *Who does he work for?* [8] would be with focus on the verb, not the preposition:

Who does he work for?

Note
In exceptional cases, contrastive stress in a word of more than one syllable may shift to a syllable which does not normally have word stress. For example, if you want to make a contrast between the two words normally pronounced *bur'eaucracy* and *au'tocracy* you may do so as follows:

|I'm afraid that bureaucracy|can be worse than autocracy.|

Given and new information
402
We can roughly divide the information in a message into

- **Given information** (something which the speaker assumes the hearer knows about already) and

- **New information** (something which the speaker does not assume the hearer knows about already).

In [7] above, 'She was speaking' is given information: it is already given by the preceding clause; in [9], 'you see him' is given information for the same reason.

As new information is obviously what is most important in a message, it receives the information focus (i.e. nucleus), whereas old information does not. Naturally, personal pronouns and other substitute words, because they refer to something already mentioned or understood, normally count as given information.

Note
Notice that given information and new information are what the speaker *presents* as given and new respectively. What *in fact* the hearer knows or assumes may be a different thing. For example, consider this dialogue:

[A] Do you like Picásso?

[B] No, I hàte modern painting.

The position of the nucleus here means that speaker [B] takes it as 'given' that Picasso is a modern painter.

Information given by situation

403

'Given information' is not just information which has already been mentioned or suggested. We may extend this notion to include information which is 'given' by the situation outside language. In this respect 'given' information is like definite meaning (*see* 82–99), and there is indeed a strong connection between given information and definiteness. In the following examples, for which we give the most natural intonation, the definite items *today, here,* and *mine* in [10], [11], [12] do not have a nuclear stress because their meaning is given by the situation. In contrast, the items *Saturday, factory,* and *sister's* in [10a], [11a], and [12a] are most likely to be new information, and therefore to receive nuclear stress:

|What are you dòing today?| [10]

|What are you doing on Sàturday?| [10a]

|I wòrk here.| [11]

|I work in a fàctory.| [11a]

|Carol is a frìend of mine.| [12]

|Carol is a friend of my sìster's.| [12a]

But the definite items *today,* etc., could have nuclear stress if some contrast were implied:

(I know what you did yesterday,)|but what are you doing todày?| [10b]

(I used to work in a factory,)|but now I work hère.| [11b]

404

In other examples, the information given by the situation outside language is more a matter of what is expected in a given context:

|The kèttle's boiling.| |The pòstman's called.|

|Is your fàther at home?| |Dìnner's réady.|

In a natural situation, the final part of each of these sentences conveys little information, and therefore does not receive the nucleus. In a home, the one thing to announce about kettles is that they are 'boiling'; and the one thing you expect the postman to do is to 'call' etc. Therefore the nucleus occurs, contrary to end-focus, on the earlier and more informative part of the sentence.

Main and subsidiary information

405

Degrees or levels of 'informativeness' are also relevant to the choice of **tone** (*see* 38–41) on the nucleus. We tend to use a falling tone to give emphasis to the main information in a sentence, and a rising tone (or, with more emphasis, a fall-rise tone) to give subsidiary or less important information, i.e. information which is more predictable from the context. Subordinate clauses and adverbials often give information which is subsidiary to the idea in the rest of the main clause:

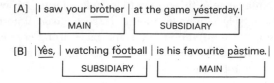

Subsidiary information may either precede or follow the main information. Speaker [B] could also say here:

|Yès, | his favourite pàstime | is watching fóotball.|

|_____MAIN_____| |____SUBSIDIARY____|

Adverbials as main and subsidiary information
406
Adverbials following the main clause often have a rising tone to indicate subsidiary information added as an afterthought:

|It was snòwing|when we arríved.|

|I will get excèedingly drunk|if I drink shérry.|

But a final adverbial clause can also occasionally contain the main information:

|She had only just finished dréssing|when her gùests arrived.|

Shorter final adverbials are often included in the same tone unit as the rest of the clause, and may bear the main focus:

|She plays the piano bèautifully.|

Main and subsidiary information in writing
407
In ⟨writing⟩, you cannot point to important information by using intonation, so you have to rely on ordering and subordination of clauses instead. The general rule is that the most important new information is saved up to the end, comparable to the **end focus** principle in ⟨speech⟩. Thus the sentence finishes with a sort of climax (here indicated by *italics*):

> Arguments in favour of a new building plan, said the mayor, included suggestions that if a new shopping centre were not built, the city's traffic problems *would soon become unmanageable.*

In reading this sentence aloud, it is natural to put a rising or fall-rise tone on all points of information except the last, which receives a falling tone.

|. . . bǔilding plan|. . . máyor|. . . suggéstions|. . . búilt|. . . tràffic
próblems|. . . unmànageable|

End-focus and end-weight
408
When deciding in which order to place the ideas in a sentence, there are two principles to remember:

- **End-focus** (*see* 399): the new or most important idea or message in a piece of information should be placed towards the end, where in speech the nucleus of the tone unit normally falls. In ⟨writing⟩ and prepared ⟨speech⟩, as we saw in 407, this principle can be applied not just to a single piece of information, but to a whole sentence containing many pieces of information. A sentence is generally more effective (especially in ⟨writing⟩) if the main point is saved up to the end.

- **End-weight**: The more 'weighty' part(s) of a sentence should be placed towards the end (*see* 409, 416, 424–7, 429). Otherwise the sentence may sound awkward and unbalanced. The 'weight' of an element can be defined in terms of its length (i.e. number of syllables or words).

409
Both end-focus and end-weight are useful guiding principles, not invariable rules. As we have said, although end-focus is normal, you are allowed in speech to shift the nucleus to an earlier position in the tone unit, for **contrastive** focus. Similarly, there are exceptions to end-weight:

> My home was that wasteland of derelict buildings behind the
>   morgue.   [1]
> That wasteland of derelict buildings behind the morgue was my
>   home.   [2]

In [1], a long complement phrase (*that wasteland of derelict buildings behind the morgue*) follows a short subject (*my home*) and a short verb (*was*). This sentence keeps to the principle of end-weight. But in [2], the long noun phrase comes first. This sentence breaks the end-weight principle, but it could easily be said by someone wanting to place the focus of information on *my home*. In such a case the two principles of end-weight and end-focus conflict. Generally, however, the two principles work together: it is usual for a short element in a sentence (e.g. a pronoun) to have less information than a longer element. For example, in

> I've been reading *a fascinating biography of Catherine the Great*

the subject (*I*) carries far less information than the long object noun phrase (in italics).

Order and emphasis

Topic
410
In the rest of this chapter, we will show that English grammar has quite a number

of ways to arrange the message for the right order and the right emphasis. Because of the principles of end-focus and end-weight, the **final** position in a sentence or clause is, usually, the most important for communication. But the **first** position is the second most important, because it is usually the part of the sentence which is familiar territory from which we begin the sentence as a mental 'journey into the unknown'. This is why we call the first element in a clause (leaving aside conjunctions and many adverbials, *see* 414, Note) the **topic**. In most statements, the topic is the subject of the sentence. If the statement has only one tone unit, usually the topic does not receive focus, because it often contains old (given) information, and links the statement in meaning to what was said before:

But sometimes topic and information focus coincide, and in this case, the topic is especially prominent:

Fronted topic

411

Instead of the subject, you may make another element the topic, by moving it to the front of the sentence. This shift gives the element a kind of psychological prominence, and has three different effects:

- emphatic topic (*see* 412)
- contrastive topic (*see* 413)
- semi-given topic (*see* 414)

Emphatic topic

412

In ⟨informal⟩ conversation, it is quite common for a speaker to front an element (particularly a complement) and to give it nuclear stress, thus giving it double emphasis:

|Very strange | his eyes looked.|⎤ (∼ His eyes looked very strange) [1]
|An utter fool I felt | too.| ⎬ (TOPIC = COMPLEMENT)   [2]
|Relaxation you call it.| ⎦   [3]
|Excellent food they serve here.| (∼ They serve excellent food here) [4]
                              (TOPIC = OBJECT)

It is as if the speaker says the most important thing in his or her mind first, adding the rest of the sentence as an afterthought. The ordering of the elements here is CSV (in [1] and [2]), CSVO (in [3]), and OSVA (in [4]), instead of the normal order SVC, SVOC, SVO (*see* 506–8).

Contrastive topic

413
Here the fronting helps to point dramatically to a contrast between two things mentioned in neighbouring sentences or clauses, which often have parallel structure:

|Sòme things | we'll tèll you| (~ We'll tell you some things)
                                    (TOPIC = OBJECT)

|but sŏme | you'll have to find out about yoursèlf.|
                    (TOPIC = PREPOSITIONAL COMPLEMENT)

|Blòggs | my náme is| (TOPIC = COMPLEMENT)
  so Blŏggs |you might as well càll me.|

|Wìllingly | he'll nèver do it| (TOPIC = ADVERBIAL)
  (he'll have to be fòrced.)

|Rìch |I mày be| (TOPIC = COMPLEMENT)
  (but that doesn't mean I'm happy.)

This construction is not very common, and is typical of ⟨rhetorical⟩ speech.

Semi-given topic

414
Another type of fronting is found in more ⟨formal⟩, especially ⟨written⟩ English:

Most of these problems a computer could solve easily.
                                    (TOPIC = OBJECT)   [1]
  (~ A computer could easily solve most of these problems.)
(A thousand delegates are too many for corporate thinking,) but
  corporate thinking there must be if all members are to have a
  voice.   (TOPIC = SUBJECT/COMPLEMENT)   [2]
Everything that can be done the administration has attended to
  already.   (TOPIC = PREPOSITIONAL OBJECT)   [3]

The fronting here is more negative: a less important idea is shifted to the front so that end-focus can fall on another, more important idea (*easily* [1], *voice* [2], *already* [3]). The word *this* or *these* (as in *most of these problems*) is often present in the fronted topic, showing that it contains given information. Nevertheless, the topic receives a kind of secondary emphasis as the starting-point of the sentence.

Note
We do not normally consider an initial adverbial to be a 'fronted topic', because many adverbials can occur fairly freely in front of the subject (*see* 451):

Yesterday John was late for school.

But some adverbials which are closely connected with the verb, such as those of manner and direction, do not usually occur in front position. These may be said to be 'fronted' for special prominence in clauses like

Willingly he'll never do it.
The moment had come. *Upon the ensuing interview* the future would depend. ⟨formal, rhetorical⟩

Inversion

415

Fronting is often accompanied by **inversion**; that is, not only the topic element, but the verb phrase, or part of it, is moved before the subject. There are two types of inversion:

SUBJECT-VERB INVERSION

SUBJECT	VERB	X	...	➤	X	VERB	SUBJECT	...
The rain	came	down	(in torrents).		Down	came	the rain	(in torrents).

SUBJECT-OPERATOR INVERSION

SUBJECT	OPERATOR	X	...	➤	X	OPERATOR	SUBJECT	...
I	have	never	seen him so angry.		Never	have	I	seen him so angry.
I	—	never	saw him so angry.		Never	did	I	see him so angry.

Subject-verb inversion

416

Subject-verb inversion is normally limited as follows:

- The verb phrase consists of a single verb word, in the past or present tense.
- The verb is an intransitive verb of position (*be, stand, lie,* etc.) or verb of motion (*come, go, fall,* etc.).
- The topic element (X in the diagram above) is an adverbial of place or direction (e.g. *down, here, to the right, away*):

Here's *a pen,* Brenda.
Here *comes McKenzie.*   ⟨informal speech⟩
Look, there *are your friends.*

There, at the summit, *stood the castle* in its mediaeval splendour.
To the right *lay the pillars* of the Hall entrance.
Away *went the car* like a whirlwind.
Slowly out of its hangar *rolled the gigantic aircraft.*

⟨more formal, literary⟩

The examples from ⟨informal speech⟩ give end-focus to the subject. In ⟨literary⟩ style, the fronted topic is more useful in giving end-weight to a long subject.

Subject-verb inversion does not take place with a fronted topic when the subject is a personal pronoun: *Here it is* (not **Here is it*); *Away they go!* (not **Away go they*).

Note
The adverb *there* is stressed in the examples above. This distinguishes it from the introductory subject *there* (*see* 590–4), which has no stress. Contrast:

'There are your friends. [*there* = adverb of place]
There are 'too many people here. [*there* = introductory]

Subject-operator inversion in statements
417
The inversion of subject and operator (*did, can,* etc.) is of course obligatory in most questions: e.g. *Can you swim?* (*see* 681–4). But here we are concerned with the obligatory subject-operator inversion when a negative element is fronted for emphasis (especially in ⟨formal⟩ and rather ⟨rhetorical⟩ style) (*see* 303):

NOT A WORD *did he say.* (= 'He didn't say a word')
UNDER NO CIRCUMSTANCES *should the door* be left unlocked. ⟨formal⟩

The negative element is in capitals above. Inversion is also obligatory after fronting of words of negative meaning such as *never, hardly, scarcely, few, little, seldom, rarely, nor, (not) only* (*see* 584–5):

HARDLY *had I* left before the trouble started. (= 'I had hardly left before . . .')
Well, she would go and see what it was all about, for ONLY IF SHE KNEW THE WHOLE STORY *could she* decide.
LITTLE *did he* realize how much suffering he had caused. (= 'He little realized . . .')

Notice that the dummy operator *do* is used for the inversion where there is no other operator in the normal-order sentence:

He little realized . . . ~ Little *did* he realize . . .

Note
In ⟨written, literary⟩ English, subject-operator inversion with *be* sometimes serves the purpose of end-weight, where the subject is long and complex:

OPPOSING HIM *was the French Admiral*, Jean de Vienne – a great sailor and an able strategist.
NEATLY RANGED AGAINST THE ROCK WALLS *were all manner of chests and trunks.*

Here the sentence begins with a participle construction (in capitals), which is then followed by the operator and finally by the subject.

Fronting with *so*
418
Notice the following constructions in which *so* is placed first:

- *So* **as a substitute form with subject-operator inversion** (for end-focus) has the meaning of 'addition' (*see* 234) in sentences like:

> [A] (I've seen the play.)
> [B] |So have I. | (= 'and I have, too') ⟨especially in speech⟩
>   (I enjoyed the play) | and so did my <u>friend</u>'.|

- *So* **as a substitute form** WITHOUT **inversion** is fronted to express emphatic affirmation:

> [A] (You've spilled coffee on your dress.)
> [B] |Oh <u>dear</u>, | so I <u>have</u>.| ⟨speech⟩
> [A] (It's raining hard outside.)
> [B] |So it <u>is</u>.|

The *so*-construction here expresses the hearer's surprise at discovering that what the speaker says is true. As with emphatic affirmation in general (*see* 272), the nucleus comes on the operator, not on the subject.

- *So* **introducing a clause of degree or amount** (*see* 231) can be fronted for emphasis, with subject-operator inversion: *So absurd did he look that everyone stared at him* (= 'He looked so absurd that. . .'). ⟨rather literary⟩

Other constructions affecting the topic
Cleft sentence (it-*type*)
419
The cleft sentence construction with introductory *it* (*see* 496) is useful for fronting an element as topic, and also for putting focus (usually for contrast) on the topic element. It does this by splitting the sentence into two halves, highlighting the topic by making it the complement of *it* + *be*:

> [A] (Would you like to borrow this book on <u>dinosaurs</u>?)
> [B] |<u>No</u>, | it's *the* <u>other</u> book | that I want to <u>read</u>.| [1]
>   (TOPIC = OBJECT; *cf* I want to read the <u>other</u> book.)

> (For centuries London had been growing as a commercial port of world
> importance.) But it was *in the north of England* that industrial power
> brought new prosperity to the country. (TOPIC = ADVERBIAL)   [2]

The contrastive meaning of the topic can be seen if we make clear the implied negative in [1] and [2]:

> It's the other book, *not that book*, that I want to read.
> But it was in the north of England, *not in London*, that . . .

The cleft sentence with *it* is particularly useful in ⟨written⟩ English, where we cannot mark contrastive emphasis by intonation.

Cleft sentence (**wh-type**)
420
A nominal relative clause (*see* 592), like an *it*-cleft sentence, can be used to highlight one element for contrast. It can be either subject or complement of the verb *be* (the subject position is more common):

NORMAL PATTERN   CLEFT SENTENCE

We need more time. ~ { |It's more time | that we need.| (*it*-type)
|What we need | is more time.| (*wh*-type)
|More time | is what we need.| (*wh*-type)

The *wh*-type cleft sentence, like the *it*-type, usually implies a contrast; e.g.

We don't need more money – what we need is more time.

Comparison of *it*-type and *wh*-type cleft sentences
421
The *it*-type and the *wh*-type cleft sentences cannot always be used in the same circumstances. For example, the *it*-type is more flexible in certain ways:

- The focus of the *wh*-type sentence normally has to be in the form of a noun phrase or nominal clause. An adverbial phrase or prepositional phrase, for example, sounds less natural in this construction than in the *it*-type sentence:

  It was *only recently* that I noticed the leak in the roof.
  It was *in 1896* that he went to Europe on his first mission.
  It was *on this very spot* that I first met my wife.
  (BETTER THAN: Where I first met my wife was *on this very spot*.)

The *wh*-type sentence sounds somewhat better when the *wh*-clause comes last:

  On this very spot is where I first met my wife.

- But if an adverbial can be put in the form of a noun phrase, it can be the focus of a *wh*-type sentence with a final *when*- or *where*-clause:

  { It is *in the autumn* that the countryside is most beautiful.
  ~ Autumn is (the time) when the countryside is most beautiful.
  { It was *at Culloden* that the rebellion was finally defeated.
  ~ Culloden was (the place) where the rebellion was finally defeated.

Note
A *wh*-type sentence using one of the *wh*-words *who, whom,* or *whose* is usually awkward or impossible:

  It was the ambassador that met us.
  BUT NOT: *Who met us was the ambassador.

We can, however, say:

  The one/person who met us was the ambassador.

422

The *wh*-type cleft sentence is more flexible than the *it*-type in the following ways:

- The *wh*-type can focus on the complement of a clause, whereas the *it*-type normally cannot:

  > She is a brilliant reporter ~ What she is is a brilliant reporter.
  > BUT NOT: *It's a brilliant reporter that she is.

- The *wh*-type can focus on the verb, by using the substitute verb *do*:

  He's spoilt the whole thing. ~ {
  What he's done is spoil the whole thing.
  BUT NOT: *It's spoil the whole thing that he's done.
  }

Notice that the complement of the *wh*-type sentence takes the form of a non-finite clause, most commonly a bare infinitive (*spoil the whole thing*).

Note

The non-finite verb may be a bare infinitive, a *to*-infinitive, an *-ed* participle, or an *-ing* participle (*see* 493):

What he'll do is	*spoil the whole thing.*	[bare infinitive]
	spoil the whole thing.	[bare infinitive]
What he's done is {	*to spoil the whole thing.*	[*to*-infinitive]
	spoilt the whole thing.	[*-ed* participle]
What he's doing is	*spoiling the whole thing.*	[*-ing* participle]

The bare infinitive is the most usual construction, except after *done* (where the *-ed* participle is just as acceptable), and after *doing* where the *-ing* participle has to be used.

Sentences with **wh-***clauses and demonstratives*

423

A common type of sentence in ⟨informal⟩ English is one in which a *wh*-clause is linked by the verb *be* to a demonstrative pronoun (*this* or *that*). These sentences are similar to *wh*-cleft sentences both in their structure and in their focusing effect:

> *This is where* I first met my wìfe.
>
> *This is how* you start the èngine.
>
> Are you trying to wreck my career? Because *that's what* you're doing.
>
> I had difficulty starting the car today. *That's what* always happens when I leave it out in cold weather.

Postponement
*Introductory-***it** *construction*

424

The introductory-*it* construction (*see* 542–6) (not to be confused with the *it*-type cleft sentence in 420) is a means of postponing a subject clause to a later position in the sentence, either for end-weight or for end-focus:

> *That income tax will be reduced* is unlikely.
> ~ It is unlikely *that income tax will be reduced.*

Here the subject is a *that*-clause: *that income tax will be reduced.* The it-construction is, in fact, more usual than the same construction without postponement. If you keep the clause in front position, this is exceptional, and suggests that you want to put special contrastive emphasis (*see* 413) on the rest of the main clause:

> |That income tax will be redǔced | is unl̀ikely; | that it will be abǒlished
> | is out of the qùestion.|

In some instances, such as the passive construction (*see* 543, 613–8), it is impossible to keep the clause in subject position:

> It is said that fear in human beings produces a smell that provokes animals to attack.
> BUT NOT: *That fear in human beings produces a smell that provokes animals to attack is said.

For other examples of *it* replacing a postponed clause as subject, *see* 542. Main focus often occurs in the postponed clause:

> It is unlikely that they will hold a refer̀endum.

But when an *-ing* clause is the postponed subject, the main focus normally falls on the rest of the main clause, and the *-ing* clause is treated as an afterthought:

> |It's hard wòrk | being a fáshion model.|

Postponing an object clause

425

Occasionally introductory *it* displaces a clause in object position. Just as in the case of subject clauses (424), the clause (here *working here*) is postponed:

> { You must find *it* enjoyable *working here.*
> { ~ You must find *working here* enjoyable.
>   (Compare: *It is enjoyable working here.*)
> I owe *it* to you *that the jury acquitted me.*
>   (Compare: *It is thanks to you that the jury acquitted me.*)
> Something put *it* into his head *that she was a spy.*
>   (Compare: *It came into his head that she was a spy.*)

This displacement MUST occur when the object clause is a *that*-clause or an infinitive clause. Thus we can have:

> I'll leave *it* to you *to lock the door.*
>   (BUT NOT: *I'll leave to lock the door to you.)

Postponing parts of sentence elements
426

The *it*-construction postpones a whole sentence element, whether a subject or object. You may also wish to postpone a 'heavy' part of a sentence element. For example you may wish to postpone part of a complement, splitting an adjective from its modifier or modifiers:

> *How ready* are they *to make peace with their enemies?*

This can avoid the awkwardness of a long or emphatic element coming in non-final position, as in *How ready to make peace with their enemies are they?* The most important cases of such postponement are discussed in 427–9.

Postponing the modifier following a noun
427

> *The time* had arrived *to leave our homes for ever.*   [1]
>   (BETTER THAN: The time to leave our homes for ever had arrived.)
> *The problem* arose *of what to do with the money.*   [2]
>   (BETTER THAN: The problem of what to do with the money arose.)
> *What business* is it *of ỳours?*   [3]
>   (MORE IDIOMATIC THAN: What business of ỳours is it?)
> We heard *the story* from her own lips *of how she was stranded for*
>   *days without food.*   [4]

This postponement avoids awkwardness particularly when the rest of the sentence is short in comparison with the subject. However, in contrast to [2], the word order is normal and fully acceptable in the following sentence with a long agent phrase:

> *The problem of what to do with the money* was discussed by all
>   members of the family.

Postponing the emphatic reflexive pronoun
428

When the reflexive pronouns *myself, himself, themselves,* etc. are used for emphasis, they normally have nuclear stress. If a reflexive pronoun is in apposition as part of the subject, it is common to postpone it for end-focus:

> The president hims̀elf gave the order.
> ~ The president gave the order hims̀elf.
>   ('It was the president, and no one else, who gave the order.')

Postponing comparative clauses, etc.
429

A comparative clause or phrase can be separated, by postponement, from the preceding word it modifies. In some cases, the same sentence without postponement would be extremely awkward:

More people own houses these days *than used to years ago.* (NOT: ?*More people than used to years ago own houses these days.)

He showed *less pity* to his victims *than any other tyrant in history.* (NOT: ?*He showed less pity than any other tyrant in history to his victims.)

Other modifiers, like comparative clauses, are sometimes postponed for end-weight. These include phrases of exception (*see* 236):

All of them were arrested *except the gang leader himself.*

Also clauses of amount or degree following *too, enough,* and *so*:

Too many people were there *for the thief to escape unseen.*
I've had *enough trouble* from those children *to last me a lifetime.*
I was *so excited* by the present *that I forgot to thank you.*

Other choices of position
The passive
430
An important example of a grammatical process which changes the positions of elements in the sentence is the rule for forming passive sentences (*see* 613–8).

[A]   (Where did these chairs come from?)
[B]   They were bought by my uncle.   [5]
The President was mistrusted by most of the radical and left wing
    politicians in the country.   [6]

In [5], the passive gives the sentence end-focus, where the active (*My uncle bought them*) would not. In [6], the passive gives end-weight, where the active sentence (*Most of the radical ... mistrusted the President*) would be awkward because of a 'heavy' subject.

You can readily use the passive for end-weight where the subject of the sentence is a clause:

I was surprised that so much had changed so quickly.
    (BETTER THAN: That so much had changed so quickly surprised me.)

The preposition *by* is omitted with the passive here because a *that*-clause cannot be complement of a preposition (*see* 740).

Position of direct object
431
In normal order, a direct object precedes an object complement or a final position adverbial (*see* 488). But if the object is long, it can be postponed to the end for end-weight:

NORMAL ORDER: We have proved *them* wrong.
FINAL OBJECT: We have proved wrong *the forecasts made by the country's leading economic experts.*

NORMAL ORDER: He condemned *them* to death.

FINAL OBJECT: He condemned to death *most of the peasants who had taken part in the rebellion.*

The same choice can be made when a noun phrase object comes before a particle (e.g. the second part of a phrasal verb such as *make up, give away, let down*):

{ He gave all his books awáy.   { She made the story úp.
{ He gave away all his bóoks.   { She made up the stóry.

The choice may be made either for end-weight, or, as in these examples, for end-focus which falls either on the phrasal verb (*gave ... away, made ... up*) or on the object. Notice that personal pronoun objects cannot be moved to the end in this way: *He gave them away,* BUT NOT **He gave away them* (*see* 631).

Position of indirect object

432

In a similar way, an indirect object can in effect be postponed, by converting it into a prepositional phrase (*see* 608, 730):

The twins told their mother all their sécrets.   [7]

The twins told all their secrets to their móther.   [8]

This change, like the others, can be used for a different end-focus. For example, [7] answers the implied question 'What did the twins tell their mother?' but [8] answers the implied question 'Who did they tell their secrets to?'

Avoiding intransitive verbs

433

Connected with the principle of end-weight in English is the feeling that the predicate of a clause should be longer or grammatically more complex than the subject. This helps to explain why we tend to avoid predicates consisting of just a single intransitive verb. Instead of saying *Mary sang,* many would probably prefer to say *Mary sang a song,* filling the object position with a noun phrase which adds little information but helps to give more weight to the predicate.

434

For such a purpose English often uses a general verb (such as *have, take, give,* and *do*) followed by an abstract noun phrase:

She's having a swim.   (Compare: She's swimming)
He's taking a bath.   (Compare: He's bathing)
They took a rest.   (Compare: They rested)

The driver gave a shout.   (Compare: The driver shouted)
She does little work.   (Compare: She works little)

The sentences on the left are more idiomatic than those on the right.

In a similar way a transitive verb can be replaced by an indirect object construction with the verb *give*, etc.:

I gave the door a kick. (= 'I kicked the door')
I paid her a visit.   (= 'I visited her')

Part Three

A–Z in English grammar

435

Part Three of this book, called 'A–Z in English grammar', covers all the important areas of English grammatical form and structure, and is arranged alphabetically under topic headings. The arrangement is alphabetical because this part of the grammar is primarily meant to be used for reference, especially as an explanation of grammatical terms and categories referred to in Part Two.

Each entry in 'A–Z in English Grammar' has a reference to the most relevant sections of *A Comprehensive Grammar of the English Language* (abbreviated *CGEL*, see preliminary page xi), so that, if required, a more detailed treatment of the topic can be consulted in that book.

Adjective patterns
(*see CGEL* 16.68–83)

436

Adjectives can have different types of complement, such as

- a prepositional phrase:

    I feel very sorry *for her.*

- a *that*-clause:

    Everybody's pleased *that she is making such good progress.*

- a *to*-infinitive:

    I'm glad *to hear she is recovering.*

Adjectives with a prepositional phrase: *Ready for lunch?*
437

Adjectives have different prepositional complements: *good at, ready for, afraid of, convinced of, interested in, keen on, close to, content with*, etc. As a dictionary will tell you, a particular adjective usually requires a particular preposition. Adjectives with prepositions are often *-ed* or *-ing* adjectives, i.e. participial adjectives like *interested (in), worried (about)*. Here are some examples:

    Planners are *worried about* the noise and dirt in our environment.
    I may have sounded a bit *annoyed at* your failing to give me the
       information.

Would you be *interested in* writing an article for my series?

The reader must be *convinced of* what is happening at one time, and not *surprised at* sudden changes of character and place.

My friends were only faintly *conscious of* foreign affairs.

Elvira was *uncertain of* what the words meant.

Industry is *independent of* natural conditions, while agriculture is continually *dependent on* the fluctuations of nature.

This product is *based on* confidential information.

Adjectives with a *that*-clause: *I'm not sure (that) I understand.*
438

Adjectives which take a *that*-clause as complement may have personal subjects or introductory *it* as subject.

Adjectives with personal subjects

That is often omitted (zero *that*):

I'm *sure* (that) she can do it.

We are *confident* that she will have a distinguished academic career.

I'm *glad* you were able to cheer her up a bit.

When the *that*-clause expresses a 'putative' idea (expressing joy, surprise, etc.), it contains *should* (*see* 280):

We're *surprised* that he should have to resign.

I'm *amazed* that somebody with his background should get the post.

Here are some other adjectives which have *that*-clauses as complement: *certain, confident, proud, sad; alarmed, annoyed, astonished, disappointed, pleased*, etc. Such adjectives can also have a prepositional phrase as complement (*see* 437): *annoyed at, certain of, pleased with*, etc. But note that, in English, a preposition cannot introduce a *that*-clause. Compare:

They were *amazed that* the cost should be so high.

They were *amazed at* the high cost.

Adjectives with introductory it *as subject*

Adjectives with *that*-clauses frequently have introductory *it* as subject (*see* 542):

It's a bit *odd* that this state has no university.

It's *possible* that we'll all be a bit late.

Is it *true* that she never turned up?

Other adjectives with *it*-constructions and *that*-clauses are, for example, *certain, curious, disconcerting, embarrassing, evident, extraordinary, fitting, fortunate, frightening, important, irritating, likely, odd, obvious, possible, probable, sad, shocking, surprising, true*. Many are *-ing* adjectives, i.e. they have the form of an *-ing* participle.

After adjectives that express a 'putative' idea (joy, surprise, etc.) the *that*-clause often contains *should*:

> The school board considered it *essential* that the opinions of teachers *should be* ascertained.

Instead of *should* + verb the *that*-clause can have the alternative constructions with the verb in the subjunctive, i.e. just the base form. This is more common in ⟨AmE⟩ than in ⟨BrE⟩ (*see* 706):

> The school board considered it *essential* that the opinions of teachers *be* ascertained.

Adjectives with a *to*-infinitive: *It's good to have you back.*

439

There are different types of adjectives which have a construction with *to*-infinitive, for example:

> She is *wrong* to say a thing like that. [1]
> Such people are *hard* to find nowadays. [2]
> I was *delighted* to make that personal contact. [3]
> Many dealers were *quick* to purchase the new shares. [4]

The meanings of the four constructions are different, as can be seen from these paraphrases:

> It's *wrong* of her to say a thing like that. [1a]
> It's *hard* to find such people nowadays. [2a]
> It's made me *delighted* to make that personal contact. [3a]
> Many dealers *quickly* purchased the new shares. [4a]

Type [1]. Other adjectives like *wrong* in [1] are *clever, cruel, good, kind, naughty, nice, rude, silly, splendid, stupid*:

> He was *silly* to go ahead with the plan.

Note the position of *not* and *never* before the *to*-infinitive:

> They were *stupid not to take* the opportunity offered.
> He was *silly never to follow* your advice.

Type [2]. Other examples of adjectives like *hard* in [2] are:

> The extent of this tendency is *difficult* to assess.
> All this is very *easy* to arrange.
> Your question is of course *impossible* to answer.
> I am rather *surprised* to learn that you have sold your stocks.

Similarly: *convenient, enjoyable, fun* ⟨informal⟩, *good, pleasant*. The construction with introductory *it* [2a] is the more common and sometimes the only possible alternative:

> It is *difficult* to assess the extent of this tendency.
> It was really *good* to see you before Christmas.

It is *important* to create a new image of the Church.
It's almost *impossible* to say this in English.
It is *necessary* to distinguish between English and Scots law.
It would be *nice* to have a portable TV at the end of one's bed.
It is now *possible* to make considerable progress in this direction.

The infinitive clause can have a subject introduced by *for*:

It is *necessary for you* to distinguish between English and Scots law.

Type [3]. Here are more examples of adjectives like *delighted* in [3]:

She'll be *furious* to see him behave that way.
I'm *glad* to see you looking so well.
If interviewed I should be *pleased* to provide further references.
I'm very *sorry* to learn that Hattie has been ill.

Other adjectives with this construction, all of which express some kind of emotion: *amazed, angry, annoyed, disappointed, surprised, worried*.

Type [4]. Other examples of adjectives like *quick* in [4]:

Nick is *willing* to do the hard work. ('He does it willingly.')
They were *careful* to avoid all mention of the child. ('carefully avoided')
They were *prompt* to act. ('acted promptly')
This student is bright but rather *slow* to pick up new ideas. ('picks up slowly')

There are also other adjectives which take an infinitive-construction but do not fit into the other types described:

I might be *able* to afford it.
She is now very *anxious* to return to the university.
There are *bound* to be social and economic differences between distant parts of the country.
He was always *ready* to listen to the views of others.
I have been *unable* to contact him during the past week or so.

Adjectives
(*see CGEL* 7.1–22, 31–44)

440
Here are four features of adjectives:

• Most adjectives can have two uses: attributive and predicative. An attributive adjective occurs before the noun it modifies:

This is a *difficult* problem.

A predicative adjective occurs as the complement of a linking verb. Linking verbs (also called copular verbs, *see* 719) are *be*, *seem*, etc.:

This problem is *difficult*.

- Most adjectives can be modified by degree adverbs like *very*, *quite*, *rather*, etc. (*see* 217):

I'm on *quite* good terms with him.

- Most adjectives can have comparative and superlative forms (*see* 500):

We have a *bigger* problem than inflation -- our *biggest* problem now is high unemployment.
He thought Linda managed to look a little *more beautiful* each year.
This must be one of the *most beautiful* buildings in Europe.

- Many adjectives are derived from nouns and can be recognized by their endings, e.g. *-ous*, *-ic*, *-y*, *-ful*: *fame* ~ *famous*, *base* ~ *basic*, *sleep* ~ *sleepy*, *beauty* ~ *beautiful*.

Attributive-only adjectives: *She's our chief economic advisor.*
441
Most adjectives can be both attributive and predicative, but some adjectives can only be used in attributive position, for example:

She was the *former* prime minister.

The adjective *former* can be related to the adverb *formerly*:

This was *formerly* a busy port.

Here are more such adjectives, where each example with an attributive-only meaning is followed by an example of its corresponding adverb:

He was a popular colleague and a *hard* worker.
~ Our students work *hard*.
Many changes occurred in Europe in the *late* 1980s.
~ I've not heard much from her *lately*.
They went to an *occasional* concert.
~ *Occasionally* they went to the theatre.

Some attributive-only adjectives are derived from nouns, for example:

A new *criminal* justice bill will soon come before Parliament. (*crime* ~ *criminal*: 'a bill concerned with the punishment of crimes')
He thought *atomic* weapons had deadened the finest feeling that had sustained mankind for ages. (*atom* ~ *atomic*)
There will be no need for a *medical* examination. (*medicine* ~ *medical*)

The predicative use of adjectives: *I feel sick.*
442

* Adjectives can be used predicatively as subject complement after linking verbs like *be, seem, look, feel* (*see* 491, 719):

    [A]: I feel *sick*.
    [B]: Yes, you do look *awful*.

* Adjectives can also be used predicatively as object complement after verbs like *consider, believe, find* (*see* 733):

    It makes me *sick* to see how people spoil the environment.

* Adjectives can be complement to a subject which is a finite clause (*see* 492):

    Whether the minister will resign is still *uncertain*.

    But the construction with introductory *it* gives end-weight (*see* 408) and is the more common:

    It is still *uncertain whether the minister will resign.*

* Adjectives can also be complement to a non-finite clause (*see* 493):

    Driving a bus isn't so *easy* as you may think.

* Although most adjectives can be used both attributively and predicatively (*see* 440), some groups of adjectives are predicative-only. One such group is 'health adjectives' like *faint, ill,* and *well*:

    Oh doctor, I feel *faint*.
    He doesn't look *well*, does he Anna?
    No matter how *well* or *ill* you are, you'll still be guaranteed acceptance
        into the pension plan up to the age of 75.

    When *faint* is not a health adjective it can be attributive:

    There's a *faint* hope on the horizon.

* Some predicative-only adjectives, including *afraid, fond, present, ready,* are often followed by clauses:

    I'm *afraid* I don't really agree with that, Bill.

    or phrases (*see* 437):

    I'm very *fond* of Hemingway.
    Most of the committee members were *present* at the meeting. ('they
        attended the meeting')
    I hope you are *ready* for some hard work. ('I hope you are prepared for
        some hard work.')

Present and *ready* can also precede a noun, but with different meanings: *a ready answer* is 'an answer which was given readily' and *the present situation* means 'the situation at the present time'.

Adjectives after the head: *all the problems* **involved**

443

- An adjective which modifies a noun is usually placed before its head (*see* 596). This is the attributive position: *a difficult problem.* But some adjectives, especially predicative-only adjectives, are placed immediately after the head they modify (*see* 641):

    All the persons *present* at the meeting were in favour of the proposal.

Such adjectives can usually be regarded as reduced relative clauses (*see* 686):

    ~ All the persons *who were present* at the meeting were in favour of the proposal.
    This is one of the problems (*that are*) *involved* in the scheme.

The two adjectives *present* and *involved* cannot be attributive with the same meaning: we cannot say *the present persons* or *the involved problems* in these sentences.

- Quantifiers (amount words) ending in *-body, -one, -thing, -where* can only have modifying adjectives after them:

    Is there *anything interesting* in the papers? ('Is there anything which is interesting in the papers?')
    How long does it take to train *somebody new*?
    His remark astonished *everyone present*.
    Think of *something nice* for us to do next weekend!

- There are adjective phrases consisting of an adjective plus an infinitive, as in

    These dogs are *easy to teach.*

Such phrases cannot come before a noun as head. We cannot say

    *The easiest to teach dogs are Labrador retrievers.

But the adjective + infinitive phrase can be placed after its noun head:

    The dogs *easiest to teach* are Labrador retrievers.

The corresponding construction with a relative clause is more common in ⟨informal⟩ English:

    ~ The dogs *that are easiest to teach* are Labrador retrievers.

The construction with the adjective placed after its head is also used for other types of complement, such as *than*-clauses:

    Our neighbours have a house *much larger than ours.*

But it is more usual to separate the adjective and its complement:

> The *easiest* dogs *to teach* are Labrador retrievers.
> Our neighbours have a *much larger* house *than ours*.

Adjectives and participles: *Her attitude is rather* **surprising.**
444
There are many adjectives that have the same form as *-ing* or *-ed* participles (*see* 574):

> Her attitude is rather *surprising*.
> The professor had been *retired* for several years.

These adjectives can also be attributive:

> We were struck by her rather *surprising* attitude.
> The *retired* professor seemed to spend most of his time on his yacht.

A verb corresponding to the adjective may have a different meaning. Compare these two uses:
Relieved used as an adjective:

> We are very *relieved* to know that you are all right. ('glad, pleased')

Relieved as the past participle of the verb *relieve*:

> The osmotic flow of water into the body is *relieved* by the pressure of
>   the heart-beat. ('eased, lessened')

The different functions of a form used as adjective and as participle are not always obvious.

- It is clear that an *-ing* form is a present participle (and not an adjective) when a direct object is present:

> She was *entertaining* students at her home together with other friends.

But *entertaining* is an adjective in:

> She was brilliantly *entertaining* in her lecture.

- For both *-ed* and *-ing* forms, modification by the adverb *very* indicates that the forms are adjectives:

> His remarks made me very *annoyed*.
> The poor attendance at the meeting is not very *encouraging*.

Adjective or adverb?
(*see* C GEL 7.6–11, 7.71–3)

445
Most adverbs in English are derived from adjectives by the addition of *-ly*: *quick* ~ *quickly*, *careful* ~ *carefully*, etc. (*see* 464). But there are some adverbs

which do not end in -*ly*: *direct, early, hard, high, late, long, straight, wrong*, etc.
These words can be used both as adjectives and adverbs. In the following pairs,
the first is an example of the word used as an adjective, and the second is an
example of the word used as an adverb:

> I think she has a *direct* line.
> ~ Why don't you call her *direct?*
> The population explosion occurred in the *early* part of the nineteenth
> century.
> ~ I'll see you after you return *early* in February.
> She is a *hard* worker.
> ~ She works *hard* at preparing new teaching materials.
> That wall is too *high* to climb.
> ~ Don't aim too *high*.
> We met in *late* August.
> ~ The modern industrial city developed relatively *late*.
> What I really need now is a *long* rest.
> ~ You mustn't stay too *long*.
> It was a long *straight* road.
> ~ The best thing would be to go *straight* back to London.
> I may have said the *wrong* thing once too often.
> ~ There's always the chance of something going *wrong*.

These adverbs are mostly connected with time, position and direction. In some
cases, there is also an adverb in -*ly* (*directly, hardly, lately, shortly*), but with a
different meaning:

> Don't hesitate to get in touch with us *directly* ('immediately').
> We've had *hardly* any replies to our advertisement. (*hardly any* =
> 'almost no')
> I haven't seen him *lately* ('recently').
> We'll be in touch with you again *shortly*. ('soon')

There is a contrast between *strong* as an adjective and *strongly* as an adverb in:

> He felt *strong* enough to win the contest.
> He felt *strongly* enough about it to object.

Adjectives as complements: *It tastes good.*
446
An adjective is used after certain verbs like *taste* and *smell*. Here we consider the
adjective to be a complement (*see* 508), not an adverbial:

> The food tasted *good*. ('The food was good to taste.')
> I thought the dish smelled absolutely *revolting*.

Well is the adverb corresponding to the adjective *good*: *She is a good writer.*
~ *She writes well*. But *well* can also be used as an adjective. In these examples
both *good* and *well* are adjectives (but with different meanings):

Those cakes look *good*. ('Those cakes look as if they taste good.')
Your mother looks *well*. ('Your mother seems to be in good health.')

Do you drive slow or slowly?
447
The difference between an adverb form and an adjective form does not always involve a difference in meaning. In the following examples the two forms are more or less equivalent (*buy cheap*~*buy cheaply*, *drive slow*~*drive slowly*, etc.), but the adjective form tends to be more ⟨informal⟩:

You can buy these things very very *cheap/cheaply* now when the sale is on.
It says here, *loud* and *clear*, that this is the road to Durham.
~I'm going to play the same chord as *loudly* as possible.
His simple philosophy is: 'Get rich *quick!*'.
~They usually made friends very *quickly*.
Why do you have to drive so *slow* when there's no speed limit here?
~The days passed and *slowly* the spring came. ⟨rather elevated⟩

The form without *-ly* is especially common in comparative and superlative constructions. Again, the adverb form is the more ⟨formal⟩:

We have to look *closer*~*more closely* at these problems.
Let's see who can run *quickest*~*most quickly*.

In their base form (i.e. when they are not comparative) these words would normally end in *-ly*: *look closely*, *run quickly*.

Adjectives as heads
(*see CGEL* 7.23–26)

448
The typical function of adjectives is to modify the head of a noun phrase: *the rich people*, *an absurd idea*. But some adjectives can themselves be heads of noun phrases: *the rich*, *the absurd*. There are two kinds of such adjectives, both with generic reference (*see* 90):

• Adjectives denoting a class of people (plural), for example *the rich* = 'those who are rich'

We must care for *the old*, *the unemployed*, *the homeless*, *the sick* and *the poor*.

• Adjectives denoting an abstract quality (singular), for example *the absurd* = 'that which is absurd':

Some people enjoy *the mystical* and *the supernatural* in literature.

The article is omitted before adjective heads in some parallel phrases (*see* 475):

Education should be for both *young* and *old*.

Adverbials
(*see CGEL* Chapter 8)

449
Adverbials tell us something extra about an action, happening, or state as described by the rest of the sentence, for example:

- the time when it happened (time adverbial):

    We got together *after dinner late in the evening*.

- the place where it happened (place adverbial):

    Will you be staying *in a hotel?*

- the manner in which it happened (manner adverbial):

    Before reaching a decision we have to study this plan *very carefully*.

There are of course many other meanings of adverbials. The meanings of adverbials are dealt with in Part Two (*see* 151). Here we will discuss the positions adverbials can have in sentences.

The forms of adverbials

450
The position adverbials can occupy depends very much on their form, and they have a number of different forms. Adverbials can be

- adverbs or adverb phrases (*see* 464):

    A colleague of mine has *very kindly* offered to baby-sit.

- prepositional phrases (*see* 654):

    I found several people waiting *outside the doctor's door*.

- clauses with a finite verb (*see* 492):

    We have to preserve these buildings *before it's too late*.

- infinitive clauses (*see* 493):

    As usual, Peter was playing *to win*.

- *-ing* participle clauses (*see* 493):

    He marched in on them, *grinning broadly*.

- *-ed* participle clauses (*see* 493):

    Three people were found dead on the roads, *presumably killed by cars*.

- verbless clauses (*see* 494):

    He admitted to driving *while under the influence of drink*.

- noun phrases (*see* 595):

    What are you doing *this afternoon?*

The positions of adverbials: front, mid or end?
451
Most adverbials are mobile, so that they can occur in different places in the sentence. We distinguish three main positions:

- Front-position is before the subject:

    Fortunately I had plenty of food with me.

- Mid-position is immediately before the main verb, if no auxiliaries are present:

    She *never* protests and she *always* agrees with him.

If there is an auxiliary verb present, the adverbial is placed after the auxiliary. If there are more than one auxiliary verb present, the adverbial is placed after the first auxiliary (called the operator, *see* 609):

    We will *never* be lonely because your family will *often* come along and pay us visits.
    This is an idea which has *never* been tried.

Occasionally a mid-position adverbial comes before the operator (*see* 261, 610). This may, for example, happen after forms of *be* when *be* is not an auxiliary but a main verb:

    It *never* was my intention to make things difficult for you.

- End-position is after the verb if there is no object or complement present:

    I went *to some second-year seminars.*

An adverbial in end-position comes after an object or complement:

    She didn't wake me up *till nine o'clock.*

The place of an adverbial depends partly on its structure (whether it is an adverb, a prepositional phrase, a clause, etc), partly on its meaning (whether it denotes time, place, manner, degree, etc). End-focus and end-weight also play a part (*see* 408).

Long and short adverbials
452
Long adverbials normally occur in end-position.

    She's going *to Chicago on Monday next week.*
    There will be delegations from several countries *at the opening meeting of the conference in London later this year.*

He was a complete failure *as far as mathematics is concerned*.

Front-position gives contrast, or provides the background or setting for the clause which follows:

> *As far as mathematics is concerned*, he was a complete failure.
> *Outside the window* a low and cold bank of cloud hung over the streets of our little town.
> *Last year* there were riots. *Now* we have strikes and demonstrations.

Long adverbials rarely occur in mid-position. Mid-position is usually restricted to short adverbs like *almost, hardly, just, never*:

> The chairman *just* resigned.

Adverbials denoting manner, means, and instrument: *Did you come by bus?*

453

Adverbials which denote manner, means, and instrument usually have end-position:

> The new hotel opens *formally* this afternoon under its new ownership.
> Will you be coming *by car?*
> He threatened the shop owner *with a big knife*.

In the passive, however, mid-position is common:

> Discussions were *formally* opened here today on the question of international disarmament.

In an active sentence like this one, *well* can only have end-position:

> She put the point *well*.

But in the corresponding passive sentence we can have either end- or mid-position:

> ∼ The point was put *well*.
> ∼ The point was *well* put.

Place adverbials: *See you at the gym.*

454

Place adverbials usually have end-position:

> The meeting will be *in room 205*.
> He showered, shaved, dressed and went down *to the dining room* for breakfast.
> He was born *in a small Danish town on the island of Langeland in the south-central part of Denmark*.

Two place adverbials can occur together in end-position, usually with the smaller location before the larger one:

> Many people eat [*in Chinese restaurants*] [*in London*].

Only the larger locational unit can be moved to front-position:

> *In London* many people eat *in Chinese restaurants.*

On place adverbials, *see further* 170.

Time adverbials: *I haven't seen her for a long time.*
455
There are three types of time adverbials (*see* 151):

- adverbials denoting time-when (*see* 456):

  > I'll write again *next week.*

- adverbials denoting duration (*see* 457):

  > I haven't seen her *for a long time.*

- adverbials denoting frequency (*see* 458):

  > This week I'll be in the office *every day.*

We will discuss these types in turn.

Time-when adverbials: *See you tomorrow.*
456
Adverbials which denote a point of time or a period of time normally have end-position:

> I'll be writing to you *again.*
> My father retired *last year.*
> The national strike ended *at 9 o'clock tonight.*

Adverbials such as *once* and *recently*, which denote a point of time, but also imply the point from which that time is measured, occur either in front-, mid- or end-position:

> *Once* you spoke about how it happened that you became a journalist.
> Shelley *once* said, in the youth of the world, all language was metaphorical.

In end-position these adverbs often have a rising-tone nucleus (*see* 406):

> |We owned an Alsatian do̱g | ónce. |

Time duration adverbials: *Don't stay too long!*
457
Time duration adverbials normally have end-position:

> I'll be in California *for the summer.*
> They were on duty *all night long.*
> This watch has not functioned correctly *since last September.*
> I've been staying here *since last Saturday.*

But single-word adverbs usually take mid-position:

> She has *temporarily* taken over the art column of the newspaper.

On time duration adverbials, *see further* 161.

Time frequency adverbials: *I jog every morning.*
458
Time frequency adverbials denoting definite frequency usually have end-position:

> Your wage will be paid *weekly*.
> Our office gets about 100 requests *every day*.
> About this question we have to think *twice*.

Time frequency adverbs denoting indefinite frequency typically have mid-position (but *see* 610 on contrastive function). Such adverbs are, for example, *always, ever, frequently, generally, never, normally, occasionally, rarely, regularly, sometimes, seldom, usually*:

> You are *always* assured of a warm and friendly welcome here.
> He *generally* leaves home at seven in the morning.
> We don't *normally* go to bed before midnight.
> He was *occasionally* carried away by his own enthusiasm.
> Important decisions can *rarely* be based on complete unanimity.
> At night the temperature *regularly* drops to minus five degrees Celsius.
> She might *sometimes* make an impression of lack of proportion.

But prepositional phrases denoting indefinite frequency have front- or end-position:

> *As a rule* it's very quiet here during the day.
> ~ It's very quiet here during the day, *as a rule*.
> *On several occasions* we've had reason to complain.
> ~ We've had reason to complain *on several occasions*.

On time frequency adverbials, *see further* 166.

Degree adverbials: *I fully agree with you.*
459
Degree adverbials like *definitely, really, very much* have a heightening effect on some part of the sentence. Degree adverbs often occur in mid-position:

> I'm *definitely* going to join the Mountaineering Club at the university.
> I *entirely* agree with your diagnosis.
> I don't think this *really* affects the situation at all.
> His frustration is *thoroughly* justified.
> I should *very much* appreciate it if you would let me know your reasons.

There are also degree adverbs like *nearly* and *scarcely* which have a lowering effect. They also have mid-position:

We can *hardly* expect people to take this election seriously.
I *nearly* missed you at the airport.
I *rather* doubt I'll be back before nine tonight.
He felt she was *scarcely* listening to what he was saying.

For emphasis, degree adverbs can occur before the operator:

I *really* don't know where we would be without you.
I *simply* can't speak too highly of her.

For some degree adverbials end-position is also possible:

Fortunately, our relationship did not cease *entirely*.

On degree adverbials, *see further* 215.

Two or more adverbials: *See you* [*in class*] [*tomorrow*].
460
Time adverbials in end-position tend to occur in the order

duration + frequency + time-when

In the following examples the different adverbials are indicated by square brackets:

Our electricity was cut off [*briefly*] [*today*].
I'm paying my rent [*monthly*] [*this year*].
I used to swim [*for an hour or so*] [*every day*] [*when I was a child*].

When more than one of the main classes of adverbials occur in end-position, the normal order is

manner/means/instrument + place + time

Examples:

We go [*to bed*] [*very early*].
I have to rush to get [*into the supermarket*] [*before they close*].

An adverbial clause normally comes after other adverbial structures (adverbs, prepositional phrases, etc.):

We plan to stop [*for a few days*] [*wherever we can find reasonable
accommodation*].

A sentence like this one with a string of end-placed prepositional phrases is 'heavy':

He was working [*on his speech*] [*in the office*] [*the whole morning*].

Some adverbials which normally have end-position can be put in front-position to avoid having too many adverbials at the end of a sentence:

[*The whole morning*] he was working [*on his speech*] [*in the office*].

It is not usual for more than one adverbial to be in front-position or mid-position, but there are exceptions. For example, to introduce a new topic in a conversation we might find sentences like this one:

> |Ányway | *the next mórning* | sòmehow or óther | I hadn't got any
> bùsiness to do.|

Sentence adverbials: *Of course I'll come.*
461
The adverbials we have discussed so far are integrated to some extent in the structure of the sentence. For example, they can modify the verb:

> He *always* drives *carefully.*

and they can be affected by negation:

> He doesn't *always* drive *carefully.*

Here both *always* and *carefully* are in the scope of the negative (*see* 269).

462
There is also another type of adverbials, **sentence adverbials**, which are not integrated but are peripheral to the sentence structure. The difference between the integrated and peripheral types becomes clear with adverbs that can have both functions:

> |It all happened quite *nàturally.*| [1]
> |*Náturally*| the population is rìsing.| [2]
>
> Haven't you finished the typing *yet?*   [3]
> *Yet* he has failed to produce any evidence to substantiate his claim.   [4]

Yet is a time adverbial ('so far') in [3] and a sentence adverbial ('nevertheless') in [4].

463
Sentence adverbials have a wide range of possible structures. For example, instead of *frankly* in this sentence

> *Frankly*, this isn't good enough.

we could use infinitive clauses like *to be frank, to put it frankly,* -*ing* participle clauses like *frankly speaking,* or finite verb clauses like *if I may be frank.*

Sentence adverbials often convey speakers' comments on the content of what they are saying:

> *Certainly* her French is very fluent.
> The document should be signed, *hopefully* by December.

Of course, nobody imagines that he'll ever repay the loan.
Strangely enough, his face reminds me vividly of Miss Peters.
To be sure, we've heard many such promises before.
Surely no other novelist can give such a vivid description.
Unfortunately that is an oversimplification of the problem.

Other sentence adverbials with this function are, for example, *actually, admittedly, definitely, fortunately, in fact, indeed, luckily, officially, possibly, preferably, really, superficially, surprisingly, technically, theoretically.*

Sentence adverbials like *however, therefore, moreover,* have a connective role (*see* 357):

The team didn't like the food. *However,* they have not complained.

The normal place for most sentence adverbials is front-position. They are often separated from what follows by a tone unit boundary in speech, or a comma in writing:

⟨Spoken⟩ |Ŏbviously | they expect us to be on tìme.|
⟨Written⟩ Obviously, they expected us to be on time.

Adverbs
(*see CGEL* 7.46–70)

464
Most adverbs are formed from adjectives with the suffix *-ly*:

frank/frankly, happy/happily, etc.

(For the change in spelling from *y* to *i* in *happy/happily*, etc., *see* 701.)
    Adverbs have two typical functions: as adverbial in sentences and as modifier of adjectives, adverbs and other phrases.

- Adverb as adverbial (*see* 449):

    The conference was *carefully* planned.

- Adverb as modifier of adjectives (*see* 465):

    She is an *extremely* talented young woman.

- Adverb as modifier of other adverbs (*see* 465):

    One has to read this document *very* closely between the lines.

- Adverb as modifier of other constructions, e.g. prepositional phrases (*see* 466):

    We live *just* outside of Chicago.

Adverbs as modifiers of adjectives and other adverbs: *That's a very good idea!*
465
Most modifying adverbs are degree adverbs like *absolutely, extremely, rather* (*see*

215, 459). When an adverb modifies an adjective, the adverb regularly precedes the adjective:

> I thought it was an *absolutely* awful show myself. ⟨familiar⟩
> He said everybody was *deeply* affected.
> It's *extremely* good of you to do this for me.
> She's *rather* tall for her age.

But *enough* is placed after its adjective:

> This just isn't good *enough*!
> They were naive *enough* to be taken in.

When *too* and *how* modify an adjective in a noun phrase, the indefinite article is placed after the adjective. Compare these two sentences:

> He's a good programmer and never makes any mistakes.
> BUT: He's *too* good *a* programmer to make any mistakes.

> *How* strange *a* feeling it was, seeing my old school again! ⟨elevated⟩

How is replaced by *what* in noun phrases where the head is a mass noun like *music* or a plural count noun like *ideas* (i.e. nouns that do not take an indefinite article):

> *What* a strange feeling it was!
> *What* strange music they play here!
> *What* peculiar ideas he has!

An adverb which modifies another adverb is placed before the adverb:

> You seem to be smoking *rather* heavily these days.

However, *enough* is an exception, and is placed after the adverb:

> Oddly *enough*, nothing valuable was stolen.

Adverbs as modifiers of prepositions, etc.: *The nail went **right** through the wall.*
466
An adverb can also modify

* a preposition:

> Her parents are *dead* against her hitch-hiking. ⟨familiar⟩

* a determiner (*see* 522):

> They seem to have *hardly* any books at home.

* a numeral (*see* 602):

> *Over* two hundred deaths were reported after the disaster.

The indefinite article can be premodified when *a* = *one*:

> My parents will stay with us for *about* a week.

- a pronoun (*see* 661):

    Nearly everybody seemed to be at the party.

The modifier *else*: *What **else** is there to do?*
467

Else can modify

- the quantifiers *much* and *little* and is placed after these head words:

    They do *little else* but watch T V in the evening.

- the pronouns ending in *-body, -one, -thing*:

    Why don't you ask *somebody else*?

- the adverbs ending in *-where*:

    You'll have to go *somewhere else*.

- the interrogatives *who, what, how* and *where*:

    What else is there to do?

With determiners like *some, other* is used instead of *else*. These two sentences
have the same meaning:

    Someone else will have to take my place.
    ~ *Some other person* will have to take my place.

Adverbs as modifiers of nouns or noun phrases: *We try to plan several years*
ahead.
468

The degree words *quite, rather, such,* and *what* (in exclamations) can modify
noun phrases:

    My grandmother told me *such* funny stories.

The noun phrase is normally indefinite, and the degree word precedes the
indefinite article (*see* 524):

    She told me *such* a funny story.
    The place was in *rather* a mess. ⟨informal⟩
    What a fool he is!

Some adverbs of place (e.g. *home*) or time (e.g. *before*) can modify nouns. The
adverb is placed after the noun (see 648):

    Our journey *home* was pretty tiring.
    The weather was fine the day *before*.
    We always try to plan several years *ahead*.

In some phrases the adverb can stand both before and after the noun:

> the *above* statement = the statement *above*
> our *upstairs* neighbour = our neighbour *upstairs*

Adverbs as complements of prepositions: *I don't know anybody around* **here.**

469
Some adverbs of place and time act as complements of prepositions such as *after, around, for, from, since*:

> **After** *today*, there will be no more concerts until October.
> I don't know anybody **around** *here.* ⟨informal⟩
> I'm saving the chocolates you gave me **for** *later.*
> He shouted at me **from** *downstairs.*
> Are we far **from** *home?*
> I haven't eaten **since** *yesterday.*

Here are more examples of the preposition *from* + adverb combinations:

> *from above, from abroad, from below, from inside, from outside.*

Several prepositions can form combinations with the place adverbs *here* and *there*, for example:

from here, from there	*in here, in there*
near here, near there	*over here, over there*
through here, through there	*up here, up there.*

Apposition
(*see CGEL* 17.65–93)

470
Two or more noun phrases which occur next to each other and refer to the same person or thing are said to be in apposition:

> *A famous author, Ted Johnson,* is coming here next week.

The noun phrases in apposition can also occur in a different order:

> ∼ *Ted Johnson, a famous author,* will be coming here next week.

In the last sentence we can regard the second noun phrase as a reduced non-restrictive relative clause (*see* 693):

> ∼ *Ted Johnson,* (who is) *a famous author,* will be coming here next week.

The meaning relation expressed by apposition is the same as that expressed by a subject and its complement:

> *Ted Johnson* is *a famous author.*

Restrictive and non-restrictive apposition: *spokeswoman Ann Guthrie*
471
Just like relative clauses, apposition can be restrictive or non-restrictive.

• Restrictive apposition:

> (Which Mr Smith do you mean?)
> |Mr Smith the ́architect| or Mr Smith the electr̀ician?|

Here *the architect* and *the electrician* restrict and narrow down the meaning of
Mr Smith.

• Non-restrictive apposition:

> |I want to speak to Mr Smìth, | the electr̀ician.|

Here *the electrician* does not restrict or limit the meaning of *Mr Smith*. The noun
phrases in non-restrictive apposition are here separated by a comma ⟨in
writing⟩, or by separate tone units ⟨in speech⟩, as in non-restrictive relative
clauses (*see* 397). Restrictive apposition is common, especially when the first
element defines the meaning of the second element:

> the famous writer Ted Johnson
> the novel *Moby Dick*
> my good friend Barbara
> this man Smith

Sometimes the determiner is omitted ⟨*esp.* written AmE⟩:

> writer Ted Johnson
> hospital spokeswoman Ann Guthrie

Here, the first noun phrase is almost like a title (as in *President Lincoln, Professor
Chomsky, see* 668).

Explicit apposition: *some poets, chiefly Shelley and Wordsworth*
472
Sometimes the appositional relation of the noun phrases is made explicit by an
adverbial such as *especially* and *chiefly*:

> They had travelled in *many countries*, especially *those in South-East Asia*.
> She had written about *the English romantics*, chiefly *Shelley and
> Wordsworth*.

Other expressions of explicit apposition: *for example, for instance, particularly, in
particular, notably, mainly* (for appositive clauses, *see* 646).

Articles
(*see CGEL* 5.10–11. 5.26–72)

473

There are two articles in English, the definite article *the* (*the book*) and the indefinite article *a* (*a book*) or *an* (*an eye*). Sometimes nouns require no article at all. This is called the 'zero article' (*books, eyes*). The articles are a subclass of the determiners (*see* 522).

It is the initial sound of the word following the article that determines how the indefinite article is spelled, and also how the definite and indefinite articles are pronounced. The unstressed definite article is always written *the*, but is pronounced /ðə/ before consonants and /ðɪ/ before vowels:

> *the* /ðə/ *car, pilot,* etc.   *the* /ðɪ/ *egg, idea,* etc.

The indefinite article is *a* /ə/ before consonants and *an* /ən/ before vowels:

> *a* /ə/ *car, pilot,* etc.   *an* /ən/ *egg, idea,* etc.

It is the pronunciation, not the spelling, of the following word that determines the choice of the indefinite article:

> *an X-ray* /ən ˈeksreɪ/
> *a UN* /əˈjuːˈen/ *spokesperson* (BUT *an EU* /ən ˈiːˈjuː/ *spokesperson*)
> *an hour, an heir* [both nouns beginning with silent *h*]

The articles are normally unstressed, but may be stressed for special emphasis. The stressed forms of the indefinite article are *a* /eɪ/ and *an* /æn/. The stressed form of the definite article is *the* /ðiː/. It is often used to denote excellence or superiority:

> The press conference will be the /ðiː/ event this week.

Article usage: *a ball, the balls, milk*

474

The general rules for the use of the articles are as follows:

- The definite article is used to express definiteness for all kinds of nouns (except proper nouns, such as *Susan, Asia* or *San Francisco*, which do not take an article; *see* 92).

> Singular count nouns:
>
> *the ball*   *the child*   *the exam*
>
> Plural count nouns:
>
> *the balls*   *the children*   *the exams*
>
> Mass nouns:
>
> *the gold*   *the knowledge*   *the milk*

- The indefinite article is used to express indefinite meaning of singular count nouns:

  a ball   *a child*   *an exam*

- Zero article (i.e. no article at all) or unstressed *some* /səm/ is used to express indefinite meaning of plural count nouns and of mass nouns.

  Plural count nouns:

  (*some*) *balls*   (*some*) *children*   (*some*) *exams*

  Mass nouns:

  (*some*) *gold*   (*some*) *knowledge*   (*some*) *milk*

The general rules of meaning for the use of articles with common nouns are discussed in Part Two (*see* 83). Here we shall give some information about article usage with common nouns that occur without an article and the use of count nouns as complements. (For proper nouns, *see* 667.)

Common nouns without article: *I felt sleepy after* **dinner.**
475
Here we list some exceptional groups of common nouns that occur without article. This usage chiefly occurs in idiomatic expressions and certain fixed combinations of words (*at night*, etc.). For contrast, examples of regular uses of the article are also given (*during the night*, etc.).

- Means of transport (with *by*)

  Did you get here *by train* or *by car*? B U T: We slept in the car.

Also: *by bus, by boat, by bike* etc.

- Times of the day and night

  These birds are mostly active *at dawn* and *at dusk*.
  We arrived rather late *at night*.

Also: *after daybreak, by sunrise, before sunset, at midnight, at twilight, at noon* (B U T: *in the afternoon, in the night*, etc.).

- Meals

  We were given scrambled eggs *for breakfast*.
  She is *having lunch* with her publisher.
  I felt sleepy *after dinner*.

- Other expressions:

> Do you *go to church* regularly?
> BUT: We walked towards the church.
> Young people should not be sent *to prison.*
> BUT: We drove past the prison.
> She was *in hospital* for six months. ⟨esp BrE⟩
> BUT: Where is the hospital?
> We met *at school* and began courting *in college.*
> We were *at university* together. ⟨esp BrE.⟩
> Let's have lunch *in town* tomorrow.
> BUT: She knows the town well.
> I like going *to bed* late.

Also: *stay in bed, get out of bed, put the children to bed, be ill in bed.* BUT: sit *on the* bed, lie down *on the* bed, etc.

- Parallel phrases

> They walked *arm in arm.*   BUT: He took her by the arm.
> We walked *hand in hand.*   BUT: What have you got in your hand?
>
> They are *husband and wife.*   BUT: She's the wife of a famous artist.
>
> We met *face to face.*   BUT: He punched me right in the face.

Count nouns as complement: *She wants to be **a doctor**.*

476

Unlike many other languages, English requires an article with singular count nouns as complement (e.g. after *be* and other linking verbs, see 508, 719). With indefinite reference, the indefinite article is used:

> Mary always wanted to be *a scientist.*

With certain verbs, e.g. *consider*, the complement follows the object or the passive:

> Everybody considered Mr Heyman (to be) *an excellent music teacher.*
> Mr Heyman was considered (to be) *an excellent music teacher.*

With other verbs, e.g. *regard*, the complement follows *as*:

> We regarded her *as a goddess.*

With definite reference, the definite article is normally used:

> Phil Moore was regarded as *the best disc jockey* in town.

However, the definite article can be omitted when the noun designates a unique role, office or task:

> Who's (*the*) *captain of the team?*
> We've elected Mr Cook (*the*) *chairman of the committee.*

In these examples the definite article can be left out because there is only one captain of a team and one chairman of a committee. The definite article can also be omitted with a noun phrase in apposition (*see* 470):

> Mrs Peterson, (*the*) *wife of a leading local businessman*, was fined for reckless driving.

Auxiliary verbs
(*see CGEL* 3.21–51)

477
Auxiliary verbs are, as their name suggests, 'helping verbs'. They are a small class of words including primary auxiliaries like *be* and modal auxiliaries like *can* and *will.* Auxiliaries do not make up a verb phrase on their own but help to make up a verb phrase in combination with a main verb (such as *work*) (*see* 735):

> I'*m working* all day today.
> I *can* even *work* at weekends if you need me.

An auxiliary verb can also occur without a main verb, but only where the main verb is omitted because it is supplied by the earlier context (*see* 384):

> I can speak French as well as she *can.*

In English, auxiliary verbs are required in certain constructions, especially questions and negative clauses:

[A] *Do* you *want* a cup of coffee?
[B] No, I *don't think* so, thank you.

- Auxiliary verbs differ from main verbs in that they can be placed before *not*:

  > I'*m* not working today. BUT: I don't *work* every day.

- Unlike main verbs, auxiliary verbs can be placed before the subject in questions:

  > *Can* I help you? BUT: Do you *want* me to help you?

478
Some auxiliary verbs have short (contracted) forms, for example: *I'm* (contracted form) instead of *I am* (uncontracted form). Contracted forms are common in ⟨spoken⟩ and ⟨informal⟩ English. Contracted forms can be used

- after pronouns:

    I'*ll* see you tomorrow.

- after short nouns:

    The *dog's* getting ready for his walk.
    The *soup'll* get cold.

- after short adverbs such as *here, there, how,* and *now*:

    Here's your key.
    How's everything with you?
    Now's the time to act.

- after introductory *there – see* 490–4:

    I think *there's* going to be trouble.

In addition, most auxiliary verbs have contracted negative forms, *isn't, can't,* etc. (*see* 582):

    The dog *isn't* here.

The auxiliary verb *do*: *What* do you say to that?
479
The auxiliary *do* has the following forms:

	Non-negative	Uncontracted negative	Contracted negative
present: 3rd person singular	*does*	*does not*	*doesn't*
present: not 3rd person singular	*do*	*do not*	*don't*
past	*did*	*did not*	*didn't*

Do is also a main verb ('perform', etc.):

    What have you been *doing* today?

In addition, *do* is a substitute verb (*see* 383), as in:

    [A] You said you would finish the job today.
    [B] I h`ave *done*. OR: I have *d`one* so.

When used as a main verb or a substitute verb, *do* has the full range of forms, including the present participle *doing* and the past participle *done,* as these examples show. (*Doing* and *done* are not included in the above table, which shows only the forms of the auxiliary *do*.)

The auxiliary verb *have*: *Have you seen today's paper?*
480
Like *do*, *have* is both a main verb and an auxiliary. It has the following forms:

	Non-negative		Negative	
	Uncontracted	Contracted	Uncontracted	Contracted
base	*have*	*'ve*	*have not,* *'ve not*	*haven't*
-s form	*has*	*'s*	*has not,* *'s not*	*hasn't*
past	*had*	*'d*	*had not,* *'d not*	*hadn't*
-ing form	*having*		*not having*	
-ed participle	*had*			

As a main verb, *have* ('possess') is sometimes constructed as an auxiliary ⟨esp BrE⟩:

> I *haven't* any money. ⟨esp BrE⟩

But this is increasingly rare. Nowadays both ⟨AmE⟩ and ⟨BrE⟩ prefer the *do*-construction:

> I *don't have* any money. ⟨AmE⟩ and ⟨BrE⟩

When used as an event verb (*see* 114) in the sense of 'take, experience, receive', the main verb *have* normally has the *do*-construction in both ⟨AmE⟩ and ⟨BrE*)*:

> *Does* he *have* coffee with his breakfast?
> *Did* you *have* any difficulty getting here?
> *Did* you *have* a good time?

481
There is also the ⟨informal⟩ *have got*, which is similar in function to *have* as a state verb, and where *have* is constructed as an auxiliary. It is particularly common in negative and interrogative sentences:

> They *haven't got* a single idea between them!
> How many students *have* you *got* in your class?

Note
⟨AmE⟩ has *gotten* as the past participle, corresponding to ⟨BrE⟩ *got* in certain senses: 'acquire, cause, come':

> He had *gotten* stuck with a job too big for his imagination.

⟨AmE⟩ makes a distinction between *We've gotten tickets* = 'acquired' and *We've got tickets* = 'possess'.

The auxiliary verb *be*: *What on earth are you doing?*
482
Be has eight different forms (which is more than any other English verb). *Be* is constructed as an auxiliary also when it functions as a main verb. For example, it has no *do*-construction (except in commands, *see* Note [b] below).

The forms of *be*

		Non-negative	Uncontracted negative	Contracted negative
base		*be*		
present	1st person singular 3rd person singular 2nd person singular and all persons plural	*am, 'm* *is, 's* *are, 're*	*am not, 'm not* *is not, 's not* *are not, 're not*	*(aren't, ain't)* [a] *isn't* *aren't*
past	1st and 3rd person singular 2nd person singular and plural, 1st and 3rd person plural	*was* *were*	*was not* *were not*	*wasn't* *weren't*
-ing form		*being*	*not being*	
-ed participle		*been*		

Note
[a] In negative questions *aren't I?*, as in *I'm right, aren't I?*, is widely used in ⟨BrE⟩, but it is felt to be somewhat affected in ⟨AmE⟩. In negative declarative sentences there is no generally acceptable contracted form for *am not*. *Ain't* is a ⟨non-standard⟩ construction used, esp. in ⟨AmE⟩, as in *Things ain't what they used to be*. As well as serving as a contracted *are not*, *ain't* is used also for *am not*, *is not* (*Ain't it the truth?*), *has not* and *have not* (*We ain't got nothing to talk about*). All these examples are taken from ⟨very informal⟩ AmE.

[b] The main verb *be* may have the *do*-construction in persuasive imperative sentences. *Do be quiet!* is more persuasive or emphatic than *Be quiet!* The *do*-construction is also required with negative imperatives (*see* 497): *Don't be awkward!*

The modal auxiliaries: *Can I use your phone?*
483
The modal auxiliaries do not have *-s* forms, *-ing* forms, or *-ed* participles. *Can, may, shall, will* have the special past forms *could, might, should, would*. The other modal auxiliaries (*must, dare, need, ought to, used to*) do not have such forms.

The modal auxiliaries

Non-negative	Uncontracted negative	Contracted negative
can	*cannot, can not*	*can't*
could	*could not*	*couldn't*
may	*may not*	(*mayn't*) [a]
might	*might not*	*mightn't*
shall	*shall not*	*shan't* [b]
should	*should not*	*shouldn't*
will, 'll	*will not, 'll not*	*won't*
would, 'd	*would not, 'd not*	*wouldn't*
must	*must not*	*mustn't*
ought to	*ought not to*	*oughtn't to*
used to [c]	*used not to*	*didn't use(d) to, usedn't to*
need [c]	*need not*	*needn't*
dare [c]	*dare not*	*daren't*

[a] *Mayn't* is rare.
[b] *Shan't* is rare, especially in ⟨AmE⟩.
[c] *Used to*, *need*, and *dare* as auxiliaries are rare in all forms.

Here are some examples of modal auxiliaries as used in conversation:

|As far as Ì *can* see | I'm sure she's a very clever wòman. |

|What he dòesn't réalize is | that not ˇeverybody else | *can* work as hard
as hè *can*.|

|I'm sure that he *would* be awfully gràteful | if you *could* see him in your
òffice sómetime.|

|What *shall* we do about this requèst then | – just write saying I'm very
sorry I cánnot | teach at the ínstitute.|

|She *should* have had her dissertation ǐn | at the beginning of Mǎy.|

|I did get a póstcard fròm her | saying that the thing is now réady | and
that she *will* send it by the end of Jùne.|

|Our chair is very stròngly of the opínion | that we àll *ought* to go on
téaching | to the end of the tèrm.|

|I think this mǎy be whý | he's so cross about the whole thìng.|

|I don't mind getting pìn money | for typing someone's thèsis | but they
might tèll me so | befòrehand.|

Dare and **need**: *You **needn't** worry about it.*
484
Dare and *need* can be constructed in two ways:
• either as main verbs (with *to*-infinitive, *-s* inflection and past forms):
It *needs to be said* that she is not to be blamed for what happened.

- or as modal auxiliaries (with bare infinitive and without the inflected forms *dares* ~ *dared, needs* ~ *needed*):

> Our country's prestige *need not suffer.*
> There *need be* no doubt about that.

The modal auxiliary construction is mainly restricted to negative and interrogative sentences, and is rare. *Dare* and *need* as auxiliaries are less common in ⟨AmE⟩ than in ⟨BrE⟩. The main verb construction can always be used, and is in fact the more common in all varieties:

> Our country's prestige *does not need to suffer.*
> There *does not need to be* any doubt about that.

Used to: *They **used** not **to** come here.*

485
As an auxiliary *used* always takes the *to*-infinitive and is pronounced /'juːstə/. *Used to* occurs only in the past tense:

> He *used to* be a racing driver.
> She *used to* come every day and talk to me for a few minutes.

This auxiliary may take the *do*-construction, in which case the spellings *use* and *used* both occur:

> He *didn't use to smoke.* OR: He *didn't used to smoke.*

In more ⟨formal⟩ style this construction is preferred:

> He *used not to smoke.*

The interrogative construction *Used he to smoke?* is ⟨esp. BrE⟩. The more ⟨informal⟩ *Did he use(d) to smoke?* is preferred in both ⟨AmE⟩ and ⟨BrE⟩. However, a different construction is often a more natural choice, for example: *Did he smoke when you first knew him?*

Clauses
(*see CGEL* 10.1–33, 14.5–9)

486
Sentences are made up of clauses. A sentence may consist of one, or more than one clause (*see* 695). There are three ways in which clauses may be described:

- In terms of the **clause elements** (subject, verb, etc.) from which they are constructed, and the verb patterns which are formed from these elements (*see* 487, 718).
- In terms of **finite clauses**, **non-finite clauses**, and **verbless clauses** (*see* 492).
- In terms of **clause function**, i.e. the function a clause performs in a sentence.

We talk about nominal clauses (clauses acting as noun phrases), adverbial clauses (clauses acting as adverbial elements), etc. (*see* 495).

We shall deal with each of these in turn.

Clause elements: S, V, O, C, A
487
A clause can be analysed into five different types of clause elements:

> S = Subject (*see* 705)
> V = Verb (or rather verb phrase, *see* 718)
> O = Object (*see* 608)
> C = Complement (*see* 508)
> A = Adverbial (*see* 449)

These clause elements can be shown in a diagram:

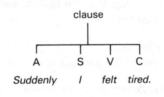

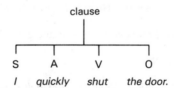

488
Among these types we may distinguish the four **main elements** of clause structure (subject, verb, complement, object) and one **modifying element** (adverbial). Adverbials differ from the other clause elements in three important ways:

- Adverbials are usually **optional**, i.e. they may be omitted (optional adverbials are given in brackets):

    (Suddenly) I felt tired.
    I (quickly) shut the door.

- Adverbials are **not restricted in number**. A clause can only have one subject, one finite verb, one complement, and one or two objects. But, there may be any number of adverbials. (This is theory, of course: in practice you will rarely find more than three adverbials in one clause.)

SV:	She awoke.
SV[A]:	She awoke [in the middle of the night].
[A]SV[A]:	[Sometimes] she awoke [in the middle of the night].

- Adverbials are often **mobile**, i.e. they can occur at different places in the clause:

[A]SV[A][A][A]	[Sometimes] I stay [a couple of extra hours] [in the office] [to finish up a job].
[A]S[A]V[A][A]	[To finish up a job] I [sometimes] stay [a couple of extra hours] [in the office].

(On the positions of adverbials, *see* 451.)

The basic verb patterns
489

If we look at the main elements in the clause (S, V, O, C), we can distinguish six basic verb patterns. (We call them 'verb patterns' rather than 'clause patterns', since it is the verb that determines the type of clause structure. For more details, *see* 718.)

- The first verb pattern occurs with linking verbs: *be, appear, look, seem,* etc. (SVC, or sometimes SVA). Linking verbs 'link together' the subject and the complement:

> His father *is* [*a lawyer*].
> Both boxers *became* [*famous*].
> The victory *seems* [a *foregone conclusion*].
> The guard posts *are* [*along the frontier*].

- The second verb pattern occurs with verbs that have one object, i.e. transitive verbs (SVO):

> She *liked* [*Hemingway's style*].

- The third verb pattern occurs with verbs that have an object + a verb (SVOV . . .):

> The manager *asked* [*me*] [*to work overtime*].

- The fourth verb pattern occurs with verbs that have two objects (which are called ditransitive verbs, SVOO):

> I'll *give* [*you*] [*the report*] on Monday.

- The fifth verb pattern occurs with verbs that have an object and an object complement (SVOC):

They *found* [*the house*] [*too expensive*].

- The sixth verb pattern occurs with verbs without object or complement, i.e. intransitive verbs (SV):

    The children just *laughed*.

The active-passive relation
490
There are certain relations between clause elements. One is the relation which makes it possible to change an active clause into a passive clause (*see* 613). The following verb patterns can occur in the passive (optional agents in round brackets):

Pattern	Active	Passive
SVO	Everybody rejected the idea.	The idea was rejected (by everybody).
SVOV ...	The manager asked me to work overtime.	I was asked (by the manager) to work overtime.
SVOO	The ambulance crew gave the casualties first aid.	The casualties were given first aid (by the ambulance crew).
SVOC	Boat owners considered the bridge a menace to navigation.	The bridge was considered a menace to navigation (by boat owners).

When an active clause is changed into a passive clause, the object of the active clause is converted into the subject of the passive clause. Therefore only those patterns which contain an object can be converted into the passive. The pattern with two objects

    I'll give you the report on Monday.

has two passive forms:

    You'll be given the report on Monday.
    The report will be given (to) you on Monday.

The complements of subjects and objects: *We found him **unhelpful**.*
491
The commonest verb in the pattern with linking verbs (SVC) is *be*. Here *be* is not an auxiliary, as in *She is leaving* (*see* 739), but a main verb (*see* 573): *She is a teacher*. Since *be* links together the subject and the complement, we call it a **linking verb**. There are also other linking verbs, such as the verbs of 'appearance' and 'sensation' *look* and *feel*, and the verbs of 'becoming' *become* and *get* (*see* 719):

    She *looks* so tired and worn, and I *felt* very worried last night when she
        rang up and said she couldn't come.
    Right from the beginning we *became* very attached to each other.

Let's hope the world will gradually *become* a better place in which to live.

The verb pattern SVOC can often be expanded by a *to be* infinitive or paraphrased by a *that*-clause (*see* 724, 727):

> We found *him unhelpful.*
> ~ We found *him to be unhelpful.*
> ~ We found *that he was unhelpful.*

The object and the complement of the SVOC verb pattern have the same relation of meaning as the subject and complement of an SVC pattern with a linking verb: *He was unhelpful.*

Finite, non-finite, and verbless clauses

492

A second way of looking at a clause is to see what kind of verb phrase acts as its V element. Here we first distinguish finite clauses and non-finite clauses.

Finite clauses are clauses whose verb element is a finite verb phrase (*see* 737). In a finite verb phrase there may be just one finite verb:

> She evidently *works* terribly hard.
> She evidently *worked* terribly hard.

If the verb phrase consists of more than one verb, the first verb is finite:

> She *has worked* in the office for six months.
> She *is working* in the office for six months.

Normally, in ⟨written⟩ language, a complete sentence has at least one independent finite verb clause.

493

Non-finite clauses are clauses whose verb element is a non-finite verb phrase. A non-finite verb phrase consists of non-finite elements such as an *-ing* participle (*see* 578), an *-ed* participle (*see* 577), or an infinitive (*see* 575). Most non-finite clauses do not have a subject:

- *-ing* clause without a subject:

  > I used to lie awake at night, *worrying about the next election.*

- *-ing* clause with a subject:

  > *His remark having been represented as an insult*, he was later forced to resign from the committee.

- *-ed* clause without a subject:

  > *Covered with confusion*, she hurriedly left the room.

- *-ed* clause with a subject:

> *The job finished*, we went home straight away.

- *to*-infinitive clause without a subject:

  > The best thing would be *to leave straight away*.

- *to*-infinitive clause with a subject. The subject of an infinitive clause is often introduced by the preposition *for*:

  > The best thing would be *for us to leave straight away*.

- bare infinitive clause (i.e. containing an infinitive without *to*) without a subject. These are much less common than *to*-infinitive clauses.

  > All I did was *hit him on the head*.

- bare infinitive clause with a subject:

  > Rather than *Joan do it*, I'd prefer to do the job myself.

494

Verbless clauses contain no verb element, and often no subject:

> Dozens of tourists were stranded, *many of them children*.
> *A sleeping bag under each arm*, they tramped off on their vacation.

They are regarded as clauses because they function like finite and non-finite clauses, and because they can be analysed in terms of one or more clause elements. We can usually assume that a form of the verb *be* or some other verb has been omitted: 'many of the tourists *were* children', 'they *had* a sleeping bag under each arm'. The subject, when omitted, can usually be understood as equivalent to the subject of the main clause:

> The oranges, *when ripe*, are picked and sorted ('when they are ripe').
> *Whether right or wrong*, Michael always comes off worst in an argument ('whether he is right or wrong').

An adjective, alone or as head of an adjective phrase, can function as a verbless clause:

> *Anxious for a quick decision*, the chairman called for a vote.
> An escort of ten horsemen waited behind the coach, *half asleep in their saddles*.

The clause is mobile, though it usually precedes or follows the subject of the main clause:

> *Even if true*, this statement would be misleading.
> ~ This statement, *even if true*, would be misleading.

An adverb may sometimes replace an adjective functioning as a verbless clause. There is hardly any difference in meaning between these two sentences:

Nervously, the gunman opened the letter.
Nervous, the gunman opened the letter.

Clause functions

495

In terms of function, i.e. what role they have in a sentence, clauses can be divided into **main clauses** and **subclauses** (subordinate clauses; *see* 709). Subclauses are part of another clause. We can also divide them into nominal clauses, adverbial clauses, etc. The various functions of clauses are treated elsewhere:

- **Nominal clauses** (*see* 588), i.e. *that*-clauses, interrogative clauses, *-ing* clauses, and infinitive clauses function as subject, object, complement, prepositional complement, etc. In this example the first *that*-clause functions as subject and the second as object:

    That he gave a false name shows *that he was doing something dishonest.*

- **Relative clauses** (*see* 686), i.e. modifying clauses introduced by *wh*-pronouns or *that* (including 'zero-*that*'), are usually modifiers of noun phrases. In this sentence the relative clause *who live opposite our house* modifies the noun phrase head *family*:

    The family *who live opposite our house* are French.

- **Comment clauses** (*see* 499) function as sentence adverbials (*see* 461), as in this sentence where *to be honest* equates with the adverb *honestly*:

    To be honest, I'm not sure what to do.

- **Comparative clauses** (*see* 505) follow a comparative item such as *more* or *less*:

    This year they've sold a lot more books *than they usually do.*

- **Adverbial clauses** have a large number of different meanings, such as time:

    I used to go to the theatre *whenever I had the opportunity.*

Adverbial clauses are discussed in Part Two: clauses denoting time (*see* 151), place (*see* 170), contrast (*see* 211), cause or reason (*see* 198, 204), purpose (*see* 203), result (*see* 202), and conditional clauses (*see* 207).

Cleft sentences

(*see CGEL* 18.25–30)

496

A single clause, such as

    Our neighbours bought that new house last year.   [1]

can be divided into two separate parts, each with its own verb:

[It *was* our neighbours] [who *bought* that new house last year.]   [1a]

A construction like [1a] is called a **cleft sentence** (*see* 419). A sentence like [1] can be changed into different cleft sentences depending on what element is considered the most important in the sentence. This has to do with focus (*see* 399). In [1a] the subject *our neighbours* is in focus. In [1b] the object *house* is in focus:

|It was that new h<u>ou</u>se that our neighbours bought last ye\`ar.| [1b]

In [1c] the adverbial *last year* is in focus:

|It was last ye\`ar that our neighbours bought that new hou\`se.| [1c]

The second part of a cleft sentence is very similar to a restrictive relative clause (*see* 687). The relative pronouns are also used in cleft sentences: e.g. *who* in [1a] and *that* in [1b].

Besides the **it-type cleft sentence**, there is also a **wh-type cleft sentence** (*see* 420). If we want to place the object *house* of [1] in focus we can use either the *it*-type in [1b] or the *wh*-type in [2b]:

|It was that new h<u>ou</u>se that our neighbours bought last ye\`ar.| [1b]
|What our neighbours bought last ye\`ar| was that new h<u>ou</u>se| [2b]

Cleft sentences are different from sentences with introductory *there* (*see* 547):

There's a lovely house for sale in our village.

and introductory *it* (*see* 542):

It doesn't cost much to buy a new radio.

Commands
(*see CGEL* 11.24–30)

497
We distinguish two types: 2nd person commands and 1st and 3rd person commands.

2nd person commands: *Behave yourself.*
A command is usually a sentence with an imperative verb, i.e. the base form of the verb, without endings for number or tense:

Come here.

Commands are apt to sound abrupt unless they are toned down by politeness signals like *please* (*see* 332):

Please *get* ready as soon as you can.
Shut the door, please.

The only auxiliary verb used in commands is *do*:

Don't stay too late, Pam.
Don't be a fool. [But in a statement we say: They *weren't* fools.]

The *do*-construction is used in such *not*-negated commands. But *do* can also occur in positive commands. If we want to make a command more emphatic or persuasive, we can say

Do sit down. (Compare: *Sit down.*]

Do tell us how you got on at your interview. [Compare: *Tell us . . .*]

In positive sentences it is only in commands that *do* can be followed by *be*:

Do be careful. [But in a statement we say: They *are* careful.]

As these examples indicate, commands usually have no **expressed** subject. When the subject is missing, we can say that there is an **implied** subject *you*. This is why we call this type of command '2nd person commands'. We can see that there is an implied subject *you* when there is a reflexive pronoun *yourself/yourselves* (*see* 619):

Behave yourself.

or a tag (*see* 684):

Be quiet, will you!

However, in commands there can sometimes be an expressed subject *you*:

You just listen to me now.
You go right ahead with your plan.

This expressed *you* is stressed in commands:

'You 'put that down. [Command] ⟨impolite⟩

Commands with *you* can sound particularly ⟨impolite⟩, as in this example. But *you* is not stressed in statements:

You 'swim well. [Statement]

498
1st and 3rd person commands: *Let's go and eat.*
There are also 1st person and 3rd person commands, but they are not as common as 2nd person commands. A 1st person command begins with *let me* in the singular or, in the plural, *let's* (the full form *let us* is rare):

Let me have a look at your essay.
Let's go and eat. ⟨informal⟩ OR *Let's* go eat. ⟨informal AmE⟩

A 3rd person command has a 3rd person subject, as in

Now *somebody* open this door. ⟨informal⟩

Commands with *let* + a 3rd person subject are ⟨formal⟩, often ⟨elevated⟩ in style:

Let each nation decide its own fate. ⟨formal⟩

Comment clauses

(*see CGEL* 15.53–56)

499
Comment clauses comment on the truth of the sentence, the manner of saying it, or the attitude of the speaker:

> The minister's proposal could, *I believe*, be a vital contribution towards
>   world peace.

Comment clauses like *I believe* are only loosely related to the rest of the main clause they belong to, and they function as sentence adverbials (*see* 462). They are usually marked off from the other clause, in ⟨written⟩ English by commas:

> *What's more*, we lost all we had.
> *Stated bluntly*, they have no chance of recovery.

In ⟨speech⟩ comment clauses are often marked off by having a separate tone unit:

> |She's an industrial desìgner | *you sée.*|
> |I'm not sure whàt to do| *to be hónest.*|

Comment clauses can occur in front-, mid- or end-position. Here are some other examples of comment clauses:

> |It's the same at the board meetings tòo *you see*| – *I mean* he takes over
>   the whole thìng|.
> |In a sense it ìs| a nèw ídea| but well – *you knów*| we're not prepared to
>   dò this|.

There are many types of comment clauses, e.g.:

> *I see, I think, I suppose, I'm afraid, as you see, as I said, to be frank, so
> to say, so to speak, what's more likely, you see, you know, you bet*
> ⟨familiar⟩.

Some such 'fillers' or 'discourse items' are very common in ⟨informal speech⟩, in particular *you see, you know, I mean, I think*, etc. (*see* 23).

Comparison

(*see* Section 225 and *CGEL* 7.74–90, 15.63–75)

500
Gradable adjectives and adverbs (*see* 216) have degrees of comparison: **comparative** and **superlative**. Comparison is expressed either by the endings *-er* and *-est* or by the words *more* and *most* before the adjective or adverb:

		Comparative	Superlative
Adjectives	tall	tall*er*	tall*est*
	beautiful	*more* beautiful	*most* beautiful
Adverbs	soon	soon*er*	soon*est*
	easily	*more* easily	*most* easily

Comparison of adjectives: *big* ~ *bigger* ~ *biggest*

501

Comparison with the endings *-er* and *-est* is generally used with short adjectives:

- One-syllable adjectives:

  great ~ *greater* ~ *greatest*

- Two-syllable adjectives ending in *-y*, *-ow*, *-le* and *-er*:

  easy ~ *easier* ~ *easiest*; also: *early, friendly, lively*, etc.
  narrow ~ *narrower* ~ *narrowest*; also: *mellow, shallow*, etc.
  able ~ *abler* ~ *ablest*; also: *simple, gentle, humble*, etc.
  clever ~ *cleverer* ~ *cleverest*; also: *bitter*, etc.

Some common two-syllable adjectives such as *common, polite, quiet* can have either type of comparison:

  common ~ *commoner* ~ *commonest* OR
  common ~ *more common* ~ *most common*

Occasionally, also one-syllable adjectives occur with *more* or *most*:

  more true ~ *most true, more proud* ~ *most proud*.

The endings sometimes involve changes in spelling (*see* 700, 703) or pronunciation (*see* 666), for example:

  pretty ~ *prettier* ~ *prettiest*
  big ~ *bigger* ~ *biggest*

Long adjectives (*awkward, possible, hopeful*, etc.), including *-ed* adjectives (*interested*, etc.) and *-ing* adjectives (*interesting*, etc.) form comparison with *more* and *most*:

  I find my new work *more challenging* and *more interesting*.
  That's one of the *most famous* places in the area.

502

A small group of highly frequent adjectives have irregular comparison:

- *bad* ~ *worse* ~ *worst*:

  Yesterday was a *bad* day for the stock market, but today seems to be the *worst* day of the week.

- *good ~ better ~ best*:

> There'd be a *better* chance to win the series with a new coach.
> To keep the children happy for the afternoon, the *best* thing to do was
> to run a film.

- *far ~ further ~ furthest* OR (less common) *far ~ farther ~ farthest*, for example

> The police never got any *further* with this problem.
> They did not relinquish their *farthest* outposts. ⟨rather formal⟩

Further elsewhere is not a comparative, but means 'additional':

> Any *further* questions?
> We stayed for a *further* three weeks. (But in ⟨informal⟩ usage usually:
> *for another three weeks.*)

Old has the regular forms *older ~ oldest*, but *elder ~ eldest* are normally used to
denote family relations:

> They've lost their two *elder* sons in the war.

Older is always used before a *than*-construction:

> Come and meet my *eldest* brother who is nine years *older than me.*

Comparison of adverbs: *well ~ better ~ best*
503
Adverbs have the same general rules of comparison as adjectives. Adverbs of
two or more syllables formed from adjectives with the *-ly* ending (*quick ~ quickly*)
have comparison with *more* and *most*:

- *quickly ~ more quickly ~ most quickly*

> The memos have to be circulated *more quickly.*

As with adjectives, there is a small group of adverbs with irregular comparison:

- *well ~ better ~ best*

> To qualify, you have to do *better* than this.
> The picture in the middle, that's the one I like *best.*

- *badly ~ worse ~ worst*

> Financially, we may be *worse* hit than some of the other departments.

- *(much) ~ more ~ most*

> You deserve a prize *more* than anyone.
> She is my *most* helpful colleague.

- *(little) ~ less ~ least*

> The older you are, the *less* strenuous the exercises should be.

The money arrived when she *least* expected it.

- *far ~ further ~ furthest* OR *far ~ farther ~ farthest*

    The sun's *further* away from the earth than the moon.
    They seem to be *farther* apart than ever before.

Comparison of quantifiers: *Waste less money!*
504
The quantifiers *much, many, little* and *few* (*see* 676) also have special comparative and superlative forms when they function as determiners:

- *much ~ more ~ most*

    We need *more* money to buy new computers for the students.
    Most of our computer equipment is ten years old.

- *many ~ more ~ most*

    We also need *more* books in the department.
    I find *most* people working in the library very helpful.

- *little ~ less ~ least*

    We now spend *less* money on periodicals than last year.
    I haven't the *least* idea what to do now.

- *few ~ fewer ~ fewest* OR *few ~ less ~ least* (On the choice of *fewer/less, see* 73.)

    · We want *fewer/less*, not more restrictions.

Comparative clauses: *Ann speaks French better than I do.*
505
The comparative form of adjectives and adverbs is used when we want to compare one thing with another in order to point out some difference (*see* 225). For this purpose, a subclause beginning with *than* can be added after the comparative word:

    His most recent book is *more interesting* than his previous ones were.

In this sentence, *more interesting* may be called the 'hinge' element of the comparison. The hinge element is the phrase which contains the comparative word. The following *than*-clause modifies the hinge element. It is called a 'hinge' because it belongs, in terms of meaning, both to the main clause and to the comparative subclause. The meaning of the hinge element *more interesting* complements *is* in the main clause and *were* in the subclause. But in terms of structure, the subclause does not contain a complement. Here are some more examples of comparative clauses:

    She looks *much younger than* her sister does.

Ann speaks French *less well than* she writes it.
We're in a hurry because prices are going up *faster than* we can buy.

Comparative phrases: *Ann speaks French better than I/me.*
506
The part of the sentence following *than* may have different structures:

Ann can speak French better *than I can.*	[1]
Ann can speak French better *than I.* ⟨formal⟩	[2]
Ann can speak French better *than me.* ⟨informal⟩	[3]

In [1] we have the subclause *than I can* (with *speak it* omitted). Other elements of a subclause can also be omitted if they repeat the information in the main clause. If the verb is omitted we are left with a comparative phrase as in [2] and [3] rather than a comparative clause. In ⟨informal⟩ English, the *than*-phrase (*than me* as in [3]) behaves like a prepositional phrase (*to me, for me,* etc.) with the following pronoun in the objective case: *me, them,* etc. (*see* 620). In ⟨formal⟩ English the subjective form of the pronoun (*I, they,* etc.) is used, if the pronoun is notionally the subject of the omitted verb: *than I* [2] (= *than I can speak it*). In ⟨informal⟩ English such clauses can be ambiguous:

He seems to like his dog more than his children.

The most likely meaning is:

He seems to like his dog more than he likes his children.

But another possible meaning is:

He seems to like his dog more than his children do.

An adverbial or adjective can follow *than* in comparative phrases:

She struck him as more beautiful *than ever.*
He said no more *than usual.*
There is higher unemployment in the north *than in the south.*

507
Some types of comparative phrases cannot be related to comparative clauses. One type is concerned with comparison of degree and amount:

There were *fewer* than twenty people at the meeting.
I have *better* things to do than watching television.

Another type is concerned with comparison of descriptions:

The performance was *more good* than bad. ('The performance was good rather than bad.')

Only comparison with *more* or *less* can be used here.
The types of structure just discussed in 505–506 are found both with

'unequal' comparisons (*more quickly, less well*), and with 'equal' comparisons (*as quickly as you can, as much as anybody else*, etc.; *see* 230):

> The voters seem to like the one candidate *as much as* the other.

Complements
(*see CGEL* 10.8, 16.20–83)

508
The term 'complement', in a general sense, means something that is necessary to complete a grammatical construction. We distinguish three types of complement: clause complements, adjective complements and prepositional complements.

Clause complements (*see* 491): *She is a very good lecturer.*
The complement of a clause can be

- a noun phrase (*see* 595):

    > She's *a very good lecturer.*

- an adjective or adjective phrase (*see* 440):

    > Her lectures are *interesting* and *easy to follow.*

- a nominal clause (*see* 588):

    > The only trouble is (*that*) *I can't read what she writes on the blackboard.*

These examples show that the complement usually comes after the verb. If there is both an object and a complement in the sentence, the complement normally comes after the object:

> This sort of behaviour made them *absolutely furious.*
> All students consider her *a very good lecturer.*

The object, but not the complement, can become subject if an active sentence is turned into a passive sentence (*see* 613):

> She is considered *a very good lecturer.*

A complement often expresses a quality or attribute of the subject or object:

> They were *absolutely furious.*

The complement can also tell us the identity of the subject or object:

> My native language is *Chinese.* ('Chinese is my native language')

The complement cannot normally be omitted. If we take away the complement, the remaining part does not make a good English sentence:

> This sort of behaviour made them absolutely furious.
> (BUT NOT: *This sort of behaviour made them.)

Adjective complements can be *that*-clauses, *to*-infinitives and prepositional phrases (*see* 436):

> I'm glad (*that*) *you think so.* (*that*-clause)
> I'm glad *to hear that.* (*to*-infinitive)
> I'm glad *of that.* (prepositional phrase)

Prepositional complements

In the last example, the prepositional phrase *of your success* is the complement of the adjective *glad*. The prepositional phrase itself consists of a preposition (*of*) and its complement (*your success*). The complement is usually a noun phrase (*see* 595):

> They argued *about the change.*

But it can also be a *wh*-clause (*see* 590):

> They argued *about what ought to be changed.*

or an *-ing* clause (*see* 594):

> They argued *about changing the wording of the document.*

Concord
(*see* C G E L 10.34–50)

509

Grammatical concord means that certain grammatical items agree with each other. Concord is therefore also called 'agreement'. There are two types: concord of number (as in singular *the film is* . . . but plural *the films are* . . .) and concord of person (as in 1st person *I am* but 2nd person *you are*).

Concord of number: *she knows ~ they know*
Subject-verb concord

With all verbs except *be*, the question of number concord arises only in the present tense:

> she *knows* ~ they *know*

In the past tense there is no concord variation:

> she *knew* ~ they *knew*

Be differs from other verbs in having many forms (*am*, *are*, *is*, etc.; *see* 482). In the present tense:

> I *am* sure ~ she *is* sure ~ they *are* sure

Be is also exceptional in that it has two forms, *was* (singular) and *were* (plural), in the past tense.

The modal auxiliaries differ from other verbs in having only one form (*must, can, will,* etc.):

> she *must* know ~ they *must* know

A clause acting as subject counts as singular:

> To treat soldiers as hostages *is* criminal.

Pronoun concord

A pronoun which refers back to a singular noun phrase is in the singular, and a pronoun which refers back to a plural noun phrase is in the plural (but *see* 96 on the singular use of *they*):

> *She* lost *her life.* ~ *They* lost *their lives.*

Notional concord: *The government is/are agreed.*

510

Sometimes we find that the singular form of a noun can be treated as plural:

> The public *are* getting tired of these demonstrations.

This is called **notional concord**, since the verb (*are*) agrees with the **idea** of plural in the group noun (*public*) rather than the actual singular **form** of the noun. But it is also possible to treat a group noun like *public* or *government* as singular:

> The public *is* getting tired of these demonstrations.

This is called **grammatical concord** because the basic grammatical rule says:

> **singular subject + singular verb** A N D
> **plural subject + plural verb.**

When the group is being considered as a single undivided body, the singular tends to be used, but it is often hard to see such a meaning distinction. Also, the plural verb after a group noun is more characteristic of ⟨BrE⟩ than of ⟨AmE⟩. Here are some more examples of actual usage:

> The *audience was* generous with *its* cheers and applause and flowers.
> A *committee has* been set up so that in the future *it* will discuss such topics in advance.
> The *committee believe* it is essential that *their* proposal should be adopted as soon as possible.
> We have a market where the *majority* consistently *wins* what the *minority loses.*
> The *majority* of the population *are* of Scandinavian descent.
> The *government has* recognized *its* dilemma and *is* beginning to devise better education in schools.
> The Irish *government* kept it to *themselves* and didn't tell the British.
> Not even the New York *public has* enough money to meet *its* needs.
> The *public are* thinking of planning *their* forthcoming annual holiday.

Attraction: *A large number of people disagree.*
511
The basic concord rule singular subject + singular verb and plural subject + plural verb is sometimes influenced by **attraction**. This means that the verb tends to agree with a noun or pronoun that closely precedes it, instead of the head word of the subject:

> A large number of *people have* asked me to stand for reelection.
> A variety of analytic *methods have* been used.

The grammatical heads of the noun phrases (*number* and *variety*) are both singular, and one would expect the verb form *has*. But the plural noun (*people* and *methods*) in the *of*-phrase modifying the head influences the form of the nearby verb. We call this feature 'attraction' or 'proximity', because the last noun attracts a certain form in the verb and upsets the rule of grammatical concord. Attraction clearly works together with notional concord in many cases, in that the head noun (*number, variety, majority*, etc.) conveys the idea of 'plural'.

Concord with coordinated subjects: *Law and order is an election issue.*
512
When a subject consists of two or more noun phrases coordinated by *and*, the verb is typically in the plural:

> *Monday and Tuesday **are** very busy for me.*

The coordination is taken to be a reduction of two clauses ('Monday is busy and Tuesday is busy'; *see* 515). But sometimes the verb is singular, as in:

> *Law and order **is** considered important in this election.*

instead of

> *Law and order **are** considered important in this election.*

Here the choice of singular or plural verb depends on how we look at these qualities in the subject, whether they are seen as separate issues (*Law and order are . . .*) or as a single, complex issue (*Law and order is . . .*). A singular verb is also used when coordinated noun phrases refer to the same person or thing:

> At the party *my colleague and long-time friend*, Charles Bedford, was the guest of honour.

When two noun phrases are joined by *or* or *either . . . or*, the general rule is that the number of the verb is determined by the number of the last noun phrase (this is the factor of attraction or proximity; *see* 511):

> Either *the workers* or *the director **is*** to blame for the disruption.
> Either *the director* or *the workers **are*** to blame for the disruption.

But such sentences are often felt to be awkward. To avoid such concord problems, it is usually possible to use a modal auxiliary verb (which has the same form in the singular and the plural), for example:

> Either the workers or the director *must be* blamed for the disruption.

Concord with indefinite expressions of amount: *None of them is/are here.*
513
- Indefinite expressions of amount, especially *any*, *no*, and *none*, often cause concord problems. The following cases follow the basic concord rule:

> *No person* of that name *lives* here. [singular count + singular verb]
> *No people* of that name *live* here. [plural count + plural verb]
> So far *no money has* been spent on repairs. [mass noun + singular verb]
> I've ordered the cement, but *none (of it) has* yet arrived.

With *none of* + a plural noun both a singular and a plural verb occur:

> *None of us wants/want* to be killed young.

In conversations, a plural verb is the more natural choice:

> *None of her boys have* been successful in the world.
> *None of the people* there *were* any more competent than we are.
> *None of my colleagues have* said anything about it.
> *None of the teachers were* graduates.

With *none of*, grammatical concord insists that *none* is singular, but notional concord invites a plural verb. A singular verb is typical of ⟨written, formal⟩ style, whereas a plural verb is more idiomatic in ⟨informal⟩ English.

- The same rule also applies to *neither* and *either*:

> I sent cards to Avis and Margery but *neither* of them *has/have* replied.
> In fact, I doubt if *either* of them *is/are* coming.

- The plural pronoun *they* is often used in ⟨informal⟩ style as a replacement of pronouns ending in *-body* and *-one*:

> *Everyone* thinks *they* have the answer to the current problems.
> Has *anybody* brought *their* camera?
> *Anybody* with any sense would have read the play in translation, wouldn't *they*?

Nowadays this use of 'unisex' *they* is becoming more current even in ⟨written⟩ English. In traditional ⟨formal⟩ English, the tendency has been to use *he* when the sex is not stated:

> *Everyone* thinks *he* has the answer.

Increasingly, writers who want to avoid male dominance in language use replace *he* with *they* or with *he or she* or with *s/he* in such cases (*see* 96).

Concord of person: *I am ~ she is ~ they are*
514
As well as concord of number, there is concord of person.

- *Be* has three forms in the present tense (*see* 482).

    I am ~ he/she/it is ~ we/you/they are

- Main verbs have only two forms in the present tense (*see* 573):

    He/she/our friend etc. *likes* cooking. [3rd person singular]
    I/you/we/they/our friends etc. *like* cooking. [not 3rd person singular]

- Modal auxiliaries have only one form (*see* 483):

    I/we/you/he/she/our friend/our friends etc. *will* cook dinner today.

Notice that *you* behaves like a plural pronoun for number concord. This is because, historically, *you* was a plural second person form: the old singular form (*thou*) is almost never used today.

Coordination
(*see CGEL* 13.1–103)

515
Coordination can occur between different grammatical units: clauses, clause elements, words. In coordination, equivalent units are linked by *and*, *or* or *but*.

Coordination of clauses: *I'm selling my car and buying a new one.*
Clauses, phrases or words may be linked together (coordinated) by the conjunctions *and*, *or*, *but*. In these examples, the conjunctions are used to link clauses:

    It's November *and* there isn't a single tourist in sight.
    When the report arrives, do you want me to put it in an envelope and
        send it to you *or* do you want me to keep it?
    Oscar is away for a couple of days, *but* (he) will be back on Monday.

When the subjects of the two clauses refer to the same person or thing, the second subject is normally omitted, as in the last example. If the clauses have matching auxiliary verbs, they are also generally omitted:

    She may have received the letter *but* (she may have) forgotten to reply.

Coordination of parts of clauses
516
Coordination can be used to link parts of clauses (e.g. subjects, verb phrases, objects) rather than whole clauses. These can often be seen as cases of clause coordination in which repeated parts are omitted. For example, this sentence

    Her mother needed a chat and some moral support.

can be expanded as

> Her mother needed a chat and *her mother needed* some moral support.

But in other cases we cannot reconstruct two complete clauses:

> My closest friends are Peter and his wife.

This does not mean:

> My closest friend is Peter and my closest friend is his wife.

In addition, there are cases of coordination by *and* which may indicate a 'reciprocal' relationship:

> By the time the first crackling of spring came around, Joan and I were hopelessly in love. ('Joan was in love with me and I was in love with Joan.')
> Last night our dog and the neighbour's were having a fight. ('Our dog and the neighbour's were having a fight with *each other*.')

Since coordination in phrases has different functions, we shall treat coordination of phrases and smaller parts in terms of what elements are *linked*, rather than what elements are *omitted*. We deal with the omission of repeated elements in 391.

But as a coordinator is more limited than *and* and *or*. For example, it cannot normally link phrases, except in combination with a negative:

> I have been *to Switzerland*, but not *to the Alps*.

or where two adjectives or adjective phrases are coordinated:

> The weather was *warm* but rather *cloudy*.

Coordination of clause elements: *Wash by hand or in the washing machine.*
517
Here are some examples of coordination within different clause elements:

- Subjects:

> *Social security* and *retirement plans* will be important election issues.

- Verb phrases:

> Many of the laws *need to be studied* and *will have to be revised*.

- Complements:

> The laws are *rather outmoded* or *totally inadequate* and *often ambiguous*.

- Adverbial:

> You can wash this sweater *by hand* or *in the washing machine*.

- Also coordination between prepositional complements:

> Our team plays in *red shirts* and *white shorts*.
> The armrest must be down during *take-off* and *landing*.

Coordination can also link phrase combinations even where these do not occur next to one another in the sentence.

Subject and verb phrase:

> *The papers say*, and *most people believe*, that the opposition party will win the next election.

Subject and complement:

> [*Dr Horgan's eyes behind his spectacles*] were [*friendly*], and [*his smile*] [*kind*].

Coordination of words: *Tomorrow will be **nice and sunny.***
518
Coordination can link two words of the same word class.

- Nouns:

> Older people think many *boys* and *girls* look the same nowadays.

- Adjectives:

> Tomorrow's weather will be *nice* and *sunny*.

- Conjunctions:

> *If* and *when* she decided to tell her parents about her experiences, she would do so unasked.

Sometimes words of different classes are linked, where they have a similar function:

> *You* and *Sandra* must visit us sometime. [noun and pronoun]
> The game can be played by *three* or *more* contestants. [numeral and quantifier]

Conjunctions omitted: *a sandwich, an ice-cream and a cup of tea*
519
When more than two items are coordinated, the conjunction is normally omitted before each item except the last. In ⟨speech⟩, a rising tone is normally used on all items in the list except the last:

> |I would like a ham sándwich, | an íce-cream | and a cup of tèa.|

In ⟨writing⟩, a comma is usually used to separate all the items except the last two, but many writers put a comma also before *and* in such a list. We often omit *and* before the linking adverbs *then, so* and *yet*:

> The car spun around again, (and) *then* violated two stop lights.
> It's a small college, (and) *yet* most students love it.

Correlative coordination: *There were reactions of* **both approval and disapproval.**

520

Sometimes the coordination of two structures is made more emphatic by the addition of a word at the beginning of the first structure: *both* X *and* Y, *either* X *or* Y, *neither* X *nor* Y, etc. This is called **correlative coordination:**

> The proposal produced strong reactions of *both* approval *and* disapproval.
> The audience last night did not respond with *either* applause *or* boos.
> The anti-trust laws are *neither* effective *nor* rational.

Another case of correlative coordination is *not (only) . . . but . . .* (see 234, 269).

Demonstratives

(*see CGEL* 6.40–44, 12.8–20)

521

The words *this, that, these* and *those* are called **demonstratives.** They can be grouped as two sets with the general meaning 'near' and 'distant' (cf. the pairs *here/there, now/then* in 100):

	Singular	Plural
'near'	*this*	*these*
'distant'	*that*	*those*

- The demonstratives have number contrast for singular and plural:

  this book ~ *these books*
  that book ~ *those books*

- The demonstratives can function as determiners in noun phrases (*see* 523):

  This time she was nervous.

- The demonstratives can also function as pronouns, i.e. as whole noun phrases (*see* 595):

  This is a public park.
  That is another story.

In ⟨more formal⟩ use, *that* and *those* (but not *this* and *these*) can function as relative antecedents, i.e. the word the relative pronoun refers to (*see* 382, 686):

> Richard took up a life similar to *that* (*which*) he had lived in New York.
> The elements which capture his imagination are *those which* make the story worth telling and worth remembering.

That cannot be an antecedent of *who* because *that* can only refer to things in this construction. For reference to people *those who* is used:

> 75 per cent of *those who* returned the questionnaire identified themselves.

Determiners

(see CGEL 5.10–25)

522

Determiners are words which specify the range of reference of a noun, e.g. by making it definite (*the book*), indefinite (*a book*), or by indicating quantity (*many books*). To understand the grammatical role of determiners, we have to see what determiners and nouns can occur together. There are three classes of common nouns relevant to the choice of determiners:

- Singular count nouns: *book, teacher, idea*, etc.
- Plural count nouns: *books, teachers, ideas*, etc.
- Mass nouns: *meat, information, money*, etc.

Proper nouns do not normally take a determiner (*see* 667).

Determiners always precede the noun they determine, but they have different positions relative to one another. The most important group of determiners is the one that includes the articles (*the, a, an*), the demonstratives (*this, that*, etc.), and the possessives (*my, your*, etc.):

> *a* book, *the* books, *these* people, *my* ideas, etc.

We call this group **central determiners**, or simply **group 2 determiners** because they may be preceded by **group 1 determiners** like *all* and *half*:

> *all* the books, *all* these people, *all* my ideas, etc.
> *half* the time, *half* a kilo, etc.

Group 2 determiners may be followed by **group 3 determiners** like *second* and *many*:

> a *second* time
> the *many* problems

The three types of determiners are listed in this table:

Group 1 determiners	Group 2 determiners	Group 3 determiners
all, both, half (*see* 524)	**Articles:** *the, a, an* (*see* 523)	**Cardinal numerals:** *one, two, three, four, . . .* (*see* 525)
double, twice, . . . *one-third, . . .* (*see* 524)	**Demonstratives:** *this, these, that, those* (*see* 523)	**Ordinal numerals:** *first, second, third, . . .* (*see* 525)
what, such, . . . (*see* 524)	**Possessives:** *my, your, his, her, . . .* (*see* 523)	**General ordinals:** *next, last, other, . . .* (*see* 525)
	Quantifiers: *some, any, no, every, each, either, neither, enough, much* (*see* 677)	**Quantifiers:** *many, few, little, several, more, less, . . .* (*see* 677)
	Wh-determiners: *what(ever), which(ever), whose* (*see* 523)	

Group 2 determiners: *the book, those people, her money*

523

(A) Determiners with count nouns and mass nouns

The following determiners can occur with all three classes of noun (singular or plural count nouns and mass nouns):

- The definite article *the* (*see* 473):

  Have you got *the book/the books/the money?*

- The possessives acting as determiners: *my, our, your, his, her, its, their* (*see* 624):

  Have you seen *my book/my books/my money?*

The genitive (*see* 530) functions like a possessive determiner. Compare:

He liked *the student's essay.*
He liked *her essay.*

The *wh*-determiners *whose, which, whichever, what, whatever* (*see* 536, 592):

She lived alone in one of those renovated houses *whose brick façade* some early settler had constructed.
Whichever way one looked at it, it was her good fortune to have a good job.

> Have you decided *what adjustments* should be made?
> We have to carry out *whatever preparations* are needed.

- *Some* and *any* when they are stressed:

> 'There must be *some misconception* in your minds', she said.
> He refused to make *any further statement*.

- The negative quantifier *no* (*see* 583):

> There was *no debate* as the Senate passed the bill.
> There were *no audience questions* after the lecture.

(B) Determiners with plural count nouns and mass nouns
(but not with singular count nouns)

- Zero article (*see* 473):

> They need *tractors and help* with farming.

- Unstressed *some* /səm/ (*see* 474, 677, 698):

> I may settle for *some makeshift arrangements* for the summer.

- Unstressed *any* (*see* 677, 698):

> |Have you *any clothes*| or *any furniture* to sell?|

- *Enough* (*see* 677):

> I don't think there's *enough money* in the department to spend on books.
> There has not been *time enough* to institute reforms.

As the last example shows, *enough* can be placed after the headword, but this is less usual.

(C) Determiners with singular count nouns and mass nouns
The demonstratives *this* and *that* can occur with singular count nouns or mass nouns (but not with plural count nouns; *see* 521):

> *This research* requires expensive equipment.
> I find *that poetry* difficult to understand.

(D) Determiners with singular count nouns only

- The indefinite article *a, an* (*see* 473):

> Wait *a minute*!

- The quantifiers *every, each, either, neither* (*see* 75, 675):

> *Every Saturday* he gets a big kick out of football.
> They took the 8.30 train to the city *each morning*.

Either way it sounds like a bad solution.
It is to the advantage of *neither side* to destroy the opponent's cities.

(E) Determiners with plural count nouns only

The plural demonstrative determiners *these* and *those* can occur with plural
count nouns only (*see* 521):

> 'I've been waiting to get *these things* done for months', she said.
> She felt it was just going to be one of *those days* when life was
>   unbearable.

(F) Determiner with mass nouns only

The quantifier *much* can occur with **mass nouns only** (*see* 676):

> Some of the young players have so *much ability*.

Group 1 determiners: *all* the time, *twice* the number

524

When combined with other determiners, **Group 1 determiners** are placed before
Group 2 determiners: *all the time, both the children, twice the number*, etc. There
are four types of Group 1 determiners:

- *All, both, half* (*see* 677)

All goes with plural count nouns and mass nouns:

> Through *all these years* she had avoided the limelight.
> During *all this time* Roy continued to paint.

With a singular count noun, *all the* + noun occasionally occurs, but *all of the* +
noun or *the whole* + noun is more common:

> *All (of) the town* was destroyed by fire.
> ~ *The whole town* was destroyed by fire.

Both goes with plural count nouns only:

> *Both (the) books* were out of the library.

Half goes with singular or plural count nouns and mass nouns:

> The bridge was *half a mile* downstream.
> More than *half the audience* departed.
> In this village, nearly *half the children* receive no education.
> He stays on the island for *half the summer*.

All, both, half occur before articles, possessives, or demonstratives.

- *Double, twice, three times, four times*, etc. occur with singular and plural
  count nouns or mass nouns denoting amount, degree, etc.:

> The party needs *double that number* of votes to win the election.

The area is approximately *three times the size* of the old location.

- The fractions *one-third, two-fifths, three-quarters,* etc. usually have the construction with *of*:

    Grains and other seed food products furnish less than *one-third of the food* consumed.

- *What* and *such* occur before the indefinite article with singular count nouns:

    She kept telling herself again and again *what a fool* she'd been.
    They had no knowledge of *such a letter.*
    At first glance the idea looked *such a good one.*

With plural count nouns and mass nouns *what* and *such* occur without an article:

    It's amazing *what beautiful designs* they come up with.
    I find it hard to believe that even our present enemies would use *such terrible and inhumane weapons.*
    I could hardly believe *such good luck* was mine.

- The degree words *rather* and *quite* behave like Group 1 determiners:

    Sometimes life can be *rather a disappointing business.*
    I've known him for *quite a while.*

Group 3 determiners: *the next few days, a great many students*
525

Group 3 determiners, which include numerals and quantifiers, occur after Group 2 determiners, but before adjectives or noun phrase heads.

- **Cardinal numerals:** *one, two, three . . .*

The numeral *one* can of course occur only with singular count nouns, and all other cardinal numerals (*ten*, etc.) only with plural count nouns (*see* 602):

    There's only (*the*) *one farm* north of here.
    (*Some*) *ten* passengers were stranded at the station.

- **Ordinal numerals:** *first, second, third . . .*

Ordinal numerals occur only with count nouns and usually precede any cardinal numbers in the noun phrase:

    He had spent *the first three years* in Edinburgh.

- **General ordinals** include *next, last, other, further,* etc., which usually precede ordinal numerals:

She spent *her next five days* at home.
This was his best match in *the last two years*.

But compare the word order of *other* with and without the definite article:

The other two projects have been scheduled for completion next year.
Two other children were seriously wounded in the highway accident.

Another is a combination of two determiners (*an* + *other*):

At the meeting, *another speaker* also came under criticism.
In *another four weeks* we are going on vacation. ('four weeks from now')

Quantifiers: *I said a few, not few friends.*
526
Quantifiers denote quantity or amount (*see 675*).

● *Many, a few, few, fewer,* and *several* occur only with plural count nouns:

I have corrected *the many spelling errors* in your report.
Here are *a few facts and figures*. ('a small number')
Probably only very *few people* are aware of this tradition. ('not many')
There are *fewer people* going to church nowadays.
I haven't seen her for *several years*.

● *Little* (like *much*, see 523) occurs only with mass nouns:

She had to work very hard with *little help* from her relatives. ('not much help')
I advise you to use *the little money you have* to some purpose.

(The adjective *little*, contrasting with *big*, is not being considered here.)

Notice the different meanings of *little* and *few* compared with *a little* and *a few*:

Can you give me *a little help*? ('some help')
　BUT: They gave *little help*. ('not much help')
She has invited *a few friends* to the party. ('some friends')
　BUT: She's got *few friends* left. ('not many friends')

● The comparative determiners *more* and *less* occur with plural nouns and mass nouns:

We are taking *more students* this year in our department.
There has been *more activity* than usual this year.

Less occurs regularly with mass nouns:

With no drunken drivers there would be *less anxiety* and *fewer accidents*.

Many people also use *less* with plural count nouns (*less accidents*) but *fewer* is preferred in ⟨more formal⟩ contexts.

527

- Also similar to determiners are some highly frequent phrases denoting number and quantity. As the table below shows, some of them can occur only with count nouns in the plural (e.g. *a large number of students*), others can occur only with mass nouns (e.g. *a large amount of money*).

Quantity phrases with count nouns in the plural:

The university had {
a (great) number of
a (good) number of
a (large) number of
a lot of ⟨informal⟩
lots of ⟨informal⟩
plenty of
} foreign students.

Quantifying phrases with mass nouns:

The safe contained {
a great deal of
a good deal of
a large amount of
a lot of ⟨informal⟩
lots of ⟨informal⟩
plenty of
} counterfeit money.

Notice that the verb has concord with the noun following *of*, not with *plenty*, *lot* and *number* (*see* 511):

Plenty of students
A lot of people
A great number of guests
} **were** at the party.

This concord rule also applies to introductory *there* constructions:

There **were** {
plenty of students
a lot of people
a great number of guests
} at the party.
There **was**   *lots of* food   on the table.

When *number* and *amount* are used in the plural, there is of course plural concord:

There **were** large *numbers of* cars on the road this morning.
Only *small amounts of* money **are** still needed for the expedition.

Exclamations
(*see CGEL* 11.31–32)

528
An exclamation is a type of sentence which is used to express the speaker's feeling or attitude. It typically occurs in ⟨speech⟩:

> *What a lovely dinner* we had last night!
> *How well* she's playing today!

The exclamation begins with the determiner *what* in noun phrases (*see* 524) or the degree word *how* with adjectives or adverbs (*see* 465). To form an exclamation, put the element of the sentence containing *what* or *how* at the beginning of the sentence (as with *wh*-questions, *see* 683), but do **not** alter the order of subject and verb:

> You have *such a good library.*
> ∼ *What a good library* you have!
> She writes *such marvellous books.*
> ∼ *What marvellous books* she writes!
> You are *so lucky* to have such a good library.
> ∼ *How lucky* you are to have such a good library!
> She sings *so beautifully.*
> ∼ *How beautifully* she sings!

On other types of exclamatory construction, *see* 254, 300.

Gender
(*see CGEL* 5.104–111)

529
English gender, in a grammatical sense, is restricted to certain pronouns (*see* 619) which have separate forms for masculine/feminine and personal/non-personal, for example as shown in the table below.

Personal: masculine	*he*	*who*	*somebody*
Personal: feminine	*she*	*who*	*somebody*
Non-personal	*it*	*which*	*something*

Nouns, adjectives, and articles have no gender distinctions. Since English nouns have no grammatical gender, the choice of *he, she,* and *it* is based on natural distinctions of meaning. The choice between *he* and *she* depends on whether the person is male or female (*see* 96 for discussion of male and female reference).

Genitive
(*see CGEL* 5.112–126, 17.37–46, 110, 119)

What's the ship's name?
530
Genitive of singular nouns
In ⟨written⟩ English, the genitive case of nouns in the singular is written *'s* (apostrophe + *s*). In ⟨spoken⟩ English, the genitive case of nouns in the singular is pronounced /ɪz/, /z/, or /s/. The pronunciation depends on the last sound of the noun (*see* the general pronunciation rules in 751):

> a *nurse's* /ˈnɜː(r)sɪz/ skills
> a *teacher's* /ˈtiːtʃə(r)z/ salary
> the *chef's* /ʃefs/ favourite dish

Genitive of regular plural nouns
In ⟨written⟩ English the genitive of nouns which have a regular *s*-plural is indicated only by an apostrophe after the plural-*s*. In ⟨spoken⟩ English the genitive is not pronounced, i.e. the singular and the plural genitive sound alike, but are not written alike:

> *nurses'* /ˈnɜː(r)sɪz/ skills
> *teachers'* /ˈtiːtʃə(r)z/ salaries
> the two *chefs'* /ʃefs/ favourite dishes

Genitive of irregular plural nouns
Nouns which do not form the plural with the *-s* ending have apostrophe + *s* in the genitive (*see* 637):

> the *child's* /tʃaɪldz/ bike   ~ the *children's* /ˈtʃɪldrənz/bikes
> the *woman's* /ˈwʊmənz/ family   ~ the *women's* /ˈwɪmɪnz/ families

Singular names
The genitive which is indicated only by the apostrophe occurs also with singular names ending in *-s: Burns, Jones,* etc. The genitive is written either *Jones'* or *Jones's,* and usually pronounced /ˈdʒəʊnzɪz/. The spelling with *s +* apostrophe is particularly common with longer names of classical or biblical origin: *Euripides' plays, St Matthias' Church.*

The genitive and the *of*-construction: *What's the name of the ship?*
531
English often offers a choice when we want to express the genitive relation between nouns. We can use either the genitive or the *of*-construction:

> What's *the ship's name?* [genitive case]
> What's *the name of the ship?* [*of*-construction]

Here the function of the noun in the genitive case (*ship's*) is similar to that of the noun as head of a noun phrase following *of* (*of the ship*). This is called the *of-*construction.

- **The *of*-construction** is mostly used with nouns denoting things. We can say *the leg of a table* but not **a table's leg*.
- **The *s*-genitive** is typically used with nouns denoting people. We can say *John's car* but not **the car of John*. But the genitive is also commonly used in such phrases as *a day's work*, *today's paper*, *a moment's thought*, *the world's economy*. (On the choice of construction, *see* 106.)

Genitives in noun phrases
532
Although we have described the genitive as a case of nouns, it is better to regard it as an ending belonging to noun phrases (*see* 595) rather than to nouns. The following examples show that the whole first noun phrase, i.e. the genitive noun phrase, modifies the head of the main noun phrase:

Genitive noun phrase	Rest of the main noun phrase
some people's	opinion
every teacher's	ambition
the Australian government's	recent decision

This is seen more clearly when we compare equivalent *of*-phrases:

> the opinion of *some people*
> the ambition of *every teacher*
> the recent decision of *the Australian government*

The genitive noun phrase occupies determiner position (*see* 522) in the main noun phrase. Thus it precedes adjectives in the main noun phrase. Compare:

> *the* longest novel
> *his* longest novel
> *Charles Dickens'* longest novel

But genitive nouns can also behave like an adjective, with a classifying role, as in *a women's university*. In such cases, they can follow adjectives modifying the head of the main noun phrase:

> a famous *women's* university in Tokyo.

Group genitives: *an hour and a half's discussion*
533
In English we often have complex noun phrases such as

> the Chairman of the Finance Committee

where the head noun (*Chairman*) is modified by a following prepositional phrase (*of the Finance Committee*; *see* 642). When we want to put such a long noun phrase in the genitive, the *-s* genitive is added to the end of the whole noun phrase (not to the head noun itself):

the *Chairman of the Finance Committee's* pointed remarks

Since the genitive ending is added to the end of the whole phrase or group, this construction is called the **group genitive**. Other examples:

They must have been acting on *someone else's* instructions.
We'll see what happens in *a month or two's* time.
The lecture was followed by *an hour and a half's* discussion.

Genitives without a head noun: *at the Johnsons'*
534
The noun modified by the *-s* genitive may be omitted if the context makes its identity clear (compare 380):

My car is faster than *John's*. (i.e. 'than John's car')
But *John's* is a good car, too.

When the *of*-construction is used instead, a pronoun is usually required (*that* for singular and *those* for plural):

A blind person's sense of touch is more sensitive to shape and size than *that of a person with normal vision.*
The new CD-players are much better than *those of the first generation.*

Omission of the head noun is typical of expressions relating to houses, shops, etc.:

We met at *Bill's/the Johnsons'*. ('at Bill's place/at the place where the Johnsons live')

The 'double' genitive: *a friend of my wife's*
535
An *of*-construction can be combined with an *s*-genitive or possessive pronoun into a **'double' genitive:**

She is a friend *of my wife's.*
His style is no favourite *of mine.*

The noun in the genitive must be both definite and personal. Unlike the simple genitive, the 'double' genitive usually implies that the meaning is not unique, i.e. that 'my wife has several friends'. Compare:

He is *Leda's brother.* [suggests she has one, or more than one, brother]
He is a brother of Leda's. [suggests she has more than one brother]

Interrogatives
(*see CGEL* 6.36–39, 11.14–23)

536
Interrogatives are words which introduce *wh*-questions (*see* 683):

What's her first name?

and interrogative subclauses (*see* 590):

> I'm not sure *what* her first name is.

The English interrogative words are *who, whom, whose, which, what, where, when, how, why, whether, if* ('whether'). We call them '*wh*-words' (since most of them begin with *wh-*). *Whether* and *if* are used only in interrogative subclauses.

Interrogatives in noun phrases: *What time is it?, What's the time?*
537
In the noun phrase, the interrogatives *which* and *what* can act as both determiner and pronoun:

> *What* as determiner: *What* time is it?
> *What* as pronoun: *What*'s the time?

The different interrogative determiners and pronouns are set out in the following table.

	Determiners	Pronouns	
	Personal and non-personal	Personal	Non-personal
Subjective case	*what, which*	*who, what, which*	*what, which*
Objective case	*what, which*	*who, whom* ⟨formal⟩, *which*	*what, which*
Genitive case		*whose*	
Interrogative ... + preposition	*what, which* ... + preposition	*who, whom* ⟨formal⟩ ... + preposition	*what, which* ... + preposition
Preposition + interrogative	preposition + *what, which* ⟨formal⟩	preposition + *whom* ⟨formal⟩	preposition + *what, which* ⟨formal⟩

Who, whom, whose, which, and **what** are used both as interrogatives and as relative pronouns (*see* 690). The relative *which* can only have non-personal reference, but the interrogative *which* is used with both non-personal and personal reference. Compare:

> The author *who* wrote my favourite novel is Greene. [relative *who*]   [1]
> *Which* is your favourite author? [interrogative *which*]   [2a]

The interrogative *who* has to be used about persons:

> *Who* is your favourite author?   [2b]

The choice of interrogative: *what* or *which*, *who* or *which*?

538

The meaning of interrogative *who*, as in [2b], is different from the meaning of interrogative *which*, as in [2a]. The difference has to do with indefinite and definite reference. The definite interrogative *which* [2a] indicates that the speaker is thinking of a definite group to choose from. *Who* [2b] and also *what* have indefinite reference, i.e. the speaker has no definite group in mind. Here are some examples:

The interrogative determiner with a personal noun
Indefinite reference:

> *What composers* do you like best?

Definite reference:

> *Which composer* do you prefer: Mozart or Beethoven?

The interrogative determiner with a non-personal noun
Indefinite reference:

> *What tax changes* are likely in this month's budget?

Definite reference:

> *Which way* are you going?
> *Which university* did you go to: Edinburgh or St Andrews?

The interrogative pronoun referring to persons
Indefinite reference:

> *Who* sent you here?

Definite reference:

> *Which* is your favourite composer: Mozart or Beethoven?

The interrogative pronoun with non-personal reference
Indefinite reference:

> *What's* the name of this song?

Definite reference:

> *Which* do you prefer: classical or popular music?
> *Which terminal* do you want: domestic or international?

- Note that *what* and *which* can go with a personal or non-personal noun when they function as interrogative determiners:

> *What/Which candidate* did you vote for?
> *What/Which party* do you support?

- *Which* can be followed by an *of*-phrase. Compare these three sentences:

> *Which of the films* do you like best?   [1]
> *Which film* do you like best?   [2]
> *Which films* do you like best?   [3]

Sentence [1] can have the same meaning as either [2] or [3]. It invites us to choose from a group: either one (singular) or more than one (plural).

The choice of interrogative: *who, whom* or *whose*
539
The pronoun *who* is personal only:

> *Who* sent you here?

Both *who* and *whom* are used for the objective case. *Whom* is ⟨formal⟩:

> *Who* did she marry?
> *Whom* did she marry? ⟨formal⟩

With a preposition the ⟨informal⟩ construction is to place the preposition at the end:

> *Who* did the generals stay loyal *to*? ⟨informal⟩

But when the interrogative follows the preposition, *whom* is obligatory. This is a ⟨formal⟩ construction:

> *To whom* did the generals stay loyal? ⟨formal⟩

The possessive interrogative *whose* can function either as a determiner or as a pronoun:

> *Whose* jacket is this?
> *Whose* is this jacket?

The noun following the determiner *whose* can be either personal or non-personal:

> *Whose children* are they?
> *Whose side* are you on?

The choice of interrogative: *what* versus *who* and *which*
540
As the following examples show, *what* has a wide range of uses.

What can have both personal and non-personal reference and can function both as a determiner (*What nationality is he?*) and as a pronoun (*What's his nationality?*):

[A] *What's* your address?	[B] (It's) 18 South Avenue.
[A] *What* date is it?	[B] (It's) the 15th of March.
[A] *What's* the time?	[B] (It's) five o'clock.
[A] *What* is he doing?	[B] (He's) painting the house.
[A] *What* was the concert like?	[B] (It was) excellent.

When *what* is a pronoun and refers to a person it is limited to questions about profession, role, identity, etc. Contrast the three possible pronouns in:

[A] *What's* her husband?
   [B] (He's) a writer. [profession]
[A] *Which* is her husband?
   [B] (He's) the man on the right with a beard. [choice from a group]
[A] *Who* is her husband?
   [B] (He's) John Miller, the author of children's books. [identity]

Interrogative adverbs and conjunctions: *Where are you going?*
541
Besides interrogative determiners and pronouns, there are interrogative adverbs and conjunctions (*see* 590): *where, when, why, how.*

- *Where* refers to place *at* or place *to* (*see* 170):

   Where is he staying? ('At what place')
   Where are you going for your vacation? ('To what place')

- *When* refers to time (*see* 151):

   When are you leaving? ('At what time')

- *Why* refers to cause, reason, and purpose (*see* 198):

   Why are you going there? ('For what reason')

- *How* refers to manner, means, and instrument (*see* 194):

   How are you travelling? ('By what means')

How is also an interrogative adverb of degree (*see* 215). In this function *how* can modify adverbs, adjectives and determiners:

   How often do you see your friends?
   How long are you staying?
   How big is your boat?
   How many people can it take?

Whether and *if* are interrogative conjunctions. Like the other interrogatives, they introduce indirect (*yes-no*) questions (*see* 259, 682).

Introductory *it*
(*see* *CGEL* 18.33–36)

It's fascinating to read her story.
542
The regular word order in English is subject + verb:

   The colour of the car doesn't matter.   [1]

Instead of a noun phrase like *the colour of the car* we may have a clause as subject (*see* 588), such as

~ *What colour the car is* doesn't matter.   [1a]

However, the construction in [1a] is less common than the construction in [1b] with an 'introductory *it*':

~ It doesn't matter *what colour the car is.*   [1b]

In [1b] the subject clause (*what colour the car is*) is placed at the end of the sentence. The normal subject position at the beginning of the sentence is filled by *it*, 'introducing' the long following subject clause. [1b] contains two subjects: the introductory subject *it* and the postponed subject *what colour the car is.* Here are some more examples of sentences with introductory *it*:

> *It's* too early *to go and visit her at the hospital.*
> *It* makes her happy *to see others enjoying themselves.*
> *It's* easy *to understand why she wanted a new job.*
> *It* made no difference *that most evidence pointed to an opposite conclusion.*
> *It's* simply untrue *that there has been another big row in the department.*
> *It's* no use *pretending everything is all right.*
> *It* would be no good *trying to catch the bus now.*

543

The introductory-*it* construction is also used in the passive

- to introduce a *that*-clause:

  > *It's* not actually been announced yet *that the job will be advertised.*
  > *It's* actually been suggested *that income tax should be abolished.*

- to introduce direct or indirect speech:

  > *It* might be asked at this point: '*Why not alter the law?*'

- to introduce a *to*-infinitive:

  > In the end, *it* may be decided *not to apply for membership.*

The infinitive may have a subject introduced by *for*:

> *It* looks impossible *for us to buy* a new car this year.

Any kind of nominal clause may have an introductory *it* except a nominal relative clause (*see* 592). There is no alternative *it*-construction for this sentence:

> *Whoever said that* was wrong.

Cases which differ from introductory *it*

544

Constructions such as *It seems that* . . ., *It appears that* . . ., *It happens that* . . . may look like introductory-*it* sentences, but they have no corresponding construction without *it*. For example, there is no such sentence corresponding to

It seems that everything is fine.
(BUT NOT: *That everything is fine seems.*)
It appeared that the theory was not widely supported by other
scientists.
It quite often *happens that* things go wrong.

Introductory-*it* constructions should be distinguished from sentences where *it* is
a personal pronoun, as in

This may not be much of *a meal*, but *it's* what I eat.

Here *it* refers back to its antecedent, the singular noun phrase *a meal* (*see* 621).

Cases related to introductory *it*: *Her story is fascinating to read.*
545
English grammar allows us to place the emphasis on different parts of sentences.
In this sentence

To read her story is fascinating.   [1]

To read her story is a nominal clause functioning as subject. But English prefers
to avoid a clause as subject. One alternative is the introductory-*it* construction,
as in [1a]:

~ *It's* fascinating *to read her story.*   [1a]

But if we want to start with *her story* as the topic of the sentence, we can say:

~ *Her story* is fascinating *to read.*   [1b]

In [1b] the object of the nominal clause, *her story* is 'lifted out' from the clause
and 'promoted' to being subject in the main clause. The same construction can
be used to 'promote' prepositional objects, such as *her* in:

To talk to her was interesting.
~ *It* was interesting *to talk to her.*
~ *She* was interesting *to talk to.*

Note that in the process, the objective pronoun *her* becomes the subjective
pronoun *she*.

546
There is a similar construction for *appear, seem, be certain, be sure, be known, be
said*, etc. + *to*-infinitive:

You *seem to* have read so much.
Our enemies *are certain to* exploit the advantage they now believe they
hold.
My parents *are sure to* find out.

He *was* never *known to* run or even walk fast.
Steele *is said to* have been indebted to Swift.
The government *appears to* be facing a difficult year.

In these cases, however, the corresponding *it*-construction requires a *that*-clause:

~ It appears that the government is facing a difficult year.

It is the subject of the *that*-clause that is 'promoted' to being subject of the main clause.

Introductory *there*
(see *CGEL* 18.44–54)

There won't be any trouble.
547
An English sentence like this one is possible but rare:

A storm is coming.

The natural way of saying this is to begin the sentence with an unstressed *there* and to postpone the indefinite subject (*a storm*):

There's a storm coming.

This is called a sentence with **introductory *there***, which is a very common type of construction. Here are some examples of different verb patterns (*see* 718) to show how they can be turned into sentences with introductory *there*, so long as the subject is indefinite and the verb phrase contains *be*:

There was something [*magical about her voice*].	(SVC)
There's no water [*in the house*].	(SVA)
There are lots of people getting [*jobs*].	(SVO)
There's something causing [*her*] [*distress*].	(SVOO)
There have been two bulldozers knocking [*the place*] [*flat*].	(SVOC)
There's somebody coming.	(SV)

In addition, *there* sometimes occurs simply with *be* and a following noun phrase:

There must be some mistake, I'm sure.

Passive sentences also occur:

There's a new novel displayed in the window.
There's been a handbag stolen in the department store.

If the postponed subject is plural, the verb is also in the plural (but *see* 548 below):

There *are* many people trying to buy houses in this neighbourhood.
There *seem* to be no poisonous snakes around here.
Were there any other drivers around to see the accident?
There *are* some friends I have to see.

Introductory *there* as subject: *I don't want there to be any trouble.*
548
Introductory *there* differs from the stressed *there* functioning as a front-placed adverb ('*There is my car = My car is 'there*, see 416). Introductory *there* is unstressed and behaves in some ways like the subject of the sentence. One example of this is the ⟨informal, spoken⟩ *there* + contracted *'s* + a plural postponed subject:

> *There*'s only four bottles left. ⟨informal⟩
> *There*'s better things to do than listen to gossip. ⟨informal⟩

(*There are* would be more formally 'correct' here.)

  Another indication of this function is that *there* can act as subject in *yes-no* questions (*see* 682) and tag questions (*see* 684), where inversion of *be* and *there* takes place:

> *Is there* any more wine?
> There's no one else coming, *is there?*

There can also act as subject in infinitive clauses and *-ing* clauses (*see* 493):

> I don't want *there to be* any trouble.
> He was disappointed at *there being* so little to do.
> Far from *there being* a trend towards free boundaries in the world, every
> single nation has given up unrestricted immigration.
> *There being* no further business, the meeting adjourned at 11.15.
>   ⟨formal⟩

Introductory *there* with relative and infinitive clauses: *There's something I*
ought to tell you.
549

- There is a further type of introductory-*there* sentence. As an alternative of this sentence

    Something keeps upsetting him.

we may have:

> ~ *There's* something (that) keeps upsetting him.

It consists of *there* + a form of *be* + a noun phrase + a clause which is like a relative clause (*see* 686). There must be an indefinite noun phrase in the sentence, but it need not be the subject:

> *Is there anyone in particular* (that) you want to speak to?
> (Compare: Do you want to speak to *anyone in particular?*)

In this construction *that* can be omitted even when it is subject, which is not possible in normal relative clauses:

> *There's* only two men in the world of golf *can play like that.* ⟨informal⟩

- Another common sentence pattern is introductory *there* + *be* + noun phrase + *to*-infinitive clause. The infinitive may have a *for*-subject:

    > Tonight *there*'s nothing else (for us) to do but watch TV.
    > *There* was no one (for us) to talk to.

This pattern also occurs in the passive:

> *There* are several practical problems to be considered.

- There is a type of *there*-sentence which is typical of ⟨literary⟩ contexts:

    > *There* may come a time when Europe will be less fortunate. ('A time may come . . .')

In this construction *there* can be followed by a verb other than *be* (such as *come, lie, stand, exist, rise*). With a place adverbial in front-position, *there* may be omitted in ⟨literary⟩ style (*see* 416):

> On the other side of the valley (*there*) *rose a gigantic rock* surmounted by a ruined fortress. ⟨formal, literary⟩

Irregular verbs
(*see CGEL* 3.11–20)

550

Most English verbs are regular, but there are over 200 main verbs that are irregular. Irregular verbs are like regular verbs in having *-s* and *-ing* forms (*see* 573). For example, the irregular verb *break* has the forms *breaks, breaking,* just as the regular verb *walk* has the forms *walks, walking*. With regular verbs we can also predict that the past tense and past participle forms are identical and formed with the *-ed* ending added to the base: *walk ~ walked ~ walked*. With irregular verbs, however, we cannot predict their past tense or past participle forms from the base: *break ~ broke ~ broken*.

We distinguish three types of irregular verbs:

- Verbs in which **all the three principal parts** (the base, the past tense, the past participle) are **identical**, for example,

    > *cut ~ cut ~ cut, let ~ let ~ let.*

- Verbs in which **two parts are identical**, for example,

    > *spend ~ spent ~ spent, come ~ came ~ come.*

- Verbs in which **all three parts are different**, for example,

    > *blow ~ blew ~ blown, speak ~ spoke ~ spoken.*

Within each type, the verbs are here arranged according to similarity: 'the *spend*-group', 'the *speak*-group', etc. The following list is not exhaustive (*see further GCEL* 3.11–20). For auxiliary verbs, *see* 477–85.

We give two lists which include the majority of the English irregular verbs.

The group list (*see* 551–71)
In the first list the verbs are grouped according to how the past tense and past participle forms differ from the base form. For example, *put* and *cut* belong to the one group where the verbs have identical forms for base, past tense and past participle: *put~put~put* and *cut~cut~cut*. *Dig* and *win* belong to another group. These two verbs are similar in that each verb has identical past tense and past participle forms and also the same vowel change: *dig~dug~dug* and *win~won~won*. This organization into groups is intended to give an idea of the different types of irregular verbs, something which is not obvious from an alphabetical arrangement.

The alphabetical list (*see* 572)
For convenient reference we also include a second list where the verbs appear in alphabetical order.

In both lists we give the three parts for each verb: the base, the past tense and the past participle.

For some verbs there are alternative forms. For example, the past form of *sweat* is given both as *sweat* (irregular) and *sweated* (regular). This means that both are used, but sometimes differently depending on context, style or variety. For example, of the two forms *dreamt* and *dreamed*, the latter is usually preferred in ⟨AmE⟩. Alternative forms in round brackets, such as *shone,(shined)*, indicate infrequent or special uses:

> The sun *shone* all day.
> BUT: He *shined* his shoes every morning.

Verbs printed in bold are high-frequency verbs (for example, *cut*, *let*, *speak*).

The group list
All three verb parts are identical
(but some verbs have alternative, non-identical forms)
551
The *put* group

bet	bet, betted	bet, betted
bid	bid, bad(e)	bid, bidden, bade
broadcast	broadcast	broadcast
burst	burst	burst
bust ⟨casual⟩	bust, busted	bust, busted
cast	cast	cast
cost	cost, (costed)	cost, (costed)
cut	cut	cut
fit	fit ⟨esp AmE⟩, fitted	fit ⟨esp AmE⟩ fitted
forecast	forecast	forecast
hit	hit	hit

hurt	hurt	hurt
knit	knit, knitted	knit, knitted
let	let	let
miscast	miscast	miscast
offset	offset	offset
outbid	outbid	outbid
put	put	put
quit	quit, quitted	quit, quitted
recast	recast	recast
reset	reset	reset
rid	rid, ridded	rid, ridded
set	set	set
shed	shed	shed
shit ⟨taboo⟩	shit, shat	shit
shut	shut	shut
slit	slit	slit
split	split	split
spread	spread	spread
sweat	sweat, sweated	sweat, sweated
thrust	thrust	thrust
typeset	typeset	typeset
upset	upset	upset
wed	wed, wedded	wed, wedded
wet	wet, wetted	wet, wetted

Two verb parts are identical

552
The *learn* group

These verbs can be either regular (*learned*) or irregular with a -*t* suffix (*learnt*). The regular /d/-form is especially ⟨AmE⟩ and the /t/-form especially ⟨BrE⟩.

burn	burned, burnt	burned, burnt
dwell	dwelled, dwelt	dwelled, dwelt
learn	learned, learnt	learned, learnt
misspell	misspelled, misspelt	misspelled, misspelt
smell	smelled, smelt	smelled, smelt
spell	spelled, spelt	spelled, spelt
spill	spilled, spilt	spilled, spilt
spoil	spoiled, spoilt	spoiled, spoilt

553
The *spend* group

bend	bent	bent
build	built	built

lend	lent	lent
rebuild	rebuilt	rebuilt
rend	rent	rent
send	sent	sent
spend	spent	spent
unbend	unbent	unbent

554
The *read* group

behold ⟨literary⟩	beheld	beheld
bleed	bled	bled
breed	bred	bred
feed	fed	fed
flee	fled	fled
hold	held	held
lead /iː/	led	led
mislead /iː/	misled	misled
overfeed	overfed	overfed
read /iː/	read /e/	read /e/
reread /iː/	reread /e/	reread /e/
speed	sped, speeded	sped, speeded
uphold	upheld	upheld
withhold	withheld	withheld

555
The *keep* group

Where there are alternative regular forms (*dreamed* besides *dreamt*, etc.), the regular forms are usually preferred in ⟨AmE⟩.

creep	crept	crept
deal /iː/	dealt /e/	dealt /e/
dream /iː/	dreamt /e/, dreamed	dreamt /e/, dreamed
feel	felt	felt
keep	kept	kept
kneel	knelt, kneeled	knelt, kneeled
lean /iː/	leant /e/, leaned	leant /e/, leaned
leap /iː/	leapt /e/, leaped	leapt /e/, leaped
leave	left	left
mean /iː/	meant /e/	meant /e/
meet	met	met
oversleep	overslept	overslept
sleep	slept	slept
sweep	swept	swept
weep	wept	wept

556
The *win* group

cling	clung	clung
dig	dug	dug
fling	flung	flung
hamstring	hamstrung	hamstrung
hang	hung, (hanged)	hung, (hanged)
restring	restrung	restrung
sling	slung	slung
slink	slunk	slunk
spin	spun, span	spun
stick	stuck	stuck
sting	stung	stung
strike	struck	struck
string	strung	strung
swing	swung	swung
win	won	won
wring	wrung	wrung

557
The *bring* group

bring	brought /ɔː/	brought /ɔː/
buy	bought	bought
catch	caught	caught
fight	fought	fought
seek	sought	sought
teach	taught	taught
think	thought	thought

558
The *find* group

bind /aɪ/	bound /aʊ/	bound /aʊ/
find	found	found
grind	ground	ground
rewind	rewound	rewound
unbind	unbound	unbound
unwind	unwound	unwound
wind /aɪ/	wound	wound

559
The *get* group

get	got	got, ⟨AmE⟩ gotten
lose /luːz/	lost	lost

| shine | shone, (shined) | shone, (shined) |
| shoot | shot | shot |

560
The *tell* group

foretell	foretold	foretold
resell	resold	resold
retell	retold	retold
sell	sold	sold
tell	told	told

561
The *come* group

become	became	become
come	came	come
outrun	outran	outrun
overcome	overcame	overcome
overrun	overran	overrun
rerun	reran	rerun
run	ran	run

562
Other verbs with two forms identical

beat	beat	beaten, (beat)
browbeat	browbeat	browbeaten
have	had	had
hear	heard	heard
lay [spelling irregular]	laid	laid
light	lit, lighted	lit, lighted
make	made	made
mishear	misheard	misheard
misunderstand	misunderstood	misunderstood
remake	remade	remade
pay [spelling irregular]	paid	paid
say	said /e/	said /e/
sit	sat	sat
slide	slid	slid
spit	spat, spit	spat, spit
stand	stood	stood
understand	understood	understood
unmake	unmade	unmade
withstand	withstood	withstood

All three verb forms are different

563

The *mow* group: The past participle can be regular (*mowed*) or irregular (*mown*).

hew	hewed	hewn, hewed
mow	mowed	mown, mowed
saw	sawed	sawn, sawed
sew	sewed	sewn, sewed
show	showed	shown, (showed)
sow	sowed	sown, sowed
swell	swelled	swollen, swelled

564

The *speak* group

awake	awoke, awaked	awoken, awaked
break	broke	broken
choose /uː/	chose /oʊ/	chosen /oʊ/
deepfreeze	deepfroze	deepfrozen
freeze	froze	frozen
speak	spoke	spoken
steal	stole	stolen
wake	woke, waked	woken, waked
weave	wove	woven

565

The *bear* group

bear /eə(r)/	bore	borne*
swear	swore	sworn
tear	tore	torn
wear	wore	worn

Born is used in constructions with *be*. Note the spelling difference: 'She has *borne* six children and the youngest was *born* only a month ago.'

566

The *know* group

blow	blew	blown
grow	grew	grown
know	knew	known
outgrow	outgrew	outgrown
overthrow	overthrew	overthrown
throw	threw	thrown

567
The *bite* group

bite	bit	bitten, (bit)
hide	hid	hidden, (hid)

568
The *take* group

mistake	mistook	mistaken
overtake	overtook	overtaken
shake	shook	shaken
take	took	taken
undertake	undertook	undertaken

569
The *write* group

arise /aɪ/	arose /oʊ/	arisen /ɪ/
drive	drove	driven
rewrite	rewrote	rewritten
ride	rode	ridden
rise	rose	risen
stride	strode	strode, stridden, strid
strive	strove, strived	striven, strived
underwrite	underwrote	underwritten
write	wrote	written

570
The *begin* group

begin	began, (begun)	begun
drink	drank	drunk
ring	rang, rung	rung
shrink	shrank, shrunk	shrunk
sing	sang, sung	sung
sink	sank, sunk	sunk
spring	sprang, sprung ⟨ΛmE⟩	sprung
stink	stank, stunk	stunk
swim	swam, swum	swum

571
Other verbs with all three parts different

cleave	cleaved, clove	cleaved, cloven, cleft
dive	dived, dove ⟨AmE only⟩	dived

do	did	done
draw	drew	drawn
eat	ate ⟨BrE⟩ /et/, ⟨esp AmE⟩ /eɪt/	eaten
fall	fell	fallen
fly	flew	flown
forbid	forbad(e)	forbidden, (forbid)
foresee	foresaw	foreseen
forget	forgot	forgotten, (forgot)
forgive	forgave	forgiven
give	gave	given
go	went	gone
lie	lay	lain
outdo	outdid	outdone
overdo	overdid	overdone
overeat	overate ⟨BrE⟩ /-et/, ⟨esp AmE⟩ /-eɪt/	overeaten
oversee	oversaw	overseen
redo	redid	redone
see	saw	seen
shear /ɪə(r)/	sheared	shorn, sheared
tread	trod	trodden, trod
undergo	underwent	undergone
undo	undid	undone
withdraw	withdrew	withdrawn

Irregular verbs in alphabetical order
572

arise	arose	arisen
awake	awoke, awaked	awoken, awaked
be (482)	was, were	been
bear	bore	borne
beat	beat	beaten, (beat)
become	became	become
begin	began, (begun)	begun
behold ⟨literary⟩	beheld	beheld
bend	bent	bent
bet	bet, betted	bet, betted
bid	bid, bad(e)	bid, bidden, bade
bind	bound	bound
bite	bit	bitten, (bit)
bleed	bled	bled
blow	blew	blown
break	broke	broken
breed	bred	bred

bring	brought	brought
broadcast	broadcast	broadcast
browbeat	browbeat	browbeaten
build	built	built
burn	burned, burnt	burned, burnt
burst	burst	burst
bust ⟨casual⟩	bust, busted	bust, busted
buy	bought	bought
cast	cast	cast
catch	caught	caught
choose	chose	chosen
cleave	cleaved, clove	cleaved, cloven, cleft
cling	clung	clung
come	came	come
cost	cost	cost
creep	crept	crept
cut	cut	cut
deal	dealt	dealt
deepfreeze	deepfroze	deepfrozen
dig	dug	dug
dive	dived, dove ⟨AmE⟩	dived
do	did	done
draw	drew	drawn
dream	dreamt, dreamed	dreamt, dreamed
drink	drank	drunk
drive	drove	driven
dwell	dwelled, dwelt	dwelled, dwelt
eat	ate	eaten
fall	fell	fallen
feed	fed	fed
feel	felt	felt
fight	fought	fought
find	found	found
fit	fitted, ⟨AmE⟩ also: fit	fitted, ⟨AmE⟩ also: fit
flee	fled	fled
fling	flung	flung
fly	flew	flown
forbid	forbad(e)	forbidden, (forbid)
forecast	forecast	forecast
foresee	foresaw	foreseen
foretell	foretold	foretold
forget	forgot	forgotten, (forgot)
forgive	forgave	forgiven
freeze	froze	frozen
get	got	got, gotten ⟨AmE⟩

give	gave	given
go	went	gone
grind	ground	ground
grow	grew	grown
hamstring	hamstrung	hamstrung
hang	hung, (hanged)	hung, (hanged)
have	had	had
hear	heard	heard
hew	hewed	hewn, hewed
hide	hid	hidden, (hid)
hit	hit	hit
hold	held	held
hurt	hurt	hurt
keep	kept	kept
kneel	knelt, kneeled	knelt, kneeled
knit	knit, knitted	knit, knitted
know	knew	known
lay	laid	laid
lead	led	led
lean	leant, leaned	leant, leaned
leap	leapt, leaped	leapt, leaped
learn	learned, learnt	learned, learnt
leave	left	left
lend	lent	lent
let	let	let
lic	lay	lain
light	lit, lighted	lit, lighted
lose	lost	lost
make	made	made
mean	meant	meant
meet	met	met
miscast	miscast	miscast
mishear	misheard	misheard
mislead	misled	misled
misspell	misspelled, misspelt	misspelled, misspelt
mistake	mistook	mistaken
misunderstand	misunderstood	misunderstood
mow	mowed	mown, mowed
offset	offset	offset
outbid	outbid	outbid
outdo	outdid	outdone
outgrow	outgrew	outgrown
outrun	outran	outrun
overcome	overcame	overcome
overdo	overdid	overdone

overeat	overate	overeaten
overfeed	overfed	overfed
overrun	overran	overrun
oversee	oversaw	overseen
oversleep	overslept	overslept
overtake	overtook	overtaken
overthrow	overthrew	overthrown
pay	paid	paid
put	put	put
quit	quit, quitted	quit, quitted
read /iː/	read /e/	read /e/
rebuild	rebuilt	rebuilt
recast	recast	recast
redo	redid	redone
remake	remade	remade
rend	rent	rent
reread /riːˈriːd/	reread /riːˈred/	reread /riːˈred/
rerun	reran	rerun
resell	resold	resold
reset	reset	reset
restring	restrung	restrung
retell	retold	retold
rewind	rewound	rewound
rewrite	rewrote	rewritten
rid	rid, ridded	rid, ridded
ride	rode	ridden
ring	rang, rung	rung
rise	rose	risen
run	ran	run
saw	sawed	sawn, sawed
say	said	said
see	saw	seen
seek	sought	sought
sell	sold	sold
send	sent	sent
set	set	set
sew	sewed	sewn, sewed
shake	shook	shaken
shear	sheared	shorn, sheared
shed	shed	shed
shine	shone, (shined)	shone, (shined)
shit ⟨taboo⟩	shit, shat	shit
shoot	shot	shot
show	showed	shown, (showed)
shrink	shrank, shrunk	shrunk

shut	shut	shut
sing	sang, sung	sung
sink	sank, sunk	sunk
sit	sat	sat
slay	slew	slain
sleep	slept	slept
slide	slid	slid
sling	slung	slung
slink	slunk	slunk
slit	slit	slit
smell	smelled, smelt	smelled, smelt
sow	sowed	sown, sowed
speak	spoke	spoken
speed	sped, speeded	sped, speeded
spell	spelled, spelt	spelled, spelt
spend	spent	spent
spill	spilled, spilt	spilled, spilt
spin	spun, span	spun
spit	spat, spit	spat, spit
split	split	split
spoil	spoiled, spoilt	spoiled, spoilt
spread	spread	spread
spring	sprang, sprung	sprung
stand	stood	stood
steal	stole	stolen
stick	stuck	stuck
sting	stung	stung
stink	stank, stunk	stunk
stride	strode	strode, stridden, strid
strike	struck	struck
string	strung	strung
strive	strove, strived	striven, strived
swear	swore	sworn
sweat	sweat, sweated	sweat, sweated
sweep	swept	swept
swell	swelled	swollen, swelled
swim	swam, swum	swum
swing	swung	swung
take	took	taken
teach	taught	taught
tear	tore	torn
tell	told	told
think	thought	thought
throw	threw	thrown
thrust	thrust	thrust

tread	trod	trodden, (trod)
typeset	typeset	typeset
unbend	unbent	unbent
unbind	unbound	unbound
undergo	underwent	undergone
understand	understood	understood
undertake	undertook	undertaken
underwrite	underwrote	underwritten
undo	undid	undone
unmake	unmade	unmade
unwind	unwound	unwound
uphold	upheld	upheld
upset	upset	upset
wake	woke, waked	woken, waked
wear	wore	worn
weave	wove	woven
wed	wed, wedded	wed, wedded
weep	wept	wept
wet	wet, wetted	wet, wetted
win	won	won
wind	wound	wound
withdraw	withdrew	withdrawn
withhold	withheld	withheld
withstand	withstood	withstood
wring	wrung	wrung
write	wrote	written

Main verbs

(see *CGEL* 3.2–6)

The forms of main verbs

573

There are two types of verbs: main verbs and auxiliary verbs (*see* 477–85). Main verbs are either regular (such as *call*, *like*, *try*) or irregular (such as *buy*, *drink*, *set*). 'Regular' means that we can state *all* the verb forms of an English verb once we know its base form. The base is the basic, uninflected form which is given as the entry form in dictionaries. The irregular verbs are listed in 550–72.

A regular English verb, such as *call*, has the following four forms:

- **the base:** *call*
- **the -s form:** *calls*
- **the -ing form:** *calling*
- **the -ed form:** *called*

The vast majority of English verbs are regular. Furthermore, all new verbs that are coined or borrowed from other languages adopt this pattern. For example, a recently coined verb *futurize* ('to implement plans based upon long-range forecasts of future developments') will have the forms *futurizes, futurizing, futurized*.

574

- The **-s form**, also called the 3rd person singular present, is formed in ⟨written⟩ English by adding *-s* or *-es* to the base (*see* 702). In ⟨spoken⟩ English, the *-s* form is pronounced /ɪz/, /z/, or /s/.

base	-s form
press /pres/	*presses* /ˈpresɪz/
play /pleɪ/	*plays* /pleɪz/
help /help/	*helps* /helps/

The rules for the choice of these alternatives are stated in 664; on changes in spelling, for example *try/tries, see* 701. Exceptions: *do* /duː/ ∼ *does* /dʌz/, *say* /seɪ/ ∼ *says* /sez/.

- The **-ing form**, or the present participle, is formed by adding *-ing* to the base of both regular and irregular verbs.

base	-ing form
press	*pressing*
play	*playing*
help	*helping*

Note
On changes in spelling, as in *beg* ∼ *begging, see* 703.

- The **-ed form** of regular verbs is formed by adding *-ed* to the base. It corresponds to two forms of many irregular verbs. Compare:

base	-ed form	
	past form	part participle
press	*pressed*	*pressed*
play	*played*	*played*
help	*helped*	*helped*
base	past form	past participle
drink	*drank*	*drunk*
know	*knew*	*known*
hit	*hit*	*hit*

The -*ed* form is pronounced /ɪd/, /d/ or /t/:

base	-*ed* form
pat	*patted* /ˈpætɪd/
praise	*praised* /preɪzd/
press	*pressed* /prest/

Note

On the choice of these pronunciations, *see* 665. On changes in spelling, as in *pat* ~ *patted*, *see* 703.

The uses of the verb forms

575

The base form is used

- in all persons of the present tense except the 3rd person singular:

  I/you/we/they/the students, etc. *like* fast food.

- in the imperative (*see* 497):

  Look what you've done!

- in the infinitive, which may be the bare infinitive (*do*) or the *to*-infinitive (*to do*):

  We'll tell them what *to do* and then let them *do* it.

- in the productive subjunctive (*see* 706):

  The committee recommends that these new techniques *be* implemented at once.

576

The -*s* form is used in the 3rd person singular of the present tense (*see* 741), which is the only person where the base form is not used:

  He/She *wants* to have a good time, that's all.

577

The -*ed* form is used for both the past tense and the past participle. These are distinct (e.g. *gave* ~ *given*) for many irregular verbs (*see* 550).

- Unlike the present tense, the past tense has only one form in all persons:

  I/you/he/she/we/they/the students/everybody, etc. *wanted* to save money but couldn't.

- The past participle is used with a form of *have* to form the perfect aspect (*see* 739):

Ms Johnson *has asked* me to contact you.

- The past participle is used with a form of *be* to form the passive (*see* 613):

  She was *given* special instructions.
  The plans were *changed*.

- The past participle is used to form *-ed* participle clauses (*see* 493):

  The codes were found *hidden in cigarette lighters in the arrested spy's apartment*.
  I also heard it *mentioned* by somebody else.

- The past participle can also become an adjective and can modify a noun:

  His *injured back* puts a stop to his career as an athlete.

578
The *-ing* form is used

- to form the progressive (*see* 739):

  She's *working* on a thesis.

- to form *-ing* participle clauses (*see* 493):

  It's a trick I learned while *recovering from the mumps*.

- The *-ing* form can also become an adjective and can modify a noun (*see* 444):

  It was a *fascinating* programme.

- The *-ing* form can also become a noun describing an action or state:
  The *telling* of stories.

Nationality words
(*see CGEL* 5.55–57, 7.25)

579
When speaking about English people **in general** we can say either *the English* (the definite article and an adjective as head, *see* 448) or *Englishmen* (plural noun without the article):

  The English have managed to hold on to their madrigal tradition better
      than anyone else.   [1a]
  Most *Englishmen* either do not know or are not concerned with the
      historical significance of the day.   [1b]

When referring to some **particular** English persons we can only use the latter form (+ the definite article):

> *The Englishmen* I met at the conference were all doctors.   [2]

We call the first, general, type of reference as in [1a, 1b], **generic reference**, and the second, specific, type as in [2], **specific reference**. In some cases, such as *English/Englishmen*, there are different forms for different types of reference. Where nationality words have no separate generic form, *the* + plural can be both generic and specific (*see* 90):

> *The Australians* are said to like the outdoors. [Australians in general]
> BUT *The Australians* I know don't particularly like the outdoors.
>   [some specific Australians]

580
Nationality words
The following table shows the names of some countries, continents etc. and their corresponding adjectives and nouns (with specific and generic reference).

Name of country, continent, etc.	Adjective	Noun with singular reference	Noun with plural reference	Noun with generic reference (plural)
China	Chinese	a Chinese	Chinese	the Chinese
Japan	Japanese	a Japanese	Japanese	the Japanese
Portugal	Portuguese	a Portuguese	Portuguese	the Portuguese
Sri Lanka	Ceylonese	a Ceylonese	Ceylonese	the Ceylonese
Switzerland	Swiss	a Swiss	Swiss	the Swiss
Vietnam	Vietnamese	a Vietnamese	Vietnamese	the Vietnamese
Iraq	Iraqi	an Iraqi	Iraqis	the Iraqis
Israel	Israeli	an Israeli	Israelis	the Israelis
Kuwait	Kuwaiti	a Kuwaiti	Kuwaitis	the Kuwaitis
Pakistan	Pakistani	a Pakistani	Pakistanis	the Pakistanis
Africa	African	an African	Africans	the Africans
America	American	an American	Americans	the Americans
Asia	Asian	an Asian	Asians	the Asians
Australia	Australian	an Australian	Australians	the Australians
Belgium	Belgian	a Belgian	Belgians	the Belgians
Brazil	Brazilian	a Brazilian	Brazilians	the Brazilians
Europe	European	a European	Europeans	the Europeans
Germany	German	a German	Germans	the Germans
Greece	Greek	a Greek	Greeks	the Greeks
Hungary	Hungarian	a Hungarian	Hungarians	the Hungarians
India	Indian	an Indian	Indians	the Indians
Norway	Norwegian	a Norwegian	Norwegians	the Norwegians
Russia	Russian	a Russian	Russians	the Russians

Name of country, continent, etc.	Adjective	Noun with singular reference	Noun with plural reference	Noun with generic reference (plural)
Argentina, (the) Argentine	Argentinian, Argentine	an Argentinian, an Argentine	Argentinians, Argentines	the Argentinians, the Argentines
Denmark	Danish	a Dane	Danes	the Danes
Finland	Finnish	a Finn	Finns	the Finns
the Philippines	Philippine	a Filipino	Filipinos	the Filipinos
Poland	Polish	a Pole	Poles	the Poles
Saudi Arabia	Saudi (Arabian)[a]	a Saudi (Arabian)	Saudis, Saudi Arabians	the Saudis, Saudi Arabians
Spain	Spanish	a Spaniard	Spaniards	the Spanish
Sweden	Swedish	a Swede	Swedes	the Swedes
Turkey	Turkish	a Turk	Turks	the Turks
England	English	an Englishman[b]	Englishmen[b]	the English
France	French	a Frenchman[b]	Frenchmen[b]	the French
Holland, the Netherlands	Dutch	a Dutchman[b]	Dutchmen[b]	the Dutch
Ireland	Irish	an Irishman[b]	Irishmen[b]	the Irish
Wales	Welsh	a Welshman[b]	Welshmen[b]	the Welsh
Britain	British	a Briton[c]	Britons	the British
Scotland	Scots, Scottish	a Scotsman[d], a Scot	Scotsmen, Scots	the Scots

Notes

[a] *Arab* is the racial and political term (*the Arab nations*, etc.). *Arabic* is used about the language and literature, as well as in *Arabic numerals* (as opposed to *Roman numerals*). *Arabia* and *Arabian* are associated with the geographical area of the Arabian peninsula (as in *Saudi Arabia*).

[b] Nouns ending in *-man, -men* refer to males. Although corresponding female nouns exist (e.g. 'Frenchwoman, 'Welshwoman), these are rather rare. There is now a tendency to avoid such gender-linked terms which could seem ⟨impolite⟩. Instead, more roundabout phrases, such as *some 'English people, a 'Welsh woman, a 'Dutch lady*, are often preferred. The avoidance of nationality nouns also extends to some other nouns such as *Spaniard* and *Pole* which, although they do not signal gender, in practice are taken to refer to males rather than females.

[c] *Brit* is a colloquial variant of *Briton*, which is not very common.

[d] The inhabitants of Scotland themselves prefer *Scots* and *Scottish* to *Scotch*, which however is commonly used in such phrases as *Scotch terrier* and *Scotch whisky*. *Scottish* denotes nationality and geographical areas: *the Scottish universities, the Scottish Highlands*.

Negation
(*see CGEL* 10.54–70)

Not-**negation:** *What he says doesn't make sense.*
581
To make a finite clause negative, place *not* immediately after the operator (*see* 609). In ⟨informal⟩ English *not* is contracted to *n't* and tagged on to the previous word:

Positive clause	Negative clause
We are satisfied with the results.	~ We *are not* satisfied with the results.
	~ We *aren't* satisfied with the results.
I have told the students.	~ I *have not* told the students.
	~ I *haven't* told the students.

In these examples, the positive sentence contains an auxiliary (*be, have*) that can serve as 'operator' (i.e. first auxiliary in a verb phrase). When there is no such operator present, the auxiliary *do* has to be introduced as operator. This is called the ***do*-construction** or ***do*-support** (*see* 611). Like modal auxiliaries, *do* is followed by the bare infinitive:

Positive clause	Negative clause
My children like to play with computers.	~ My children *do not* like to play with computers.
	~ My children *don't* like to play with computers.
What he says *makes* sense.	~ What he says *does not* make sense.
	~ What he says *doesn't* make sense.

(On the constructions with *be* and *have* as main verbs in negative sentences and on the forms of the modal auxiliaries, *see* 480.)

Contracted negation: *She won't mind.*
582
Besides the ⟨informal⟩ contracted negative *n't* there are contracted verb forms *'s* for *is*, *'re* for *are*, *'ll* for *will*, etc., also ⟨informal⟩ (*see* 478). The contracted verb forms can be tagged on to the subject (if it is a pronoun or short noun): *he's, you're, she'll*. Consequently, there are two forms of ⟨informal⟩ negation possible, one with a contracted verb, and the other with a contracted negative:

Contracted verb + full form of *not*	Full form of verb + contracted negative
It's *not* their fault.	~ It *isn't* their fault.
You*'ve not* read the book, have you?	~ You *haven't* read the book, have you?
She*'ll not* mind if you stay.	~ She *won't* mind if you stay.
They*'re not* in school today.	~ They *aren't* in school today.

But in general, especially with a long noun as subject, the *n't* form is more likely:

> The children *aren't* in school today.

Both sets of contracted forms are used in ⟨informal⟩ English. In ⟨formal⟩ English, the full forms are used for both verb and negative: *It is not their fault*, etc. In questions with inversion, *not* can be placed either after the auxiliary in its contracted form *n't*, or after the subject in its full form *not*:

> Have*n't* you written to the publishers? ⟨informal⟩
> ~ Have you *not* written to the publishers? ⟨formal⟩

Negative pronouns and determiners: *There's no time left.*

583

Any-words (*see* 697) are frequently used after negation. Compare:

> I have *some* time left.
> I have*n't any* time left.

Instead of the construction with *not*-negation and *any*:

> There is*n't any* time left.

we may equally well say:

> There is *no* time left.

No is a negative determiner (*see* 522). In English there are a number of negative expressions with different functions, as can be seen in the table below.

NUMBER	FUNCTION	COUNT		MASS
		PERSONAL	NON-PERSONAL	
singular	pronoun	*no one* *nobody*	*nothing*	
			none (of)	*none* (of)
	pronoun and determiner		*neither* (of)	
plural	pronoun		*none* (of)	
singular and plural	determiner		*no*	

As the table shows, *none* can be treated as either singular or plural as far as concord is concerned (*see* 513):

> *None of them has arrived.* OR
> *None of them have arrived.*

Other negative words: *Neither of them is correct.*
584
There are also other negative words beginning with *n: neither, never, nowhere,* etc.:

neither (determiner, pronoun, adverb of addition, *see* 234):

> You've given two answers. *Neither* is correct.

neither . . . nor (coordinating conjunction, *see* 520):

> *Neither* the government *nor* the market can be blamed for the present economic situation.

never (adverb of time-when or frequency):

> I *never* believed those rumours.

nowhere (adverb of place):

> This tradition exists *nowhere* else in Africa.

Also, there are certain words which are negative in meaning and behaviour although they do not appear negative in form:

barely ('almost . . . not'):

> The dormitories could *barely* house one hundred students.

few ('not many'):

> Some people work very hard but there seem to be *few* of them left.

hardly ('almost not'):

> There is *hardly* any butter left. ('almost no butter')

little ('not much'):

> He seems to be doing very *little* research.

rarely ('almost never'):

> We now know that things *rarely* ever work out in such a cut-and-dried fashion.

scarcely ('almost not'):

> There was *scarcely anything* she did that did not fascinate me. ('almost nothing')

seldom ('not often') ⟨rather formal⟩:

> This subject is *seldom* properly taught to undergraduates.

The effect of negative words: *She never seems to care, does she?*
585
The usual effect of negative words is to make the whole clause in which they occur negative (but *see* 261). Negative clauses have certain characteristics:

- After a negative item there are normally *any*-words instead of *some*-words (*see* 698).

Positive clause:

> I had *some* doubts about his ability.

Negative clauses:

> ~I didn't have *any* doubts about his ability. ('I had *no* doubts about his ability.')
> I *seldom* get *any* sleep after the baby wakes up.
> I've spoken to *hardly anyone* who disagrees with me on this point.

- Negative words are followed by positive rather than negative tag-questions (*see* 684):

> |She *never* seems to c`a`re | d`o`es she?|
> |That *won't* happen ag`a`in | w`i`ll it?|
> |You *won't* forget the sho̬pping | w`i`ll you?|

Compare:

> |You'll remember the sho̬pping | w`o`n't you?|

- A negative item placed at the beginning of a clause brings about the inversion of subject and operator, i.e. the order is operator + subject:

> *Only* after a long argument *did* he agree to our plan.   [1]
> *Rarely* in American history *has* there been a political campaign that clarified issues less.
> *Never was* a greater fuss made about any man than about Lord Byron.

This inversion does not happen where the negative is part of the subject:

> *No one* appears to have noticed the escape.

The inverted construction, as in [1], sounds rather ⟨elevated⟩ and ⟨rhetorical⟩ (*see* 417). If the negative item is **not** placed at the beginning of the clause, the word order is regular (subject + verb), and there is no *do*-construction (*see* 611). Both [1a], [1b] are more common than [1]:

~ He agreed to our plan *only* after a long argument.   [1a]
~ It was *only* after a long argument that he agreed to our plan.   [1b]

Not in phrases and in non-finite clauses
586

Sometimes the negative word *not* is attached to a noun phrase instead of the verb phrase. There is no inversion when the negated noun phrase is subject:

She likes big cities. *Not all* her paintings, however, are of cities.

But inversion and the *do*-construction are required when the negated and front-placed noun phrase is object:

Not a single painting did she manage to sell.

To make non-finite clauses negative (*see* 493), we place the negative word *not* before the verb phrase:

They had no opinions about Kafka, *not having* read him.
The motorist was on probation and under court order *not to drive.*
The important thing now is *not to mourn* the past but to look ahead.

Transferred negation: *I don't believe we've met.*
587

We expect to find the negative item in the clause it negates. But instead of saying

I believe we have*n't* met.   [1]

we may say

I do*n't* believe we've met.   [2]

In [2] *not* has been transferred from the subclause to the main clause. This construction, which is called **transferred negation**, occurs after verbs like *believe, suppose,* and *think*:

I *don't suppose anybody* will notice the improvement.
    ~ I suppose nobody will notice the improvement.
She *doesn't think* it's very likely to happen.
    ~ She thinks it's not very likely to happen.

Nominal clauses
(*see CGEL* 15.3–16)

588
Nominal clauses function like noun phrases (*see* 595). This means that nominal clauses may be subject, object, complement, or prepositional complement.

- As subject:

    Whether I take a degree or not does not matter very much.
    ~ It doesn't matter very much *whether I take a degree or not.*
    [*it*-construction, *see* 542]

- As object:

    I don't know *whether we really need* a new car.

- As complement:

    What they worry about is *whether to stay here or move elsewhere.*

- As prepositional complement:

    This raises the question *as to whether we should have better student grants.*

Nominal clauses can also occasionally take an appositive function similar to that of a noun phrase in apposition:

    Our latest prediction, *that Norway would win the match*, was totally disbelieved.
    Let us know your college address, i.e. *where you live during the term.*

There are five main types of nominal clause, which will be discussed in the following sections:

- *that*-clauses (*see* 589)
- interrogative subclauses (*see* 590)
- nominal relative clauses (*see* 592)
- nominal *to*-infinitive clauses (*see* 593)
- nominal -*ing* clauses (*see* 594)

That-clauses: *I'm sure that she'll manage somehow.*
589
That-clauses can occur as subject, direct object, subject complement or adjective complement.

- As subject:

    That you're still alive is sheer luck.

- As direct object:

    No one can deny *that films and TV influence the pattern of public behaviour.*

- As subject complement:

    The assumption is *that things will improve.*

- As complement of an adjective:

    One can't be sure *that this finding is important.*

In ⟨informal⟩ use, *that* is often omitted when the *that*-clause is object:

    I knew *I was wrong.*

or complement:

    I'm sure *she'll manage somehow.*

or postponed subject (*see* 542):

    It's a pity *you have to leave so soon.*

Wh-interrogative subclauses: *Nobody seems to know* **what to do.**
590
Interrogative subclauses are introduced by *wh*-interrogative words (*see* 536). They can function as subject, direct object, subject complement or adjective complement.

- As subject:

    How the book will sell largely depends on its author.

- As direct object:

    I don't know *how she managed to do it.*

- As subject complement:

    This is *how he described the accident.*

- As complement of an adjective:

    I wasn't certain *whose house we were in.*

Wh-clauses can have all the functions of *that*-clauses. In addition, *wh*-clauses can be prepositional complement (which *that*-clauses cannot be):

    None of us were consulted about *who should have the job.*

When the *wh*-element is a prepositional complement, the preposition can be in either initial position ⟨formal⟩ or final position ⟨informal⟩:

    He couldn't remember *on which* shelf he kept the book. ⟨formal⟩
    ~ He couldn't remember *which* shelf he kept the book *on.* ⟨informal⟩

An infinitive *wh*-clause can be formed with all *wh*-words except *why*:

> Nobody knew *what to* do. ('what they were supposed to do')
> They discussed *where to* go. ('where they should go')
> He explained to me *how to* start the motor. ('how one should start the motor')

Yes-no interrogative subclauses: *She wondered **whether Stan would call.***
591
Yes-no interrogative subclauses are formed with *if* or *whether*:

> She wondered *if/whether Stan would call.*
> Do you know *if/whether the shops are open today?*

The alternative question (*see* 242) has *if/whether . . . or*:

> Do you know *if/whether the shops are open or not?*

Only *whether* can be directly followed by *or not*:

> *Whether or not Wally lost his job* was no concern of mine.

Nominal relative clauses: *What we need is something to get warm.*
592
Nominal relative clauses are also introduced by different *wh*-words. They have the same functions as noun phrases:

- As subject

> *What we need* is something to get warm. ('the thing that we need . . .')
> *Whoever owns this boat* must be rich. ('the person who owns . . .')

- As direct object:

> I want to see *whoever deals with complaints.*
> You'll find *what you need* in this cupboard. ('the things that . . .')
> I can go into a shop and buy *whatever is there.*

- As subject complement:

> Home is *where you were born, reared, went to school and,* most particularly, *where grandma is.*

- As object complement:

> You can call me *what(ever) names you like.*

- As complement of a preposition:

> You should vote for *which(ever) candidate you like the best.*

Nominal relative clauses are introduced by a *wh*-determiner or *wh*-pronoun (*see* 523), as in this proverb:

> *Whoever* laughs last, laughs longest.

This sentence can also be put in the form:

> ~ *Those who* laugh last, laugh longest.

Whoever is here replaced by the demonstrative pronoun *those* and the relative pronoun *who*. *Who* alone hardly occurs in this nominal relative function.

As we see above, a nominal relative clause can be introduced by a *wh*-word ending in *-ever*, e.g. *whatever*. These words have general or inclusive meaning. Thus the pronoun *whatever* means roughly 'anything which'. Other expressions containing relative clauses can be used instead, as in *anyone who*, *the person who*:

> *Whoever* told you that was lying.
> ~ *Anyone who* told you that was lying.
> ~ *The person who* told you that was lying.

Nominal *to*-infinitive clauses: *I was only glad **to be able to help.***
593
Nominal *to*-infinitive clauses have a number of different functions in the clause:

- As subject:

  > *To say there is no afterlife* would mean a rejection of religion.

- As direct object:

  > He wants *everyone to be happy.*

- As subject complement:

  > The minister's first duty will be *to stop inflation.*

- As complement of an adjective:

  > I was very glad *to help in this way.*

The subject of a *to*-infinitive is normally introduced by *for*. A pronoun subject here has the objective form:

> What I wanted was *for them to advance me the money.*

Nominal *-ing* clauses: *I don't like **people telling me how to do things.***
594
Nominal *-ing* participle clauses have the same range of functions as nominal *to*-infinitive clauses. In addition, they can act as complement of a preposition:

- As subject:

  > *Telling stories* was one thing he was well-known for.

- As direct object:

  > I don't mind *people telling me how to do things better.*

- As subject complement:

  What he likes best is *playing practical jokes*.

- As prepositional complement:

  She sparked off the opposition by *telling a television audience it was gossip*.
  She is quite capable of *telling her employers where they are wrong*.

When the *-ing* clause has a subject there is sometimes a choice between two constructions. The genitive case of nouns and the possessive form of pronouns are typical of ⟨formal⟩ style:

  Winston was surprised at *his wife's reacting so sharply*.
  Winston was surprised at *their reacting so sharply*.

In ⟨informal⟩ style, the normal form of nouns and the objective case of personal pronouns are more common:

  Winston was surprised at *his wife reacting so sharply*.
  Winston was surprised at *them reacting so sharply*.

Noun phrases
(*see CGEL* Chapter 17)

595
A noun phrase is called a noun phrase because the word which is its head (i.e. main part) is typically a noun. In the following two sentences there are several noun phrases:

  On Tuesday a German passenger liner rescued the crew of a trawler. It found them drifting on a life raft after they had abandoned a sinking ship.

Here are the noun phrases with a description of their grammatical functions:

1. *Tuesday* in the prepositional phrase *On Tuesday*, which functions as a time-when adverbial. *Tuesday* itself is a prepositional complement (*see* 654).
2. *a German passenger liner* is the subject of the first sentence.
3. *the crew of a trawler* is the object. This noun phrase contains another noun phrase, *a trawler*, which is prepositional complement in the prepositional phrase *of a trawler*.
4. *It*, a personal pronoun referring to *a German passenger liner* and functioning as the subject of the second sentence.
5. *them*, a plural personal pronoun referring to *the crew of a trawler*. The reason why the plural *them* can refer to the singular *crew* is that this is a group noun (*see* 510).
6. *a life raft*, the prepositional complement in *on a life raft*, which functions as a place adverbial.

7. *they*, a plural personal pronoun referring to *the crew of a trawler* and functioning as subject of the subclause beginning with *after*.
8. *a sinking ship* functioning as object of the subclause beginning with *after*.

596

A head noun can be accompanied by determiners (*a, the, his*, etc.) and one or more modifiers: *passenger* modifies *liner* and *German* modifies *passenger liner*. This type of modification is called **premodification** because the modifiers stand **before** the head noun. When there is modification **after** the head, it is called **postmodification**. An example of this is in *the crew of a trawler*, where the head *crew* is postmodified by the prepositional phrase *of a trawler*. Often there exists a choice between the two types of modification: we could also say *the trawler's crew*, using premodification (*see* 650) instead of postmodification (*see* 641).

Pronouns such as *it* and *them* typically have a function equivalent to that of a whole noun phrase. In this book, in fact, we regard pronouns as the heads (and often the only words) of noun phrases.

The structure of the English noun phrase can be written:

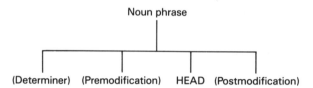

Noun phrase

(Determiner)   (Premodification)   HEAD   (Postmodification)

The brackets indicate that the determiners and modifiers can be left out. But determiners are more essential to noun phrase structure than modifiers. The only situation in which a noun phrase has no expressed determiner is where it has a 'zero article' (*see* 473). Here are some examples of noun phrases:

Determiner	Premodification	HEAD	Postmodification
the		BOOKS	
a	*good*	BOOK	
some		BOOKS	*to read*
all those	*good*	BOOKS	*I want to read*
a	*sinking*	SHIP	
a	*German*	PASSENGER LINER	
the		CREW	*of a trawler*

The different parts of noun phrase structure are treated separately in this part of the grammar: determiners in 522, premodifiers in 650 and postmodifiers in 641. Apart from nouns, pronouns (*see* 661) and adjectives (*see* 448) may act as head of a noun phrase.

Number
(*see CGEL* 5.73–103)

Singular and plural number: *this problem ~ those problems*
597
In English, there is singular number (denoting 'one') and plural number (denoting 'more than one'). Number is a feature of nouns (*book/books*), demonstrative pronouns (*this/these*, *see* 521), and personal pronouns (*she/they*, *see* 619). It is also shown through concord with singular or plural forms of the verb (*see* 575).

The regular plural of nouns is formed by adding *-s* or *-es* to the singular (see 635).

- **Count nouns** can be singular or plural (*see* 58), as in:

  one daughter ~ two daughters
  a fast train ~ fast trains
  this problem ~ these problems

But many nouns do not have plural number. They include **mass nouns** (also called **non-count nouns** or **uncountables**) and **proper nouns** (names).

- **Mass nouns** such as the following are singular only (*see* more examples in 62): *advertising, advice, applause, cash, evidence, food, furniture, garbage, hospitality, information, knowledge, money, music, pollution, refuse, rubbish, waste.*

  Our *advertising* is mainly concentrated on the large national newspapers.
  It's wise to have *cash* in the bank before cheques are drawn.
  The lawyer said *evidence* would show that her clients were entirely innocent.
  Our city is known for its fine *food*, good *music* and colourful *hospitality*.
  Is this your *money*? – No, it's my sister's.

- **Proper nouns** such as *Margaret, Stratford, Mars, the Mississippi, Broadway* are also singular:

  Are you living in *Stratford* at the moment?

For some exceptions, such as *the Wilsons* (= the Wilson family), *the West Indies*, *see* 671).

Singular nouns ending in -s: *What's the big news?*
598
There are some nouns which are exceptional or require special comment, such as singular nouns ending in *-s*.

- *News* is always singular:

    That's good *news!*
    Instead of being depressed by *this news*, she was actually relieved by *it*.

- **Subject names in** *-ics* are singular: e.g. *classics* ('classical languages'), *linguistics, mathematics, phonetics, statistics*:

    Statistics is not as difficult as some people think.

But *statistics* is treated as a plural when it is not a subject but = 'figures':

    The official *statistics show* that 6 per cent are unemployed.

- **Names of games** ending in *-s* are singular, e.g. *billiards, darts, dominoes, fives, ninepins*:

    Billiards is my favourite game.

- **Proper nouns** ending in *-s* are singular, e.g. *Algiers, Athens, Brussels, Flanders, Marseilles, Naples, Wales. The United Nations* (*the UN*) and *the United States of America* (*the USA*) have a singular verb when considered as single units:

    There is no evidence to suggest that *the United States is* weaker than other nations in this respect.

- **The names of some diseases** ending in *-s* are usually treated as singular, e.g. *measles, German measles, mumps, rickets, shingles.* Similarly *AIDS* (which is an acronym of 'acquired immune deficiency syndrome'):

    AIDS is an illness which destroys the natural system of protection that the body has acquired against disease.

Plural-only nouns: *How much are **those sunglasses?***
599
There are some nouns which occur only in the plural (sometimes only in certain senses), for example *people, police, trousers*.

- *People* as the plural of *person*:

    Many qualified young *people* are not going into medicine because they can't afford the schooling costs.

But *people* has the plural *peoples* when it is a group noun, in the sense of 'men and women of a particular country, race', etc.:

    The speaker said that by leaving our country's doors open we give other *peoples* the opportunity to see us and compare.
    This country has been settled by many *peoples* of many heritages.

- *Police*:

> The *police* have dropped the case.
> When we entered the building the *police* were no longer there.

But 'a member of the police force' = *policeman, policewoman*:

> My father's a *policeman* and makes less than fifteen thousand a year.

- *Cattle*:

> Holstein *cattle* aren't a beef breed and they are rarely seen on a ranch.

600
Some nouns denoting a tool or an instrument (e.g. *scissors*) consisting of two equal parts which are joined together:

> (A) Have you seen my new *sunglasses*? (B) Here they are.

To express one or more items of such nouns we can use *a pair of, two pairs of*:

> I'd like a *pair of scissors*, please.

Other nouns that behave like *scissors*: *binoculars, glasses, pincers, pliers, tongs, scales* [for weighing], *shears, tweezers*.

Nouns for articles of dress consisting of two parts (e.g. *trousers*) are also treated as plural:

> Where are my *trousers*?

But such plural nouns can be 'turned into' ordinary count nouns by means of *a pair of* or *pairs of*:

> I need to buy a new *pair of trousers*.
> How many *pairs of blue jeans* do you have?

Other nouns that behave like *trousers* are: *briefs, jeans, pants, pajamas* ⟨AmE⟩, *pyjamas* ⟨BrE⟩, *shorts, slacks, tights, trunks*:

> My *pants* were soaking wet.
> She was dressed in the tightest-fitting pair of *slacks* I had ever seen on a
> woman.

Further examples of nouns that are plural-only, or mainly plural: Many thanks!

601
There are many nouns which, in a given sense, only occur in the plural, for example **contents** (as in *the contents of a book, the contents of a cupboard, a list of contents*, etc.):

> The *contents* of this 195-page document are not known to many.
> The minister has to work through the *contents* of a bulging briefcase in
> the evenings.

The singular form *content* denotes what is contained by a text or by a particular substance:

> The *content* of a text frequently influences its style.
> The average nickel *content* of the alloy is about 2.5 per cent.

Here are some other examples of plural-only, or mainly plural, nouns:

arms ('weapons'): *Arms* were distributed widely among the civilian population.
ashes: After the fire many a ranch-house lay as a square of blackened *ashes*.
   (BUT: *cigarette ash*)
funds ('money'): Our *funds* are too scarce to permit this plan. (BUT: *a fund*, 'a
   source of money': *The family set up a fund for medical research.*)
oats: The *oats* were sown early this year. (BUT: *corn, barley* are singular.)
odds: The *odds* are not very strongly in favour of a temporary tax cut.
outskirts: They met in a place on the *outskirts* of the city.
premises ('building'): She discovered the residential *premises* were on fire.
quarters, headquarters: The proposal aroused violent opposition in some
   quarters. ['circles'] (BUT: *the third quarter of 1990* = 'three-month period')
spirits ('mood'): She got home in high *spirits*, relaxed and smiling. (BUT: *These
   people have retained their pioneering spirit.*)
stairs: She was about to mount a wide flight of marble *stairs*.
steps: They stood on the *steps* of the ambassador's home.
surroundings: The *surroundings* of their house are rather unattractive.
thanks: My warmest *thanks* are due to your organization.

To make *thanks* singular one can use expressions like these:

> *A vote of thanks* was proposed to the retiring manager. ⟨formal⟩
> And now, let's give a big *thank-you* to our hostess! ⟨informal⟩

Numerals
(*see CGEL* 6.63–69)

Cardinals and ordinals
602
The **cardinal numerals** (*one, two, three,* etc.) and the **ordinal numerals** (*first, second, third,* etc.) are shown in the following list. The ordinals are normally preceded by another determiner, usually the definite article (*see* 525):

> [A]   How many people are taking part in the competition?
> [B]   There are *ten* on the list, so you are *the eleventh*.   [1]
> They have *five children* already, so this will be *their sixth child*.   [2]

Numerals can be used either as pronouns [1], or as determiners [2]. Cardinal numerals also function as nouns, when they name a particular number, e.g. (playing with dice):

> You need a *six* or two *threes* to win the game.

Cardinals		Ordinals	
0	zero, nought ‖ naught		
1	one	1st	first
2	two	2nd	second
3	three	3rd	third
4	four	4th	fourth
5	five	5th	fifth
6	six	6th	sixth
7	seven	7th	seventh
8	eight	8th	eighth
9	nine	9th	ninth
10	ten	10th	tenth
11	eleven	11th	eleventh
12	twelve	12th	twelfth
13	thirteen	13th	thirteenth
14	fourteen	14th	fourteenth
15	fifteen	15th	fifteenth
16	sixteen	16th	sixteenth
17	seventeen	17th	seventeenth
18	eighteen	18th	eighteenth
19	nineteen	19th	nineteenth
20	twenty	20th	twentieth
21	twenty-one (etc.)	21st	twenty-first (etc.)
24	twenty-four (etc.)	24th	twenty-fourth (etc.)
30	thirty	30th	thirtieth
40	forty	40th	fortieth
50	fifty	50th	fiftieth
60	sixty	60th	sixtieth
70	seventy	70th	seventieth
80	eighty	80th	eightieth
90	ninety	90th	ninetieth
100	a/one hundred	100th	hundredth
101	a/one hundred and one (etc.)	101st	hundred and first (etc.)
120	a/one hundred and twenty	120th	hundred and twentieth (etc.)
200	two hundred	200th	two hundredth
1,000	a/one thousand	1,000th	thousandth
2,000	two thousand (etc.)	2,000th	two thousandth (etc.)
100,000	a/one hundred thousand	100,000th	hundred thousandth

0 = *zero, nought, naught, oh, nil, nothing, love*

603

The numeral 0 is spoken or written out in different ways: *zero, nought, naught, oh, nil, nothing,* and *love.*

- **Zero** /ˈzɪərəʊ/ is used especially in mathematics and for temperature (*see* 606):

  This correlation is not significantly different from *zero.*
  Her blood pressure was down to *zero.*
  The temperature dropped and stood at *zero* in the daytime.

- **Nought** ‖ **naught** /nɔːt/ occurs chiefly as the name of the numeral 0:

> To write 'a million' in figures, you need a one followed by six noughts
> ‖ naughts.

- Read as /oʊ/, sometimes written **oh**, used for example in telephone and fax numbers. In ⟨AmE⟩ telephone numbers are more often read as 'zero' than 'oh':

  > Dial 7050 ['seven oh five oh'] and ask for extension 90 ['nine oh'] ⟨esp BrE⟩.
  > Who used to play Agent 007 ['double oh seven']?

- *Nil* or **nothing** is used in contexts such as these (especially football scores):

  > The visitors won 4–0. ['four nil, four nothing, four to nothing', *see* 606 below]
  > Now her influence was reduced to *nil*.
  > The training promises to be arduous and the pay will be *nil*.

- *Love* is used in tennis, squash, etc.:

  > The champion leads by 30–0 ('thirty love').

In general use, zero is replaced by the negative determiner *no* or the pronoun **none**:

> There were *no* survivors from the air disaster.
> *None* of the passengers or crew survived.

Hundred, thousand, million and billion
604

One or *a* must be used with *hundred, thousand, million* and *billion* when they are spoken or written out:

100	*one hundred* OR *a hundred*
1,000	*one thousand* OR *a thousand*
1,000,000	*one million* OR *a million*
1,000,000,000	*one billion* OR *a billion* OR *one thousand million*

These numerals have the singular form following both singular and plural numbers or quantifiers. But all four have the *-s* plural when they denote an indefinite number:

four *hundred* soccer fans	BUT: *hundreds of* supporters
ten *thousand* books	BUT: *thousands of* books
several *million* yen	BUT: *millions of* yen

> Tok Pisin is used by more than *three million* people in Papua New Guinea today.

BUT: [A]   How many children are born each year?
       [B]   I don't know – *millions and millions.*
       Hundreds of thousands of people had to be evacuated during the monsoon.

Fractions, decimals, superscripts, etc.
605
Fractions, decimals, superscripts, etc. are written and read out as follows:

Fractions

$\frac{1}{2}$ *(a) half*: They stayed (for) half an hour. OR They stayed for a half hour.
$\frac{1}{4}$ *a quarter*: They stayed (for) a quarter of an hour.
$\frac{1}{10}$ *a/one tenth*: a tenth of the population
$\frac{3}{4}$ *three quarters* OR *three fourths*: three quarters of an hour
$1\frac{1}{2}$ *one and a half*: one and a half hours, an hour and a half
$3\frac{2}{5}$ *three and two fifths*: three and two fifths inches
$\frac{3}{568}$ *three over five six eight* [in mathematics]

Decimals

0.9   *nought point nine* ⟨esp BrE⟩ OR *zero point nine* ⟨esp AmE⟩
2.5   *two point five*
3.14   *three point one four*

Superscripts

10^2 *ten squared*
10^3 *ten cubed*

Arithmetic

$4 + 4 = 8$ *four plus four equals eight* OR *four and four makes/is eight*
$5 \times 2 = 10$ *five multiplied by two equals ten* OR *five times two makes/is ten*
$6 \div 2 = 3$ *six divided by two equals/makes/is three*

606
Temperatures

$-15°$ *fifteen (degrees) below (zero)* OR *minus fifteen (degrees Celsius)*
85°F   *eighty-five (degrees (Fahrenheit))*

Currency

25c   *twenty-five cents* OR *a quarter*
$4.75   *four dollars seventy-five* OR *four seventy-five*
20p   *twenty pence* OR *twenty p* /piː/
£9.95   *nine pounds ninety-five (pence)* OR *nine ninety-five*

Sports scores

5–1   *five to one* OR *five one*
3–0   *three to nil* OR *three nil* OR *three (to) nothing* ⟨BrE⟩ OR *three (to) zero* OR
       three blank ⟨AmE⟩
2–2   *two all* OR *two two* OR ⟨AmE⟩ *two up* (i.e. it's a tie or a draw)

Dates and times of the clock
607
Years
1996   (*the year*) *nineteen ninety-six* OR (*the year*) *nineteen hundred and ninety-six*
          ⟨more formal⟩
2000   *the year two thousand*
2010   (*the year*) *two thousand* (*and*) *ten* OR (*the year*) *twenty ten*

Decades
Decades can be written: *the 1990s* OR *the 1990's* OR *the 90s* OR *the '90s*. They
are also written, and read out, as *the nineteen nineties* OR *the nineties*.
    The plural *twenties* denotes an age or a period between 20 and 29; similarly
with *thirties* (30–39), *forties* (40–49), etc.:

> He looked like a man *in his early/mid/late forties.*

Dates ⟨written⟩:

> Our daughter was born
> > *on 18 August 1993.* ⟨BrE⟩
> > *on August 18, 1993.* ⟨esp AmE⟩
> > *on August 18th, 1993.* ⟨AmE⟩

The alternative written forms are *18/8/93* (day + month) ⟨in BrE⟩ BUT *8/18/93*
(month + day) ⟨in AmE⟩.

Dates ⟨spoken⟩:

> Our daughter was born
> > *on the eighteenth of August, nineteen ninety-three.*
> > *on August the eighteenth, nineteen ninety-three.* ⟨BrE⟩
> > *on August eighteenth, nineteen ninety-three.* ⟨AmE⟩

Times of the clock
Times of the clock are read out in full as follows:
> at 5   *at 5* (*o'clock*)
> at 5.15   *at five fifteen* OR *at a quarter past five* OR *at a quarter after five*
> > ⟨AmE⟩
> at 5.30   *at five thirty* OR *at half past five*
> at 5.45   *at five forty-five* OR *at a quarter to six* OR *at a quarter of six*
> > ⟨AmE⟩
> at 5.50   *at five fifty* OR *at ten* (*minutes*) *to six*
> at 6.10   *at ten* (*minutes*) *past six* OR *at ten minutes after six* ⟨AmE⟩ OR
> > *at six ten* [for instance in referring to a timetable]

Objects

(*see CGEL* 10.7–8, 27–32, 16.25–67)

608

The object of a clause can be a noun phrase (*see* 595):

> Can you see *that white boat* over there?

But the object can also be a nominal clause (*see* 588):

> Now we can see *that too little has been spent on the environment.*

The object usually refers to the person, thing, etc., affected by the action of the verb:

> She kissed *him* gently on the cheek.
> He parked *his car* outside a café.

The object normally follows the verb phrase. English typically has SVO (subject + verb + object) order in both main clauses and subclauses:

> After the chairman announced *the takeover bid,* the stock exchange council banned *dealings in the company's shares.*

But on variations of word order, *see* fronted topic (411), exclamations (528), *wh*-questions (683) and relative clauses (687).

The object of an active sentence can usually be turned into the subject of a passive sentence (*see* 613):

Active: A dog owner *found* little Nancy yesterday at about 11 a.m.
Passive: Little Nancy *was found* yesterday at about 11 a.m. (by a dog owner).

When a clause has two objects, the first is an indirect object and the second a direct object. The indirect object is typically personal, as in these examples: *me, the patient.*

> 'Nobody gives [*me*] [*flowers*] anymore', she said.
> She bought [*the patient*] [*fruit, meat and cheese*].

The indirect object is often equivalent to a prepositional phrase with *to*:

> Nobody gives flowers *to me* anymore.

or a prepositional phrase with *for* (*see* 730):

> She bought fruit, meat and cheese *for the patient.*

However, an alternative prepositional construction is not always possible, as in these sentences:

> We all wish *you better health.*
> Isabelle leaned down and gave *him a real kiss.*

Operators
(see CGEL 2.48–50, 3.21–30, 34, 37)

What is an operator?

609

Auxiliary verbs have different meanings and functions in the verb phrase (*see* 735). But they have one important feature in common: they all occur before the main verb. When finite (*see* 737), they are placed first in the finite verb phrase. We call the first auxiliary of a verb phrase the **operator**. Compare the following interrogative sentences with the matching declarative ones (the operator is in bold):

> ***Will*** you *be* back after the weekend?
> ~ You ***will*** *be* back after the weekend.
> ***Were*** they *showing* any comedy films?
> ~ They ***were*** *showing* some comedy films.
> ***Was*** he *lecturing* on English grammar?
> ~ He ***was*** *lecturing* on English grammar.
> ***Have*** you *met* the new students?
> ~ You ***have*** *met* the new students.
> ***Have*** I *been asking* too many questions?
> ~ I **have** *been asking* too many questions.
> ***Would*** a more radical decision *have been* possible?
> ~ A more radical decision ***would*** *have been* possible.

In each case, the first auxiliary (operator) of the finite verb phrase is placed first, and isolated from the rest of the verb phrase, no matter how complex the phrase is.

Be acts like an operator even when it is a main verb, and so the term 'operator' will be used also in cases like this one:

> *Is* she a good student?

Note

In ⟨BrE⟩ also *have* sometimes acts like an operator even when it is a main verb:

> *Have* you any money?

However, there is an alternative *do*-construction, which is used in both ⟨AmE⟩ and ⟨BrE⟩ (*see* 611):

> *Do* you *have* any money?

Operators in interrogatives and negatives

610

Operators are important in English because they are generally used in the construction of interrogative and negative sentences. In *yes–no* questions the operator stands before the subject. (This is called **inversion** of subject and operator.) In negative statements the operator stands before *not*:

> I *will not* be going to the seminar tomorrow.
> Chris *is not* playing so well this season.
> She *has not* got the full-hearted consent of her parents.

Or, in ⟨informal⟩ English, the auxiliary is combined with the negative contraction *n't* (see 582):

> ~ I *won't* be going to the seminar tomorrow.
> ~ Chris *isn't* playing so well this season.
> ~ She *hasn't* got the whole-hearted consent of her parents.

Adverbs with mid-position, such as *always, never* (see 458), usually take the same position as *not*, just after the operator:

> Things *will* **never** *be* the same again.
> That sort of attitude *has* **always** *appealed* to me.

Such adverbs are also found before the operator, especially for contrast:

> I submit that this is the key problem of international relations, that it **always** h<u>as</u> been, that it **always** w<u>ill</u> be.

The *do*-construction: *Does he know the way?*
611
In a verb phrase which has no auxiliary verb there is no word that can act as operator, for example:

> He *knows* the way.
> You *need* some advice.
> The delegates *arrived* yesterday.

In such cases, we have to introduce the special 'dummy' operator *do* in *yes–no* questions (see 682) and *not*-negation (see 581). This is called **the *do*-construction** or ***do*-support.**

Yes–no questions	Not-negation
Does he *know* the way?	He *doesn't know* the way.
Do you *need* any advice?	I *don't need* any advice.
Did the delegates *arrive* yesterday?	The delegates *didn't arrive* yesterday.

Do as operator is followed by the infinitive of the main verb (or of the second auxiliary verb).

612
Other constructions with an operator
Apart from *yes–no* questions and *not*-negatives, there are some other constructions which also require an operator, including the 'dummy' operator *do*. Such constructions are:

Emphatic sentences (*see* 300):

> Dŏ *be* quiet! (More emphatic than *Be quiet!*)
>
> I dĭd *enjoy* that meal last night! ('I really enjoyed that meal')

Tag questions (*see* 684):

> |He won the men's dŏubles lást year| dĭdn't he?|
>
> |She's got a very distinctive accent as wĕll | hăsn't she?|

Wh-*questions* where the *wh*-element is **not** the subject:

When *did* you come back from Spain?	[*when* = adverbial]
How long *did* she stay in Egypt?	[*how long* = adverbial]
What *did* she do so long in London?	[*what* = object]
Who *did* you want to speak to?	[*who* = prepositional complement]

But no operator and no *do*-construction are needed when the *wh*-element is subject:

> Who is this on the picture?
>
> Which guests are coming by train?
>
> What took you so long?

Compare:

Who met you at the airport?	[*who* = subject]
Who did you meet at the airport?	[*who* = object]

Statements with subject-operator inversion, which occurs when a negative expression is placed first in the sentence (*see* 417):

> Only after a long delay *did* news of Livingstone's fate *reach* the coast. ⟨rather formal⟩

A cleft sentence with introductory *it* (*see* 496) would be more natural in most contexts:

> It was only after a long delay that news of Livingstone's fate reached the coast.

Passives
(*see CGEL* 3.63–78)

613
The term **passive** is the name of verb phrases which contain the construction *be* + past participle (*see* 739):

is accepted, has been shown, will be covered, etc.

The passive is not very common in ⟨informal speech⟩ but is a regular feature in ⟨formal, especially scientific written⟩ texts, as in the following extract from a paper on odontology (with passive verb phrases in italics):

> It *is* generally *accepted* that, when it *is exposed* in the oral cavity, any natural or artificial solid surface *will* quickly *be covered* by thin organic films. It *has been shown* in several studies that these films contain material of salivary origin.

The opposite of 'passive' is 'active'. Here are some pairs of examples of different verb types to show the contrast between active clauses and their corresponding passive clauses:

> Everyone *rejected* the bold idea.
> ∼ The bold idea *was rejected* (by everyone).
> The ambulance crew *gave* the casualties first aid.
> ∼ The casualties *were given* first aid (by the ambulance crew).
> Boat owners *considered* the bridge a menace to navigation.
> ∼ The bridge *was considered* a menace to navigation (by boat owners).
> The committee *asked* him to become director of the institute.
> ∼ He *was asked* (by the committee) to become director of the institute.

Turning actives into passives
614
To change an active clause into a passive clause:

1. replace the active verb phrase by the matching passive one;
2. make the object of the active clause the subject of the passive clause;
3. make the subject of the active clause the agent of the passive clause. The agent is the noun phrase which occurs after the preposition *by* in the passive clause. The agent is an optional part of the passive construction: *by* + agent can be omitted altogether, as indicated by round brackets in the examples.

These three changes can be pictured as follows:

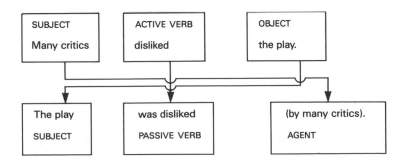

615

The effect of the change into the passive is to reverse the positions of the noun phrases acting as subject and object in the active sentence. Active sentences which have a noun phrase or pronoun as object can be made passive. However, a few verbs which take an object do not have a passive: they include *have* (as in *I have a small car*, and *hold* (as in *This jug holds one litre*). Also, the passive is sometimes not possible when the object is a clause.

With verbs like *give*, which can have two objects, it is usually the first object (the indirect object) that becomes subject of the passive clause:

> The department *gave* him no authority to take such a decision.
> ~ He *was given* no authority to take such a decision.
> Our school *did not give* general subjects enough time.
> ~ General subjects *were not given* enough time.

But there is also another passive construction where the direct object is made subject and *to* is added before the object:

> ~ Enough time *was not given* to general subjects.

Passives without agents: *Nobody was injured in the crash.*
616

The *by*-phrase containing the agent of a passive clause (and corresponding to the subject in an active clause) is only required in specific cases. In fact, only about one out of five English passive clauses has an expressed agent. The passive is especially associated with ⟨impersonal⟩ style, such as ⟨scientific and official writing⟩. Here the question of who is the agent (i.e. who performs the action described by the verb) is often unimportant and need not be stated:

> The question *will be discussed* at a meeting tomorrow.

The passive may be a convenient construction to choose also when we do not know who the performer of an action is:

> A police officer *was killed* last night in a road accident.

The *get*-passive: *I hope you didn't get hurt.*
617

As we have seen in the examples given so far, the passive auxiliary is normally *be*. There is also a passive with *get*:

> The boy *got hurt* on his way home from work.
> It's upsetting when a person *gets punished* for a crime that they didn't commit.

The *get*-passive is found only in ⟨informal⟩ style, and normally in constructions without an agent.

Passives with prepositional verbs and with non-finite verb phrases:
This matter will have to be dealt with.
618
The passive also occurs with prepositional verbs (e.g. *deal with, ask for, believe in, cater for, look at, stare at, talk about, wonder at*; *see* 632). The prepositional object, i.e. the noun phrase following the preposition of the active sentence, then becomes the subject of the passive sentence:

> The members also *talked about* other possibilities at the meeting.
> ~ Other possibilities *were* also *talked about* at the meeting.   [1]
> Someone *will have to deal with* this matter right away.
> ~ This matter *will have to be dealt with* right away.   [2]
> I just don't like people *staring at* me.
> ~ I just don't like *being stared at*.   [3]
> An improvement in relations between our countries *is to be hoped*
>   *for* as a result of the conference.   [4]

As the examples [2], [3] and [4] show, the passive can also occur in non-finite verb phrases. Compare:

> I want everybody *to understand* this.   [active *to*-infinitive]
> ~ I want this *to be understood* by everybody.   [passive *to*-infinitive]
> Without anybody *asking* her, Joan did the job
>   herself.   [active *-ing* clause]
> ~ Without *being asked*, Joan did the job herself.   [passive *-ing* clause]

Personal and reflexive pronouns
(*see CGEL* 6.15–31)

The range of forms
619
Personal pronouns (e.g. *she, they*) and reflexive pronouns (e.g. *herself, themselves*) are related. Both distinguish between personal and non-personal gender and, within personal gender, between masculine and feminine (*see* 529):

	Singular	Plural
1st person	*I* ~ *myself*	*we* ~ *ourselves*
2nd person	*you* ~ *yourself*	*you* ~ *yourselves*
3rd person	*he* ~ *himself*	*they* ~ *themselves*
	she ~ *herself*	
	it ~ *itself*	

For the 2nd person the same form is used in the singular and plural of personal and possessive pronouns (*you, your, yours*), but there is a separate plural of reflexive pronouns: *yourself* (singular) and *yourselves* (plural). *We*, the 1st person plural pronoun, denotes 'I plus one or more others' (*see* 97).

620

Five personal pronouns have both subjective and objective forms:

> *I/me, we/us, he/him, she/her, they/them* (but *you* has only one form).

Some personal pronouns also have two genitive forms:

> *my/mine, our/ours, you/yours, her/hers, their/theirs*
>   (but *his* has only one form).

The genitives of the personal pronouns are usually called **possessive pronouns** (*see* 623). The following table gives all the forms of personal and reflexive pronouns.

		Personal pronouns				Reflexive pronouns
				Possessives		
		subjective case	objective case	acting as deter-miner	acting as pronoun	
1st person	singular	*I*	*me*	*my*	*mine*	*myself*
	plural	*we*	*us*	*our*	*ours*	*ourselves*
2nd person	singular plural	*you*		*your*	*yours*	*yourself* *yourselves*
3rd person	singular masculine	*he*	*him*	*his*		*himself*
	singular feminine	*she*	*her*	*her*	*hers*	*herself*
	singular non-personal	*it*		*its*		*itself*
	plural	*they*	*them*	*their*	*theirs*	*themselves*

Personal pronouns

621

Personal pronouns, as we see from this table, are classified according to

- **person:** 1st, 2nd, 3rd person
- **number:** singular, plural
- **gender:** masculine, feminine, non-personal
- **case:** subjective, objective, genitive (or possessive)

The choice of person, number and gender is decided by meaning (*see* 82–5), which is supplied either by context outside language, or by the sort of noun phrase to which the pronoun 'refers' (or 'points back'; *see* 375). Pronouns generally point back to a noun phrase, as in this example and in [1] and [2] below:

> *My brother* is out, but *he* will be returning soon.

But a personal pronoun in a subclause can also 'point forward' to a noun phrase in the following main clause, as *it* pointing forward to *the plane* in [3] below. Compare the different order in the following three alternative sentences.

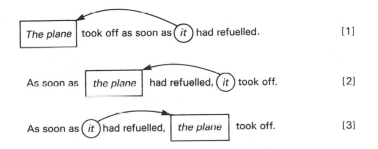

It is especially in ⟨formal written⟩ English that the personal pronoun precedes the noun phrase (as in [3]).

Subjective and objective forms
622
The choice of subjective and objective case is made on the basis of grammatical position. The simplest rule to use is that the subjective form is the one used in subject position with finite verbs, and the objective form is the form used in all other positions.

Subjective case:

> *She* was very helpful.

Objective case:

> ~I found *her* very helpful. (*her* = direct object)
> She gave *him* her home number. (*him* = indirect object)
> I haven't had the opportunity to speak to *them* about it. (*them* = prepositional complement)
> She must have been about five years older than *him*. (*him* = prepositional complement)
> [In a telephone conversation]
> [A] Who's t̀hat?
>   [B] It's m̀e – Àgnes. (*me* = subject complement)

Datrx International Limited
Fri Mar 18 10:49:37 1994 comgra **gra001 -333**
prism ch1459 total55140 jn

In the last two examples, *older than him* and *it's me* are ⟨informal⟩ English. It is sometimes stated that the subjective form is the correct one here. But *older than I* and *it's I* sound rather stilted, and are avoided in ⟨informal⟩ use (*see* 506).

Possessives
623
There are two kinds of possessives, each with its separate function. *My, your, her*, etc. act as determiners before noun heads. *Mine, yours, hers*, etc. act as pronouns, i.e. as independent noun phrases:

> Determiner function: This is *her* book.
> Pronoun function: This book is ʹ*hers*.

In pronoun function, the possessive is stressed. Compare the two corresponding genitive noun constructions (*see* 530):

> This is *Joan's* book.
> This book is ʹ*Joan's*.

Possessives as determiner: Have you changed **your** *mind again?*
624
Unlike many other languages, English uses determiner possessives with reference to parts of the body and personal belongings:

> She broke *her* leg when she was skiing in Austria.
> Don't tell me they've changed *their* minds again!
> Don't lose *your* balance and fall into the water!
> I can't find *my* glasses.

The definite article is usual in prepositional phrases related to the object:

> She took the little girl by *the* hand. (The hand belongs to the little girl.)
> Something must have hit me on *the* head. (The head is mine.)

In passive constructions, the prepositional phrase is related to the subject:

> He was shot in *the* leg during the war.

Possessives as pronoun: Is that paper **yours?**
625
The forms *mine, hers, theirs*, etc., can act in all the main positions where a noun phrase is possible:

- A possessive as subject:

> *Yours* is an international company, *mine* is just a small local firm.

- A possessive as subject complement:

> Is that my copy or *yours*?

- A possessive as object:

> Philip wanted a screwdriver, so I let him borrow *yours*.

- A possessive as prepositional complement:

    > This is a special policy of *theirs*, is it?
    > What business is it of *hers*? (*cf.* 535)

- A possessive is also used in comparisons after *than* and *as*:

    > Your car looks faster than *ours*. ('our car')

Reflexive pronouns: *Have you locked **yourself** out?*
626
Reflexive pronouns are used as objects, complements, and (often) prepositional complements where these elements have the same reference as the subject of the clause or sentence:

> We have to find *ourselves* a new home.
>
> Have you locked *yourself* out?
>
> He works too hard. He'll burn *himself* out.
>
> I hope she enjoyed *herself*.
>
> Most authors start by writing novels about *themselves*.
>
> This is a word Indians use among *themselves*.
>
> He certainly has a high opinion of *himself*.
>
> Carolyn got a seat all by *herself*.

Notice that in some cases the reflexive pronoun receives nuclear stress, and in other cases not.

The indefinite pronoun *one* (*see* 680) has its own reflexive, as in

> One mustn't fool *oneself*.
>
> It's just a journey one does by *oneself*.

Reflexives are also used in imperative and non-finite constructions, where they point back to the element which is understood to be the subject of the verb:

> Make *yourself* at home.
> I've asked everyone to help *themselves*. [On concord here, *see* 96.]

But the ordinary personal pronouns are used in many prepositional phrases denoting place:

> He turned around and looked *about him*.
> Have you any money *on you*?
> We examined all the documents *in front of us*.

Personal or reflexive pronoun: *someone like **you** ~ someone like **yourself***
627
The reflexive pronouns (*myself, ourselves*, etc.) are sometimes used as alternatives to the objective forms of personal pronouns (*me, us*, etc.). This happens after *as for, like, but for, except for*, and in coordinated noun phrases:

As for *me/myself*, I don't mind what you decide to do.

For someone like *me/myself*, one good meal a day is quite enough.

The picture she showed us was of *her/herself* and Brian on the terrace.

Emphatic use: *I'll do it **myself**.*
628

The reflexive pronouns also have an emphatic use, where they follow a noun phrase or another pronoun, and reinforce its meaning:

I spoke to the manager *himself*.

The question was how she *herself* was to achieve this goal.

She's getting a divorce: she *herself* told me.

If the premises *themselves* were improved, the college would be much
   more attractive.

We can also postpone the reflexive pronoun to the end of the sentence (*see* 428):

She told me so *herself*.

He'll be here *himself*.

Without being asked, Joe fixed the lock *himself*.

Alternative constructions: *my **own** house ~a house **of my own***
629

After a possessive determiner, *own* can be used for reflexive or emphatic meaning: *my own, your own, his own* etc.:

He cooks *his own* dinner ('He cooks dinner *for himself*')
We'll have to make *our own* decisions.
The government is encouraging people to buy *their own* homes.

The intensifying adverb *very* can be added before *own* for added emphasis:

Do you like the soup? The recipe is *my very own*.

The combination possessive + *own* can also occur in an *of*-phrase (*compare* 535):

I'd love to have a house *of my own*.
It's so much easier for a student to work in a room *of his or her own*.

Phrasal and prepositional verbs
(*see CGEL* 16.3–16)

Phrasal verbs: *Go **on**!*
630

Verbs may form combinations with adverbial particles such as *down, in, off, on, out, up*:

Aren't you going to *sit down*?
I usually *get up* quite early and *get on* with my own work.

Did he *catch on?*
We expect this project to *go on* another three years.
My interview *went off* very smoothly.
The plane has just *taken off*.
When will they *give in?*
The doctor thinks by the end of next week you could *get out* in the air a little.
Drink up quickly.
It's a pity their marriage did *break up*, and whose fault was it?
I stood there for another ten minutes but she didn't *turn up*.

Such verb-adverb combinations are called **phrasal verbs**, and they are usually ⟨informal⟩. Most adverbs in phrasal verbs are place adverbs identical in form to prepositions (*down, in, up*, etc.; *see* 192). Verbs can also combine with prepositional adverbs which function like prepositional phrases (*see* 654):

> They *walked past* (the place). [1]
> She *ran across* (the street). [2]

In [1] and [2], the noun phrases are omitted by ellipsis. Like these, some phrasal verbs retain the individual meanings of the verb and the adverb (for example *sit down*). Other phrasal verbs are idiomatic: the meaning of the combination cannot be built up from the meanings of the individual verb and adverb, for example *catch on* ('understand'), *give in* ('surrender'), *turn up* ('appear, arrive').

Alternative adverb positions: **Turn on** *the light!,* **Turn** *the light* **on!**
631
Many phrasal verbs can take an object:

> I'll *get out* my old pair of skis.
> His parents were forced to *make up* the deficit.
> She is *bringing up* her brother's children.
> The union *called off* the strike.
> We've got to *find out* what's going on here.

With most phrasal verbs, the adverb can either come before or follow a noun object:

> They *turned on* the light.
> ~ They *turned* the light *on*.

But when the object is a personal pronoun it always has to come before the adverb:

> ~ They *turned* it *on*.

Other examples of phrasal verbs with objects are:

> The new government was unable to *bring about* immediate expansion.
> The president decided to *break off* diplomatic relations immediately.
> He couldn't *get over* the fact that she died.
> The enemy *blew up* the bridge.

In the end it's the taxpayers who are forced to *make up* the deficit.

In some cases phrasal verbs with objects look identical to verbs followed by a prepositional phrase. Compare:

> They *ran over* the bri̇̀dge. ('crossed the bridge by running')
> [verb + preposition]
>
> They *ran 'over* the cȧt. ('knocked down and passed over')
>
> [phrasal verb]

Prepositional verbs: *Will you attend to that?*
632
A verb may also form a fixed combination with a preposition (*see* 744), for example:

> He's *applied for* a new job.
> Would you like to *comment on* the situation?
> The article also *hinted at* other possibilities.
> I don't *object to* this proposal in principle.
> The mayor announced that he would not *run for* re-election.

The noun phrase following the preposition is called the **prepositional object**. Here are some other examples of prepositional verbs:

> The plan must be flexible enough to *allow for* technological
>   breakthroughs.
> What is called a plan for action *amounts to* doing nothing.
> At the meeting she told him not to bother about the contract – she
>   would *attend to* that.
> The new hospital is equipped to *care for* all patients.
> We must give small shops a chance to *compete with* large supermarkets.
> These statements can be interpreted to *conform to* our own point of
>   view.
> She said she was not adequately trained to describe or *enlarge on* these
>   difficult questions.
> The personal pronouns are normally unstressed because they *refer to*
>   what is prominent in the immediate context.
> The minister stated categorically that we should under no circum-
>   stances *resort to* the use of such weapons unless they are first used
>   by our enemies.

Notice that prepositional verbs are commonly 'stranded' at the end of the sentence (*see* 659) when they are part of prepositional verbs:

> That's exactly what I'm *hoping for*.
> He had a poor salary but he didn't need much to *live on*.

Phrasal and prepositional verbs compared: *call* her *up* but *call on* her
633
Phrasal and prepositional verbs may seem very similar, for example:

> He *called up* his wife to tell her he'd met some old friends and could be
> home late. [1]
> She went to the hospital to *call on* a friend after a serious operation. [2]

But phrasal verbs, such as *call up* in [1], and prepositional verbs, such as *call on*
in [2] are different in several ways:

- The adverb in a phrasal verb [1] is usually stressed and has nuclear stress in
  end-position. The preposition in a prepositional verb [2] is normally unstressed. Compare:

  > All young men were *called ùp* | for military sèrvice. [1]
  > We'll c`all on you | as soon as we arr`ive. [2]

- The preposition in a prepositional verb must come before the prepositional
  object. Compare again the phrasal verb [3] with the prepositional verb
  [4]:

  > We'll *call up* our friends. [3]
  > ~ We'll *call* our friends *up*.
  > ~ We'll *call* them *up*.
  > We'll *call on* our friends. [4]
  > ~ We'll *call on* them. (BUT NOT: *We'll *call* our friends *on*.)

- Only the prepositional verb allows an adverb to be placed between the verb
  and the preposition:

  > They *called* early *on* their friends. (BUT NOT: *They *called* early *up* our
  > friends.)

Unlike some languages, English allows the prepositional object to become the
subject of a passive sentence (*see* 613). Compare:

> Some employees *looked upon* the manager almost as a saint.
> ~ The manager was *looked upon* almost as a saint (by some employees).

Phrasal-prepositional verbs: *This noise is hard to* **put up with**!
634
In ⟨informal⟩ English, some verbs can combine as an idiom with both an
adverb and a preposition, for example:

> She seems to *put up with* almost anything. ('tolerate')
> You shouldn't *break in on* a conversation like that. ('interrupt')
> What a preposterous idea! She'll never *get away with* it. ('succeed')
> He *walked out on* the project. ('abandoned')
> I'm trying to *catch up on* my own work. ('bring . . . up to date')
> We shouldn't *give in to* their arguments so easily. ('yield')

We call these combinations **phrasal-prepositional verbs**. Like prepositional verbs, some phrasal-prepositional verbs can be turned into the passive by changing the prepositional object into the subject of the clause (*see* 618):

> They thought such tendencies would increase rather than be *done away with*. ('be abolished')

We cannot insert an adverb between the preposition and the object, but we can do so between the adverb and the preposition:

> Oddly enough he *puts up* willingly *with* that secretary of his.

In relative clauses, and other fronting constructions where the (prepositional) object is front-placed, the adverb and preposition stay after the verb:

> Is this something the police are *checking up on*? ('investigating')
> You don't realize what I've had to *put up with*. ('tolerate')

(Compare the 'stranded' preposition with prepositional verbs, *see* 659.)

Other examples of phrasal-prepositional verbs in ⟨informal⟩ English are:

> You can't just *back out of* an agreement like that!
> Why don't you just *drop in on* the new neighbours? ('call on' ⟨casual⟩)
> The first thing you've got to do, to be happy, is to *face up to* your problems. ('confront')
> Now let's *get down to* some serious talk. ('give some serious attention to')
> What does it all *add up to*? ('amount to')
> You should never *look down on* people in trouble. ('have a low opinion of')
> They managed to *make away with* most of the bank's money. ('escape with')
> Somebody's got to *stand up for* those principles! ('defend')

Plurals
(*see CGEL* 5.73–103)

Regular plurals: *one dog* ∼ *many dogs*
635
Most nouns are count nouns: they can occur in both the singular, denoting 'one', or in the plural, denoting 'more than one' (*see* 58). Most count nouns have the regular *-s* plural, which is formed by adding an *-s* to the singular:

> *one dog* ∼ *two dogs.*

In some cases spelling changes occur when *-s* is added (*see* 702). For the pronunciation of the *-s* ending, *see* 664.

In most compounds the ending is added to the last part:

> *assistant district attorney* ∼ *assistant district attorneys*

So also: *breakdowns, check-ups, grown-ups, stand-bys, take-offs,* etc. But in a few compounds where the head noun comes first, the ending follows the first part:

> *editors-in-chief, lookers-on* (BUT: *onlookers*), *mothers-in-law, notaries public, runners-up, passers-by,* etc.

A few compounds, such as *woman doctor,* have both the first and the last part in the plural:

> *women doctors, women writers, men students,* etc.

Irregular plurals
Voicing + -s *plural: knife ~ knives*
636
Some singular nouns which end in the voiceless /f/ or /θ/ sound (spelled -*f* and -*th*) change to the corresponding voiced sound /v/ or /ð/ in the plural before the regular /z/ ending.

- **Some nouns in** -*f(e)*. The voiced plurals /-vz/ are spelled -*ves*:

calf ~ calves	*half ~ halves*
knife ~ knives	*leaf ~ leaves*
life ~ lives	*loaf ~ loaves*
shelf ~ shelves	*thief ~ thieves*
wife ~ wives	*wolf ~ wolves*

Other nouns in -*f* have the regular plural /fs/: *beliefs, chiefs, cliffs, proofs, roofs, safes,* etc. Compare also reflexive pronouns: *herself ~ themselves* (see 619).

- **Some nouns in** -*th*. With a consonant before the -*th*, the plural is regular:

> *month* /mʌnθ/ ~ *months* /mʌnθs/

With a vowel before the -*th*, the plural is also often regular, as with *cloths, deaths, faiths.* But there is voicing in

> *mouth* /maʊθ/ ~ *mouths* /maʊðz/, *path ~ paths*

In some cases we find both regular and voiced plurals:

> *oath* /oʊθ/ ~ /*oaths* /oʊθs/ or /oʊðz/

Similarly: *truths, wreaths.*

- *House* /haʊs/ has the voicing in the plural: /ˈhaʊzɪz/, but the spelling is regular: *houses.*

Change of vowel in the plural: foot ~ feet
637
The following nouns form the plural by a vowel change instead of an ending:

> *foot* /fʊt/ ~ *feet* /fiːt/[a]   *tooth* /tuːθ/ ~ *teeth* /tiːθ/

goose /gu:s/ ~ *geese* /gi:s/   man /mæn/ ~ *men* /men/
mouse /maʊs/ ~ *mice* /maɪs/[b]   woman /ˈwʊmən/ ~ *women*
                                              /ˈwɪmɪn/

Child /tʃaɪld/ has the plural *children* /ˈtʃɪldrən/.

Note
[a] On *six foot/feet two inches*, see 638.
[b] For the hand-held device used with a computer, both *mice* and the regular *mouses* occur.

No plural ending: *one sheep ~ many sheep*
638
Some nouns can be used both with a singular and a plural meaning without change in form ('zero plural'), as in *one sheep ~ many sheep.*

- *Sheep* and some other animal names are always unchanged, but with other names there is great variation. Most animal nouns are regular: *bird ~ birds, hen ~ hens, rabbit ~ rabbits*, etc.
    Always unchanged: *deer, sheep, plaice, salmon, grouse* (e.g. *several deer*, etc.).
    Usually unchanged: *pike, trout, carp, moose* (e.g. *a lot of fine trout*).
    With both the regular and the unchanged plurals: *antelope(s), fish(es), flounder(s), herring(s)* (e.g. *several herring/herrings*).

- *Dozen* and *foot* have no plural form in many expressions of quantity:

    He scored a *dozen* goals (BUT: He scored *dozens of* goals.)
    [A] How tall are you?
        [B] I'm six *foot* [Also written: 6 *ft*]. (BUT: I'm six *feet* tall) I'm six *foot/feet* two (inches). [Also written: *6 ft 2 in.*]

- Plural expressions like *five days* do not have a plural *-s* when they modify a noun (*see* 651), as in *a five-day week, a six-cylinder engine, an eight-month-old baby.*

- *Series* and *species* can be used as either singular or plural:

    She gave *one series/two series* of lectures.

Foreign plurals: *analysis ~ analyses*
639
Some nouns borrowed from foreign languages (including Latin and Greek) keep their foreign plurals, instead of adopting regular English plurals. Other foreign nouns can have both a regular plural and a foreign plural.

- **Nouns in -*us*** (Latin): The foreign plural is *-i* /aɪ/ in

    stimulus ~ stimuli /ˈstɪmjʊlaɪ/.

Only regular plurals occur in

    bonus ~ bonuses, campus ~ campuses, circus ~ circuses.

Both plurals are used in

> *cactus ~ cactuses/cacti, focus ~ focuses/foci, radius ~ radiuses/radii,*
> *terminus ~ terminuses/termini, syllabus ~ syllabuses/syllabi.*

Only foreign plurals are:

> *alumnus ~ alumni, bacillus ~ bacilli, stimulus ~ stimuli.*

- **Nouns in -*a*** (Latin): The foreign plural is *-æ* (also written *-æ*, both pronounced /i:/), as in *alumna ~ alumnae*. But only the regular plural occurs in

> *area ~ areas, arena ~ arenas*, etc.

Only foreign plurals are used in

> *alga ~ algae, larva ~ larvae*

but both plurals occur in

> *formula ~ formulas/formulae, antenna ~ antennas/antennae.*

Foreign plurals tend to be more common in technical usage, whereas the *-s* plural is more natural in everyday language. We find *formulas* in general use, as in *the formulas of politicians, milk formulas*. But often *formulae* is used in fields such as mathematics:

> This relationship is best expressed in algebraic *formulae*.

Similarly, *antennas* occurs in general uses and in electronics (*directional antennas*), but *antennae* in biology.

- **Nouns in -*um*** (Latin): The foreign plural is *-a* /ə/, as in *curriculum ~ curricula*.

Only the regular plural occurs in

> *album ~ albums, museum ~ museums*, etc.

Usually regular are

> *forum ~ forums, stadium ~ stadiums, ultimatum ~ ultimatums.*

Both plurals occur in

> *memorandum ~ memorandums/memoranda,*
> *symposium ~ symposiums/symposia.*

Medium always has *media* in the *mass media* sense. These days *media* (in the sense of 'the newspapers, television and radio') and also *data* 'information' or 'facts' are often used as if they were singular mass nouns:

> The media *are/is* giving a biased account of this story.
> My data *show/shows* that the hypothesis was right.

- **Nouns in -*ex*** and **-*ix*** (Latin): The foreign plural is *-ices* (pronounced /-ɪsiːz/), as in *index ~ indices*. Both regular and foreign plurals occur in

>
> *apex ~ apexes/apices, appendix ~ appendixes/appendices,*
> *matrix ~ matrixes/matrices.*

Codex has only the foreign plural: *codices.*

640

- **Nouns in *-is*** (Greek): The foreign plural is *-es* (/-i:z/), as in *basis ~ bases.* The regular plural occurs in *metropolis ~ metropolises.* The foreign plural is used in

  > *analysis ~ analyses, axis ~ axes, crisis ~ crises, diagnosis ~ diagnoses,*
  > *ellipsis ~ ellipses, hypothesis ~ hypotheses, oasis ~ oases,*
  > *parenthesis ~ parentheses, synopsis ~ synopses, thesis ~ theses.*

- **Nouns in *-on*** (Greek): The foreign plural is *-a* /ə/, as in

  > *criterion ~ criteria, phenomenon ~ phenomena.*

Only regular plurals are used in

> *demon ~ demons, neutron ~ neutrons, proton ~ protons.*

Both plurals are used in *automaton ~ automatons/automata.*

Note
There are also some less common types of irregular plurals from Latin and Greek, e.g. *corpus ~ corpora* (besides *corpuses*), *schema ~ schemata.*

Postmodifiers
(*see* CGEL 17.9–64)

Different types of postmodifiers
641
A noun can be modified by another word (often an adjective) placed before the noun (noun phrase heads are printed in SMALL CAPITAL LETTERS, modifiers in **bold**):

> *the* **red** *HOUSE.*

Such words are called **premodifiers**. A noun can also be modified by a following phrase or a clause, often a relative clause:

> *the HOUSE* **which is red.**

Modifiers after the noun head are called **postmodifiers** (*see* 596). We have the following types of postmodifiers:

- Relative clauses (*see* separate entry 686):

  > The parents wanted to meet *the BOY* **who was going out with their daughter.**

- Prepositional phrases (*see* 654):

A *nice young* W O M A N *in jeans* was watching me.

- Non-finite clauses equivalent to relative clauses (*see* 643):

  They wanted to meet *the* B O Y *going out with their daughter*.

- Appositive clauses (*see* 646):

  The F A C T *that such a move on our part would be unpopular* is well-known.

- Clauses of time, place, manner and reason (*see* 647):

  In Stratford-on-Avon we visited *the* H O U S E *where Shakespeare lived*.

- Adverbs (*see* 648):

  Where is *the* W A Y *out?*

- Adjectives (*see* 649):

  There's N O T H I N G *new* about these techniques.

Two or more postmodifiers can modify the same noun:

  Have you seen the H O U S E [*in Stratford-on-Avon*] [*where Shakespeare lived*]?

Prepositional phrases as postmodifier: *a week of hard work*
642
Prepositional phrases (*see* 654) are by far the most common type of postmodifier in English. Prepositional phrases can often be expanded to relative clauses:

  Is this *the* R O A D *to Paris?* ('Is this the road *that leads to Paris?*').
  These are *economic* A C T I O N S *far beyond the normal citizen's control.*
    ('. . . actions which are far beyond . . .')

Other examples of nouns followed by a prepositional phrase:

  This message is scarcely *a* C A U S E *for regret*.
  The government seems to have *no* C O N T R O L *over capital movement*.
  This seems *a better* W A Y *of doing it*.

(On *of*-phrases, *see also* 70, 106, 531.)

Non-finite clauses as postmodifier: *a girl sitting opposite me*
643
All three types of non-finite clause (*-ing* participle clauses, *-ed* participle clauses, and *to*-infinitive clauses) can function as postmodifiers similar to relative clauses. Here are some examples:

- **-ing** *participle clauses*: PEOPLE *working with computers*

> PEOPLE **working in the advertising business** are often young. ('who are working in the advertising business')
> Do you know any of *those* PEOPLE *sitting behind us*?
> *A good-looking* MAN **wearing a grey suit** sat opposite me.
> Last Friday I got *a* LETTER **saying that there was trouble afoot.**

The participle clause does not have tense (*see* 128, 392), so that it can be interpreted, according to context, as past or present. But the *-ing* participle clause need not carry the meaning of the progressive aspect (*see* 132, 740). A progressive form (*are belonging) could not be used here:

> All ARTICLES **belonging to the college** must be returned. ('all articles that belong . . .')

644

- **-ed** *participle clauses*: *the* SUBJECT *discussed in the book*

> *The* QUESTION **debated in Parliament yesterday** was about the new tax. ('that was debated in Parliament')
> We have seen *the* DAMAGE *to the pine* **done by the deer**. ('that *has been done/had been done/was done* by the deer')

The participle clause corresponds in meaning to a passive relative clause, but the participle clause contains none of the distinctions that can be made by tense and aspect.

645

- **to-***infinitive clauses*: *the best* THING *to do*

> If you can't think of *a* THING **to do**, try something – anything.
> I've got SOMETHING **to say to you.**

The *to*-infinitive clause is often preceded by *next, last,* ordinal numerals or superlatives:

> *The next* TRAIN **to arrive** was from Chicago. ('the train which arrived next')
> John is *the last* PERSON **to cause trouble**. ('the person who would be the last to cause trouble')
> Amundsen was *the first* MAN **to reach the South Pole**. ('who reached the South Pole first')

In many infinitive clauses, the head of the noun phrase is the implied object or prepositional object of the infinitive verb:

> *The (best)* PERSON **to consult** is Wilson. ('the person you/one, etc. should consult')
> There are *plenty of* TOYS **to play with**. ('which you can play with')

In these cases, a subject preceded by *for* may be added:

> There are *plenty of* TOYS *for the children to play with*.
> It's TIME *for you to take over the family business*.

(On other infinitive clauses, such as *the time to arrive, see* 728.)

Appositive clauses as postmodifier: *Have you heard the* NEWS *that our team won?*
646
Appositive clauses are nominal clauses which have a relation to the head similar to that between two noun phrases in apposition (*see* 470). They can be *that*-clauses (*see* 589) or *to*-infinitive clauses (*see* 593):

> We will stick to *my* IDEA *that the project can be finished on time*.
>   (Compare: 'My idea *is that* . . .)   [1]
> It is reported that there has been *a* PLOT *to overthrow the government*.
>   [2]

The noun phrase can be related to a subject + *be* + complement construction:

> My idea is *that the project can be finished on time*.   [1a]
> The plot was *to overthrow the government*.   [2a]

The head of an appositive clause is an abstract noun such as *fact, idea, reply, answer, appeal, promise*:

> We were delighted at *the* NEWS *that our team had won*.
> We gratefully accepted *his* PROMISE *to help them*.
> The mayor launched *an* APPEAL *to the public to give blood to the victims of the disaster*.

The examples of appositive clauses given so far have been restrictive (*see* 687). There are also non-restrictive appositive clauses:

> His main ARGUMENT, *that scientific laws have no exceptions*, was considered absurd.
> His last APPEAL, *for his son to visit him*, was never delivered.

On the distinction between restrictive and non-restrictive meaning, *see* 110.

Clauses of time, place, manner, and reason: *There's no* REASON *why you should accept*.
647
There are a number of postmodifying clauses which denote adverbial relations: time (*see* 151), place (170), manner (194) and reason (198).

Finite clauses introduced by a wh-word, such as when, where, why:

TIME: Can you give me *a* TIME *when you will be free?*

PLACE: They wanted to take a vacation in *a* PLACE *where people could speak English.*

REASON: There's *no* REASON *why you should have to do a thing like that.*

Finite clauses introduced by **that** or **zero** (i.e. with *that* left out):

TIME: I'll never forget *the* TIME *(that) we've had together here.*

PLACE: That's hardly a PLACE *(that) one wants to go (to) for a holiday.*

MANNER: *The* WAY *(that) you said it in that broadcast* was misjudged.

REASON: That's *the only* REASON *(that) they are called fortified wines.*

To-infinitive clause: *the best* PLACE *to go*

TIME: I'll have plenty of TIME *to deal with this problem.*

PLACE: That's probably *the best* PLACE *to go (to) for trout-fishing.*

MANNER: There's really *no other* WAY *to do it.*

REASON: I have *no* REASON *to believe he can finish his thesis this year.*

Adverbs as postmodifier: *Can you find the* ROAD *back?*
648
Some adverbs are also used as postmodifiers of nouns (*see also* 468):

> Can you find the ROAD *back?*
> *The* PEOPLE *outside* started to shout.
> Have you written your paper for *the* SEMINAR *tomorrow* ('tomorrow's seminar')?

Adjectives as postmodifier: *There's* SOMETHING *odd about him.*
649
Adjectives which modify a noun usually stand before the noun: *That was an odd experience.* But in some constructions, e.g. with a pronoun like *something* or *everyone*, they follow the noun (*see* 443):

> There was SOMETHING *odd* about his behaviour.
> ANYONE *keen on modern jazz* should not miss this opportunity.

Premodifiers
(*see CGEL* 17.94–120)

The different types of premodifiers
650
Modifiers which are placed after determiners (*see* 522) but **before** the head of a noun phrase are called **premodifiers**. There are different types of premodifiers:

- *Adjectives* as premodifiers (*see* 440):

> We had *a **pleasant*** HOLIDAY *this year.*
> There are plenty of ***bright*** PEOPLE *here.*

An adjective can itself be modified by degree adverbs (*see* 459):

> We had *a **very pleasant** HOLIDAY* this year.
> There are a number of ***really quite bright young** PEOPLE*.

- **-ing** *participles* as premodifiers:

> We can see this as *an **accelerating** PROGRAMME* under the new government.
> The cost of painting and decorating *an old **converted** WAREHOUSE* would be too high.

- *Nouns* as premodifiers:

> Are *the **removal** EXPENSES* paid by your company?
> *The **passenger** LINER* dropped anchor in the harbour.

Compounds as premodifier: *camera-ready* COPY
651

Compounds often function as premodifiers of nouns. Compounds are combinations of words which function as a single adjective or noun, for example:

> I've just bought *a **brand-new** COMPUTER*.
> Do you have to submit ***camera-ready** COPY*?
> That's an absolutely *first-class IDEA*!
> These are all ***hard-working** STUDENTS*.
> Is that *a **new-style** CARDIGAN*?
> She has *some pretty **old-fashioned** NOTIONS*.

There are also modifiers which consist of more than two words, e.g. *out of date*. They are not hyphenated when they occur as complements (after the verb in a clause):

> This dictionary is *out of date*.

But they are often hyphenated when they are placed as modifiers before a noun:

> an *out-of-date* DICTIONARY
> a *ready-to-wear* SUIT
> thick *red-and-white-striped* WALLPAPER

Sequences of three, four, or even five nouns occur quite commonly in a noun phrase, e.g.:

> *a Copenhagen airline ticket office*.

These are formed either through noun premodification or through noun compounds, or through a combination of both. We can show the way in which this example is built up as follows:

airline ticket ('a ticket issued by an airline')
airline ticket office ('an office which sells *airline tickets*')
Copenhagen airline ticket office ('*an airline ticket office* in Copenhagen')

The structure of this noun phrase can be indicated by bracketing:

a [Copenhagen [[airline ticket] office]]

More than one premodifier: *the American spring medical* CONFERENCE
652
When a noun head has two or more premodifiers, these tend to occur in a certain order. We deal with them in a right-to-left order, i.e. starting from the head (which is indicated by SMALL CAPITAL LETTERS, modifiers in **bold**).

The item that comes next before the head is the type of classifying adjective which means 'consisting of', 'involving', or 'relating to':

This is not *a **political** PROBLEM*, it's *a **social** PROBLEM*.

Next closest to the head is the noun modifier:

We always attend *the **spring medical** CONFERENCE*.

Before the noun modifier comes the adjective derived from a proper noun:

I mean *the **American spring medical** CONFERENCE*.

However, most noun phrases have a simpler structure with no more than two modifiers, for example:

*the **Italian telephone** COMPANY*
***Scandinavian furniture** DESIGNS*

653
Before these modifiers we can find a variety of other modifiers: participles (*printed*), colour-adjectives (*red*), adjectives denoting age (*young*), etc.:

***printed** Scandinavian DESIGNS*
***red** oriental CARPETS*
*a **young** physics STUDENT*
*a **large** lecture HALL*

These premodifiers can themselves have modifiers:

***badly** copied Scandinavian furniture DESIGNS*
***really** attractive deep-red oriental SILK*
*a **very, very** young physics STUDENT*
*a large **enough** lecture HALL*

Notice the middle position of *little*, *old* and *young* when they are unstressed:

She lives in *a* '***nice** little* 'VILLAGE.
This is indeed *a* '***fine** old* 'WINE
He looks like *a* '***serious** young* 'MAN.

Prepositional phrases
(*see* CGEL Chapter 9)

The different complements of prepositions
654
A prepositional phrase consists of a preposition (*see* 657) followed by a prepositional complement. The complement is usually a noun phrase, but can also be another element, as we see below:

- Preposition + a noun phrase (*see* 595):

  As usual, her bright smile greeted me *at the breakfast table.*

- Preposition + a *wh*-clause (*see* 590):

  She came *from what she called 'a small farm' of two hundred acres.*

- Preposition + an *-ing* clause (*see* 594):

  Warren tried to shake off his fears *by looking at the sky.*

- Preposition + an adverb:

  You can see the station *from here.*

655
There are two types of nominal clauses which cannot be the complement of a preposition: *that*-clauses (*see* 589) and *to*-infinitive clauses (*see* 593). With such clauses, the preposition is omitted:

> I was surprised *at the news.*
> I was surprised *that things changed so quickly.* (*at* is omitted)
> I was surprised *to hear you say it had been raining.* (*at* is omitted)

Compare these constructions with preposition + a *wh*-clause:

> I was surprised *at what happened next.*
> I agree *with what you say,* Amy.

Sometimes, the addition of *the fact* (*that*) can serve to convert the *that*-clause construction into a form suitable for a prepositional complement. Compare:

> I think everybody's aware *of these problems.*
> ~I think everybody's aware *that there are problems.*
> ~I think everybody's aware *of the fact that there are problems.*

The functions of prepositional phrases
656
Prepositional phrases have many different grammatical functions. The main functions are the following:

- **Prepositional phrases as adverbial** (*see* 449):

We may need you to do some work *in the evening.*
To my surprise, the doctor phoned the next morning.
Finally I went back *to my old job.*

- **Prepositional phrases as modifier in a noun phrase** (*see* 596):

    She felt she had no CHANCE *of promotion.*
    We've rented this COTTAGE *in the country* for peace and quiet.
    The NOISE *from the sitting-room* was deafening but tuneful.

- **Prepositional phrases as verb complement:**

    You mustn't *worry* too much *about* this.

- **Prepositional phrases as complement of an adjective** (*see* 437):

    How can you remember when that novel came out? I'm terribly *bad at dates.*

A prepositional phrase may occasionally function as subject, complement, etc.:

    Before lunch is when I do my best work.

Prepositions and prepositional adverbs
(*see CGEL* 9.65–66)

Simple prepositions: *for, in, of, with,* etc.
657
Prepositions are very frequent words like *at, for* and *by* that are placed before a noun phrase (*by his work*), or sometimes before an *-ing* clause (*by working hard*), to form a prepositional phrase. The most common English prepositions are simple, i.e. they consist of one word. Here are the most common simple prepositions:

about	*above*	*after*
along	*around*	*at*
before	*below*	*beside*
between	*by*	*down*
for	*from*	*in*
into	*of*	*off*
on	*over*	*past*
since	*till*	*through*
to	*under*	*until*
up	*with*	*without*

In the following examples, the brackets [ ] enclose prepositional phrases:

    Do you know anything more definite [*about* her]?
    Temperatures hardly rose [*above* freezing] [*for* three months].
    When Miranda went to see him [*after* the accident] he was [*in* bed] [*with* a drip feed].

As she was walking [*up* the street] the van stopped [*beside* her] and one [*of* the men] lifted her [*into* it] and shut the door.

One prepositional phrase can be included in another:

The fire was discovered [*at* about five [*past* seven]].
A new scheme may be announced [*before* the end [*of* this month]].
[*After* walking [*up* the lane]] they made a sharp turn [*to* the right] [*past* some buildings].
It must be a nasty surprise [*for* a motorist] going [*along* a moorland road] [*at* the end [*of* the night]] to suddenly find a kangaroo jumping out [*at* one].

Complex prepositions: *as for, because of, except for,* etc.
658
There are also prepositions consisting of more than one word, so-called complex prepositions:

along with	*as for*	*away from*
because of	*due to*	*except for*
instead of	*out of*	*up to*
by means of	*in comparison with*	*in front of*
in relation to	*on top of*	(etc.)

Here are some examples of both simple and complex prepositions:

[*Because of* family circumstances] Michael was kept [*in* the hospital] [*for* a time].
Certain trades are [*in* many communities] closed areas [*of* employment], [*except for* a lucky few].
The boy said the blast knocked him [*out of* bed] and [*against* the wall].
It's [*up to* the government] to take action [*against* them].
Decide what the place is worth [*to* you] [*as* a home] [*in comparison with* what it would cost] to live [*in* town].
The training has not been enough [*in relation to* the need].
I grinned, feeling supremely [*on top of* things].

Stranded prepositions: *What is she looking at?*
659
Normally a preposition must come before its complement:

I came *in my brother's car.*   [1]

But there are cases where this does not happen, as in this *wh-* question:

Which car did you come *in?*   [1a]

In *wh*-questions, relative clauses and exclamations, the preposition can stand either at the end, as in [1a], or at the beginning, as in [1b], which is ⟨formal⟩:

~ *In which car* did you come?   [1b]

Prepositions which are deferred to the end of the sentence are sometimes called 'stranded prepositions'. Here are some further examples of the choice between 'stranding' and 'non-stranding':

- **In relative clauses** (*see* 688):

    That's a job you need special training *for*. [⟨informal⟩ with zero *that*]
    ~ This is a post *for which* one needs special training. ⟨formal⟩
    The means *through which* the plan may be achieved are very limited.
        ⟨formal⟩

- **In *wh*-questions** (*see* 683, including indirect questions, *see* 259):

    Who do you work *for*?
    ~ *For whom* do you work? ⟨formal⟩
    I asked her *which company* she worked *for*?

- **In exclamations** (*see* 528):

    What a difficult situation he's *in*!
    With what amazing skill this artist handles the brush! ⟨formal⟩

There are some clauses where there are no alternative positions for the preposition. In nominal *wh*-clauses, passive clauses, and most infinitive clauses, the preposition must occur at the end:

- *wh*-clauses (*see* 590, 592):

    What I'm convinced *of* is that the world's population will grow too fast.

- Passive clauses (*see* 618):

    The old woman was cared *for* by a nurse from the hospital.

- Infinitive clauses (*see* 593):

    Our new manager is an easy man to work *with*.

Prepositional adverbs: *A police car just went **past**.*
660
A prepositional adverb is an adverb which behaves like a preposition with the complement omitted (*see* 192):

    I walked *past the entrance*. (*past* = preposition)
    I got a quick look at their faces as we went *past*. (*past* = prepositional
        adverb)

Prepositions consisting of one syllable are normally unstressed, but prepositional adverbs are stressed. Compare:

    She stayed *in the house* all dày. ~ She stayed ìn.

All the words listed in 657 (except *at, beside, for, from, into, of, till, to, until, with*) can act as prepositional adverbs (*see* 185).

Pronouns
(*see CGEL* 6.1–13)

661

Pronouns are words like *I, me, this, those, everybody, nobody, each other, who, which*. A pronoun can function as a whole noun phrase, for example in being subject or object of a clause: *I love you*. Many of them act as substitutes (*see* 375) or 'replacements' for noun phrases in the context. A singular noun phrase is replaced by a singular pronoun and a plural noun phrase is replaced by a plural pronoun:

[A]:   **What sort of car** is *this?*   [B]:   *It's* called a hatchback.
[A]:   **What cars** are *those?*   [B]:   *They're* called hatchbacks.

Since a pronoun functions as a whole noun phrase, it does not normally have any determiners or modifiers. But many words can function both as determiners (which require a head) and as pronouns (which do not require a head).

Which car is yours? [*Which* is a determiner]
Which is yours? [*Which* is a pronoun]
This bike is mine. [*This* is a determiner]
This is my bike. [*This* is a pronoun]

Some items, e.g. *she, herself, one another, each other*, cannot be determiners but are pronouns only:

She had to support *herself* while attending school.
At first they didn't recognize *one another*.
The members of the family were separated from *each other* for several months.

662

Pronouns are treated under different headings in this part of the grammar:

- **Demonstratives:** *this, that, these, those* in 521.
- **Interrogatives:** *who, which, what, where*, etc. in 536–41.
- **Negatives:** *none, nobody, no one, nothing*, etc. in 581–7 (negation) and 675–80 (quantifiers).
- **Personal and reflexive pronouns:** *I, my, mine, myself*, etc. in 619–21.
- **Reciprocal pronouns:** *each other* and *one another* in 685.
- **Relative clauses:** *who, whom, whose, which, that* in 686–94.
- **Quantifiers:** *some, any, someone, everything, anybody, each, all, both, either, much, many, more, most, enough, several, (a) little, (a) few, less, least*, etc. in 675–80.

Pronunciation of endings
(*see CGEL 3.3–10, 5.80, 5.113, 7.80*)

The five endings of English
663
English has very few grammatical endings (inflections). The only five endings regularly used are *-s, -ed, -ing, -er, -est*. But some of them are used for more than one word-class. Here we deal with rules for the pronunciation of grammatical endings, whether they are added to nouns, verbs, or adjectives.

The -s ending: She works hard.
664
The *-s* ending has three different grammatical functions:

- **plural:** *She stayed for two* **weeks.** (*see* 635)
- **genitive:** *It was a* **week's** *work.* (*see* 530)
- **3rd person singular present tense:** *She* **works** *hard.* (*see* 574)

However, the rules for pronouncing the ending are the same in all functions:

Function	Pronunciation		
	/ɪz/-ending	/z/-ending	/s/-ending
Plural of nouns	*horse ~ horses*	*dog ~ dogs*	*cat ~ cats*
Genitive of nouns	*George ~ George's*	*Jane ~ Jane's*	*Ruth ~ Ruth's*
3rd person singular of verbs	*catch ~ catches*	*call ~ calls*	*hit ~ hits*

- The pronunciation is /ɪz/ after bases ending in voiced or voiceless sibilants. They are /z/, /s/, /dʒ/, /tʃ/, /ʒ/, /ʃ/. Examples of plurals, genitives and 3rd person singular present tense:

  /tʃ/: *church ~ churches*   /s/: *prince ~ prince's*
  /dʒ/: *Reg ~ Reg's*   /ʒ/: *barrage ~ barrages*
  /z/: *praise ~ praises*   /ʃ/: *wash ~ washes*

- The pronunciation is /z/ after bases ending in a vowel and voiced consonants other than /z/, /dʒ/, /ʒ/:

  boy ~ boys /bɔɪ/ ~ /bɔɪz/, *pig ~ pig's, read ~ reads*

- The pronunciation is /s/ after bases ending in voiceless sounds other than /s/, /tʃ/, /ʃ/:

  month ~ months /mʌnθ/ ~ /mʌnθs/, *week ~ week's, pick ~ picks*

Note the irregular pronunciations of the verbs *do* and *say* in the 3rd person singular present tense:

do ~ *does* /du:/ ~ /dʌz/ (stressed), /dəz/ (unstressed)
say ~ *says* /seɪ/ ~ /sez/

The -ed ending (see 574): She worked hard.
665
The *-ed* ending of regular verbs has three spoken forms:

- /ɪd/ after bases ending in /d/ and /t/:

pad ~ *padded*	/pæd/ ~ /ˈpædɪd/
pat ~ *patted*	/pæt/ ~ /ˈpætɪd/

- /d/ after bases ending in vowels and voiced consonants other than /d/:

mow ~ *mowed*	/moʊ/ ~ /moʊd/
praise ~ *praised*	/preɪz/ ~ /preɪzd/

- /t/ after bases ending in voiceless sounds other than /t/:

press ~ *pressed*	/pres/ ~ /prest/
pack ~ *packed*	/pæk/ ~ /pækt/

Consonants before the -er, -est and -ing endings
666
Normally the endings *-er*, *-est*, *-ing*, pronounced /ə(r)/, /ɪst/, and /ɪŋ/, are simply added to the base (see 501). But note these special changes of pronunciation:

- Syllabic l is no longer syllabic before *-er* and *-est*:

  simple /ˈsɪmpl/ ~ *simpler* /ˈsɪmplə(r)/ ~ *simplest* /ˈsɪmplɪst/

- Three adjectives ending in /ŋ/ change /ŋ/ to /ŋg/ before *-er* and *-est*:

  long /lɒŋ/ ~ *longer* /ˈlɒŋgə(r)/ ~ *longest* /ˈlɒŋgɪst/
  strong ~ *stronger* ~ *strongest, young* ~ *younger* ~ *youngest*

But compare: *sing* /sɪŋ/ ~ *singing* /ˈsɪŋɪŋ/.

- Whether or not speakers pronounce final r in words like *pour* and *poor*, the r is always pronounced before *-ing*, *-er* and *-est*:

  The rain is *pouring* /ˈpɔːrɪŋ/ down.
  It would be *fairer* /ˈfeərə(r)/ to take a vote.

Proper nouns and names
(see CGEL 5.60–72)

The unique reference of proper nouns
667
Proper nouns have 'unique' reference, and usually have no article in English *(see 92)*. The following list gives examples of article usage with some classes of proper nouns.

Proper nouns without an article: *Professor Chomsky*
668
Personal names (with or without titles) have no article:

> *Miranda, Paul, Helen Lee, Shakespeare, Mr and Mrs Johnson, Lady Macbeth,*
> *Dr Clark, Judge Powell* ⟨mainly AmE⟩, *Professor Chomsky*

Contrast names with 'unique' descriptions, for which *the* is needed:

> *President Roosevelt* (BUT: *the President of the United States*)
> *Lord Nelson* (BUT: *the Lord* ['God']; *see* 83).

Family terms with unique reference often behave like proper nouns:

> Hello *Mother/Mummy/Mum/Ma*! (The last three terms are ⟨familiar⟩.)
> *Father/Daddy/Dad* will soon be home. (The last two terms are ⟨familiar⟩.)

669
Calendar items have no article.
Names of festivals: *Christmas (Day), Independence Day, Easter (Sunday)*
Names of the months and the days of the week: *January, February. . ., Monday,*
  Tuesday . . .
Names of seasons may have the article omitted ⟨esp. BrE⟩:

> I last saw her *in (the) spring.* BUT: *in the spring of* 1975 (*see* 83).

670
Geographical names usually have no article:

- Names of continents: *(North) America, (mediaeval) Europe, (Central) Australia,*
  (East) Africa
- Names of countries, counties, states, etc.: *(modern) Brazil, (Elizabethan)*
  England, (eastern) Kent, (northern) Florida
- Cities and towns: *(downtown) Washington, (suburban) Long Island, (ancient)*
  Rome, (central) Tokyo. BUT: *The Hague, the Bronx, the City, the West End, the*
  East End (of London)
- Lakes: *Lake Michigan, (Lake) Windermere, Loch Ness*
- Mountains: *Mount Everest, Vesuvius, (Mount) Kilimanjaro.* BUT: *The Matterhorn*
- In combinations of name and common noun denoting buildings, streets,
  bridges, etc., the second noun usually has the main stress: *Hampstead* '*Heath.*
  But names ending in *Street* have the main stress on the first noun: '*Oxford*
  Street.

Madison '*Avenue*	*Westminster* '*Bridge*
Park '*Lane*	*Leicester* '*Square*
Russell '*Drive*	*Greenwich* '*Village*
Reynolds '*Close*	*Kennedy* '*Airport*
Portland '*Place*	*Harvard Uni*'*versity*

BUT: *the Albert Hall, the Haymarket* (a street name in London), *the George*

Washington Memorial Parkway, the Massachusetts Turnpike, the University of London

Proper nouns with the definite article: *the Wilsons*
671
Plural names take the definite article:

> *The Netherlands* (B U T : *Holland*)
> *the Midlands, the Bahamas, the Canaries, the Hebrides*
> *the Alps, the Himalayas, the Pyrenees, the Rockies*
> *the Wilsons* ('the Wilson family')

672
Some geographical names take the definite article:

> Rivers: *the (River) Avon, the Danube, the Mississippi, the Ganges, the Nile, the Rhone, the Amazon, the Thames,* etc.
> Seas: *the Atlantic (Ocean), the Baltic (Sea), the Mediterranean, the Pacific,* etc.
> Canals: *the Panama Canal, the Erie Canal, the Suez Canal*

673
The following *institutions* and other facilities take the definite article:

> Hotels, pubs and restaurants: *the Grand (Hotel), the Hilton, the Old Bull and Bush,* etc.
> Theatres, cinemas, etc.: *the Apollo Theatre, the Globe, the Odeon, the Hollywood Bowl.* B U T : *Drury Lane* (theatre), *Covent Garden* (opera house)
> Museums, libraries: *the Huntingdon (Library), the British Museum, the National Gallery, the Uffizi*

674
Newspapers usually take the definite article:
The Daily Express, The Independent, The New York Times, The Observer. After genitives the article is dropped: *today's Times.*

Magazines and periodicals normally have no article: *English Today, Language, Nature, Newsweek, New Scientist, Scientific American, Time.*

Quantifiers
(*see CGEL* 5.10–25, 6.45–62)

The grammatical functions of quantifiers
675
Quantifiers are words such as *all, any, some, nobody,* which denote quantity or amount (*see* 60). They have different grammatical functions.

Quantifiers can be **determiners** in the noun phrase:

- Words like *some*, *no* and *any* can function as determiners (i.e. **Group 2 determiners**, *see* 523): *some friends*.
- Words like *all* can function as determiners and can precede *the*, *this*, etc. in the noun phrase (i.e. **Group 1 determiners**, *see* 524): *all the time*.
- Words like *few* can function as determiners and can follow *the*, *these*, etc. (i.e. **Group 3 determiners**, *see* 525): *the few facts*.

Quantifiers can also function as **pronouns** (*see* 661), e.g. *somebody*:

> ***Somebody*** called this morning.

Quantifiers which have determiner function and pronoun function (alone or with an of-phrase):

(N = noun)	Count				Mass	
	Singular		Plural		Singular	
	Determiner function	Pronoun function	Determiner function	Pronoun function	Determiner function	Pronoun function
Group A: Words with inclusive meaning (*see* 80)	*all* N	*all* (of N)	*all* N	*all* (of N)	*all* N	*all* (of N)
	every N	*every one* (of N)				
	each N	*each* (of N)				
			both N	*both* (of N)		
	half N	*half* (of N)	*half* N	*half* (of N)	*half* N	*half* (of N)
Group B: *Some-* and *any*-words (*see* 697)	*some* N	*some* (of N)	*some* N	*some* (of N)	*some* N	*some* (of N)
	any N	*any* (of N)	*any* N	*any* (of N)	*any* N	*any* (of N)
	either N	*either* (of N)				
Group C: Words denoting degrees of quantity and amount (*see* 70)			*many* N	*many* (of N)	*much* N	*much* (of N)
			more N	*more* (of N)	*more* N	*more* (of N)
			most N	*most* (of N)	*most* N	*most* (of N)
			enough	*enough* (of N)	*enough* N	*enough* (of N)
			few N	*few* (of N)	*little* N	*little* (of N)
			a few N	*a few* (of N)	*a little* N	*a little* (*of* N)
			fewer N *less* N	*fewer* (of N) *less* (of N)	*less* N *less* N	*less* (of N) *less* (of N)
			fewest N	*fewest* (of N)	*least* N	*least* (of N)
			several N	*several* (of N)		
Group D: Unitary	*one* N	*one* (of N)				
Group E: Negative words	*no* N	*none* (of N)	*no* N	*none* (of N)	*no* N	*none* (of N)
	neither N	*neither* (of N)				

Some pronouns can have an *of*-construction:

>   *some of her friends*

Many quantifiers have the same form, whether they are determiners or pronouns: compare

>   *some people* (*some* = determiner)
>   *some of the people* (*some* = pronoun)

Determiners: *fewer jobs, less income*
676
The table opposite shows five groups of quantifiers (A–E) which have determiner function and/or pronoun function (alone or with an *of*-phrase).

677
• *Group (A) determiners* (*see* 75). In the following examples, determiners are printed in **bold**, and noun phrase heads in SMALL CAPITAL LETTERS:

>   The missionary obligation to proclaim the gospel to *all* the WORLD
>   was once left to zealous individuals and voluntary societies. (BUT:
>   *the whole world* is more usual than *all the world*.)
>   *Every* STUDENT must attend ten of the meetings *each* YEAR.
>   *Every* SALESMAN was to read a sheet containing a description of the
>   product.
>   Liberals and conservatives in *both* PARTIES should form independent
>   parties.

All, *both* and *each* can also occur after their heads. If the head is subject, they have the mid-position of adverbs (*see* 451):

>   *All* his FRIENDS were on vacation.   ~ *His friends* were *all* on
>   vacation.
>   *Both* of THEM love dancing.   ~ *They* *both* love dancing.
>   *Each* of the ROOMS have a telephone. ~ *The rooms* *each* have a
>   telephone.

• *Group (B) determiners* (*see* 697). *Some* and *any* can be used as determiners with singular count nouns when they are stressed (on unstressed *some, see* 523):

>   There was '*some* 'BOOK or other on this topic published last year.
>   I didn't have '*any* I'DEA they wanted me to make a speech.

In ⟨familiar⟩ style, stressed *some* means '*a wonderful . . .*' etc.:

>   That's '*some* 'CAR you have there!

However, *some* and *any* are usually used with plural nouns and mass nouns:

> It's unfair to mention *some PEOPLE* without mentioning all.
> His resignation has been expected for *some TIME*.

- *Group (C) determiners* (*see* 80):

> The company lost *many MILLIONS of dollars*.
> They've been spending too *much MONEY* on speculation.
> The chairman asked for *more INFORMATION* to be brought at the
>   next meeting.
> She was *a few MINUTES* late.
> There are *far fewer FACTORIES* going to come to our part of the
>   country.
> It has been said that good writing is the art of conveying meaning with
>   the greatest possible force in *the fewest* possible *WORDS*.
> Why is it that some people pay *less INCOME TAX* than any of us?

Enough can occur both before and after its head:

> The election left no party with *enough STRENGTH* to form a govern-
>   ment on its own.
> There hasn't been *TIME enough* to institute reforms.

- *The group (D) determiner one:*

One is used as an indefinite determiner in such expressions as *one day, one morning, one night*:

> *One* day she'll change her mind. ('at an indefinite time')

One is also a numeral (*see* 602):

> *One* ticket, please.

and a pronoun (*see* 680):

> How does *one* deal with such problems?

- *Group (E) determiners:*

> They had *no KNOWLEDGE* of secret negotiations.
> There were *no CONDITIONS* laid down in the contract.

Pronouns with an *of*-construction: *all* of the *PEOPLE*, *all* of the *TIME*
678

- As the figure on page 360 shows, most of the quantifiers can also be followed
  by an *of*-phrase, e.g. *all the people* ~ *all of the people*:

> You can fool *all the PEOPLE some of the TIME*, and *some of the
>   PEOPLE all the TIME*, but you cannot fool *all the PEOPLE all of the
>   TIME*. (Abraham Lincoln in a speech made in 1858)
> You see so *much of this STUFF* in the newspapers nowadays.

Both of is normally followed by a pronoun or a definite noun phrase:

> Do sit down. *both of you.*
> People seem to have money to spend on entertainment and food, ***both of** which* are expensive.
> ***Both of** those picturesque tales* originated in newspaper reports.

- The *of*-phrase may be omitted if the quantifier acts as a substitute for an earlier noun phrase (*see* 379):

> McGregor had paused to say something to his wife, and Jane was able to address ***both***.

> [A] Would any of you like *some more soup?*
> [B] Yes, I'd love ***some***.

> *Many of them* are competent people, but *a few* are not.
> I've got *most of the data* now for my conference paper, but ***some*** is still missing.

- *Every* and *no* cannot act as pronouns. Instead we use *every one* and *none*:

> [A] Did you say you pay ***no*** INTEREST on this loan?
> [B] Yes, ***none*** at all.

> ***None of** the* MEMBERS was excited by the thought of higher fees.

(On verb concord after *none of*, see 513. The corresponding determiner construction would be: *No member was . . .* or *No members were . . .*)

Pronouns ending in *-body, -one, -thing*
679
The following quantifier pronouns are singular and have either personal or non-personal reference:

	Personal reference	Non-personal reference
GROUP (A)	*everybody, everyone* *somebody, someone*	*everything* *something*
GROUP (B)	*anybody, anyone*	*anything*
GROUP (E)	*nobody, no one*	*nothing*

There are two sets of pronouns with personal reference: one set ending in *-body* (*everybody, somebody, anybody, nobody*) and another set ending in *-one* (*everyone, someone, anyone, no one*). Both sets with personal reference have a genitive form: *everybody's, everyone's*, etc. There is no difference of meaning between the two sets, but pronouns ending in *-body* are less frequent than pronouns ending in *-one*. Here are some examples:

> *Everybody* says she's an unusual woman.
> *Everybody* made *their* contribution to the good cause.
>   (On concord here, *see* 513.)
> We chatted about the news, and so did *everyone* else in the department.
> I first heard this thing mentioned by *somebody* else.
> If *anybody* rings I'll say you're too busy to come to the telephone.
> We wouldn't be on speaking terms with *anyone* if we made this proposal.
> Is there *anyone* we can give a lift?
> Are you writing this paper in collaboration with *someone*? (on *some-* forms in questions, *see* 243.)
> As *someone* said, one goes into academic life because one can't stand office hours.
> Give me *something* to do that's in line with what I like doing.

One: *Are there any good* ones?
680

One is a numeral (*see* 602) and a pronoun. The pronoun *one* has three uses:

- The pronoun *one* can follow certain other quantifiers and be followed by *of* (*see* 678): *every one of* (with *every* and *one* written as separate words) and *each one of*.

> What is happening in this country now concerns **every one of** us.
> There are many ways of making an omelette, **only one of** WHICH is right.

With *each* and *any*, *one* is optional:

> The doctors came to **each** (**one**) in turn and asked how the patients felt.
> **Each** (**one**) **of** the big manufacturing divisions has its own board of directors.

- As a pronoun *one* (with the plural form *ones*) may substitute for an indefinite noun (*see* 380):

> I want a map of Tokyo – but *a really good* **one**.
> We haven't got a textbook of our own. We have to use *English and American* **ones**.
> The managers that are going to join this sort of rat race are *the really ambitious* **ones**.

- As an indefinite personal pronoun, *one* means 'people in general' (*see* 98). In this use *one* has a genitive form *one's* and a reflexive form *oneself*:

> I've always believed in having the evenings free for doing **one's** *hobbies*.
> This is just a journey *one* does by **oneself**.

Questions
(*see CGEL* 11.4–23)

Different types of questions
681
There are direct and indirect questions:

> 'How did you get on at your interview?', she asked.   [direct question]
> She asked me how I got on at my interview.   [indirect question]

Indirect questions are always signalled by an interrogative word such as *how* or *what*. But direct questions need not contain an interrogative word (on interrogative words, *see* 536, on indirect questions, *see* 259).

We also distinguish between three main types of questions: *yes-no* questions, *wh*-questions and tag questions (*see* 241).

Yes-No questions: *Did you find the file?*
682
The answer to a *yes-no* question is *yes* or *no*, which explains the name '*yes-no*' question. To make a statement into a *yes-no* question, put the operator (*will, is,* etc.) before the subject.

> She will be in the office later today.
> ~ Will she be in the office later today?

Yes-no questions usually have rising intonation (*see* 40). Here are some examples of *yes-no* questions:

> Will you be around at lunch time?
> Is he married?
> Have you replied to the letter?
> Does she still live in Australia?

The last example has the 'dummy operator' *does* (*see* 611). A form of *do* has to be used here because there is no operator in the corresponding statement:

> ~ She still lives in Australia.

Wh-questions: *How are you feeling today?*
683
Wh-questions begin with an interrogative word: *who, what, when,* etc. (*see* 536) and normally have falling intonation. Starting from a statement, this is how to form *wh*-questions: Put the sentence element which contains the *wh*-word at the beginning of the sentence. If the element containing the *wh*-word is object, complement or adverbial, place the operator (i.e. the first auxiliary in a verb phrase or the finite verb *be*) in front of the subject.

- *Wh*-element is object:

> They bought a Volvo. ~ *Which car* did they buy?

John asked a question. ~ *What question* did John ask?

The operator normally comes just after the *wh*-element. In these examples the *do*-construction has to be used, because the corresponding statements have no operator.

- *Wh*-element is complement:

  The subject of the lecture is lexicology.
  ~ *What's* the subject of the lecture?

- *Wh*-element is adverbial:

  They'll leave tomorrow. ~ *When* will they leave?

- *Wh*-element is subject. If the element containing the *wh*-word is the subject, the verb phrase remains the same as in the corresponding statement, and no inversion or *do*-construction is necessary (*see* 611):

  Jane said she might be late. ~ *Who* said that?

Here are some other examples of a *wh*-word as subject:

  Who's calling?
  Who's that?
  What made you decide to take that secretarial course?

See 659 on cases where the *wh*-element is a prepositional complement, e.g.

  What's she like?

Tag questions: *You're coming, **aren't you?***
684
Tag questions are tagged on to the end of a statement:

  She's a doctor, *isn't she?*   [1]
  She isn't a doctor, *is she?*   [2]

Tag questions are shortened *yes-no* questions and consist of operator plus pronoun, with a negative (*isn't she* in [1]) or without a negative (*is she* in [2]). The choice of operator depends on the preceding verb phrase. The pronoun repeats or refers back to the subject of the statement. Usually the tag question is in a separate tone unit:

You are staying here	are you?
Tom is younger than you	isn't he?
She had a rest	didn't she?
That would be difficult	wouldn't it?

On tag questions, *see further* 245.

Reciprocal pronouns
(*see CGEL* 6.31)

685
We can bring together two sentences such as *Ann likes Bob* and *Bob likes Ann* into a reciprocal structure:

> EITHER: Ann and Bob like *each other*.
> OR: Ann and Bob like *one another*.

Each other and *one another* are both reciprocal pronouns. *Each other* is the more frequent alternative, but when more than two people or things are involved, *one another* is often preferred.

> We looked at *each other*. ~ We looked at *one another*.
> When we got to know *each other* he wanted to know where I lived.
> Their children are all quite different from *each other*.
> You have a great deal in common, which enables you to communicate with *one another*.

The reciprocal pronouns can be used in the genitive:

> We were all victims of *one another's tastes*.
> They're all determined to cut *each other's* throats.

Relative clauses
(*see CGEL* 6.32–35, 17.10–25)

The grammatical function of relative clauses
686
The main function of a relative clause is to modify a noun phrase (*see* 595):

> They read every book *that they could borrow in the village*.

Here the relative pronoun is *that* and the whole relative clause is *that they could borrow in the village*. The relative pronoun *that* points back to the head of the noun phrase (*book*), which is called the **antecedent**.

The term **relative clause** is used for various types of subclauses which are linked to the main clause. The linking is achieved with a back-pointing element (*see* 84), usually a relative pronoun (but *see* 592 on nominal relative clauses).

The relative pronouns in English are *who*, *whom*, *whose*, *which*, *that*, and zero. A 'zero pronoun' is not expressed. Although it is not pronounced, the pronoun still 'exists' in that it fills a grammatical position in the clause. These two sentences are alternatives:

> The records **which** he owns are mostly classical.
>   [The relative pronoun *which* functions as object of *owns*]
> ~ The records he owns are mostly classical.
>   [The zero relative pronoun functions as object of *owns*]

The choice of relative pronouns
687

There are several relative pronouns to choose from. The choice depends on different factors.

- The choice of relative pronoun depends on whether the clause is **restrictive** or **non-restrictive** (*see* 110).

Restrictive relative clause:

> There's always a place for people *who can speak foreign languages well.*

Non-restrictive relative clause:

> The younger people, *who have lost all faith and convictions*, are now parents.

- The choice of relative pronoun also depends on whether the head of the noun phrase (i.e. the antecedent) is **personal** or **non-personal**.

Personal antecedent:

> This is the message we want to communicate to the men and women *who will soon be going to help the hunger-stricken areas.*

Non-personal antecedent:

> We need to find a house *which is big enough for our family.*

- The choice of relative pronoun also depends on what role the pronoun has in the relative clause: whether it is **subject**, **object**, etc. This determines the choice between *who* and *whom*.

Relative pronoun as subject:

> Have you met the man *who is going to marry Diana?*   [1]

Relative pronoun as object:

> Have you met the man *whom Diana is going to marry?*   [2]

Note that the object, when it is a relative pronoun, is fronted, i.e. is placed before the subject (OSV) rather than after the verb (SVO).

Instead of the ⟨rather formal⟩ *whom* in [2], we can also have *who* [2a] or, more common, zero (i.e. *who* omitted), as in [2b]:

> Have you met the man *who Diana is going to marry?* ⟨less formal, rare⟩
> [2a]
> Have you met the man *Diana is going to marry?* ⟨informal⟩   [2b]

Relative pronouns as prepositional complement: *in which*, etc.
688

There is an even greater choice of constructions when the relative pronoun acts as prepositional complement (*see* 659):

Do you know the man Diana is engaged *to?* ⟨informal⟩

~Do you know the man *whom* Diana is engaged *to?* ⟨formal, rare⟩

~Do you know the man *who* Diana is engaged *to?* ⟨less formal, rare⟩

~Do you know the man *to whom* Diana is engaged? ⟨very formal⟩

Once again, the relative pronoun is fronted, and the preposition may or may not precede. However, the construction preposition + relative pronoun may be the only one available, as in

Maurice wrote me a letter *in which he said*: 'I'm not interested in how long a bee can live in a vacuum or how far it can fly.'

In other cases, the construction with the end-placed, 'stranded' preposition (*see* 659) may be the only one available:

The plan *they've come up with* is an absolute winner.

The uses of relative pronouns
689
The uses of relative pronouns are given in this table:

	Restrictive and non-restrictive		Restrictive only
	personal	non-personal	personal and non-personal
subjective	*who*	*which*	*that*
objective	*who(m)*		*that*, zero
genitive	*whose*	*of which, whose*	

We will now discuss the use of three forms of relative pronouns: *wh-* pronouns, *that*, and zero.

*Wh-*relative pronouns
690
The **wh-relative pronouns** are *who, whom, whose* and *which*. They reflect the personal/non-personal gender of the antecedent (printed in SMALL CAPITAL LETTERS):

- **who, whom** *for personal*:

  There's a MAN outside *who* wants to see you.

- **which** *for non-personal*:

  I want a WATCH *which* is waterproof.

But this distinction does not exist with *whose*. If a pronoun is in a genitive relation to a noun head, the pronoun can have the form *whose* for both personal and non-personal antecedents:

> The NEIGHBOUR *whose* car we borrowed is Danish.
> On the road this morning there were CARS *whose* drivers apparently had something more important to catch than I had.
> This was an enormously long BUILDING *whose* walls were made of rocks.

In the examples where the antecedent is non-personal (such as *cars, building*), there is some tendency to avoid the use of *whose* by using the *of*-phrase, but this construction can be awkward ⟨formal⟩:

> ~This was an enormously long BUILDING *the walls of which* were made of rocks. ⟨formal⟩

With a personal antecedent, the relative pronoun can show the distinction between *who* and *whom*, depending on its role as subject of the relative clause, or as object, or as prepositional complement.

That and zero as relative pronouns
691

That is used with both personal and non-personal reference. However, it cannot follow a preposition, and is not usually used in non-restrictive relative clauses.

The zero relative pronoun (i.e. with no pronoun expressed) is used like *that*, but it cannot be the subject of a clause.

- *That* as subject cannot be left out:

> The POLICEMAN *that caught the thief* received a commendation for bravery.

- *That* as object or prepositional complement can be left out:

> The MAN *(that) he caught* received a jail sentence.
> That's the kind of PROBLEM *(that) I can live with.*

Restrictive relative clauses
692

All the relative pronouns can be used in restrictive relative clauses, particularly *that* and the zero relative, but also *who* (*whom, whose*) and *which*. We can now complete the picture of the possible choices among all the relative pronouns in restrictive clauses by four sets of examples.

- Relative pronoun as subject and with personal antecedent:

> He is the sort of PERSON *who* always answers letters.
> ~He is the sort of PERSON *that* always answers letters.

- Relative pronoun as subject and with non-personal antecedent:

    This author uses lots of WORDS *which* are new to me.
    ~ This author uses lots of WORDS *that* are new to me.

- Relative pronoun as object and with personal antecedent:

    Our professor keeps lecturing on AUTHORS *whom* nobody's ever read.
      ⟨formal⟩
    ~ Our professor keeps lecturing on AUTHORS *who* nobody's ever read.
    ~ Our professor keeps lecturing on AUTHORS *that* nobody's ever read.
    ~ Our professor keeps lecturing on AUTHORS nobody's ever read.

- Relative pronoun as object and with non-personal antecedent:

    I need to talk to you about the FAX *which* you sent me.
    ~ I need to talk to you about the FAX *that* you sent me.
    ~ I need to talk to you about the FAX you sent me.

- Relative pronoun as prepositional complement and with personal antecedent:

    I know most of the BUSINESSMEN *with whom* I am dealing. ⟨formal⟩
    ~ I know most of the BUSINESSMEN *whom* I am dealing *with*. ⟨formal, rare⟩
    ~ I know most of the BUSINESSMEN *who* I am dealing *with*. ⟨rare⟩
    ~ I know most of the BUSINESSMEN *that* I'm dealing *with*.
    ~ I know most of the BUSINESSMEN I'm dealing *with*.

- Relative pronoun as prepositional complement and with non-personal antecedent:

    Is that the ORGANIZATION *to which* she referred? ⟨formal⟩
    ~ Is that the ORGANIZATION *which* she referred *to*?
    ~ Is that the ORGANIZATION *that* she referred *to*?
    ~ Is that the ORGANIZATION she referred *to*?

Non-restrictive relative clauses
693
Only *wh*-pronouns are usually used in non-restrictive clauses. The meaning of a non-restrictive relative clause is often very similar to the meaning of a coordinated clause (with or without conjunction), as we indicate by paraphrases of the examples:

    Then he met a GIRL, *who* invited him to a party.
    ~ Then he met a girl, and she invited him to a party.
    Here is JOHN SMITH, *who(m)* I mentioned to you the other day.
    ~ Here is John Smith: I mentioned him to you the other day.

(On intonation and punctuation here, *see* 111.)

Sometimes in non-restrictive clauses *which* is followed by a noun, and therefore functions as a relative determiner, not a relative pronoun:

> The fire brigade is all too often delayed by traffic congestion, and arrives on the scene more than an hour late, by *which time* there is little chance of saving the building.

Sentence relative clauses
694

The sentence relative clause is a special type of non-restrictive clause. It does not point back to a noun but to a whole clause or sentence. The relative pronoun in such clauses is *which*:

> THE COUNTRY IS ALMOST BANKRUPT, *which is not surprising.* ('and this is not surprising')
> HE IS NOW BACK IN PRISON, *after which we'll start again.* ('and after that we'll start again')

These clauses have the function of sentence adverbial (*see* 461).

Sentences
(*see CGEL* 10.1, 11.1–2, 13.3)

Clauses and sentences
695

Sentences are units made up of one or more clauses (*see* 486). Sentences containing just one clause are called **simple**, and sentences containing more than one clause are called **complex**. Here are two simple sentences:

> She heard an explosion.
> She phoned the police.

- They may be joined into a complex sentence by **coordination**, i.e. coordinating the two clauses by *and*:

> She heard an explosion and (she) phoned the police.

- The two simple sentences can also be joined into a complex sentence by **subordination**, i.e. making one clause into a main clause and the other into a subclause:

> When she heard an explosion, she phoned the police.

For coordination, *see* 515; for subordination, *see* 709.

Four kinds of sentence
696

A simple English sentence, i.e. a sentence consisting of only one clause, may be a statement, a question, a command, or an exclamation.

Statements are sentences in which the subject is present and generally comes before the verb (but *see* fronted topic, 411):

> I'll speak to the manager today.

Questions (*see* 681) are sentences which differ from statements in one or more ways:

- The operator is placed immediately before the subject:

  > *Will* you see him today?

- The sentence begins with an interrogative word (*see* 536):

  > *Who* do you want to speak to?

- The sentence has subject + verb order but with rising intonation in ⟨spoken⟩ English (*see* 40, 244) and ending with a question mark in ⟨written⟩ English:

  > You'll speak to the mánager today?

Commands (*see* 497) are sentences with the verb in the imperative, i.e. the base form of the verb (*see* 573). In ⟨written⟩ English, command sentences do not normally end with an exclamation mark, but with a full stop (period):

> Come here.

Commands usually have no expressed subject but sometimes take the subject *you* (*see* 497):

> (You) speak to the manager today.

Exclamations (*see* 528) are sentences which begin with *what* or *how*, without inversion of subject and operator. In ⟨written⟩ English, exclamations usually end with an exclamation mark (!):

> *What* a noise they are making in that band!

Communication in complete sentences is typical of ⟨formal⟩ or ⟨written⟩ language. In ⟨speech⟩ and ⟨informal writing⟩ it is common to use less fully structured units (*see* 254, 299). For example, *What a noise!* is a typical spoken exclamation, in which the verb and other parts are omitted.

Some-words and *any*-words
(*see* CGEL 6.59–62, 10.60–63)

697
Some and *any* can function both as determiners (*see* 522) and pronouns (*see* 661). But in both functions the choice between *some* and *any* depends on the

grammatical context: *some* is the normal word in positive statements, and *any* is the normal word in *yes-no* questions and after negatives:

Ann has bought *some* new material.	[positive statement]
Ann hasn't bought *any* new material.	[after a negative]
Has Ann bought *any* new material?	[question]

There are a number of items which behave like *some* and *any* in this respect. Therefore we need to distinguish two classes of words, which we call *some*-words and *any*-words:

- **Some-words** are:

  some, someone, somebody, something, somewhere, sometime, sometimes, already, somewhat, somehow, too (adverb of addition).

- **Any-words** are:

  any, anyone, anybody, anything, anywhere, ever, yet, at all, either.

698

The following figure illustrates the contrasts between matching *some-* and *any-*words.

Some-words	*Any*-words	
Positive statements	After negatives	Questions
DETERMINER They've had *some* lunch.	They haven't had *any* lunch.	Have they had *any* lunch?
PRONOUN He was rude to *somebody*.	He wasn't rude to *anybody*.	Was he rude to *anybody*?
PLACE ADVERB They've seen her *somewhere*.	They haven't seen her *anywhere*.	Have they seen her *anywhere*?
TIME-WHEN ADVERB I'll see you again *sometime*.	I won't *ever* see you again.	Will I *ever* see you again?
FREQUENCY ADVERB He *sometimes* visits her.	He doesn't *ever* visit her.	Does he *ever* visit her?
DEGREE ADVERB She was *somewhat* annoyed.	She wasn't *at all* annoyed.	Was she *at all* annoyed?

There are similar contrasts between *somehow* and *in any way*, between *already* and *yet*, and between *still* and *any more*.

In negative clauses, *any*-words follow not only *not* and its shortened form *n't*, but also other negative words such as *nobody, no, scarcely*, etc. (*see* 585):

Nobody has *ever* given her *any* encouragement.

When *any*-words are stressed and have distributive meaning they can occur also in positive statements (*see* 77). e.g.:

> `Ànyone` can do thát!   Phone me 'any time you like.

Any-*words in other contexts*
699
There are also grammatical contexts other than *yes-no* questions and negatives where *any*-words occur:

- In *yes-no* interrogative subclauses:

> I sometimes wonder whether examinations are *any* use to anyone.

- In conditional clauses (*see* 210):

> If there is *anything* we can do to speed up the process, do let us know.

- After verbs, adjectives and prepositions with negative implication:

Verbs: *deny, fail, forget, prevent*, etc.

> Some historians deny that there were *any* Anglo-Saxon invasions *at all*.
> I'm sorry that my work prevents me from doing *anything* with you
>   today.

Adjectives: *difficult, hard, reluctant*, etc.

> I think it's difficult for *anyone* to understand what he means.
> I really feel reluctant to take *any* more duties at this time.

Prepositions: *against, without*, etc.

> She can hold her own against *any* opposition.
> The bill is expected to pass without *any* major opposition.

- With comparisons (*see* 500) and constructions with *as* and *too*:

> She sings this very difficult part better than *anyone* else.
>   ('Nobody sings this part better.')
> It's too late to blame *anyone* for the accident.

Spelling changes

(*see CGEL* 3.5–10, 5.81, 5.113, 7.79)
700
There are some changes in the spelling of endings of nouns, verbs, adjectives, and adverbs. It will be convenient to deal with all such spelling changes here in one place. They involve three types of change: replacing, adding, and dropping letters.

Replacing letters: *carry ∼ carries*
701
Changing y *to* i(e). In bases ending in a consonant + *y*:

- *y* becomes *ie* in verbs before 3rd person singular present -*s* (*see* 574):

    they *carry* ∼ he *carries*

- *y* becomes *ie* in nouns before plural -*s* (*see* 635):

    one *copy* ∼ several *copies*

- *y* becomes *i* in adjectives before comparative -*er* or -*est* (*see* 500):

    early ∼ *earlier* ∼ *earliest*

- *y* becomes *i* in verbs before -*ed* (*see* 574):

    they *carry* ∼ they *carried*

- *y* becomes *i* in adverbs before the -*ly* used to form adverbs from adjectives (*see* 464):

    easy ∼ *easily*

But *y* is kept after a vowel:

    journey ∼ *journeys, play* ∼ *played*

In three verbs there is a spelling change from *y* to *i* also after a vowel:

    lay ∼ *laid, pay* ∼ *paid, say* ∼ *said*

(In *said* there is also a change of vowel sound: /seɪ/ ∼ /sed/.) Also: *day* ∼ *daily*. Y is kept in a few words such as *standbys, laybys*, and in proper nouns: *the Kennedys*.

Changing -ie *to* -y. Before the -*ing* ending (*see* 574), -*ie* is changed to -*y*:

    they *die* ∼ they are *dying*

Adding letters: *box ∼ boxes*
702
Adding e *to nouns ending in sibilants*
Unless already spelled with a final silent *e*, bases ending in sibilants receive an additional *e* before the -*s* endings.

The sibilants are /z/, /s/, /dʒ/, /tʃ/, /ʒ/, /ʃ/. The added *e* occurs

- in the plural of nouns:

    one *box* ∼ two *boxes*, one *dish* ∼ two *dishes*

- in the 3rd person singular present of verbs:

    they *pass* ∼ she *passes*, they *polish* ∼ he *polishes*

An additional -*e* is also added in two irregular verbs ending in -*o*:

> they *do* /duː/ ~ she *does* /ˈdʌz/
> they *go* /goʊ/ ~ she *goes* /goʊz/

Adding e *to nouns ending in* -o

The following nouns ending in -*o* have the plural spelled -*oes*:

> *echoes, embargoes, goes, heroes, noes, potatoes, tomatoes, torpedoes, vetoes.*

Many nouns ending in -*o* can have either -*oes* or -*os*, for example:

> *archipelagoes* or *archipelagos, cargoes* or *cargos.*

The plural -*os* spelling is always used after a vowel (*radios, rodeos, studios,* etc.) and in abbreviations:

> *hippos* (~ *hippopotamus*), *kilos* (~ *kilogram*), *memos* (~ *memorandum*), *photos* (~ *photograph*), *pianos* (~ *pianoforte*).

Doubling of consonants: *hot* ~ *hotter* ~ *hottest*
703
Final consonants are doubled when the preceding vowel is stressed and spelled with a single letter. There is no doubling when the vowel is unstressed or written with two letters. Doubling occurs in the following cases:

- in adjectives and adverbs before -*er* and -*est*:

> *big* ~ *bigger* ~ *biggest*   BUT: *quiet* ~ *quieter* ~ *quietest*
> *hot* ~ *hotter* ~ *hottest*   BUT: *great* ~ *greater* ~ *greatest*

- in verbs before -*ing* and -*ed*:

> *drop* ~ *dropping* ~ *dropped*   BUT: *dread* ~ *dreading* ~ *dreaded*
> *stop* ~ *stopping* ~ *stopped*   BUT: *stoop* ~ *stooping* ~ *stooped*
> *perˈmit* ~ *perˈmitting* ~ *perˈmitted*   BUT: *ˈvisit* ~ *ˈvisiting* ~ *ˈvisited*
> *preˈfer* ~ *preˈferring* ~ *preˈferred*   BUT: *ˈenter* ~ *ˈentering* ~ *ˈentered*

In ⟨BrE⟩ *l* is doubled also when it is in an unstressed syllable:

> *cruel* ~ *crueller* ~ *cruellest* ⟨BrE⟩   BUT: *crueler* ~ *cruelest* ⟨AmE⟩
> *travel* ~ *travelling* ~ *travelled* ⟨BrE⟩   BUT: *traveling* ~ *traveled* ⟨AmE⟩

Dropping letters: *hope ~ hoping ~ hoped*
704
If the base ends in silent *-e*, the *e* is dropped

- in adjectives and adverbs before *-er* and *-est*:

    brave ~ braver ~ bravest
    free ~ freer /ˈfriːə(r)/ ~ freest ˈfriːɪst/

- in verbs before *-ing* and *-ed*:

    create ~ creating ~ created
    hope ~ hoping ~ hoped
    shave ~ shaving ~ shaved

Compare the spelling of

    hoping ~ hoped (*~ hope*) with *hopping ~ hopped* (*~ hop*), and of
    staring ~ stared (*~ stare*) with *starring ~ starred* (*~ star*).

Verbs ending in *-ee*, *-ye*, *-oe*, and often *-ge*, do not drop the *e* before *-ing* (but they drop it before *-ed*):

agree ~ agreeing	BUT: *agreed*
dye ~ dyeing	BUT: *dyed*
singe ~ singeing	BUT: *singed*

Compare

    dyeing (*~ dye*) with *dying* (*~ die*)
    singeing /ˈsɪndʒɪŋ/(*~ singe*) with *singing* /ˈsɪŋɪŋ/ (*~ sing*)

Subjects
(*see CGEL* 10.6, 10.18–26)

705

- The subject of a clause is generally a noun phrase (*see* 595): either a full noun phrase or a pronoun:

    The secretary will be late for the meeting.
    Jane will be late for the meeting.
    She will be late for the meeting.

The subject can also be a non-finite clause (*see* 593):

    Playing football paid him a lot more than working in a factory.

or a finite nominal clause (*see* 589):

    That there are dangers to be dealt with is inevitable.

Starting a sentence with such a long clause makes it 'top-heavy' and it is more common to have a construction with introductory *it* (see 542):

> ~ It is inevitable *that there are dangers to be dealt with.*

- The subject normally occurs before the verb in statements:

> *They've* had some lunch.

In questions, the subject occurs immediately after the operator (*see* 609):

> Have *they* had any lunch?

- The subject has number and person concord with the finite verb (*see* 509):

> *I'm* leaving. ~ *The teacher* **is** leaving.

With modal auxiliaries there is no difference in the form of the verb:

> *I* **must** leave. ~ *The teacher* **must** leave.

- The most typical function of a subject is to denote the actor, i.e. the person, event, etc. causing the happening denoted by the verb:

> *Joan* drove Ed to the airport.

- When an active sentence is turned into a passive sentence (*see* 613), the subject of the active sentence becomes the agent of the passive. The agent is introduced in a *by*-phrase, but the agent need not be expressed. In most passive sentences the agent is omitted (*see* 616):

> Everybody rejected the proposal.
>
> ~ The proposal was rejected (by everybody).

Subjunctives
(*see CGEL* 3.58–62)

706
Productive subjunctives: *Public opinion demanded that an inquiry be held.*
After a verb like *insist* followed by a *that*-clause as complement we may find two different verb constructions:

She insists that he *left* before she did.	[1]
She insists that he *leave* immediately.	[2]

The reason is that *insist* has two different meanings: in [1] it means 'declare firmly' and the verb in the *that*-clause is the normal past form (*left*); in [2] it means 'demand insistently' and the following verb is in the subjunctive, which is the uninflected base form (*leave*). We call this second construction the 'mandative' subjunctive, or the 'productive' subjunctive (to mark it as different from subjunctives that are formulaic expressions like *Come what may, see* 708).

The subjunctive is used in ⟨rather formal⟩ English after governing expressions which express will (or volition). They are verbs like *insist*, adjectives like *insistent* and nouns like *insistence*.

- Here are some **verbs** which govern a subjunctive in the following *that*-clause:

  advise, ask, beg, decide, decree, demand, desire, dictate, insist, intend, move, order, petition, propose, recommend, request, require, resolve, suggest, urge, vote.

Examples:

  Some committee members *asked* that the proposal *be* read a second time.
  Public opinion *demanded* that an inquiry *be* held.
  Ann *suggested* that her parents *stay* for supper.
  Then I called her up and *proposed* that she *telephone* her lawyer.

- **Adjectives** which are often followed by a verb in the subjunctive can have a personal subject. Examples are: *anxious, determined, eager*, e.g.:

  She was *eager* that they *stay* together during the storm.

Adjectives with a subjunctive verb can also have an impersonal *it*-construction, for example *advisable, appropriate, desirable, essential, fitting, imperative, important, necessary, urgent, vital*:

  It is *necessary* that every member *be* informed about these rules.

- **Nouns** which take a following verb in the subjunctive are, for example, *condition, demand, directive, intention, order, proposal, recommendation, request, suggestion*:

  The Law Society granted aid on the *condition* that he *accept* any
    reasonable out-of-court settlement.
  Further offences will lead to a *request* that the official *be* transferred or
    withdrawn.

The use of the uninflected base form means there is lack of the usual concord between subject and finite verb in the 3rd person singular present. Also, there is no distinction between present and past tenses (*see* 740). The use of the subjunctive is more common in ⟨AmE⟩ than in ⟨BrE⟩, and in ⟨written⟩ than in ⟨spoken⟩ English.

Alternatives to the subjunctive
707

- There is an optional construction, 'putative *should*' (*see* 280), which in ⟨BrE⟩ is more common than the subjunctive. Compare the following *should*-constructions [1a, 2a] as alternatives to the subjunctive construction [1, 2]:

Public opinion *demanded* that an inquiry *be* held.   [1]

~ Public opinion *demanded* that an inquiry ***should be*** held.   [1a]

Ann *suggested* that her parents ***stay*** for supper.   [2]

~ Ann *suggested* that her parents ***should stay*** for supper.   [2a]

- ⟨BrE⟩ has in fact a third option, the indicative, which is rarer in ⟨AmE⟩:

  He has *demanded* that the vehicle *undergoes* rigorous trials to test its efficiency at sustained speeds.

  It is *essential* that more decisions *are taken* by majority vote.

- To avoid the somewhat ⟨formal⟩ subjunctive there is the further possibility of a construction with *for* + infinitive:

  It is *necessary for* every member *to be informed* of these rules.

Formulaic and *were*-subjunctives: *Come what may; I wouldn't do it if I were you.*
708

- The subjunctive constructions discussed so far are fully productive and quite common, especially in ⟨AmE⟩. There is also a **formulaic subjunctive**. It consists of the base form of the verb, but is used only in certain set expressions:

  Come what may, I'll be there. ('whatever happens')

  Heaven *help* us! (an exclamation of despair)

- There is also a type of construction where *were* is used (instead of the expected *was*), called the ***were*-subjunctive** (*see* 277):

  If I *were* you, I wouldn't do it.

The *were*-subjunctive occurs in clauses expressing a hypothetical condition (especially *if*-clauses) or after verbs such as *wish*. Usually the expected form *was* can also be used, and is more common in ⟨informal⟩ style:

  If the road *were/was* wider, there would be no danger of an accident.

  Sometimes I wish I *were/was* someone else!

Subordination
(*see CGEL* Chapter 14)

What is subordination?
709
Two clauses in the same sentence may be related either by coordination or subordination. Compare these two sentences:

Joan arrived at the office by ten but no one else was there.
[coordination]
Joan arrived at the office by ten before anyone else was there.
[subordination]

In coordination, the two clauses are 'equal partners' in the same structure:

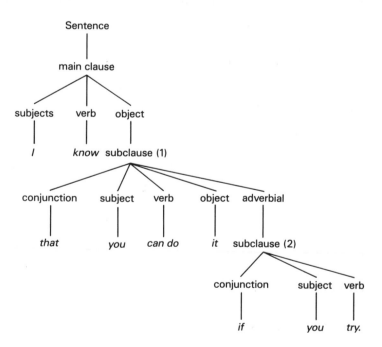

710

A subclause can also have another subclause inside it, which means that the first subclause behaves as a 'main clause' with respect to the second subclause. For example, the sentence *I know that you can do it if you try* is made up of three clauses, each within the other:

Subclauses can have various functions in their main clause. They may be subjects, objects, adverbials, prepositional complements, postmodifiers, etc.

Finite, non-finite and verbless subclauses

711

A main clause is almost always a finite clause. A subclause, on the other hand, can be a finite, non-finite, or verbless clause:

- A finite subclause (*see* 492)

    This news came *after the stockmarket had closed.*

- A non-finite subclause (*see* 493)

    They could still see the ship, *drifting on the remorseless tide.*

- A verbless subclause (*see* 494):

    She invited him into the special lounge, *cool, quiet and empty.*

All three types of clause (finite, non-finite, and verbless) may of course themselves have subclauses inside them. Here is a non-finite clause containing a finite subclause (in bold face):

> *Having left **before the letter arrived**, he was surprised to find his
> wife at the station.*

Here is a verbless clause containing a non-finite subclause:

> *Never slow **to take advantage of an opponent's weakness**,* the Australian
> moved ahead confidently to win the fourth set.

Signals of subordination

712

A subclause is not usually capable of standing alone as the main clause of a sentence. Subclauses are usually marked as subclauses by some signal of subordination. The signal may be

- *that*, which is often omitted ('zero *that*'):

    I hope (*that*) *the department will cooperate on this.*

- another subordinating conjunction, for example *before, if, when* (*see* 207):

    I'd not have been at all surprised *if the entire roof had collapsed.*

- a *wh*-word (*see* 536):

    I asked her *why she wanted to move to another university.*

- inversion ⟨rather formal⟩ (*see* 278):

    Had I been a royal princess, they couldn't have treated me better.

- lack of a finite verb:

    I hope *to phone you back at the very beginning of next week.*

Apart from *that*-clauses with *that* omitted (including relative clauses, *see* 691) there is only one type of subclause that contains no expressed signal of subordination. This is a comment clause (*see* 499):

> He must be at least sixty years old, *I suppose.*

It can be related to the main clause of a *that*-clause:

> ~ I suppose (that) he must be at least sixty years old.

The various uses of subordinating conjunctions are discussed in Part Two (*see* 360). Some subordinating conjunctions (*after, as, before, but, like, since, till, until*) also function as prepositions (*see* 656). Compare:

> I haven't seen her *since the end of the war.* [*since* = preposition]
> I haven't seen her *since the war ended.* [*since* = conjunction]

Simple subordinating conjunctions: *as, that, though, when . . .*
713
We can distinguish between simple, compound, and correlative conjunctions.

Here are some simple subordinating conjunctions:

> *after, although, as, because, before, however, if, like* ⟨familiar⟩, *once, since, that, though. till, unless, when, whenever, where, wherever, whereas, whereby, whereupon, while, whilst* ⟨especially BrE⟩.

Examples:

> This news came *after the stockmarket had closed.*
> *Although extensive inquiries were made at the time,* no trace was found of any relatives.
> A stranger came into the hall *as he opened the front door.*
> The party opposed the missiles *because they were out of date.*
> The election result was clear *before polling closed.*
> Paul seemed a bit moody, *like he used to be years ago.* ⟨familiar⟩
>   [many people prefer *as* to *like* here]
> *Once you begin to look at the problem* there is almost nothing you can do about it.
> I'm ashamed *that I can't remember her first name.*
> I didn't have glasses *till I was ten.*
> You can't be put on probation *unless you are guilty.*
> You will not be transferred *until they get someone to take your place.*
> You have to crack the head of an egg *when you take it out of the pan* – otherwise it goes on cooking.
> She said I could use her notebook computer *whenever I wanted.*
> I don't know *where to start.*
> *Wherever I go* I hear you've been very successful.

They need some facts and figures *whereby they can assess alternative strategies.*

After the adjournment, the lawyer requested Parker to visit him, *whereupon Parker burst into tears.* ⟨formal and rare⟩

I've got a colleague taking my classes *while I'm away*, you see.

We must realize that *whilst God could erect a cocoon around us to protect us*, our faith would be worthless if he did. ⟨*whilst* is especially BrE and rare⟩

Compound subordinating conjunctions: *except that, in order that . . .*

714

Compound subordinating conjunctions contain more than one word, although one of these words may be omitted if it is *that*. We can distinguish the following types:

• *Compound conjunctions ending with* **that**, *where* **that** *cannot be omitted:*

> *except that, in that, in order that (in order to with infinitives), so that, such that.*

Examples:

> The horse reared and threw the officer from the saddle, *except that one booted foot caught in the stirrup.*
>
> Did you consider the fact that your brother possibly died *in order that you can live?* ⟨formal and rare⟩
>
> They've got social inbreeding *in that this is probably a self-perpetuating system.*
>
> I try to have a look at the student files *so that I know what everybody's doing.*
>
> We're all trying to pull our wits together to submit papers *such that they will pay our fares to the congress next year.* ⟨rather formal⟩

• *Compound conjunctions ending with* **that**, *where* **that** *may be omitted.* Most of these compound conjunctions are ⟨rather formal⟩:

> *assuming (that), considering (that), granting (that), granted (that), now (that), provided (that), providing (that), supposing (that).*

Examples:

> By the end of next year, *assuming that a general business recovery gets under way*, interest rates should begin to edge upwards again.
>
> *Granting that there are only a few problems to be solved*, these problems make great demands.
>
> The grass in the meadows was growing fast, *now that the warm weather was here.*
>
> The government will endorse increased support for public education, *provided that such funds can be received and expended.*

- *Compound conjunctions ending with* **as:**

715

> as far as, as long as, as soon as, insofar as, inasmuch as ⟨very formal⟩,
> so as + *to*-infinitive, *so far as, so long as.*

Examples:

> *As far as they were aware*, the association had not officially opposed the
> bill's passage.
> This is a solution most people try to avoid, *as long as they can see an*
> *alternative approach to the problem.*
> He ate little that morning, and his mother became concerned, *inasmuch*
> *as he usually ate heartily.* ⟨formal⟩
> *Insofar as science generates any fear*, the fear stems chiefly from the fact
> that new unanswered questions arise. ⟨formal⟩
> Like Caesar he has only one joke, *so far as I can find out.*
> Our politicians generally vote *so as to serve their own constituency.*

- *Compound subordinating conjunctions ending with* **than,** e.g. *rather than*
  + a non-finite clause:

> It was an audience of at least a couple of thousand who came to hear
> music *rather than go to the beach.* (*See* 310 on the use of the base form
> *go* here.)

- *Other compound subordinating conjunctions:* **as if, as though, in case.**

> It began to look *as if something was going to happen.*
> She hesitated, *as though hunting for words and ways of putting them.*
> A man like Jess would want to have a ready means of escape *in case it*
> *was needed.*

Correlative subordinating conjunctions: *if . . . then, no sooner . . . than*

716

Correlative conjunctions consist of two markers: one marking the main clause,
and the other marking the beginning of the subclause. The second marker, if it
is *that*, is sometimes omitted. These conjunctions include

if . . . then	comparative . . . *than*
no sooner . . . than	*as . . . as*
so . . . as	*so . . . (that)*
such . . . (that)	*whether . . . or*
the . . . the	

Examples:

> *If* it is true that new galaxies are forever being formed, *then* the
> universe today looks just as it did millions of years ago.
> I can be *as* stubborn *as* she can. ⟨formal⟩

No sooner were the guards posted *than* the whole camp turned in for a
  night of sound sleep. ⟨rather formal⟩
We are getting *such* high yields per acre *that* many are being forced to
  buy new harvesting machines.
The more you jog, *the* more you get hooked by the habit of taking
  regular exercise. (*See* 233)

Whether ... *or* ... is an exception: here both words mark alternatives in a
subclause:

  She didn't care *whether* she got him *or* not.

The functions of subclauses

717

Subclauses may function grammatically as subject, object, complement, or
adverbial in a main clause.

- As subject:

    What I like doing most in my spare time is playing around with my
      computer.

- As direct object:

    It may interest you to know *that Sue and I are engaged.*

- As indirect object:

    I gave *whoever it was* a drink.

- As subject complement:

    The idea is *that we meet and work at his home in the mornings.*

- As object complement:

    I can't imagine John *overcome with grief.*

- As adverbial:

    When we first lived in the country my wife worried about who would
      clean our windows.

Subclauses also have other functions:

- As postmodifier in a noun phrase:

    The friend *who shared her room* was an art student.

- As complement of a preposition:

    Their loyalty will depend on *which way the wind is blowing.*

- As complement of an adjective:

    The curtain was now ready *to go up.*

Nominal clauses (*see* 588) can function as subject, object, complement, or complement of a preposition, i.e. in general they can have the same function as noun phrases. (On these and other types of subclauses, *see* 495.)

Verb patterns
(*see CGEL* 16.18–85)

Six basic verb patterns
718
The part of a clause following the verb phrase depends on the verb for its basic structure. For example, we can use the verb *find* with these different contexts:

> I found her in the library.
> I found her a new job.
> I found her to be a very competent person.

We distinguish six basic verb patterns in English:

- Linking verbs with subject complement (719–20): (SVC)

    She *is* [A DOCTOR].

- Verbs with one object (721–6): (SVO)

    She *wants* [SOME HELP].

- Verbs with object + verb (727–9): (SVOV . . .)

    She *wants* [YOU] [TO HELP].

- Verbs with two objects (730–2): (SVOO)

    She *gave* [HER SISTER] [SOME RECORDS].

- Verbs with object and object complement (733): (SVOC)

    She *found* [THE TASK] [IMPOSSIBLE].

- Verbs without object or complement (734): (SV)

    The door *opened*.

Within each basic verb pattern, we can distinguish a varying number of subpatterns. It is not possible to list here all the verbs which can occur in each pattern. For this you will need to consult a dictionary. The patterns are given in the active, but where passives (*see* 613) are common, we also include passive examples.

Linking verbs with subject complement: *Sorry I'm* LATE.
719
A linking verb (also called 'copular verb') has a following complement consisting of a noun phrase, an adjective etc. The most common linking verb is *be*. In the following examples, complements and objects are printed in SMALL CAPITAL LETTERS.

Sorry I'*m* LATE.
Was he A PERSONAL FRIEND OF YOURS?

Among other linking verbs there are two groups: **current linking verbs** and **resulting linking verbs**.

- **Current linking verbs** (such as *appear, feel, look, remain, seem*) are like *be* in that they indicate a state:

    He always *appears* HAPPY AT SOMEBODY ELSE'S MISFORTUNE.
    I never *lie* AWAKE at night.
    I hope this will *remain* A CONTINUING TRADITION.
    That did not *seem* A GOOD IDEA to me.
    You *sound* A BIT DUBIOUS.
    I'd love to go on with this job as long as I can *stay* ALIVE ON IT.
    The things that are poisonous we don't eat, so we don't know if they
        taste NICE or not.

- **Resulting linking verbs**, such as *become* and *get*, indicate that the role of the verb complement is a result of the event or process described in the verb:

    The situation *became* UNBEARABLE.
    Quite unexpectedly, her parents *fell* SICK and died.
    Why did they *get* SO ANGRY?
    We have to learn to *grow* OLD because we are all going to *grow* OLD.
    She said she'd seen her dog *turn* NASTY just once.

720

- The complement of a linking verb can be a noun phrase or adjective phrase, as in the examples above, or else a nominal clause (*see* 588):

    The answer *is* THAT WE DON'T QUITE KNOW WHAT TO DO NOW.

- The complement of a linking verb can also be an *-ed* adjective (such as *puzzled, depressed*) or *-ing* adjective (such as *amusing, interesting*):

    Some of the spectators *looked* RATHER PUZZLED.
    Her lectures *were* not very CLEAR but rather AMUSING.

- With some verbs, *to be* can occur between the linking verb and the complement:

    There doesn't *seem to be* ANY TROUBLE WITH THIS CAR.
    Everybody *seems* (*to be*) VERY DEPRESSED at the moment.
    What they did *proved* (*to be*) MORE THAN ADEQUATE.

- As a linking verb, *be* is often followed by an adverbial, particularly an adverbial of place:

    I'd like to *be* IN TOWN for a few weeks.

Verbs with one object
*The object is a noun phrase: Did you **telephone** THE DOCTOR?*
721
The object of verbs with one object (ordinary transitive verbs) can be a noun phrase:

> Let me just *finish* THE POINT.
> Where did you *hear* THAT RUMOUR?
> Do you *believe* ME now?
> Did you *telephone* THE DOCTOR?
> This event *caused* GREAT INTEREST in our village.

- The verb may be a phrasal verb (*see* 630), i.e. verb + adverbial particle + object. When the object is a full noun phrase, it may be placed either before or after the adverbial particle:

  > They **blew up** THE BRIDGE.
  > ~ They **blew** THE BRIDGE *up*.

If the object is a pronoun, it may only be placed before the particle:

> ~ They **blew** IT *up*.

In the passive:

> ~ The bridge/It **was blown up.**

- The verb may be a prepositional verb (*see* 632), i.e. verb + preposition + object:

  > Then he *called on* THE GOVERNOR to explain why.
  > As she was going up the stairs Mr Middleton accidentally *bumped into* HER.
  > He *came across* SOMEONE WHOSE NAME HE HAD FORGOTTEN.

- The verb may be a phrasal-prepositional verb (*see* 634), i.e. verb + adverbial particle + preposition + object:

  > The statement was firm enough to *do away with* ALL DOUBTS.

Like other verbs in this pattern, prepositional verbs and phrasal-prepositional verbs can also appear in the passive:

> Then the governor was *called on* to explain why.
> Things like that would increase rather than *be done away with.*

However, this construction is exceptional rather than normal.

*The object is an infinitive: We **agreed** TO STAY.*
722
The object of a transitive verb is often a *to*-infinitive:

> We *agreed* TO STAY overnight.

The company has *decided* TO BRING OUT A NEW MAGAZINE.
Don't *expect* TO LEAVE WORK BEFORE SIX O'CLOCK.
I'd *like* TO DISCUSS TWO POINTS IN YOUR PAPER.
I've been *longing* TO SEE YOU.
He brought a manuscript I had *promised* TO CHECK THROUGH.

Among other verbs which take a *to*-infinitive as object we find (*can't*) *afford*, *ask*, *dislike*, *forget*, *hate*, *help*, *hope*, *learn*, *love*, *need*, *offer*, *prefer*, *promise*, *refuse*, *remember*, *try*, *want*.

Help can also be used with a bare infinitive (i.e. without *to*):

After her mother died she came over to *help* (to) settle up the estate.

This construction without *to* is rare for main verbs, but it is normal with the modal auxiliaries (*see* 483).

The object is an -ing form: I enjoyed *TALKING TO YOU.*
723
One group of transitive verbs is followed by an -*ing* form:

We ought to *avoid* WASTING money.
Obviously there would be just a few people one would *enjoy* TALKING to at the party.
The secretarial school was awful because they *disliked* TEACHING graduates.
Why did she *stop* TALKING?

Other such verbs are *admit*, (*can't*) *bear*, *confess*, *deny*, *finish*, *forget*, *hate*, (*can't*) *help*, *keep*, *like*, *love*, (*not*) *mind*, *prefer*, *remember*, (*can't*) *stand*.

The object is a that-clause: I agree *THAT THE PROSPECTS ARE GLOOMY.*
724

• The object of the verb can be a *that*-clause (where *that* is often omitted):

I *agree* (THAT) THE ECONOMIC PROSPECTS ARE PRETTY GLOOMY AT THE MOMENT.
After school I *discovered* (THAT) I HADN'T GOT ANY SALEABLE SKILL.
I always *thought* (THAT) THEY GOT ON SO WELL TOGETHER.

Passive with introductory *it* (*see* 543):

It would still have to be *agreed* THAT THESE ACTS WERE HARMFUL.

Among verbs which take a *that*-clause are: *admit*, *announce*, *bet*, *claim*, *complain*, *confess*, *declare*, *deny*, *explain*, *guarantee*, *insist*, *mention*, *object*, *predict*, *promise*, *reply*, *say*, *state*, *suggest*, *warn*, *write*.

- The *that*-clause can sometimes be replaced by *so*:

  > [A] Is it worth seeing the manager about the job?
  > [B] I *believe* so./I don't *believe* so.
  > [A] Would you like to live in this country?
  > [B] Yes, at least I *think* so./No, I don't *think* so.

- *Not* may replace a negative *that*-clause:

  > [A] Does that symbol stand for 'cold front'?
  > [B] No, I don't think *it does*.
  >
  > ∼ No, I don't think *so*.
  >
  > ∼ No, I think *not*.

Verbs which allow the use of *so* and *not* in this way include *believe, hope, say, suppose, think*.

725

The verb may have a *that*-clause with putative *should* (*see* 280) or a subjunctive verb (*see* 706). *That* is rarely omitted in these constructions:

> The prosecuting attorney *ordered* THAT THE TALL STORE DETECTIVE (SHOULD) BE SUMMONED FOR QUESTIONING.
> The lawyer *requested* THAT THE HEARING (SHOULD) BE POSTPONED FOR TWO WEEKS.
> The officer *suggested* THAT THE PETITIONER (SHOULD) BE EXEMPT ONLY FROM COMBATANT TRAINING.

Other verbs which can have this construction are *ask, command, decide, demand, insist, intend, move, prefer, propose, recommend, require, urge*.

The object is a wh-*clause: I* wonder WHY HE DID IT.
726

- Some verbs take a finite clause introduced by a *wh*-word (*see* 536): *how, why, where, who, whether* (or *if*) etc.

  > The department *asked* IF/WHETHER IT COULD GO AHEAD WITH THE EXPANSION PLANS.
  > We flew in rickety planes so overloaded that we *wondered* WHY WE DIDN'T CRASH.

Other verbs with a *wh*-clause as object are, for example, *care, decide, depend, doubt, explain, forget, hear, mind, prove, realize, remember, see, tell, think*. The verbs *know, notice* and *say* usually occur in negative sentences:

> We don't *know* IF THESE ANIMALS TASTE NICE OR NOT.

- Some verbs, for example *forget, know, learn, remember, see*, can take an infinitive clause introduced by a *wh*-word:

I don't *know* WHAT TO DO NEXT.
She *forgot* WHERE TO LOOK.

Verbs with object + verb

727
Verb with object + infinitive: Have you **heard** *HER SING?*
Many transitive verbs have an object which is followed by another non-finite verb.

- A few verbs (*hear, help, let, make*) have an object + infinitive without *to*:

    Have you *heard* [PROFESSOR CRAY] [LECTURE on pollution]?
    Just *let* ME FINISH, will you?
    Her letter *made* ME THINK.

Help occurs with or without *to*:

    Will you *help* ME (TO) WRITE the invitations?

The *to*-infinitive is always used in the passive:

    The former Wimbledon champion *was made* TO LOOK ALMOST A
    BEGINNER.

- Most verbs which take an object + infinitive have the *to*-infinitive:

    Henrietta *advised* HIM TO RISE at five in the morning as she did.
    When he was 15 his parents *allowed* HIM TO ATTEND classes at the
        Academy of Fine Arts.
    Can I *ask* HIM TO RING you back?
    I *want* YOU TO GET BACK as soon as possible.

Passive examples are common:

    HE *is* not *allowed* TO DRIVE A CAR, but I saw him driving a car!
    I *was advised* by a psychiatrist NOT TO HELP MY COLLEAGUE.

Some other verbs in this pattern are: *believe, force, help, order, permit, require, teach, tell, urge*. There is no passive with *want* in this construction.

728
Verb + object + -ing form: We **got** *THE MACHINE WORKING.*

    In the end we *got* [THE MACHINE] [WORKING].
    I can't *imagine* HIM INTERRUPTING anybody.
    The announcement *left* THE AUDIENCE WONDERING whether there
        would be a concert.
    I *resent* HIM SPREADING rumours about us.

Other verbs in this pattern include *catch, find, hate, like, love, (don't) mind, prefer, see, stop*.

729
Verb + object + -ed form: *We finally* **got** THE ENGINE STARTED.

> I must *get* [MY GLASSES] [CHANGED].
> We've just *had* OUR HOUSE REBUILT.
> I like your hair. You've *had* IT CURLED.

Verbs with this construction include the perceptual verbs *feel, hear, see, watch,* the volitional verbs *like, need, want* and the causative verbs *get* and *have.*

Verbs with two objects
730
Both objects are noun phrases

- The verb has an indirect object + a direct object:

> *Let* me *give* [YOU] [AN EXAMPLE OF THIS].
> Did you manage to *teach* THEM ANY ENGLISH?
> I'll *write* HIM A LITTLE NOTE.

With a verb like *offer* this construction can be replaced by a direct object + *to* + noun phrase:

> They *offered* [MY SISTER] [A FINE JOB].
> ~They *offered* A FINE JOB TO MY SISTER.

Passive:

> MY SISTER *was offered* A FINE JOB.
> ~A FINE JOB *was offered* TO MY SISTER.

Verbs which can take the alternative construction with *to* include *bring, give, hand, lend, offer, owe, promise, read, send, show, teach, throw, write.*

- Some verbs which take the construction with an indirect object + a direct object can have an alternative construction with direct object + *for* + noun phrase:

> I'll *buy* YOU ALL A DRINK. ~I'll *buy* a drink for you all.
> Can I *get* YOU ANYTHING? ~Can I *get* anything for you?

Other such verbs are: *find, make, order, save, spare.*

- Some verbs with two objects, such as *ask* and *cost,* cannot be replaced by prepositional constructions with *to* or *for*:

> He *asked* ME SOME AWKWARD QUESTIONS.

In the passive, only the second object (in this example SOME AWKWARD QUESTIONS) can appear alone.

> I *was asked* SOME AWKWARD QUESTIONS.

There is no corresponding passive with *cost*:

It's going to *cost* ME A FORTUNE to buy all these course books.

Verb + object + **that-***clause: The pilot* **informed** US THAT THE FLIGHT WAS DELAYED.

731

The verb has an indirect object + a *that*-clause (*see* 589), where *that* is often omitted:

> I *told* [HIM] [I'D RING AGAIN].

Other such verbs are: *advise, assure, bet, convince, inform, persuade, promise, remind, show, teach, warn, write.*

So can substitute for the *that*-clause after *tell*:

> [A] Did you *tell* HER THAT I AM BUSY BOTH EVENINGS?
> [B] Yes, I *told* HER SO.

Verb + object + **wh-***clause: We* **asked** HIM WHAT HE WAS GOING TO DO.

732

The verb has an object + a finite or non-finite *wh*-clause (*see* 590):

> We used to *ask* [HIM] [WHAT HE WAS GOING TO DO].
> Perhaps you'd like to *tell* US WHAT YOU WANT.
> Nobody *taught* THE STUDENTS HOW TO USE THE MACHINES.

Passive:

> EACH DEPARTMENT *was asked* WHETHER IT COULD GO AHEAD WITH THE EXPANSION PLANS.

Verbs with object and object complement

733

Verbs such as *call, find* and *consider* have an object and an object complement and are called **complex-transitive verbs.**

* The complement following the object is a noun phrase in:

> Would you *call* ['OTHELLO'] [A TRAGEDY OF CIRCUMSTANCE]?

With some verbs, *to be* may be inserted before the complement:

> We *found* HER (*to be*) A VERY EFFICIENT SECRETARY.
> They *considered* HIM (*to be*) THE BEST PLAYER ON THE TEAM.

Passive:

> ~HE *was considered* (*to be*) THE BEST PLAYER ON THE TEAM.

Other such verbs: *appoint, elect, imagine, make, name, suppose, think, vote.*

* The complement is more likely to be an adjective with verbs like *declare, find, judge, keep, leave, make* and *wash:*

If you do that it will *make* [HER] [VERY ANGRY].
I had to quit because I *found* MY WORK IN THE OFFICE SO DULL.

- With verbs such as *believe, feel, imagine, suppose* and *think, to be* is usually inserted before an adjective complement:

Many students *thought* THE EXAM (*to be*) RATHER UNFAIR.
They *believed* HIM (*to be*) INNOCENT.

Passive:

~HE *was believed to be* INNOCENT.

Verbs without object or complement

734
Verbs which have no object or complement are called **intransitive verbs:**

Her heart *sank.*

Intransitive verbs are usually followed by one or more adverbials (in these examples enclosed by brackets):

You are *teaching* [at college], aren't you?
The Argentinian *leads* [by three games to one].
Did you *go* [to his lectures]?

The verb may be a phrasal verb without an object:

Don't ever *give up* ('surrender').
He used to *come in* late in the morning.

Verb phrases
(*see* CGEL 3.21–56, 4.2–40)

735
Verb phrases can consist of just the main verb (*see* 573):

She *writes* several letters every day.

Verb phrases can also contain one or more auxiliary verbs before the main verb. Auxiliary verbs such as *be, have, might* are 'helping verbs' and help the main verb to make up verb phrases:

She *is writing* a long letter home.
She *has been writing* letters all morning.
Those letters *might* never *have been written*, if you hadn't reminded her.

There are two types of auxiliaries: primary auxiliary verbs and modal auxiliary verbs.

		write, walk, frighten, etc. *do, have, be*
	Main verbs	
Auxiliary verbs	Primary auxiliaries	*do, have, be*
	Modal auxiliaries	*can, could, may, might, shall, should, will, would, must, used to, ought to, dare, need*

736

There are three **primary auxiliary verbs**: *do, have,* and *be.* As the table shows, these verbs can also act as main verbs.

- *Do* helps to form the *do*-construction (also called *do*-support, see 611):

    She *didn't write* many letters.

- *Have* helps to form the perfect aspect:

    She *has written* only one letter.

- *Be* also helps to form the progressive aspect:

    She *was interviewing* somebody or other when it suddenly started to rain.
    You *must be joking!*

- *Be* also helps to form the passive:

    I was talking to a colleague of mine whose uncle *was killed* and whose father *was put* in jail.

The **modal auxiliary verbs** help to express a variety of meanings, for example intention (*see* 141), future time (140) and ability (287), as in:

    I was teaching classics and then thought I *will cease* to teach classics. I *will go* abroad and teach English.
    If we *can catch* that train across there we*'ll save* three minutes.

The modal auxiliaries are: *can, may, shall, will, could, might, should, would, used to, must, ought to, need, dare* (*see* 483).

Finite and non-finite verb phrases

737

There are two kinds of verb phrase: finite and non-finite.

- **Finite verb phrases** may consist of just a finite verb:

    He *worked* very hard indeed.

In finite verb phrases consisting of more than one verb, the finite verb is the first one (*was* and *had* in these examples):

He *was working* for a computer company at the time.
The enemy's attack *had been planned* for fifteen years.

The finite verb is the element of the verb phrase which has present or past tense. In the given examples *working* and *been planned* are non-finite verb forms, but they function in finite verb phrases: *was working* and *had been planned*.

Finite verb phrases occur as the verb element of main clauses and most subclauses (*see* 709). There is usually person and number concord between the subject and the finite verb. Concord of person is particularly clear with *be* (*see* 509):

> *I am ~ you are ~ he is*

With most finite main verbs, there is no concord contrast except between the 3rd person singular present and all other persons:

> *she reads ~ they read*

Modal auxiliaries count as finite verbs, although they have no concord with the subject:

> *I/you/he/they can do it.*

738

The non-finite forms of the verb are:

- **the infinitive:**   (*to*) *call*
- **the -*ing* participle:**   *calling*
- **the -*ed* participle:**   *called*

Many irregular verbs (*see* 550) have different forms for the past tense (*did, went,* etc.) and -*ed* participle (*done, gone,* etc.). Regular verbs, however, have the same -*ed* form for both functions: *worked* (past tense) and *worked* (-*ed* participle). The -*ed* participle (or 'past participle') is so called because of its -*ed* ending with regular verbs.

Compare finite and non-finite verb phrases.

- **Finite verb phrases:**

> She *works* in a laboratory.
> She's *working* for a degree in German.
> She'*ll be working* with overseas students.

- **Non-finite verb phrases:**

> I actually like *to get up* early in the morning.
> She heard the door *open*.
> My father got a degree through *working* in the evenings.
> *Having bought* this drill, how do I set about using it?
> When *asked* to help she never refused.

Non-finite verb phrases have no finite verb form but one (or more than one) non-finite verb form (in these examples: *to get up, open, working, having bought, asked*).

Combinations of verbs

739

When a verb phrase consists of more than one verb, there are certain rules for how the verbs can be combined. There are four basic verb combinations:

(A) **Modal** – a modal auxiliary followed by a verb in the infinitive:

> We *can do* nothing else.

(B) **Perfect** – a form of *have* followed by a verb in the *-ed* participle form:

> I *have* never *heard* of him.

(C) **Progressive** – a form of *be* followed by a verb in the *-ing* form:

> We *are getting* on well together.

(D) **Passive** – a form of *be* followed by a verb in the *-ed* participle form:

> He *was* never *forgiven* for his mistake.

These four basic combinations may also combine with each other to make up longer strings of verbs in one single verb phrase. The order is then alphabetical: A + B + C + D, for example:

A + B: He *must have typed* the letter himself.
A + C: He *may be typing* at the moment.
A + D: The letters *could be typed* by Mrs Anderson.
B + C: He *has been typing* all morning.
B + D: The letters *have been typed* already.
C + D: The letters *are being typed*, so please wait a moment.
A + B + C: He *must have been typing* the letters himself.
A + B + D: The letters *must have been typed* by the secretary.

As we can see in the figure below, the verbs in the middle of the phrase serve both as the second part of the previous combination and as the first part of the following combination:

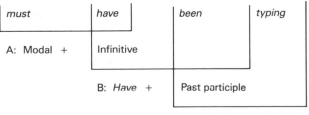

Verb phrases

| must | have | been | typing |

A: Modal + Infinitive

B: *Have* + Past participle

C: *Be* + *-ing* form

Tense and aspect
740

By **tense** we understand the correspondence between the form of the verb and our concept of time (past, present, or future). English has two simple tenses: the present tense (*see* 116) and the past tense (*see* 123).

- The present tense:

    How *are* you today?

- The past tense:

    Fine thanks, but yesterday I *felt* awful.

Aspect concerns the manner in which a verbal action is experienced or regarded, for example as complete or in progress. English has two marked aspects: the progressive aspect (*see* 132) and the perfect aspect (*see* 125).

- **The progressive aspect:**

    How *are* you *feeling* today?

- **The perfect aspect:**

    I'*ve* never *felt* better, thanks.

741

The present and past tenses can form combinations with the progressive and perfect aspects. The letters in [square brackets] denote the basic combinations (*see* 739).

Present time

- **The simple present:**

    Our teacher *uses* a blackboard and *writes* illegible things on it.

- **The present progressive [C]:**

    What'*s* he *writing* now?

Past time

- **The simple past:**

    I *wrote* a letter and almost by return post I *got* an answer.

- **The past progressive [C]:**

    I could neither read what he *was writing* nor hear what he *was saying*.

- **The present perfect [B]:**

    Here you find that all kinds of people you meet *have written* at least one
    book – if not two.

- **The present perfect progressive [B + C]:**

   He is a journalist and *has been writing* a novel about the condition of slum dwellers.

- **The past perfect [B]:**

   For the first time after her visit to America I *had spoken* to her on the phone but I *hadn't seen* her in the flesh.

- **The past perfect progressive [B + C]:**

   That's what people *had been saying* for a long time.

The passive (*see* 613) is formed by adding combination type [D], for example:

- **The passive simple past [D]:**

   This book *was written* for people who have a sense of humour.

- **The passive past perfect [B + D]:**

   The attack on this small friendly nation *had been planned* for fifteen years.

There is no future tense in English corresponding to the time/tense relation for present and past, but there are several expressions available for expressing future time (*see* 140), notably the modal auxiliary *will*.

The operator in the verb phrase
742
We have now described structures and contrasts of the verb phrase, in terms of modals, tense, aspect, and active-passive. There are also other constructions where the verb phrase plays an important part. For these constructions, the first auxiliary verb of the verb phrase has a special function as operator (*see* 609–12).

- In *yes-no* questions (*see* 682) the auxiliary verb functions as operator:

   Will you *be staying* long?

- In negation with *not* (*see* 581) the auxiliary verb functions as operator. Compare:

   I *have received* some letters this morning.
   ~I *haven't received* any letters this morning.
   She *speaks* fluent French but she *doesn't speak* a word of English.

- Emphasis is frequently produced by *do* as operator (*see* 264, 300, 611):

   One change was likely to happen. Whether it *dìd* happen, I just don't knòw.

- The *do*-construction can be used in imperatives (*see* 498):

   Dò be careful.

- The operator can stand alone (without the main verb) when it acts as a substitute form (*see* 384):

> [A] *Have* you *seen* these photographs?
> [B] Yes I *have*, thanks.

Word-classes
(*see* CGEL 2.34–45)

743
We can make a distinction between major word-classes and minor word-classes. Check the references here for further information about word classes given elsewhere in this grammar.

Major word-classes
744
The major word-classes are also called **open class words**. Major word-classes are 'open' in the sense that new members can easily be added. We cannot make a complete inventory of all the nouns in English, because no one knows for sure all the nouns used in English today, and new nouns are continually being formed. The major word-classes are:

- **Main verbs:** *get, give, prefer, put, say, search, walk*, etc. (*see* 573).
- **Nouns:** *belief, car, library, room, San Francisco, Sarah, session*, etc. (*see* 597).
- **Adjectives:** *afraid, blue, happy, large, new, round, steady*, etc. (*see* 440).
- **Adverbs:** *completely, now, really, steadily, suddenly, very*, etc. (*see* 464).

Minor word-classes
745
Words that belong to the minor word-classes are also called **closed-class words**. Minor word-classes are 'closed' in the sense that their membership is limited in number, and they can be listed. A minor word-class cannot easily be extended by new additions: for all practical purposes, the list is closed. Minor word-classes (such as determiners, pronouns, and conjunctions) change relatively little from one period of the language to another. Minor word-classes are:

- **Auxiliary verbs:** *can, may, should, used to, will*, etc. (*see* 477).
- **Determiners:** *a, all, the, this, every, such*, etc. (*see* 522).
- **Pronouns:** *anybody, she, some, they, which*, etc. (*see* 661).
- **Prepositions:** *at, in spite of, of, with, without*, etc. (*see* 657).
- **Conjunctions:** *although, and, because, that, when*, etc. (*see* 515, 709).
- **Interjections:** *ah* /ɑː/, *oh* /oʊ/, *ouch* /aʊtʃ/, *phew* /fjuː/, *ugh* /ʊχ/, *wow* /waʊ/, etc. (*see* 299).

746
Many English word-forms belong to more than one word-class. For example,

love is

- both a verb:

    Do you *love* me?

- and a noun:

    What is this thing called *love?*

Since is

- both a conjunction:

    Since the war ended living conditions have improved.

- and a preposition:

    Since the war living conditions have improved.

Round belongs to five word-classes:

- preposition:

    She put her arms *round* him.

- adverb:

    All the neighbours came *round* to admire our new puppy.

- adjective:

    That's a nice *round* sum.

- noun:

    The champion was knocked out in the second *round.*

- verb:

    The cattle were *rounded* up at the end of the summer.

Zero

747

We use the term 'zero' in grammar to mark the position where an item has been omitted. In the following examples, ∅ marks the position of the zero item:

- Zero *that* as a relative pronoun (*see* 686):

    Joan is the person ∅ I like best in the office.

    ~Joan is the person *that* I like best in the office.

- Zero *that* as a subordinating conjunction (*see* 712):

    I hope ∅ you'll be successful in your new job.

    ~I hope *that* you'll be successful in your new job.

- Zero article with mass nouns and plural count nouns (*see* 523):

    The possession of ∅ *language* is a distinctive feature of the human
      species.

    My best subject at school was ∅ *languages.*

Index

References are to section numbers, not pages.

- Individual words and phrases treated in the Grammar are printed in italics (e.g. *proper, because of*).
- Grammatical terms are entered in small capitals (e.g. PROPER NOUN)
- Functions or meanings appear in ordinary type (e.g. proportion, female, purpose).
- References to language varieties are given in angle brackets, e.g. ⟨spoken⟩, ⟨AmE⟩.